GOD AND GOVERNMENT

"No one is more on top of the challenges facing the first amendment than Barry Lynn. We are lucky he is paying attention, for no one sees more clearly how important it is that our government and whatever religion you choose to practice remain separated. By doing so, he is one of those who is keeping the lamp of liberty lit. With intelligence, wisdom, humanity, and a devilish wit, Lynn makes the issues come alive, and thereby we all become wiser. It is a book you should grab and read. You won't regret it."

—Lewis Black, comedian

"Before I fled the religious right Barry Lynn would have been a deadly enemy. I'd have seen him as someone standing between us and the theocracy we were trying to turn America into. This book is literally a defense of freedom against the theocratic illness. As Lynn writes 'From cradle to grave, the Religious Right is concerned about every choice you make.' It is up to us to stop them from dominating every aspect of American life too. This book is a good place to start."

—Frank Schaeffer, author of *Crazy for God*

"This book is a must-read for feminists and for all Americans who support women's rights—especially reproductive rights. Increasingly "religious liberty" is being used to block women's access to abortion and birth control. That is "religious liberty" for everyone—employers, right-wing politicians, bishops—except women who need access. Barry Lynn knows all the tricks, twists, and turns of those who want to turn the clock back several centuries. When he speaks, I take notes. His insights from twenty-five years on the front lines are extremely valuable."

—Eleanor Smeal, President of the Feminist Majority Foundation

"Barry Lynn has the extraordinary ability to demonstrate how religious fundamentalism poisons almost every public policy debate that matters. His new book, *God and Government*, explores a quarter century of his work standing up for the marginalized and the disadvantaged, and carefully explores why it is critical to never throw anyone under the bus for what they do or do not believe about religion."

—Jill Soloway, creator of the Golden Globe winning
Amazon series *Transparent* and Sundance Film Festival awardee
as Best Director for *Afternoon Delight*

GOD AND GOVERNMENT

Twenty-Five Years of Fighting for
EQUALITY, SECULARISM, *and* FREEDOM OF CONSCIENCE

REV. BARRY W. LYNN

Prometheus Books
59 John Glenn Drive
Amherst, New York 14228

Published 2015 by Prometheus Books

Lyrices from "The Christians and the Pagans," © Dar Williams (1996), reprinted with permission.

Cover design by Nicole Sommer-Lecht

Prometheus Books recognizes the following registered trademarks mentioned within the text: Norplant®, Plan B®, and U-Haul®.

Inquiries should be addressed to
Prometheus Books
59 John Glenn Drive
Amherst, New York 14228
VOICE: 716–691–0133
FAX: 716–691–0137
WWW.PROMETHEUSBOOKS.COM

19 18 17 16 15   5 4 3 2 1

Library of Congress Cataloging-in-Publication Data

Lynn, Barry W.
    God and government : twenty-five years of fighting for equality, secularism, and freedom of conscience / by Barry W. Lynn.
        pages cm
    Includes bibliographical references and index.
    ISBN 978-1-63388-024-5 (paperback) — ISBN 978-1-63388-025-2 (e-book)
    1. Church and state—United States. 2. Christianity and politics—United States.
3. Religious right—United States. 4. Freedom of religion—United States. 5. Religious pluralism—United States. 6. Religious tolerance—United States. I. Title.

BR516.L96 2015
322'.10973—dc23

                                                                                                                2015004942

Printed in the United States of America

CONTENTS

HOW I GOT INTO FIGHTING
THE RELIGIOUS RIGHT

I was sitting at the Values Voter Summit, sponsored by the Heritage Foundation, the Family Research Council, and a panoply of other far-right organizations, in the fall of 2014. Speakers kept exclaiming that they wanted to "take our country back." Right. But to where: the sixteenth century?

Voter apathy and a trending toward Republican conservatives in key Senate races was on the minds of the sponsors and, in fact, they were victorious on Election Day 2014, flipping the Senate to Republican control and placing any "legacy" of Barack Obama in serious jeopardy. Is this a temporary setback for progressive secularists or a bona fide statement that we are returning to a past time when religious minorities and nontheists are at risk of losing gains made over the past quarter century? The good news: I think it is the former. The bad news: If we "secularists" don't get our act together, it could turn out that everything is lost.

This book is a collection of columns, testimony, speeches, and other writings that I've done over the past twenty-five years of "in-trench" engagement for the preservation of the separation of church and state. In addition, it seeks to update the issues I've written about over those decades and show where we have made progress, where we have lost ground, and where we are treading water. It is not a textbook or legal treatise. It is also not a comprehensive history of First Amendment matters over the past twenty-five years. It is selective and personal and, I think, quite funny at times.

I first became aware of the problems of separation of church and state in college when I asked one of my roommates how he was going to spend spring break. He said he and his girlfriend would be flying to London. Why? To get a safe and legal abortion. This was in 1967—pre *Roe v. Wade* and pre-New York State's loosening of abortion restrictions. I was flabbergasted that so many "liberal" states at that time barred reproductive choice.

The more I looked into it, the clearer it became that the Roman Catholic Church had an inordinate amount of clout when it came to writing the laws, even in places like Massachusetts and New York. The Church was successfully turning its theological views into the basis for state law, restricting reproductive options, passing anti-LGBT bills, censoring books, films, and even comedy routines. (Lenny Bruce was convicted of obscenity in the city of New York in 1968.)

As a person who opposed the Vietnam War, marched with Dr. Martin Luther King, Jr. and otherwise considered myself a "liberal," I couldn't believe that the power of religious groups was so great and that I knew so little about it.

Well, I learned my lesson and became a staunch church/state separationist. After failing my Army physical, I decided to go to seminary at Boston University rather than to law school. The clergy at that time seemed thoroughly engaged in issues of social justice, but the legal profession (except for the National Lawyers' Guild and the ACLU) seemed to have little interest in such matters.

After spending time working on the First Amendment for the United Church of Christ's Washington office and later for the ACLU—and after a disturbing and debilitating few years dealing with our son's cancer—my wife and I decided to leave Washington and its rats racing and move to Dartmouth College in New Hampshire. This turned out to be a fiasco for me, and I let the legislative director at Americans United know how unhappy I was. She told me that the AU Board had been seeking a new director and that the candidate they had chosen had unexpectedly decided not to move and take the job. She offered to let the search committee know I was willing to consider a move back to DC.

The rest is history.

This book is set in two typefaces. The first Perpetua, a serif font, is the "all-new connective tissue" that updates issues and ideas. The second, Futura, a sans serif font, includes previously published or spoken materials I have used. The political and social landscape of church-state separation is always changing. Even as I write this, the Supreme Court is in the process of listening to oral arguments and deciding upon the status of a case regarding same-sex marriage. Unfortunately, I will not be able to include the result of the case, and any subsequent actions, as all work on this book was completed in April 2015.

Chapter 1

SCHOOLS ARE STILL A BATTLEFIELD, BUT WE ARE WINNING

NEVER USE THIS LINE WHEN DISCUSSING CHURCH AND STATE ISSUES: "AS LONG AS THERE ARE MATH TESTS, THERE WILL BE PRAYER IN SCHOOLS"

In 1962 and 1963, the United States Supreme Court invalidated, first, the daily recitation in New York public schools of a prayer written by the New York State Board of Regents, and then the recitation of the Lord's Prayer (at least a better crafted theological work, by my standards) in Pennsylvania and Maryland schools. President John F. Kennedy urged respect for the rule of law, even though there was an enormous outcry by many religious groups about the Court having "kicked God out of public school," a fairly dramatic conclusion for those believers in an otherwise omnipotent deity.

The anti-Supreme Court sentiment, though, boiled over into consistent efforts from 1963 until 1999 to have Congress pass a proposed constitutional amendment allowing public school prayer out to states for ratification. This process would require a two-thirds vote of both the House and Senate and then the approval of three-quarters of the states' legislatures.

During the 1980s, when I worked for the American Civil Liberties Union, there was a tremendous push to pass such a measure in the Senate. Indeed, during my first day of employment there, I was sent out for an interview with CNN, in the middle of a massive rainstorm. I'm sure the image projected to the network's more conservative viewers was clearly: "Look at that idiot from the ACLU—he doesn't even know enough to come in out of the rain!"

That proposal was ultimately defeated—liberal Republicans and a plurality of Democrats voted no. Even Mr. Conservative, Arizona senator Barry Goldwater, was opposed, arguing that it would be impossible to come up with appropriate language in a state that had Christians and numerous Native American communities side by side.

What follows are my first two columns for *Church and State* magazine after my selection as Executive Director of Americans United for Separation of Church and State, both about the central constitutional fear in 1992—that new momentum in Congress and a waffling newly elected President Bill Clinton—would propel a prayer measure to the even more conservative quilt of state legislatures.

Religious Freedom and Church-State Separation: Keeping Our Balance[1]

Once, when my daughter was seven years old, she happened to begin a sentence at the family dinner with the phrase: "When I prayed at lunch today . . ."

Nearly dropping my forkful of spaghetti, I thought: "This is a school day and she is in a public school." Visions of protest, and perhaps litigation, danced in my head. I was so surprised, I didn't allow her to finish the sentence before my interrogation began.

"Did the teacher tell you what to say?"

"No," she replied.

Undaunted, I continued. "Well, did somebody in the lunch room tell you this was the *time* to pray?"

Again, the answer was no.

"Well," I queried, "why did you pray?"

She gave me one of those looks that I see more regularly now that she is a teenager and announced: "You know—to thank God for the food."

Pretty good answer.

Somehow, my daughter hadn't gotten the misinformation promoted by the Religious Right that "God had been expelled from public schools" because she expected God to hear her just fine. On the other hand, her religious education at home and church was apparently sufficient that she didn't need a government to tell her how or when to practice her faith.

WELCOME TO WASHINGTON, PRESIDENT CLINTON[2]

The Washington newspapers are filled these day with tales of the coming of Bill Clinton. There is speculation about everything from his cabinet appointments to how the "open house" at the White House can avoid becoming a duplicate of Andrew Jackson's inaugural open house, where rowdy crowds forced him to escape through a window.

Church-state separationists look to President-elect Clinton as a compatriot on some issues and a mystery on others. Like many other issues, church-state separation was a largely invisible topic during the presidential campaign, but some important facts did emerge.

On the matter of government-sponsored religious observances in public schools, the incoming president enters without a complete understanding of what is at stake. While he supports the Supreme Court ban on religious devotions in the classroom, he told *Reader's Digest* he questions the *Lee v. Weisman*[3] decision, which rejected the constitutionality of school-sponsored graduation prayers. "The issue of prayer at public events is whether it is in any way coercive or oppressive to non-believers," he said. "In an open public event like a commencement, I don't really think that it is—at least nine times out of ten."[4]

Since Americans United was founded, we have seen nine presidents come and go. (President-elect Clinton will be the tenth.) Some have been favorable to First Amendment values; some have misunderstood the concept. In each case, our organization has done its best to make the case for church-state separation. Our commitment remains firm.

President Clinton eventually made it clear that he wouldn't support such an amendment (which he would not have had to sign for it to be sent to the states for possible ratification) and the movement again lost its momentum. Clinton did a brilliant Saturday morning Oval Office address on this topic. I attended, discussed country music with him briefly, and met his dog, Buddy, on the way out.

Republicans who captured the House in 1994, led by the ever-insufferable Newt Gingrich, backed a quixotic campaign beginning in 1995 for the "real deal"—an allegedly noncoercive Constitutional amendment. The weight of this exercise fell to Oklahoma Congressman and former television commentator Ernest "Jim" Istook.

Praying for Common Sense in Congress[5]

To the surprise of many political pundits, Election Day 1994 brought the Republican Party into power in both house of Congress.

I am more than a little disturbed over the comments being made by soon-to-be Speaker of the House Newt Gingrich about prayer in public schools. The Georgia Republican's remarks indicate that he is not the type of conservative who understands that one important component of "conserving" American principles means not aiding religion or subsidizing its mission.

Indeed, Gingrich has already called for action by July 4, 1995, on an amendment to the Constitution to permit governmental-sponsored prayer in public schools. Sure, Gingrich and his backers call it "voluntary prayer" and say it won't be written by the state and that no one will be forced to pray. But that's all smoke. What they really want is majority rule in religious matters in the public schools. In other words, the majority decides what prayer goes into the school, and everyone else is out of luck.

Gingrich admitted this last October during a speech at the Heritage Foundation when he acknowledged that under his scheme "you might well have a prayer that was offered by a person who was not necessarily praying in exactly the way that you would personally pray."

Yes, you might well. To me that quite obviously flies in the face of religious freedom and usurps parental rights; Gingrich seems untroubled by it.

This amendment has one purpose: to allow schools to set aside a time for group, vocal prayer each and every school day. Perhaps the school will be nice enough to let your child get up and walk out to the hall every morning if he or she would find the activity inconsistent with your family's tradition. Maybe the school won't even force your child to have his or her head bowed on the way out, but that's exactly what will happen—not out of reverence but out of discomfort from the ostracism that child will feel every day.

The amendment will probably say that no government body will write the prayer. It won't say that the school board, a committee of administrators, or a group of parents can't *select* it, though. Perhaps there will be contests to write the best prayer, with the winner chosen by a school official. Perhaps communities will vote on whether the Protestant Lord's Prayer will be used over its Roman Catholic counterpart, the Our Father.

These are not far-fetched examples. One allegedly conservative talk radio show host told me recently that the problem of which prayer to use could be solved by having students utter a prayer to a different deity every day. (Yes, he was serious.) Does he actually believe that prayers to the Christian God on Monday, Allah on Tuesday, and to Odin of Norse mythology on Wednesday is sound theology? What parent who is a person of faith tells his or her children to pray to random deities?

As many of you know, I cohost the *Pat Buchanan and Company* radio show most afternoons. On a recent show, a woman called in to say she supports a school prayer amendment. I asked her how she would feel if the prayer chosen to be recited read, "Dear Lord, we thank you for the diversity you have created, making us male and female, black, white, gay, and straight. Amen." She was outraged and declared the prayer unacceptable. But I've actually heard such prayers used by people of various religious backgrounds over the years. Although I find no fault with such a theological stance, others obviously do. Who is going to judge the quality or acceptability of the prayer being said?

The amendment was introduced, as promised. Americans United flew into action. Our government relations staff lobbied Capitol Hill for months. Our communications department blitzed the media with information about why this was a bad idea. Our field department engaged and energized our grassroots supporters. And every week, staffers were traveling to (or returning from) meetings where they spoke against the measure.

In addition to the unconstitutionality of the amendment, we were also motivated by stories like the ones below, which popped up every time I spoke about the issue.

First there was "Sam," whom I encountered at a convention in Texas. He grew up in Chicago in the late '20s/early '30s. As the only Jewish kid in his class, his teacher, Mrs. Smith, would excuse him from the morning prayers that she conducted in her homeroom, but she desperately wanted "her only Jewish student to come to know Jesus." One day, after school, a dozen of Sam's classmates broke his nose because they were tired of "praying for the different kid."

Then there was Jo Ann Bell, the Oklahoma mother who was assaulted in a parking lot and whose house was burned down after she spoke out against school-sponsored religious activity at her child's public school. Ms. Bell had a lot in common with the Wybles, who were driven from their home in North Carolina because they protested sectarian Bible classes at their son's public elementary school. And there were many others.

So when the day for a vote on the amendment eventually came in early June of 1998, I could not have been happier with the result.

One of the congressional leaders of the anti-amendment forces had told me a few hours earlier that a last-minute half-million-dollar ad campaign by the Christian Coalition was "costing us votes."[6] With this in mind, I had in my head a list of members whose votes would be pivotal. These folks had indicated they would oppose the Istook Amendment, but were feeling the heat. If enough of them changed their votes from no to yes, it could spell disaster for our side.

I watched in amazement as these swing members cast their votes and the lights blinked on the big board. They were all red (no), as were a surprising number of the votes of those who called themselves hopelessly undecided until the day of the vote. When the opposition vote total went over 190—eventually reaching 203—it was clear that Istook and his Religious Right allies had suffered a humiliating defeat. Not only had they fallen short by 61 votes of the two-thirds majority needed to pass the measure, but our side got 33 votes more than in 1971, the last time a prayer amendment hit the House floor.

The last prevote debate I had with Istook (and I had so many I sometimes felt he was a member of my family) illustrated, in about six minutes, why the amendment campaign failed. As Istook complained that children can't pray in school, the Fox News Channel was running footage of a large group of Minnesota high schools students at their regular voluntary Bible study club, praying away. The image put the lie to the comments of the congressman. I really didn't need to say a thing. Clearly, Istook's unnuanced assessment, though, was incorrect—and the message was clear. The need for this amendment was built on an insupportable house of cards.

Now, before too much excitement sets in, we must all remember that a simple majority of the House did vote to amend the Bill of Rights. Even though some will privately concede that Religious Right pressure, not the merits, compelled their yes votes, such profiles in cowardice don't square with the vow taken by members to uphold the Constitution and to make independent judgments about the constitutionality of any action.

Congressman Istook attempted to revive this himself a year later, but in spite of the support of such moral giants as Tom DeLay and Dick Armey, the whole effort petered out. Although the Constitutional amendment route was not revisited, prayer issues still emerge in public school districts across the country.

The courts have had to address the issue of prayer at school board meetings,[7] clergy-led school-sponsored prayer at graduation ceremonies,[8] and student-led speech over school public address systems,[9] each time finding it unconstitutional if the speech is religious and it carries any hint of school sponsorship or support. One might think, after reading this, that prayer has been completely eradicated from the public schoolhouse. That would be an incorrect assumption. Provided that faculty and outsiders don't participate, there are a number of ways that like-minded students can organize together for prayer or spiritual fellowship. Students can organize anywhere on the school grounds, including the flagpole or the cafeteria, and pray together.[10] Students can also pray before games, competitions, or other school events, provided that faculty do not participate.[11]

At the time of this writing, there are two issues that have not been clearly resolved. The first is to whether schools must provide temporary accommodations to those whose religion requires them to pray during the school day. The courts' decisions seem to imply that this will be permitted if the space provided is not set aside exclusively for prayer.

The second unresolved situation is whether student speakers at graduations or events can open with a prayer, make religious comments during their speech, or deliver sermons to the attendees. The Ninth Circuit court found this to be unconstitutional.[12] The Eleventh Circuit Court did not.[13] Some case will need to come forward, and probably make it all the way up to the Supreme Court, before we will get a definitive ruling.

STEALTH EVANGELISM—TROUBLING ENCOUNTERS WITH "UNEQUAL ACCESS"

When it became apparent that Constitutional amendments would not fly, the Religious Right started pushing for something called the "Equal Access Act." I was not happy that so many moderate and liberal groups supported it, because initially it only allowed for "religious" clubs in public schools. At the ACLU, I pushed to make it a "free speech" bill, including the phrase "religious, political, philosophical, or other content." On balance, it hasn't worked out as badly as some of us feared. The statute was upheld 8–1 in *Westside School District v. Mergens*[14] in 1990.

MEMO TO GOVERNMENT: IF YOU DON'T WANT "WEEDS," DON'T PLANT A GARDEN[15]

Everybody loves the "marketplace of ideas." Everyone believes that "a thousand flowers should bloom." Free speech is great, isn't it? The problem is that it's often more appealing in theory than in practice. At least, that's the lesson in Salt Lake City, Waynesboro, Pennsylvania, and Titusville, Florida, these days.

In 1984, Congress passed the Equal Access Act, which guarantees that public secondary schools cannot discriminate against student clubs on the basis of "religious, political, philosophical, or other content of speech." Consistent with this open-door policy, Salt Lake City high schools have welcomed debate clubs, chess clubs, a Bible club, and even a steak-eating club.

No longer. On a 4–3 vote the school board recently canceled all clubs. This bizarre decision was prompted because a support group for gay students was about to be established at East High School. Gay and straight students simply wanted to be able to meet to talk through the sometimes painful experiences of life in a homophobic society. The majority of the school board—all of whom apparently loved the idea of "equal access" when initially passed at the urging of religious groups—suddenly had a change of heart. Realizing that failure to comply with the Act could lose the state over $100 million in federal aid, board members decided to throw all the clubs off the cliff.

Senator Orrin Hatch (R-UT), a big supporter of the federal law, is now arguing that the law might not need to be read to require gay-related clubs, apparently because clubs may be prevented if they pose "order and discipline" problems. Even a first-year law student knows that you can't curtail the right of one person to speak because other people get disorderly. None of the students who wanted to form the group had any illegal or disorderly interest. To his credit, even Jim Henderson, counsel for Pat Robertson's American Center for Law and Justice, on a radio show with me, conceded that "equal access" preserves the right of any lawful group—no matter how much he disagrees with them—to meet. The lesson for high school is one of "all or none."

First Amendment controversies can have differing resolutions. Two propositions, in my view, ought to help our dilemma. One, every public space (say, an elementary school hallway) does not have to become a literature bazaar. Two, once a public forum—a "thousand-flower garden"—is set up, it's not constitutionally acceptable to allow a school board, city council, or other governmental body—to tear out some of the plants by deciding they are weeds.

The Equal Access Act has led to hundreds of "gay-straight student alliance" clubs—and only in an outlier case from a federal court in Texas was such a club not allowed to meet.

This "all or nothing" approach next emerged in an unusual Supreme Court case involving student clubs at a law school.

In the Supreme Court case *Christian Legal Society v. Martinez*[16] the Christian Legal Society at the Hastings College of the Law claimed that it was the subject of discrimination because it did not receive official school recognition and a cut of the student fees like other student-run clubs. The law school argued that the Christian group was not being treated differently, but that because the CLS refused to not discriminate on the basis of status or belief it was not a recognized club. CLS insisted that full membership not be open to non-Christians and (at least) "unrepentant homosexuals."

I admit that the policy of requiring a student-run club to admit everyone sounds strange to some people. Why does an environmental group have to admit members who want to chop down the California redwoods? Why does the Republican Club have to admit Democrats?

Hastings's rules may not be the best-constructed policy out there. The policy may even be "crazy" (as Justice Antonin Scalia characterized it during the oral argument), but that does not mean it's also unconstitutional.

To be constitutional, the policy need only be "viewpoint neutral"—a legalistic way of saying it treats all groups the same. Hastings's policy is certainly neutral, requiring all groups to admit all comers. This means school officials don't have to decide whether a student was rejected for club membership by some "forbidden" reason: it is wrong if she was rejected for any reason.

In 2010, the Supreme Court ruled 5–4 that the policy is reasonable and viewpoint neutral. Since this case, forty-one Intervarsity Christian Fellowships have been defunded, although not prohibited from meeting. Several schools, including private ones like Vanderbilt, have added similar nondiscrimination policies.

Although school prayer seems to be a battle won, other religious issues still emerge when parents demand inclusion of religious messages, or national or local crises lead to public prayer sessions.

Religious Right groups and their allies are now seeking ways to chip away First Amendment rights while spouting platitudes about "free speech" at the same time.[17] Enter Zachary Hood, who as a first grade student at a New Jersey public school was told he could not read a story from a children's Bible to his classmates after he had been chosen to bring something from home to share with the class.

Zachary's mother decided to literally make a federal case out of this matter, and his lawyers have been in court for years, trying to prove that their client was "censored." Add to the mix that the particular story, about Jacob and Esau, did not contain any direct reference to God, and even columnists like Nat Hentoff have been boosters of Hood's claim.

But the federal courts have found the young boy's case less persuasive. In fact, four federal judges, including the trial court judge and three appellate court judges, have ruled against Zachary's claim of "censorship." They have sided with the teacher's discretion in handling the delicate issue of the appearance of government promotion of religion. They found no anti-religious bias on her part and no hostility toward her student.

Here was a teacher trying to be careful in dealing with this delicate subject in a classroom full of young children of various faiths. She was concerned that since this was a school assignment and she was introducing the student to the class, it could appear that she was promoting religion. After all, six-year-olds are not constitutional scholars able to readily separate the imprimatur of the school from the personal views of a fellow student. Zachary's teacher allowed him to read the story to her as a means of reasonably accommodating his oral presentation of an important story. In other words, when courts looked at these facts, they saw a teacher exercising reasonable judgment, not the tyrannical actions of a bigot.

In Times of Trouble, The Watchdogs Must Bark Even Louder[18]

The chickens have come home to roost. More specifically, my own son's high school was the site of an unusually flagrant violation of church-state separation a few days after the September 11 terrorist attacks.

The Rev. Jesse Jackson invited himself to speak at Thomas Jefferson High School for Science and Technology in Northern Virginia. Since his schedule allegedly did not permit him to come to the regular Friday assembly period, the principal dutifully "accommodated" his need to speak on Thursday by shortening all the academic class periods to encourage maximum attendance. Jesse then used the occasion to launch a prayer session, followed by a speech on peacekeeping liberally laced with Bible stories.

My son's friend Ankur Shah, a Hindu, posed the right question (and got quoted in *Time* magazine): "Can he do that?"

What was the principal thinking? What was Jackson thinking? Does this mean that anybody who is famous (or used to have a cable TV show, or is a minister) can now address this public school whenever he or she feels like it? I am awaiting a response from the school and its attorneys. It is one example, though, of the apparent feeling of some school and government leaders that the First Amendment is partially suspended in times of national crisis.

I believe just the opposite: it is in such times that our real commitment to fundamental principles should be highest. You might even say that this is a time when love of country demands renewed commitment to the separation of church and state as the first principle of constitutional democracy. This is the preeminent defining principle that stands in starkest contrast to the conduct of those against whom President George W. Bush has declared "a new kind of war."

Was the Jackson appearance at my son's school the most egregious incident of "suspending" religious liberty? Probably not, but it was certainly an incident that didn't need to happen, or that should properly have been the subject of an immediate apology.

The school eventually conceded that the Rev. Jackson's appearance was not appropriate.

RELIGIOUS RIGHT ACTIVISTS: EVER INSATIABLE, EVER INNOVATIVE

It is perhaps faint praise, but I would concede that the Religious Right remains "inventive" when it comes to sneaking religion into schools.

The culprit can be Congress or state legislatures who try to pass "get religion in the schoolhouse door" statutes, as illustrated by a 1999 effort to have the Ten Commandments—at least some version of them—up in every classroom.

MEMO TO CONGRESS: YOU'RE ON CAPITOL HILL, NOT MT. SINAI[19]

Lately, many people have been asking me the same question—in San Diego when I moderated a debate on vouchers at a national meeting of the American Civil Liberties Union, in Salt Lake City when I spoke to the Unitarian Universalist Association General Assembly, and in casual conversations on airplanes en route. The question: "Do they really believe it?"

"They" in this case is Congress, and the belief is the sincerity to which I am asked to assess, that posting the Ten Commandments in public schools is a cure for youth violence at Colorado's Columbine High School and elsewhere.

On June 17, 1999, 248 members of the House of Representatives voted to permit states to allow the Ten Commandments to be put up in all public buildings, including schools. What everyone wants to know is, did the House members who voted for this proposal really think it would help?

I have a basic rule of thumb that about 2 percent of any large group will believe literally anything, no matter how preposterous it seems to the rest of us. Therefore, almost five House members honestly think posting the Ten Commandments will do the trick. The rest, I suggest, just knew a no vote would look bad on their next Religious Right "voter guide" separating the "godly" sheep for the "unholy" goats.

I did so many radio and television shows in the forty-eight hours following the vote that I thought I had been given a job as a permanent guest on some networks. The debates were mesmerizingly bizarre. One spokeswoman for the Family Research Council was so abrasive I had to remind her that although "thou shalt not be rude" was not officially a commandment, it was probably a good standard for TV show debates.

On another show, I asked Georgia congressman Jack Kingston to discuss the meaning of the Second Commandment, which relates to graven images. He began spouting off about gun control, as if I had asked about the Second Amendment. Conservative talk show host Oliver North seemed to think if the First Commandment (barring the worship of "false" gods) was too controversial in some states, it could be eliminated from the posting. "You mean," I said, "we should let the states edit God?" I saved perhaps my favorite quip for the new president of the Southern Baptist Convention, telling him that I believe, frankly, that most Americans would be happier if members of Congress just tried to obey most of the commandments instead of launching them as political footballs.

In the midst of these comments, I was able to make this core point for religious liberty advocates: The House of Representatives is wasting its time with this foolish grandstanding because this issue is settled. The Supreme Court, back in the 1980 *Stone v. Graham*[20] case, said the commandments are "undeniably a sacred text" and therefore could not be posted in Kentucky's public schools.

Several Religious Rights groups have launched campaigns with names like "Hang Ten" (a somewhat oblique reference to surfing) but they have had only marginal successes. For example, in December of 2014, the principal of Harding High School in Marion, Ohio, removed a community plaque donated by a private group. He told a local paper: "Our responsibility, when we are challenged is to do what's in line under the law." One disgruntled freshman told the same paper that he was so upset he would not participate in any school-related activities, go to class, and "won't even wear my Harding Marching Band shirt." Life will probably go on.

But if not for "religion," where will our values come from? This question, when coming from the Religious Right, is usually followed by the fatuous answer: "there will be no values" because of "cultural relativism." Baloney.

Public schools *do* teach and can teach values Americans commonly share. You might say that many commonly shared values are found right in the United States Constitution.

PUBLIC SCHOOLS TEACH VALUES EVERY DAY[21]

Former Moral Majority Communications Director, and then TV talk show host, Cal Thomas wrote a new book called *The Things That Matter Most*. The cover describes it as a work that "debunks fuzzy-headed liberalism," and in it are cleverly written essays on what Cal sees as the failed promises of the 1960s.

Cal has a wonderful sense of humor. I only wish it was equaled by a parallel sense of logic and analytical clarity. One essay in the book that I found particularly muddled deals with the "Promise of Progressive Education." He asserts, "As for learning about a moral code in school, one by which people should live in order to benefit themselves and society, the notion that such a moral code even exists, or ought to exist, has been abandoned."

This assertion echoes a constantly recurring notion I hear in question periods after speeches I give and on talk radio shows I do around the country. The Religious Right says it so often that many people think it's true: Public schools don't teach values.

Is that so? Do public schools really have no interest in "values" or the search for a "moral code"? Repetition of a complaint, of course, doesn't mean there is really something to it.

Unlike many leaders of the Religious Right, I actually have children who attend public schools. I'm aware that all kinds of positive ideas are being generated in them, and children are even encouraged to believe these ideas are normative, that they ought to inform the way they live—for self and others.

The problem with critics like Cal is that they hold such a limited view of what "values" are they don't acknowledge any effort at moral instruction that doesn't fit into that narrow definition. For example, virtually every public school corridor from elementary school to high school, has a poster communicating the message, "Don't Use Drugs!" Some would be happier if the poster had a "proof-text" from the Bible at the bottom of it, but for me it is important enough that the widely shared community value of not having fourteen-year-olds try crack cocaine be plugged as official policy.

Contrary to the common talk-show assumption, even when sex is discussed in school, it is a rare course that doesn't promote abstinence before it discusses condoms.

One could even argue that every time a student is told to stop talking in class, receives praise for solving a problem, or gets a low grade for turning in a sloppy reports, values are transmitted. After all, these actions are designed to make students learn that good behavior brings rewards, bad behavior brings sanctions. In other words, children are taught the difference between right and wrong in the classroom every day.

In a sense, the real values "taught" in public schools are not deliberately articulated parts of any lesson plan. Instead, they are examples set by a school's teachers and administrators. Does the administration respect the views of students, giving some responsible mechanism for grievances and suggestions? Is there a sense of fairness in disciplinary proceedings? Are students with differing backgrounds treated with equal respect? I remember more about the character of math teachers I had thirty years ago than the relationship between sines and tangents.

All of this probably sounds too mushy, too "touchy-feel" for people like Cal Thomas. So may be the fact that my son in the fourth grade is taught to respect the environment; is told about the similarities—and differences—between United States residents and people in Africa and Japan (Cal probably sees "one-world government" propaganda running rampant); or that my daughter in high school is actually writing a paper on images of African-Americans in films. (She also reads Steinbeck.)

This values issue came up recently when I spoke to a Chicago group organized by the National Council of Jewish Women. I explained how last December, Americans United got a Pennsylvania school district to halt daily Bible reading and praying over the intercom, practices the Supreme Court ruled unconstitutional thirty years ago. What "value" is taught when school administrators thumb their noses at the highest court in the land and continue illegal practices? That is the ultimate example of "relativism" gone amok; it's even got a name: anarchy. So, Cal, shouldn't we put the "rule of law" somewhere among the "things that matter most?"

There are also routine attacks on sex education by ultraconservative religious critics. I summarized some of the nonsense being promoted by the

Religious Right at a meeting called Save Our Schools: The People's Education Convention in August of 2012 in Washington, DC:

A second area of concern where social conservatives have success-fully worked their own agenda into the public schools, is sex education.[22] Since 1994 public schools have been stuck with federal funding only for "abstinence" programs. While some states forgo this federal funding, many can't afford to, and we now spend over half a billion dollars on a plan of action that has not a single reputable scientific study to validate it. Presi-dent Obama, with some reluctance, even had to put more money into the program in order to pass his healthcare bill. At best, for some populations it may postpone the first sexual activity for six to eight months, but then, tragi-cally, young people engage in the riskiest behavior (in no small measure because they have been left in the dark about safer alternatives). A few years back, Congressman Henry Waxman commissioned a study of the materials taught in these abstinence classes and some of the information there is embarrassing. A textbook example: One out of every seven uses of a condom fails; which, if true, would create a birthrate high enough to sink the United States into both oceans, even without global warming. But we know condoms are, in actuality, 98 percent effective.

And there are many other absurd examples. Some materials assert that condom use has no effect in mitigating the health risks of unprotected sex (what these materials refer to categorically as "premarital sex") like the con-traction of sexually transmitted diseases. They say condoms fail to prevent HIV transmission 31 percent of the time, when in fact they are proven to reduce transmission over 85 percent of the time. And some materials also claim that condoms are ineffective because students who can't "exercise self-control to remain abstinent" are not likely to "exercise self-control" and use a condom. That's like saying we shouldn't teach our kids safe drinking techniques because those who choose to drink underage can't control them-selves anyway—so we should just let them binge drink without any guidance at all. Alarmingly, drawing on the inaccurate "one in seven condoms fail" statistic, some programs compare the use of condoms to playing Russian roulette—arguing that "if one continues to perform this act, the chamber with the bullet will ultimately fall into position under the hammer, and the game ends as one of the players dies. Relying on condoms is like playing

Russian roulette." But instead, running a curriculum about health like this, based on religious beliefs, is playing Russian roulette with our children.

So, when all is said and done, where do we stand on the issue of how much, if any, religious promotion can occur within the hallowed halls of America's public schools. I tried to summarize it all to the Secular Student Association Convention in the summer of 2013 in Columbus, Ohio:

I have a question[23]. How many of you are in law school or thinking about going to law school? Great. I am exactly one week from being covered by Medicare, but I will only offer one bit of grandfatherly advice: if you pick the right subject matter you won't have to remember much of what you are actually taught in law school. I have built most of my career on just two phrases: the sixteen words in the First Amendment that note, "Congress shall make no law respecting an establishment of religion or prohibiting the free exercise thereof," and Article 3's prohibition on any religious test for public office. Pick environmental law and you'll spend every waking hour on regulations about land use, air, water, and something called the "Federal Insecticide, Rodenticide, and Fungicide Act." Choose wisely.

I'm going to try to distill the history and future of the law of religion and secularism in public schools in the next fourteen minutes so we have five more for questions. Until the 1930s Americans didn't even know that an individual could challenge government actions by claiming it violated an individual guarantee in the Constitution. Once we figured that out, the dam broke open. But it was still just fifty years ago last month that a man named Ellery Schempp, with the full support of his parents, challenged the required public school practice in Pennsylvania of reading ten verses from the Bible and reciting the Lord's Prayer. I was in a Pennsylvania junior high school at the time and one year—all of a sudden—the religiosity was gone from home room. I was a very religious young person; I still am a religious person. Those practices in school—particularly any dealing with Jesus—seemed to make my Jewish friends uncomfortable. At that time, atheists hadn't been invented yet but I'm sure they would have been upset. The whole process became increasingly silly as classmates managed to find the strangest passages to read, including the famous lineage sections that all go "So and so begat so and so who begat so and so . . ." or the section of Song of Solomon that mentioned breasts. We were idiots.

No prayer privately uttered (or even voluntary groups of students praying in a nondisruptive manner) is unconstitutional. No child saying her prayers over cookies and milk has been sent to prison. However, many other forms of government prayer—where the school sets the time, the place, the manner, the content, or the opportunity for prayer—have been held unconstitutional. If you have a "moment of silence," which the legislative history of the policy shows was designed not for thinking about stuff generally but to have you consider the divine, even that is unconstitutional. You can't have prayers by clergy at high school graduations or even prayer by students at sporting events over the public address system. After the Supreme Court found such prayers at Texas football games unconstitutional, I was on ESPN one morning with Senator Lindsey Graham, who was all upset about the case and was saying that he expected people to "spontaneously" rise up in prayer in the stands; I told him as a public official he should be trying to explain the case, not avoid its conclusion, but I said: "here's an idea if you want to keep evading the law—have parrots trained to say the Lord's Prayer and release them right before kickoff." Lindsey Graham really didn't like me to start with.

Can students offer a prayer at graduation? Most courts say no but it is not fully settled. You may have seen stories of a young man in South Carolina just last month who ripped up the valedictory speech he had cleared with the school and instead led the audience in the aforementioned "Lord's Prayer." The crowd went wild. Fox News acted like this was the moral equivalent of standing up in front of a tank in Tiananmen Square or saving Anne Frank; when in fact it was just a display to make the guy popular. He's probably already running for office down there. What the school should have done—turned off the microphone and not given him his diploma until he at least appeared at a hearing. Yeah, I know; I'm a hard ass.

Legislatures are now passing bills to protect such religious activities as "free speech" of students. Although this sounds better, it is not constitutional to characterize evangelizing student utterances, sponsored or promoted by the school, as if they were football scores or announcements about where to pick up the school newspaper. Religious speech is in that way different from other speech—and it is the First Amendment that makes that distinction. Congress and (through the Fourteenth Amendment) the states can hold opinions about lots of things, but must be neutral about one thing: religion.

Okay—in theory no school prayer with the blessing of the school. How about other religious activities, like school clubs? A federal law called the Equal Access Act, passed in 1984 and upheld 8–1 by the Supreme Court stated that if a high school has any "noncurricular" clubs (chess club, philately club—does anyone still collect stamps) then you can't keep out any club on the basis of "religious, political, philosophical, or other content." This is why there are Bible clubs and Gay-Straight Student Alliances in so many high schools. Only one court has ruled that an LGBT club wasn't permitted, and that was in Texas, home of the Ted Cruz, W., and of course Governor Rick "God Told Me I'd Be President" Perry. (Go ahead and laugh at Texas—this is the Eastern Secular Student Alliance conference; the Western people had theirs a few weeks ago in Las Vegas—Columbus, Vegas, same difference except there are more magicians in Nevada.) These clubs can't have faculty participation, can't regularly invite outsiders come in; in other words, they are truly student initiated and student run. Based on the reasoning of a recent Supreme Court case regarding student clubs at a law school, a high school club probably can't bar students because of their religion or absence of it or their sexual orientation.

And, of course, you can have secular clubs. We represented a young man named Micah in Michigan, who wanted to start an atheist club. The school at first refused, but then offered him the opportunity to lead a "world religions club." We gave them his answer: "No, my point is I don't believe in any of them!" He won.

Since these clubs must be student-initiated and run, there are other avenues sometimes adopted to sneak religious evangelism into public schools. There are schools that just happen to allow a local minister to come into the schools at lunchtime, wander around looking for apparently lost souls and then counseling them. There are schools that still allow the Gideons to distribute Bibles in public schools, although we can generally stop that with a complaint letter, not even having to go to court. I will give the Gideons credit for trying, though. After they were no longer allowed to roam the halls at one school, they decided to go to the bus parking lot, ask students to roll down the windows, and then threw the Bibles through the windows.

Finally, there is the "school assembly" scam. This is where a school allows a local minister to do an assembly about why you shouldn't be a stoner. And he doesn't mention God at all. However, on the way out the doors his assistants pass out leaflets about how you can come to a local pizza parlor after school for free food (which may sound really good if you didn't buy into the "no pot" message) and that's where the Jesus chats happen. Schools have no business facilitating that or variations that include demonstrations by Christian bodybuilders or motorcycle riders.

One of the biggest issues beyond these is whether schools need to "accommodate" individual student religious claims. This gets a little trickier. If a school has not banned all "expressive" tee shirts, for example, and you can wear shirts advertising your favorite gun brand or political candidate, the school probably can't bar a Christian student from wearing a shirt that says "Gay Is Not Great" or other minitheological sentiments. In several states, including California, Sikh students can bring ceremonial daggers required by their religion to school if the blades are welded into the sheath and thus rendered unusable as a weapon. If you are a secular "knife" aficionado, although it may not be right, that same school can probably prevent you from carrying even a welded Harry Potter-themed blade.

But what if you want to be religiously accommodated not for doing something but for avoiding something? Let's say your parents do not want you to learn about sex in school? Schools are permitted—but probably not required—to allow opt-outs from specific parts of a course (in the sex education context, what is referred to as "the good stuff"), but in an important case in Tennessee fifteen years ago, a federal court pretty much disposed of the idea that schools were required to allow "opt-outs" of entire swaths of the curriculum. In that case, a parent didn't like the English reading choices. In other states, parents have not been allowed to refuse to allow their child to be exposed to, for example, Othello because it has an interracial love affair. If that school had allowed this stab at Shakespeare, can you imagine how the parents would have next gone after Macbeth, which has three witches and obviously condones demon worship?

School displays can cause litigation as well. The general rule is: no religious imagery is allowed unless it has a distinct and separate historical value. Even my friend Michael Newdow, who brought the case challenging the use of "under God" in the Pledge of Allegiance to the Supreme Court, doesn't object to the frieze of famous lawgivers that is at the top of the Supreme Court chamber, even though it depicts Moses with tablets and Confucius. A student in Oklahoma just successfully challenged Ten Commandments posters, which had been put up in most classrooms. A Religious Right group has been distributing these in a campaign cleverly labeled "Hang Ten"—

dude. A young woman in Rhode Island won a case last year challenging a long-hanging banner on a school wall that contained a prayer. We won a case in West Virginia where students objected to a portrait of Jesus praying that happened to hang right outside the principal's office for the last forty years, presumably sending the message that you didn't need to just fear the academic power structure, but the cosmic one as well.

When it comes to holiday time in December, manger scenes of the Nativity standing alone are impermissible, but if you find a crèche amidst a menorah, an evergreen tree, and a Festivus pole, the school might be able to get away with it under current law. I have a neighbor who used to put up a display on her front yard (and I am not making this up), where the baby Jesus was in a cradle, surrounded by shepherds, wise men, and Santa Claus looking down at the baby. See, nothing I've ever seen from an atheist is more insulting to the spiritual significance of Christmas than seeing St. Nick at the manger.

So, we've been through prayers, clubs, displays, and assemblies. What about the curriculum of public schools? Many high schools have done away with art, music, geography, and even civics. But there are both well-meaning and not-so-well-meaning people who want to have classes in "comparative religion" or, even more problematically, the Bible. Even some liberals point out that there are so many biblical references in art, music, and literature that a well-rounded education requires instruction in religion generally or Christianity specifically. My response to this line of thinking is why not address religious imagery when it in fact comes up in the regular flow of teaching. When your English literature class comes up to William Faulkner's *Absalom, Absalom*, it's fine to mention that this is a character's name in the Bible who did something. Even with comparative religion, are we going to give equal time to all two thousand religions in this country along, with the beliefs of humanists, freethinkers, agnostics, atheists, and disbelievers? Of course not—we'll focus on the majority faiths only and claim to be balanced. We'll really end up teaching about Christianity, because in the latest poll on the subject nearly 40 percent think we should declare the United States a Christian nation.

Finally, did any of you have "sex education" classes in public schools? If you had a good course, you are in the minority. Like evolution, fact-based teaching on human sexuality is always under attack. I used to debate the late Dr. Jerry Falwell all the time, and he always claimed that you should teach alternatives to evolution and "let the children decide." So one night I asked him on TV if he felt the same about sex education. We could have students decide whether to read the abstinence brochures on one end of a table or watch the condom and banana demonstration on the other end. He never liked me even before that night.

So you can see we are still in a major fight to keeping religious evangelism out of our nation's supposedly secular, religiously neutral public schools. We depend on courageous students to let us know what is going on in their schools so we can help remedy unconstitutional activities. Let us know if we can be of help.

Chapter 2

THE EVOLVING DEBATE
. . . ON EVOLUTION

America faces an enormous literacy problem when it comes to many topics but perhaps none is as dangerous as our ignorance of science. I don't mean that we all need to understand the intricacies of molecular biology or be able to graph linear equations. I simply fear that basic high-school-level genetics, statistics, and geology are missing from most high school graduates' education. There is almost a knee-jerk sense that if an "expert" in science tells us something we don't want to believe, he or she is an elitist snob who is probably fudging some numbers and is almost certainly an antireligious bigot to boot.

Nowhere is this view more relevant than in the never-ceasing debate over how the universe began or, as Jim Holt queries in the title of his extraordinary book, *Why Does the World Exist?*[1] Most readers are familiar with the actual facts of the historic Scopes "Monkey Trial," or at least the fictionalized account in the play and film "Inherit the Wind." Fewer realize how little good it did for getting creationism out of the classroom, which didn't happen until forty-three years later with *Epperson v. Arkansas.*[2]

Regrettably, the evolution debate continues, with a rabid 42 percent of Americans still unconvinced of its veracity. Between the Scopes trial in 1925 and today, some terribly important Supreme Court cases have been decided in regard to various attacks on the teaching of evolution. In 2003, I had the opportunity to summarize them in a presentation to the National Association of Biology Teachers convention in Portland, Oregon. The hall was set up for hundreds of people to come to my session on "Creationism and the Law," but only about twenty-five people showed up. When I asked several of the participants what happened to the anticipated "crowd," I was told with varying degrees of whispered responses: "Many of us are here with other teachers in our school district. In many places, it wouldn't be a good idea to be seen coming into a session on this topic."What I had told them, as you can see below, was hardly an assault on religion; it was just a chronicling of what the highest court in the country had ruled:

Let me begin by summarizing how current constitutional law deals with the evolution question.[3] I realize that many of you may have thought the strictly legal issues involving the teaching of "creationism" had been resolved. In a rare example of being both right and wrong, you would be right and wrong. In 1968, less than one month after it was argued before the Supreme Court, that court ruled, without dissent, that a tenth-grade teacher in Arkansas should not have been fired for teaching about human evolution, despite a 1928 state law that had prohibited such instruction.[4] Justice Abe Fortas wrote plainly: "Arkansas has sought to prevent its teachers from discussing the theory of evolution because it is contrary to the belief of some that the Book of Genesis must be the exclusive source of doctrine as to the origin of man." This was the death knell for statutes born around the time of Tennessee's infamous "monkey trial."

However, opponents of evolution then turned to a theory of "inclusiveness" instead of "exclusion." That approach reached the Supreme Court nineteen years later in Edwards v. Aguillard,[5] a challenge to Louisiana's "Balanced Treatment for Creation Science and Evolution Science in Public Schools Instruction Act." The act essentially forbade the teaching of evolution in public schools unless accompanied by instruction in "creation science." Although the Supreme Court acknowledged that the stated purpose of the law was to "protect academic freedom," the Court concluded that the entire legislative history of the measure demonstrated that the real purpose was quite different. The majority of the Court wrote: "The Louisiana Creationism Act advances a religious doctrine by requiring either the banishment of the theory of evolution from public school classrooms or the presentation of a religious viewpoint that rejects evolution in its entirety. The Act violates the Establishment Clause of the First Amendment because it seeks to employ the symbolic and financial support of government to achieve a religious purpose." Clear enough? Not quite.

Now, you are all biologists to whom I can obviously teach nothing about biology. But—I can teach a little law. Lengthy opinions often contain what we lawyers call "dicta," words that help to arrive at a ruling, but which are not essential to reach the result. Some would call them "gratuitous comments." Here are a few slivers of "dicta" from that *Edwards* case I just mentioned: "We do not imply that a legislature could never require that scientific critiques of prevailing scientific theories be taught." A second comment of note was: ". . . teaching a variety of scientific theories about the origins of humankind to schoolchildren might be validly done with the clear secular intent of enhancing the effectiveness of science instruction."

These words paved the way for, shall we say, "innovative," future attempts to incorporate antievolution material in the curriculum of public schools. Those attempts have borne fruit, including lawsuits, but none has been ultimately successful. In two federal appeals courts, teachers lost claims that their first amendment rights were being violated by constraints on teaching nonevolutionary theories of creation in the classroom. In a case brought by a junior high school social studies teacher in New Lenox, Illinois, the court said there was legitimate concern that his comments promoting creation science could be viewed by reasonable people as an establishment of religion.[6] As to his more grandiose claim that his "academic freedom" was being suppressed, the court reiterated that the First Amendment is not a "teacher license for uncontrolled expression at variance with established curriculum content."

A few years later in the Ninth Circuit Court of Appeals, John E. Peloza, backed by a raft of so-called "Religious Right" groups, argued the flip side of the Illinois case, claiming that by requiring him to teach what he called "evolutionism," he was being coerced through a conspiracy of state officials to teach what he categorized as a "religious belief system" with which he disagreed.[7] The Court fairly briskly reminded Mr. Peloza that there is no religion called "evolutionism" and that the school is not establishing said nonreligion by teaching an "established scientific theory." Remember dicta, though? The Court commented that "evolution" means "higher life forms evolve from lower ones. The concept has nothing to do with how the universe was created; it has nothing to do with whether or not there is a divine Creator (who did or did not create the universe or did or did not plan evolution as part of a divine scheme)." More on this later.

If teachers can't successfully make a First Amendment argument, what about students? In one illustrative case a fourteen-year-old named Rebecca Moeller in Muscogee County, Georgia, claimed that a passage from her science textbook disparaged her religious beliefs.[8] The offending section merely said that many cultures had creationist beliefs but that these could not be tested using the scientific method. The appeals court ruled: "The use of the textbook in question in no way forces Moeller to refrain from practicing her religious beliefs."

So: if a state can't prohibit teaching evolution or require side-by-side instruction in evolution and creationism; and if neither teachers nor students can claim a First Amendment right to avoid the issue, what legal avenues are left? Next case: official disclaimers placed on textbooks or recited whenever the issue of evolution is raised in a classroom discussion. In *Freiler v. Tangipahoa* (even harder to pronounce that "angiosperm") *Parish Board of Education,*[9] several federal courts examined a Louisiana school board policy requiring a disclaimer that noted that any lessons about evolution are "not intended to influence or dissuade belief in the biblical version of creation or any other concept." The trial judge noted in his ruling that: "While encouraging students to maintain their belief in the Bible, or in God, may be noble aim, it cannot be one in which the public schools participate, no matter how important this goal may be to its supporters." This decision was upheld by a federal appeals court and the Supreme Court chose not to hear the case (as it does, with roughly 98 percent of the cases presented to them).

Another disclaimer still appears in Alabama biology textbooks, after its approval by a 6–1 vote in 1995 by the State Board of Education. It has not been challenged in court, but it is extraordinarily misleading in its 250 words. One sentence describes evolution as a "controversial theory some scientists present as a scientific explanation for the origin of living things, such as plants, animals and humans." Actually, there is virtually no controversy among scientists, but this makes it sound again like there is fifty-fifty split in scientific opinion. The statement then expands its ignorance to note: "no one was present when life first appeared on earth. Therefore, any statement about life's origins should be considered as theory, not fact." Here, too, the false implication is left that there is some set of scientific "facts" that are higher on the intellectual food chain than "mere" theories. In truth, it is almost precisely the opposite: only after the review of many facts does one reach the position of crafting a "theory," so the "theory" is the culmination of observation and experiment, not some kind of hunch that came to you after a little too much wine.

This was the state of the law until a seminal event in 2005—the filing of a challenge to the inclusion of "intelligent design" (ID) materials in a high school biology curriculum in the small city of Dover, Pennsylvania. Intelligent design is a non-scientific view that the careful "design" of the universe must be attributable to a "cause" (God) and not the undirected process of natural selection. Americans United and the Pennsylvania affiliate of the American Civil Liberties Union joined with the firm of Pepper Hamilton LLP to represent parents challenging the inclusion of antievolution "supplementary" materials—particularly a book called *Of Pandas and People*—in their public high school's library.

The Dover case was the source of vast international press attention from the day of the filing until weeks past the final disposition. On December 20, 2005, Judge John E. Jones III, appointed by President George W. Bush, with the strong endorsement of Pennsylvania's staunch conservative senator Rick Santorum, ruled for our plaintiffs in a superbly written 139-page opinion that shocked many observers. The ruling concluded that intelligent design was not science and permanently barred the school board from "maintaining the ID Policy in any school within the Dover Area School District, from requiring teachers to denigrate or disparage the scientific theory of evolution, and from requiring teachers to refer to a religious, alternative theory known as ID."

Judge Jones was not merely convinced of the unconstitutionality of the "intelligent design" materials being included in the biology class, he also learned some unpleasant lessons about the conduct of the Religious Right. He blasted the board for not being honest about its goals and for trying to cover up the fact that the copies of *Pandas* were paid for by a church offering:

> [T]he inescapable truth is that both Bonsell and Buckingham [two school board members] lied at their January 3, 2005 depositions about their knowledge of the source of the donation for Pandas. . . . This mendacity was a clear and deliberate attempt to hide the source of the donations by the Board President and the Chair of the Curriculum Committee to further ensure that Dover students received a creationist alternative to Darwin's theory of evolution. We are accordingly presented with further compelling evidence that Bonsell and Buckingham sought to conceal the blatantly religious purpose behind the ID Policy. . . . The citizens of the Dover area were poorly served by the members of the Board who voted for the ID Policy. . . . It is ironic that several of these individuals, who so staunchly and proudly touted their religious convictions in public, would time and again lie to cover their tracks and disguise the real purpose behind the ID Policy.[10]

In a strange footnote, Judge Jones and I had both attended the well-respected liberal arts college, Dickinson, in Carlisle, Pennsylvania. In 2007, the college put out a list of its twenty-five most important alumni, and the judge and I were both on that list. It was quite an honor. Dickinson only graduated one person who went on to the presidency, James Buchanan. He was also on that list. You pretty much have to put a president-graduate on any such list, although Buchanan is widely considered by historians to be the worst chief executive in American history, given his failure to avert the Civil War.

Although the issue of "creationism" did not go away after the events in Dover, and later, an Americans United case in El Tejon, California, there was a sharp pullback of the seriousness with which right wing legislators pursued the matter. "Creationism" lawsuits are really expensive to lose. And, of course, evolution deniers have been working on other projects.

Advocates of "intelligent design" and so-called "Young Earth Creationism" (a non-scientific belief that asserts that, based on a literal reading of the biblical texts, the Earth is only about six thousand years old and that all life on Earth was created over a relatively brief period) are still out there promoting their beliefs and even occasionally seeking financial aid for their ideas. Nothing, however, is stranger than the "Ark Park"—a planned attraction by Answers in Genesis founder Ken Ham, the founder of the Kentucky Creation Museum which I almost got to see, until I realized that the only road into the place had been blocked earlier in the day by the crash of a double-wide house trailer. (I did not make this up, even though, to some readers, this may sound like a crass reflection of anti-southern stereotyping.) Ham and I had a lively chat about this on CNN in 2011 before an astonished Anderson Cooper, discussed in this column:

I debated Ken Ham, the head of the group Answers in Genesis.[11] His latest project is to be a partner in the construction of a "Noah's Ark" theme park near his Creation Museum in Grant County, Kentucky.

With his own money, Ham can build an ark-sized water slide if he wants, but unfortunately he wants taxpayers to subsidize this effort by giving him a sales tax rebate—up to about $43 million.

Ham was offended that I considered this a "subsidy" at all, but I maintained that the difference between his effort and the construction of a sports stadium was that the purpose of his facility would be to convert people to his religious perspective. When Cooper asked him if he wanted to convert people, Ham—like so many of his peers—wouldn't admit that was the purpose of the project. (For the biblically inclined, this kind of dodge always reminds me of Peter's trifecta denial that he knew this fellow Jesus when asked by the Roman soldiers.)

Ham was clear that dinosaurs would be depicted on the ark since he claims they obviously lived in Noah's time, but got a bit standoffish about inclusion of unicorns, a species he notes on his website also existed at the time.

Although Ham's proposed project got no direct state funding because of delays in private funding and subsequent construction problems, another issue arose in 2014 that appears to have put the kibosh on his whole government funding effort—a blatantly discriminatory hiring policy at the venue.

In August 2014, an online post went up advertising a position for a computer-assisted-design technician to work at Ark Encounter. Interested applicants were required to submit, in addition to the usual documents, a "[c]reation belief statement," as well as "[c]onfirmation of [their] agreement with the AiG Statement of Faith." For those unfamiliar with the Ark Park's "statement of faith," it requires potential employees to affirm their belief that homosexuality is a sin on par with bestiality and incest, that the earth is only six thousand years old, and that the Bible is literally true, among other things. The post was taken down quickly, but the Ark Park's hiring practices are still a cause for concern.[12]

As of this writing, the waterslides and the unicorn-infested Ark Park remain unbuilt and largely unfunded. But, like so many bad things, Ham is convinced that he can still sail on to victory. In mid-December 2014, he launched an aggressive billboard campaign, both in Kentucky and New York City's Time Square. It notes: "To All Our Intolerant Liberal Friends: Thank God You Can't Sink This Ship"—alongside a photo of an ark under construction.

Except that we did. Or rather, Kentucky did. The Kentucky Tourism Secretary decided that the Ark Park would not be eligible for tax incentives, an important source of funding for the park.

It looks like his ship might be sunk after all. Nevertheless, in early February 2015, Ham sued the commonwealth of Kentucky for "discriminating" against this project. He directly blamed Americans United for his funding problems.

In other words, creationism, although sputtering, endures. However, there is a silver lining. In the same 2014 survey cited at the beginning of this chapter reporting that 42 percent of Americans believe in creationism, young Americans were, notably, the most skeptical of the creationists' story.[13] Only 28 percent of young Americans aged eighteen to twenty-nine believe that humans have always existed in their present form, versus the 50 percent of Americans aged sixty-five years or older who feel the same way. There is an inverse correlation between the number of years individuals spend in school and their support for creationism. Twenty-seven percent of college graduates report believing that "God created humans in present form within the last 10,000 years." This is in stark contrast to the 57 percent of Americans who did not graduate from high school reporting that they believe in creationism. These two trends foretell a brighter future: As younger Americans who are attending college in increasing numbers begin to make policy decisions, creationism only stands to fail.

This is perhaps best illustrated by the ongoing fight over creationism in Louisiana spearheaded by Zack Kopplin, a native of Baton Rouge and student at Rice University in Texas. Since 2010, Kopplin has been fighting the Louisiana Science Education Act—a bill signed into law by Governor Bobby Jindal in 2008. The first of its kind in the nation, this law permits public schools to supplement traditional biology classes with materials that incorporate creationism into their curricula. Americans United and the Louisiana affiliate of the ACLU have already announced a lawsuit against any school district in the state that tries to implement this statute.

Chapter 3

IF WE CAN'T CHANGE PUBLIC SCHOOL CURRICULA, LET'S JUST DESTROY PUBLIC SCHOOLS

The late Dr. Jerry Falwell once wrote, "I hope I live to see the day when, as in the early days of our country, we won't have any public schools. The churches will have taken them over again and Christians will be running them. What a happy day that will be!"[1] His angst, and that of many of his supporters in other right-wing groups and in political circles, can be summarized as deciding that if you can't control what is taught in publicly funded schools, perhaps it would be best to simply get rid of them.

On my speaking tours, I often discuss the destructive ways alternatives to public school funding would operate. School vouchers and other forms of aid to private (and primarily religious) schools were a hot topic when I spoke to a Unitarian Fellowship in South Carolina in February 2013. (South Carolina's proposals were defeated—but this discussion merely illustrates how these proposals would operate.)

The goal of many in the Catholic hierarchy and their friends in the Protestant Religious Right is an affirmative demand for funds for their missions and ministries, including their parochial schools. In South Carolina, there has been a great deal of money given from out of the state by individuals and foundations that are trying to gin up enthusiasm for school vouchers or tuition tax credits (most accurately characterized as "back door vouchers"), which would indisputably primarily assist religious schools. Legislation to give tax credits for private school tuition and the cost of "home schooling" has also been introduced. The efforts in South Carolina would allow tax deductions for tuition spent at private schools and for certain costs of home schooling. In addition, it would create a program where corporations could give financial assistance to private school students instead of paying as much in taxes. The corporations would actually give the money to specific charities, which would then dole out the funds. All this is done in the name of "educational choice," a corruption of language.

The evidence on the lack of success of these programs is also mounting. The latest studies in Milwaukee (home of the oldest voucher program), Cleveland (the subject of the Supreme Court case that allowed them), and the voucher program forced on the residents of the District of Columbia all show that students in voucher schools do no better on academic tests than students in public school, and in DC students don't even express any greater sense of safety or satisfaction in those private schools. We know a 5 member majority of the Supreme Court of the United States got it wrong when it ruled that vouchers were not a way to promote religion, but it also helps to look at this data and see they were equally wrong about the presumed value of the vouchers.

These days, a real hero of the antivoucher movement is the woman who is often considered the "godmother" of the movement: Dianne Ravitch, an academic researcher in New York. About a year ago, she wrote a book in which she described the failures of vouchers (and of their kissing cousins, tuition tax credits), conceding that much of her life's work was erroneous. When asked by the New York Times why she altered her position, she quoted the great economist John Maynard Keynes: "when the facts change, I change my mind." Hers is an act of rare and substantial courage. And yes, for the first time in history a national public opinion poll shows that 63 percent of Americans now oppose school vouchers.[2]

How could it be otherwise? In that Milwaukee program, 90 percent of the students in the voucher program who go to private schools are not proficient in the state test in reading and math; the public schools there (viewed as some of the worst in the nation) are doing better.

But what is so fraudulent about calling it "educational choice" is that any choice for students and parents is almost always hypothetical and only the institutions getting the "vouchers" and "scholarships" are exercising any real choice.

In Washington, DC, many of the roughly fifty schools that receive voucher aid for students are not even accredited and others are in so-called "unconventional" spaces, like a K–12 school run by one family out of a storefront. The school chose to accept the money; in some cities these schools actually hire young people to pass out DVDs about how great a particular school is, choosing to spend money on misleading promotional materials rather than certified instructors. Some home schooling parents actually "teach" their children primarily through the showing of Christian DVDs—perhaps funding under the proposed bill in South Carolina could allow them to upgrade to 4K, super-high-definition television with THX-certified Dolby 7.1 Surround Sound.

These schools get another kind of "choice": which students to accept and, later, those to retain. In our public schools, we deal with all kinds of children, those with special needs and even ones with disciplinary problems. Private schools have the luxury of dumping "problem kids" right back into the public schools if they don't feel like dealing with them: just a simple "refund" of unused voucher aid and that child is out. Even where there is a system for requiring nondiscriminatory admissions based on race, gender, religion, there is one other big choice problem for parents. In DC, the voucher can be worth up to $6,000, but the private schools presidents send their children to, like Sidwell Friends, cost $34,000. So choice, without that extra $28,000, is not much choice at all.

Finally, the school often "chooses" whether to follow the dictates of civil rights statutes. For example, Title IX of the federal civil rights act has allowed thousands of female high school students to be engaged in athletics on equal par with men, opening all kinds of new doors of opportunity for women in seeking scholarships for higher education and economic advancement. Many private schools do not follow this mandate because legislation exempts them from such a requirement.

Many of the facts, however, seemed ignored when the Supreme Court had examined the constitutionality of vouchers in 2002.

Voucher Vendetta: A Heated Debate at the High Court[3]

Wednesday, February 20, 2002, was the day when the constitutionality of the Cleveland voucher program—now with 99 percent of voucher recipients in private religious schools—was argued before the United States Supreme Court.

A piece of paper worth $2,250 can sure cause a ruckus. It is because that piece of paper has something to do with religion that the feelings are so strong. Claims of "ultimate truth" often have that effect. When one group thinks it has it and wants everybody else to pay for it, you have a recipe for conflict.

In Cleveland, the largest amount of voucher funding goes to the Roman Catholic school system. Like most other inner-city parishes, Cleveland was having trouble attracting enough Catholics to send their children to the schools there. Many parents moved to the suburbs and found religious or public schools there. Most of the inner-city schools now have very high minority enrollments, and most of those students are not Catholic. This voucher program was designed as a government bailout for those schools.

Here's the problem: Our constitutional system never envisioned having taxpayers pay to keep religious institutions from failing. If the sermons are bad at the local Baptist church and people start going elsewhere, Baptists wouldn't expect the local governing body to give them some tax funds to make up the shortfall in the collection plate. Why, then, should religious schools get a comparable helping hand from government?

Voucher advocates would say my analogy is unfair. Besides being promoters of the faith, these religious schools are good schools, they argue. It turns out, however, that they aren't better than the public schools in terms of academic performance for children with academic troubles. Even if they were, the right question is how to make sure the public schools do the best job possible. You can't blame the victim for looking pale when you are bleeding him yourself.

Cleveland public schools do not have funds to implement tested and successful programs for "at risk" students because the state has blessed the siphoning off of $11 million from the public school budget. Ohio has also resolutely failed to comply with court orders to fund suburban and inner-city schools more comparably and has supported many other financial benefits for private schools throughout the state. Instead of making hard choices, the state chose a gimmick—vouchers.

I had a chance to be reviled by a number of the parents whose kids are in the Cleveland voucher program at a debate at the libertarian Cato Institute the afternoon before the argument. One mother complained that her daughter had been threatened at a public school. She was delighted to get a voucher to put her daughter in a private school.

Of course, no parent should tolerate such activity at any school, but possibly protecting one child and leaving your neighbor's kids vulnerable can't be the final answer either. At the end of the day, of course, you have to be able to say you did everything possible for your family. I said to that mother, though, I think you have to say you did something for other peoples' families too.

In education, that means demanding that public schools work and fighting any group, individual, or political force that says otherwise. In some places, that might even mean spending more to make the system work. If that is what it takes, we're past due paying the bill.

After a somewhat lackluster oral argument, I had the distinct feeling that my side was going to lose—and that is, in fact, what happened on June 27, 2002. I discussed the consequences of this decision at a rally in Florida, as that state took up legislation to direct state funds to even more private schools.

There is one major similarity between decisions of the United States Supreme Court and baseball games: the side with one more vote or one more run wins.[4] Late in June, the Supreme Court let the "other side" win. The good news is that one game is not the whole season, and it certainly isn't next season. Frankly, taxpayer-funded vouchers for private religious academies are as miserable and as useless and as unconscionable and as dangerous to kids today as they were an hour before the Supreme Court issued its ruling!

But you all knew that. Here's some other news: they are still just as unconstitutional as well, if by unconstitutional we mean inconsistent with the premise of our nation that religious institutions and the ministries they establish (like schools) must make it on their own, without subsidy from government taxpayers.

I live in a simple world; I think it is the real one. Since this is a rally, I have made up some signs. This gentleman has a sign with the word STATE TREASURY on it. I go to him and I can get a sign that reads VOUCHER. I have some of the people in the front row with other signs that read: GROCERY STORE; ELITE PRIVATE SCHOOL; RELIGIOUS SCHOOL. I'm going to go into the audience. Can I cash in my voucher to buy groceries? Of course not. These are "education" vouchers. Can I cash it in at the ELITE private school? Yes, but only if I have another $6,000 in cash to pay the growing tuition. I can only use it at this RELIGIOUS SCHOOL. In the back is a guy with one other paper: FLY BY NIGHT PRIVATE SCHOOL. I can also use my voucher there, but he's not too sure that the school will get enough kids to stay open past Thanksgiving. If not, he says he'll be happy to dump them back into the public school system.

Now, tell me this. How is it not a direct payment to the treasury of this religious school for me to take my voucher there and have them cash it in for up to $4,000 of taxpayer funds? Why is this any different from the treasury just handing them the money directly? They get it and can use it for any purpose, including buying Bibles, crucifixes, prayer rugs, creationist biology textbooks, sex ed courses that never mention condoms, hymnals, religion teachers, chapel services, and anything and everything religious.

Those five members of the Supreme Court found a nonsensical distinction; that doesn't mean that Florida state legislators or state supreme court judges are required to play the semantic games that Clarence Thomas and Antonin Scalia did to reach the result they desired. Indeed, the first court that looked at vouchers after the Supreme Court decision was a Florida court—and it ruled that the state constitution barred what the US Supreme Court had permitted. More on that later.

Many of you may have seen Clint Bolick, the "godfather" of modern vouchers, on CNN with me after the decision was announced saying, "This is the most important educational decision since *Brown v. Board of Education*"[5] He's right, if you're trying to reverse *Brown*, and cause even more segregation than we have now.

Of course, he meant it would "open opportunities." The problem with his approach is that vouchers are not now, have never been, and will never become, a tool for civil rights protections. The whole voucher movement started right after *Brown* precisely as a way to continue to fund segregationist schools in the south. That's right, while Bolick and other voucher advocates claim that their top priority is the future of inner-city children, the fact remains that vouchers were used to prop up segregationist academies forty years ago when white families didn't want their kids going to school with African America kids. At that time, courts saw through the charade and struck vouchers down. Regrettably, five Supreme Court justices weren't as wise on June 27th.

I don't mind telling you that I find the comparison between the voucher ruling and *Brown v. Board of Education* offensive and disingenuous. Voucher proponents use bumper-sticker slogans and poll-tested rhetoric to say they care deeply about the education of children in poverty. Call me a cynic, but I find their claims incredibly hard to believe. It is wrong, they argue, for poor families to be denied the same educational opportunities as wealthy children. Oh really? What about poor children getting the same access to healthcare as wealthy children? Or perhaps the same access to quality housing? Or quality nutrition? Or quality transportation? What about giving poor families vouchers to get the same political influence as wealthy families? For some reason, despite all their talk about desperately caring for families in need, their silence on these issues is deafening.

Now, even people who worked to get voucher schemes passed in their communities are beginning to have second thoughts.

In Milwaukee, Wisconsin, some of the same advocates who lobbied aggressively for vouchers in 1995 are expressing frustration with the program because it did not turn out to help the poorest of the poor, as had been promised. Making matters worse, there are several expansion efforts for the voucher scheme under consideration—and all of them are aimed at the suburban middle class, which now wants to find ways for the state to pay all or part of the tuition those folks are already paying themselves.

A study from the Civil Rights Project at Harvard University[6], released just a day before the shameful Supreme Court action, found that the most segregated schools in the country were private, religious schools. In fact, the same research found that most students in Catholic and other religious schools encounter a "heavily segregated educational experience." When one looks at the history, the reasons become clear. Public schools have taken specific and deliberate steps to desegregate over the last half century. Schools run by religious ministries have not. The practical reality is that voucher programs will actually promulgate—not alleviate—racial segregation.

Now, the war is not over. You know that those of us against vouchers all over the United States are going to be heading to many statehouses next session and insisting that no new voucher plans are adopted. Our goal nationally should be to see that not a single new voucher program starts anywhere. When Clint Bolick heard me say that outside the Supreme Court this summer, he said it was "sour grapes." No, that is an affirmation that we know snake oil when we see it; we aren't going to sit back and let the voucher weed strangle the vitality of genuine school reform around the country.

Can we win? Of course we can. In fact, we have been winning the voucher argument for decades. In twenty-three state referenda in the past twenty years vouchers, and some of their kissin' cousins like tax credits, have been defeated every single time.

Dr. James Witte studied the Milwaukee voucher program for five years. After he concluded that the plan produced no statistically significant changes in most subjects for most grade levels[7], the Wisconsin legislature could have said, "Whoa, maybe we made a mistake here." Instead, in a move that would be laugh-out-loud funny if it weren't so pathetic, lawmakers reacted to the report by cutting off the funds to continue the testing of students so nobody would know if there was any improvement. This even turns free marketism on its head: Create an expensive government program with tax-payer money, and when the data suggests the program isn't working, hide the data and make sure consumers don't get any similar data in the future.

Voucher supporters were already being forced to acknowledge the very day of the Supreme Court decision that the battle wasn't even over in the courts. The Supreme Court's ruling dealt specifically, and exclusively, with the legality of vouchers under the US Constitution. The decision, however, has nothing to do with whether vouchers may violate provisions of state constitutions. In fact, thirty-six state constitutions—including, of course, yours—have very clear prohibitions against use of public funds for any religious purpose.

Americans United, the PTA of Florida, and teachers groups were already litigating in Florida under that kind of provision in its state constitution to terminate your inaptly named "Opportunity Scholarship Program." The Supreme Court's ruling on the Cleveland program has no bearing on whether Florida's voucher plan violates the state constitution. On August 5, Circuit Judge P. Kevin Davey ruled that Article I, Section 3 of the Florida Constitution said, "The language utilized in this provision is clear and unambiguous." And it is: "No revenue of the state or any political subdivision or agency thereof shall ever be taken from the public treasury directly or indirectly in aid of any church, sect, or religious denomination or in aid of any sectarian institution." Pretty clear, and very wise. I don't see how your Supreme Court, when it hears the appeal, can rule any differently from Judge Davey.

There are a few more lawsuit-ready issues. Under current law, a private religious school that receives no taxpayer subsidies can hire or fire teachers based on their religious affiliation or belief. In one case, a Catholic school fired a single but pregnant mother, and a federal court upheld their right to do so under a "religious" exemption in the Civil Rights Act of 1964. I believe that if that school is now the beneficiary of tax dollars (even if the court accepts the fiction of this intermediary) it can't do that anymore. We'd love to help someone in that situation.

Or, how about a student with disabilities? Public schools in my state have to find ways to accommodate disabilities. Special-needs children can require up to 30 percent of the budget in some school systems. Right now, religious schools don't have to take any disabled students—and very few do. A journalist went out to Milwaukee a few years ago and interviewed the principal of a well-run private high school, with fine science facilities. He noted to her that the labs were all on the second floor and that there was no elevator in the building. He wondered how a student in a wheelchair would be able to use them. Without any venal purpose, she just said, "Somebody like that really wouldn't be comfortable here." If a school like that gets a voucher that I helped to pay for, the "comfortable" argument just does not cut it. You will be required to alter your facilities and be able to serve all if all of us are paying for it! No voucher-receiving entity ought to be able to treat a single student like a second-class citizen.

There is no quick fix for that minority of public schools that are not meeting the needs of their students.

In a broader sense, school vouchers don't make sense, as I stated at my alma mater, Dickinson College in 2001:

Let's look at the general illogic of this idea of vouchers. It makes the curious assumption that if there is a new flow of state or federal money for schools, competitive high-quality facilities will just be popping up all over America's inner cities. Where in South Central Los Angeles, or Harlem, or Detroit is this phenomenon occurring with any other institution? Are there banks opening there? Grocery store chains or department stores? New money might lead to new construction somewhere, but it won't be in the same neighborhoods now missing banks and groceries. It simply won't be viewed as cost effective. This argument that vouchers are to help low-income parents is absolute nonsense. If the pro-voucher moguls didn't want to expand the program to everybody, there would be no pro-voucher movement. Even the chief liberal support of the Milwaukee plan, African-American legislator Polly Williams, has repudiated the way that plan is being implemented, claiming that it is already abandoning the poorest of the poor. You know, yesterday five hundred thousand homeless children, address "not fixed," attended America's public schools, which probably fed them and counseled them as well. Almost no private schools take even one such child.

I used to do a national syndicated radio show with Pat Buchanan. One day, in discussing a ballot initiative in California, our first caller was a recently retired school principal from a Catholic high school. She asked Pat if he knew what she would have done first with any financial help from the government. Pat failed to answer quickly enough, so she gave him the correct answer: "I would have given myself a raise." Of course, many private religious school teachers and administrators earn $8,000 a year less than their already underpaid public school counterparts. But if they were paid equitably, tuition costs would by necessity rise, and the value of the voucher would decline accordingly. By the way, although I don't think money is the solution for everything, there is a certain truth to the adage "you get what you pay for." This country isn't paying for much. Of the sixteen major industrialized nations, the United States ranks tenth in school spending as a percentage of our gross domestic product and an appalling fourteenth in expenditures as a percentage of per capita income. Think about that when you see the next comparison of test scores in Japan and those in the United States.

Speaking of cost effectiveness, that Cleveland program was a pretty strange example of it. One year, a full quarter of the costs of the program were expended on taxicabs to take children from home to school. It was determined that the cost of a cab was about eight times that of a normal school bus. Exacerbating the problem was the fact that about $400,000 were spent on students who never actually took the cabs, but for whom the cab companies billed the city anyway. It may sound petty, but a community probably ought to see an injustice in a program that sends some kids to school in luxury while the school buses may soon be traveling without a tire.

Perhaps the most pernicious argument about vouchers is that if we don't have them, we are consigning children in the worst schools to a perpetual life in squalor. Ladies and gentlemen, the choice is not between vouchers and doing nothing. Secretary of Education Richard Riley pointed out recently that a proposed $7 million worth of "so-called" scholarships for students in DC, the latest euphemism for vouchers, would reach a mere two thousand students, leaving the other seventy-five thousand without any extra funds. His alternative was a wise one: use half of the money to match fifty-eight district schools with proven educational success programs like the Laboratory for Success, developed at Temple University, or the "Success for All" program at Johns Hopkins in Baltimore. These are track-record-proven programs to turn around failing inner-city schools. And then with the $3.5 million left, support seventy new after-school programs for seven thousand students. Commonsense and local police tell the same story: it is the hours between 3 and 6 pm that present the greatest danger for children's safety. So please don't let anybody tell you that it is vouchers or nothing changes.

I was speaking in Philadelphia recently and the idea of leaping to vouchers to "fix" education had a particularly bizarre ring. Many of the problems there are those directly addressable through increased funding. A year ago, I was shocked to learn that a state Senator who was visiting Philadelphia schools found a high school that did not have a single computer for student use. She said that a graduating senior told her she didn't feel prepared to get a job without knowing anything about computers. Of course, she was right. Is there no money for computers? No. This state has a "rainy day" fund of over $1.1 billion. Not damp enough when your students can't find one computer? The administration of Governor Tom Ridge had a budget surplus of $777 million dollars last year. Yet the state got an F—which, when I went to Dickinson meant "failure"—in *Education Week*'s "Quality Counts" report for the funding disparities between rich and poor communities. How disparate? The richest school district spends $190,125 more per classroom of twenty-five students than the poorest district. Poor children in the inner cities and rural districts don't stand a chance.

As I said, the progress of public school has not been fully linear. But I like the directions it is going. In the 1950s, segregation was the lawfully sanctioned norm and we bussed students away from their closest school so we could maintain the practice. Now segregation is seen as the sin and constitutional shame it always was. In the 1950s, persons with disabilities were relegated to a hidden corner of the basement, but now, by law, their special needs must be accommodated. In the 1950s, girls were discouraged from bothering with math and science. Now, young women win prestigious awards in every field of study. We are not going back by funding a web of right-wing religious academies that harken back to some new dark age of educational pseudo-reform.

So here are the facts:

Most states are afraid to test voucher students on a regular basis because "school choice" advocates know the results won't be to their liking. When tests are actually administered, however, students at voucher schools normally score worse than their public school peers—particularly in reading and math.

How poorly? Here is the data:

- Louisiana: When it comes to the latest scores for the Louisiana Educational Assessment Program (LEAP), voucher students did worse than those in public school. In 2014, 44 percent of voucher students passed the tests compared with 69 percent in public schools.[8]
- Wisconsin: Of the 272 voucher students enrolled in grades that required testing in 2013–2014, just 33.2 percent scored proficient or better in both reading and math. Unfortunately sixty-one students who should have been tested—almost 25 percent of the pool—opted out of the tests, showing once again how little oversight comes with voucher money. By contrast, 48.6 percent of public school students scored proficient or advanced in math and 36.6 percent scored that in reading.[9]
- Cleveland: In the 2009–2010 school year, almost all voucher students tested in third through eighth grades performed worse on reading and math tests than their public school counterparts. None performed better in math, though some performed slightly better in science and reading.[10] The biggest gaps were as follows:
  - ◊ Fifty-one percent of public school third graders scored proficient or better in math, compared to just 31 percent of voucher students;
  - ◊ 45.6 percent of public school fourth graders scored proficient or better in math, compared with just 22.1 percent of voucher fourth graders;
  - ◊ 54.4 percent of public school third graders scored proficient or better in reading, while only 46.3 percent of voucher students did so;

◊ 26.7 percent of fifth graders scored proficient or higher in science while 24.5 percent of voucher students achieved the same level.

- Washington, DC: In 2010, test data showed that over four years, students who had received vouchers achieved scores in reading and math that were not better than their public school peers in any statistically significant way. Researchers thus concluded the program had "no significant impact" on student academic achievement.[11]

Using provisions of state constitutions, we can often win. Thirty-eight states have provisos that indicate, without equivocation, that no state funds may be used, directly or indirectly, to subsidize religious ministries, missions, or clergy. Other states contain language that requires equitable distribution of tax dollars.

State constitutional provisions have been used successfully to terminate a Louisiana voucher program in 2013, Florida's "Opportunity Scholarship" program in 2006, Arizona's "Scholarship for Pupils with Disabilities" program in 2008, and (as of December 2014) put the kibosh on a North Carolina program as well.

Various state constitutional provisions have been unsuccessfully invoked in challenges to an Indiana voucher plan and (so far) a school district program in Colorado's Douglas County.

When one looks at the facts and applies commonsense legal standards, voucher schemes drop like flies. Texas senator Ted Cruz, a new member of the Senate Subcommittee on the Constitution stated in December 2014, "When it comes to civil rights, I think there is no civil right more important than the right of every child to access a quality education and . . . the most compelling civil rights issue of the 21st Century is the need to expand school choice and educational options."[12]

Charter schools pose a special kind of problem because they are publicly funded but privately run. From a church-state standpoint, the most common issue with these schools is the use of textbooks that promote creationism and undermine evolution. In many cases, these books promote ideas about God and include scripture to back up their claims. Such texts often provide a distorted or inaccurate view of history as well—at least one textbook used by a chain of charter schools in Texas and Arkansas said the holocaust was caused by ideas about evolution.[13]

A second problem with charter schools occurs when a private religious school doesn't have the funds to survive on its own, so it makes a deal with a state to reopen as a charter school. Despite receiving taxpayer funds, in many cases these charter schools are located in the same building(s) as their former religious school, employ the same teachers, and are attended by the same students as before. As a result, it is not uncommon for sectarian instruction to continue—but on the public dime. Schools that make this transition must be closely monitored to ensure that the curriculum becomes secular once the school goes public.

Tuition tax credits are a kind of "kissing cousins" to vouchers. In 2011, the US Supreme Court ruled 5–4 that Arizona taxpayers had no "standing" to challenge the constitutionality of that state's "tax credit scholarship" program. Regrettably, the use here of state constitutions has not been as successful as I had hoped in my too-optimistic take on litigation in New Hampshire.

LOVE YOUR FAITH? THEN PAY FOR IT.[14]

Some years ago, I lived in New Hampshire. I vividly remember two things about the state: the rock formation known as the "Old Man of the Mountain" and the great public schools my children attended.

Sadly, the rock formation collapsed in 2003—and now it looks like the state's public schools may be headed down the same road. New Hampshire's legislators seem determined to siphon money away from public schools and into the coffers of private religious institutions.

It's too late to save the rock, but we can still rescue the schools. Like a lot of states, New Hampshire has a constitution that bans tax support for sectarian enterprises. It also has a law making it easy for taxpayers to challenge unconstitutional forms of government spending. Both are being put to use by the organization I represent, Americans United for Separation of Church and State, which has just filed a lawsuit in state court to free taxpayers from being forced to support religion.

New Hampshire has adopted an increasingly popular (but convoluted) tax-credit scheme that works like this:

Corporation A makes a large donation to a "scholarship" program. It then receives a tax credit—sometimes equivalent to the amount it donated, sometimes slightly less—from the state. The money is parceled out to parents who want to send their children to private schools and hand the bill to someone else.

If your head is spinning right about now, you're not alone. I'm always amazed at the shell games some legislators can come up with when they don't want to follow the clear commands of their governing charters.

And, yes, I put "scholarship" in quotation marks for a reason. That word is a euphemism designed to make what's going on in New Hampshire— taxpayer-funded religion—sound warm and fuzzy.

It's neither warm nor fuzzy. Most private schools in America are religious in nature. They're largely free from government oversight. Most of them teach dogma. Fundamentalist academies, for example, substitute creationism for science and base all instruction on a narrow reading of the Bible. Don't even get me started on what they teach about LGBT Americans and the rights of women.

Parents have the right to send their children to these schools. They have no right to expect you to pay for it. They have no right to expect you to subsidize a sectarian worldview with which you may vehemently disagree. In short, they have no right to tax you to pay for their religion.

Yet that's exactly what is happening in New Hampshire and in other states that have adopted tax credit and voucher plans. Private schools that openly admit they exist primarily to spread a certain faith and indoctrinate children in it are receiving tax windfalls. In some cases, Catholic schools that were on the verge of closing received new life thanks to taxpayer-funded vouchers.

Let's call this what it is: a bailout. The government can choose to bail out General Motors; it can't bail out the Catholic Church.

With any luck, this won't be going on in New Hampshire much longer. Americans United and the American Civil Liberties Union argue in their lawsuit that the tax credit plan is just a back-door method to do something that the New Hampshire Constitution plainly forbids: award taxpayer money to religion.

Part I, Article 6, of that document guarantees that "no person shall ever be compelled to pay towards the support of the schools of any sect or denomination." Furthermore, Part II, Article 83, states that "no money raised by taxation shall ever be granted or applied for the use of the schools or institutions of any religious sect or denomination."

What part of "no money raised by taxation" did New Hampshire legislators not understand?

For more than two hundred years, religion in America has been voluntarily supported, and it has done quite well under that system. The churches
I have been involved with over the years have undertaken many projects
designed to spread our beliefs, help the hurting, and draw people to what we
do, but we've always been guided by one bedrock principle: If the men and
women sitting in the pews can't be persuaded to pay for it, we don't do it.

Regrettably, the New Hampshire Supreme Court ultimately ruled in favor
of this plan in mid-2014, using the somewhat bizarre argument that because
the residents of New Hampshire, who were also taxpayers, could not show any
"personal" injury, they couldn't challenge the program.[15] This result came about
in spite of a New Hampshire statute that appeared to broadly grant "standing"
to citizens who allege that virtually any actions violated the state constitution.

Chapter 4

THE RELIGIOUS RIGHT

The More Things Change,
the More the Weirdness Continues

What follows is one of my "Top 10" lists. This was a speech given to the annual dinner of the Texas Civil Liberties Union back in 2002. As you will see after you read it, any church/state separationist could pretty much give the same speech with very current examples of the same reasons for distrust.

TEXAS: TEN REASONS TO BE SUSPICIOUS OF THE RELIGIOUS RIGHT[1]

Thanks for the introduction; there are some places where I wouldn't get such a positive description. I was interviewed recently by a journalist who asked if I got hate mail. It was as easy to answer yes to that question as it would be for any of you to answer no to the question, "Does Florida have good voting machines?" I regret that my hate mail so often includes vulgarity and/or bad spelling. But it is even worse when it expresses abject ignorance. Here is a recent e-mail: "If the founding fathers of this country were alive today, they would have Lynn on trial for witchcraft." I thought this country was founded to move away from such activities.

My daughter was actually kind enough to send me a website devoted entirely to attacking me. It has a message board. (I am not making this up.) One message read: "I used to be proud of my name—Lynn—but now I am embarrassed because people might think I'm related to Barry"; a few days later, "I've done some research—two boats of Lynn's came over from Ireland—Barry Lynn's relations were on the boat of 'bad Lynn's,' and your relatives must have been on the other one." Thank Heaven for the Internet! It saved me a huge amount of money on genealogical research.

What I'd like to do this evening is something I rarely do: give a presentation called "The Top 10 Reasons You Should Not Trust the Religious Right." Actually, this address is so inflammatory that I am only allowed to give it at ACLU dinners, library conventions, and meetings of the Religious Right —in the latter case, because they don't understand it!

Why distrust? First, the Religious Right sees things that aren't there! In the movie *The Sixth Sense*, the little boy saw dead people and they WERE really there. The Religious Right sees things that aren't really there. Let me explain. You probably know that the Right is obsessed with images. They are offended by all kinds of things. They don't like rap music; they don't like *Playboy* or *Cosmopolitan* covers to be visible in stores, so they keep demanding that brown wrappers be put over them; they don't like anything connected to Hollywood. But they also have found reasons to demand the censorship or destruction of things that many of us don't see as remotely controversial. Pastor Jack Brock of the Christ Community Church in Alamogordo, New Mexico, sponsored a book burning to celebrate the New Year. At this event at least thirty Harry Potter books were tossed into a bonfire. Although Brock admitted that he had not read any of the four J. K. Rowling fantasy novels about a young wizard, he nevertheless formally declared to CNN that "Harry Potter is the devil" who "is destroying people" and that the books are "a masterpiece of satanic deception . . . that encourage our youth to learn more about witches, warlocks, and sorcerers, and those things [that] are an abomination to God." By the way, he also burned the *Collected Works of William Shakespeare*; wait a minute, that only makes sense—there are three witches in *Macbeth* alone! If this is all that Religious Right fundamentalists did, they might be the subject of David Letterman jokes, but the First Amendment would not face a serious threat. My only interest would be if my backyard was downwind of his fire. Regrettably, too many of these literal book burners are not satisfied with persuading people to do things; they seek to invoke the power of the state to stop everyone from exercising their own judgment. See, you didn't know. But it gets worse. The American Life League announced that in the video of Disney's *Lion King* the word SEX is visible in a cloud formation as the lion king is standing on a cliff. Ridiculous—I can't remember that. I've seen it a lot—just about every weekend I pick my wife up on Friday and we buy a bottle of wine and rent *The Lion King*.

Reason number two is that these folks do not always understand irony and have a startling lack of any sense of humor. We took out an ad in the Colorado Springs *Gazette* a few years back that just read, in block letters, "MAYBE WE SHOULD LET RADICAL RELIGIOUS FUNDAMENTALISTS RUN AMERICA (AFTER ALL IT HAS WORKED SO WELL IN IRAN)." It then had a special 800 number we sometimes used—man, did we get some interesting messages the next day, most of them unrepeatable. My personal favorite was from a guy who said: "I'm just going to waste your money because I know you're paying for this. So I'll just keep on costing you money, by staying on the line." Then he began to whistle. Then he put the receiver up to a radio playing really bad country music, and then up to a TV blaring a soap opera. Now, we have a cutoff after five minutes, but because he was having too much fun to hear it click off, I visualize that to this very moment there is a guy in Colorado still waltzing around his house holding his telephone up to household appliances—the trash compactor, the vacuum cleaner, the humming device in his wife's bottom drawer, still thinking he's on our dime.

Reason number three: They are careless. There is a minister out in Buena Vista, California, named Wiley Drake. For several years, he has been praying "imprecatory" prayers—basically prayers for my death. He decided to get a member of Congress—Congressman Jay Dickey of Arkansas—to hold a "pastors' summit" in the Capitol, basically to pray for the election of Republicans. Somehow, Pastor Drake must have gotten his list of friends and enemies mixed up, and I ended up getting invited to attend the pastors' summit. When I walked into that room and went up to Wiley Drake to say "hello" he nearly turned to stone, as if the largest skunk in this universe had just arrived at his family reunion picnic. See, that was just pure sloppiness—I wasn't supposed to be there. Congressman Dickey was a big hit, though, with these pastors—particularly when he explained that Satan was often on the floor of the House of Representatives causing members to cast bad votes. Attendees were constantly praying for Mr. Dickey (which is ok by me), until it shaded into praying for his reelection (that offends my personal view of the purpose of prayer). Just a footnote: On January 6, we began referring to Mr. Dickey as "former Congressman" Jay Dickey, since he lost his reelection Tuesday night. I do not wish to impose my religion on you: You can decide if God works in mysterious ways!

Reason number four: They are a tad hypocritical, and that makes them untrustworthy. The members of Congress supported by the RR often tote their perfect scorecards on "family issues" prepared by groups like the

Christian Coalition and the Traditional Values Coalition, but sometimes have trouble explaining their own life choices. For example, in a five-year period, ending in 2002, Congress has spent almost $400 million on programs whose "exclusive purpose" is the promotion of abstinence and, in the words of the federal law, teach that monogamy in the context of marriage is the "expected standard of human sexuality."[2] I know what this guy over at that table is thinking! Who supported the standard? Yes, Newt "I used to be important" Gingrich, who was, of course, having an affair with a staff member during the entire period he was chastising the president for his sexual indecencies.[3] Then there was Bob Livingston, who would have been Speaker of the House but for his numerous amorous escapades.[4] And the list goes on; we need not belabor it. What is fascinating is not just the hypocrisy but the lameness of the excuses for it. Judiciary Chairman Henry Hyde, presider over Clinton's impeachment, admitted to an affair but described it as a "youthful indiscretion" at the tender age of forty.[5] At least Bush uses thirty as the cutoff age for youth. And, of course, Georgia congressman Bob Barr is so "profamily" he's already had three of them![6]

Reason number five: When the Religious Right doesn't get what it wants through the normal processes of constitutional democracy, they often try to get it through tactics of pressure, lawlessness, and intimidation. I have been having a running feud with a minister (I know it sounds like ministers don't like me) in Texas named Robert Jeffress because of his manner of dealing with books he doesn't like. He goes to the local library, checks out books he finds offensive, and never returns them. Normally, we call this theft: There is even one of the Ten Commandments directly on point—it is against it. What the pastor then does is goes to the city council to demand that the library not be permitted to repurchase the "lost" item[7].

Reason number six: Their prognostications are often wrong. Recently, when the city of Orlando, Florida, allowed rainbow flags to be flown from city light poles and, when the Disney company had a "Gay Day" at Disney World, Pat Robertson went ballistic. He said on his syndicated TV show *The 700 Club* that Orlando could be hit by tornadoes, earthquakes, terrorist attacks, and "possibly a meteor."[8] We at Americans United were afraid that this prediction hadn't gotten its proper recognition, so we reported it in a press release titled, "Duck, Donald." When all was said and done, Orlando didn't have any of these problems and was actually spared from disastrous forest fires that occurred in much of the rest of the state.

Reason number seven: They always have simple answers for almost every problem, but they are simply wrong. Following the Columbine tragedy two and a half years ago, Congress managed to avoid passing any legislation about guns or funding programs for troubled youth. The House, however, did pass a resolution supporting the posting of the Ten Commandments in all schools and public buildings. I doubt that Moses has been waiting for several millennia for this affirmation of his work. That's simplistic and useless. If placing holy words next to people turned them from sinners to saints, the mere presence of Gideon bibles in motel nightstands would have terminated adultery by now.

Reason number eight: The Religious Right really doesn't like most of us. Take Pat Robertson, for example. Here are a few of his observations about people of different faiths. On Hindus: "What is Hinduism but devil worship, ultimately?"[9] On Muslims: "To see Americans become followers of, quote, Islam, is nothing short of insanity. . . . Why would people in America want to embrace the religion of the slavers?"[10] What a remarkably short historical memory he has. Did he just forget that there were a lot of Christians piloting those boats from West Africa? He has suggested that the Roman Catholic understanding of Holy Communion is akin to cannibalism. He doesn't think much of fellow Protestants, noting: "You say, you're supposed to be nice to the Episcopalians and the Presbyterians and the Methodists and this, that and the other thing—nonsense! I don't have to be nice to the spirit of the Antichrist. . . . I don't have to be nice to them."[11] His book *The New World Order* uses classic anti-Semitic sources and reeks of anti-Jewish sentiment.

It is not just religious bigotry for which he stands. He's not very high on women. He noted in one fundraising letter: "The feminist agenda . . . is not about equal rights for women. It is about a socialist, anti-family political movement that encourages women to leave their husbands, kill their children, practice witchcraft and become lesbians."[12] He later noted that he couldn't consider women the intellectual equivalents of men because they can't play chess as well.[13] He didn't know that at the time we had a woman national chess master, and we've had a few since. I really don't think he's changed his mind. The facts rarely seem to matter to him. I have heard a rumor that he is checking into new competitive games for gender comparison—and is leaning toward bowling.

Gay people also aren't particularly appreciated. As recently as four months ago at the annual Christian Coalition convention in Washington,

DC, he was selling a work by George Grant called *Legislating Immorality*, which called for the execution of all gay people, but was kind enough to qualify it in a footnote by saying that in our judicial system we would have to give them a trial first. As we know, because of Matthew Shepherd and Brandon Teena, some people don't read the footnotes. See, you can't peddle hate literature out of the back of your bookstore and then take no moral responsibility for the actions of others who seem to take those words into their cold hearts.

And what of race? Pat Robertson has tried to make inroads into the African-American community. Briefly, he even created something called the Samaritan Project to work with black churches; he, of course, dumped the project as soon as it made demands on his own bank account. Pastors were a little unhappy to learn that Robertson had been one of the last Americans willing to go on state television in South Africa to support apartheid, arguing that he wasn't sure that the rights of the white minority would be protected by a new system.[14] If that is viewed by some of you as ancient history, his racial insensitivity continues. The keynote dinner speaker at his 1998 Christian Coalition "Road To Victory" convention in Washington was Charlton Heston, representing both Moses and the NRA, I believe. Heston gave a barn-burning speech about how many things are wrong with the country, culminating in his prayerful lament, "Heaven help the God-fearing, law abiding, Caucasian middle class." No criticism by the Coalition of that. The speech was noted, however, by fascist David Duke, who put the speech up on his own website, and asked readers why it was okay for Heston to say this, but if he said it he would be called a racist. Good question, David; although I think he and all of you would have different answers. Despite all the hate-filled rhetoric that we have had to endure from Robertson, one of the chief purveyors of religious bigotry in America, we now learn that he is to be rewarded with a 1.5 million dollar grant from the so called Compassion Capital Fund! Of course, the fact that Robertson had been a harsh critic of the program on the grounds that religious minorities such as the Church of Scientology and Hare Krishnas may receive tax dollars had no effect on his willingness to accept the cash.[15] It appears that thirty pieces of silver was enough to change his mind.

Reason number nine: They aren't clear about their real agenda until they have suckered a lot of folks far down the primrose path. A major focus of their efforts toward restricting reproductive choices right now is on banning third-trimester abortions, or, as they characterize it, killing a fetus in the process of birth. And the procedure they describe is couched in some lurid language that even normally pro-choice folks sometimes decide to draw that line. Do you think for a moment that this is all the Religious Right wants? Of course not. The official question for candidates on most of those phony voters' guides they distributed in churches the Sunday before election day was usually phrased, "Do you agree that abortion should be illegal under all circumstances?" Overturning *Roe v. Wade* is their goal; outlawing all abortions in each state is their next goal. Dr. James Dobson says women who have abortions have committed a "crime against humanity [that] will not go unpunished."

Reason number ten: Inconsistency. Although they detest government, they want to use government power to promote their religion. The real enemy of the Christian Right is not Americans United or the ACLU; it is themselves.

I don't think the Religious Right understands that religion thrives best where government takes no sides and offers no "help." There are two thousand different religious groups in the United States and tens of millions of Americans who choose no spiritual path. We all live in relative harmony. Look at Iran; look at Northern Ireland; look at Afghanistan—state-sponsored religion and the wars against other faiths it engenders should teach us all that we have a pretty good thing going here. In fact, the separation of church and state is probably the single best idea that our two-hundred-year experiment in democracy has engendered.

I don't want, or need, the help of government to pray the prayers I believe in. Politicians always talk about "nonsectarian prayers." What do they say: "To a God or gods unknown. Thanks. Amen"? I think most people of faith want to pray in their own manner. I don't want the government giving out money or vouchers to corrupt the integrity of the ministries of the church I attend or any other faith community. I don't want to see a day when Methodists, Baptists, Catholics, Scientologists, and Christian Scientists battle for the biggest piece of funding for their religious missions.

Indeed, this is precisely what is so terribly wrong with the Bush initiative on "faith-based organizations"—it will amount to the funding of programs that are by their very character "religious." You cannot be spiritual when a private dollar is in your hand and secular when it is a government dollar. By the way, George Bush really is being hypocritical about this. On the first

Monday in office he reinstated the so-called "Mexico City Policy," which barred all federal funds to family-planning groups that operated abroad if they—even with privately raised funds—counseled or performed abortion. Money is fungible; if the government buys the soup for the soup kitchen the religious provider can just buy more Bibles.

That's what Robertson thought he would achieve during the last election—a president to select and an overwhelming Republican Senate to ratify selections to the Supreme Court. The speech given by his spouse, Dede Robertson, to the Christian Coalition convention in September included the stern warning that without a new Supreme Court—and Dave Barry, I am not making this up—we would soon have "SEX IN THE STREETS"! (Talk about traffic tie-ups).

He didn't quite get what he wanted. If there are Supreme Court appointments to fill a majority of the Senate—Democrats and Pro-First Amendment Republicans—can stop bad appointments. Clarence Thomas, a man of no known intellect, did NOT have to be on the Court; spineless senators put him there. Bad proposals of George W. Bush—about public school vouchers, about prayer in school, about limits on reproductive choice—can be blocked through the procedures of the Senate if the will to protect the Constitution is there. Your senators aren't going to help, I know, but others have the power to do what one of the greatest defenders of the First Amendment in modern political history—former Republican senator of Connecticut Lowell Weicker—said was the Senate's greatest role: be the last best defender of the Constitution for the American people.

In 1999 I was having lunch with a congressman from Oklahoma named Ernest Istook. We had just had a debate in Texas about his proposal to bring government-sponsored prayer back to public schools. After finishing the main course, he says: "Barry, the conservative Republican caucus had a meeting the other day and we've solved the problem of the Y2K bug." I can be a straight man, so I say, "Gee, so what did you guys decide." He answers, "Well, when the computers can't recognize the year 2000, they flip back to 1900, and we like it better that way." There is a lot of sad truth in that joke. But, you know, I don't get the impression that most of you are willing to go gently back into that night when women couldn't vote and couldn't make reproductive choices; when those with mental and physical disabilities were shunted aside to basement classrooms as early as elementary school so their disability would be complete; when gays and lesbians were third-class citizens everywhere; and when the shame of racism was often celebrated as a virtue.

The bottom line—the Religious Right still wants to run your life from the moment of conception until the moment of "natural death"—as well as pretty much every moment in between. What a nation we'd have then.

IMAGINE THE RIGHT'S RELIGION[16]

For decades I've been told by my adversaries in the Religious Right that they only seek a "place at the table" for their Christian worldview—well, their version of Christianity, that is.

But evidence has mounted recently that what they really want is something else entirely: to own the table, determine what goes on it, and force-feed everyone the same gruel they consume.

Consider the outcry over the US Air Force Academy's decision to alter the Honor Oath cadets take every academic year. It formerly concluded, always, with the phrase "So help me God."

The problem is that some cadets didn't want to say a religious oath. Since it makes no sense to force a person to swear an oath that he or she disbelieves, academy officials made the eminently sensible decision to make the God part optional.

Religious Right groups immediately went ballistic. The Tupelo, Mississippi, based American Family Association is urging its legion of followers to write to the commandant of the Academy to "preserve religious liberty by defending the oath and recommending the Academy keep the current language intact."[17]

The Family Research Council's Tony Perkins asserted in a radio broadcast that even giving nonbelievers the option not to say "God" would somehow reflect an "anti-Christian bias."[18] According to Perkins, making these four words optional would not be "inclusive" since it would not include military personnel like George Washington, whom he claims initiated that phrase. (Washington didn't do that, but that's another column.)

Think about this for a moment. How does it protect "religious liberty" in this multicultural and multireligious nation to force all cadets to affirm support for something an increasing number of them do not believe is true?

In fact, isn't it silly—and perhaps even blasphemous—to demand that newly minted defenders of the republic lie about their belief in God? This is an "honor code" after all. The pedestal on which to erect a system of moral commitment is probably not perjury. (Nevertheless, a member of Congress has actually introduced legislation to make it illegal for the military to alter such oaths without congressional approval.[19])

Furthermore, since no one is told they cannot say "So help me God" how does this change to an individual option possibly harm some future military leader who is devout and includes the phrase as she or he is still permitted to do?

Perkins holds a so-called Values Voter Summit every autumn in Washington and has been known to actually have Jewish people on the platform. Does the fact that US House Majority Leader Eric Cantor (R-VA) may bow his head but not pray in the name of Jesus mean that the assembled Christian masses at the conference are suddenly having their rights violated? Person A's decision to opt out of Person B's theology in no way lessens Person B's right to participate.

Our second table-grabber is Sarah Palin. She has returned to the talk-show circuit with a new book called *Good Tidings and Great Joy: Protecting the Heart of Christmas*. This tome asserts that our nation is at war with Christianity, with the secularist assault on Christmas becoming the bloody Antietam of the conflict.

According to the former governor, one of the many fronts in this anti-yuletide blitzkrieg is the tendency by in-store greeters and advertising executives at certain big box stores to replace "Merry Christmas" with "Happy Holidays."

Like the oath defenders, Palin seems to assume that a retailer's failure to affirm a certain aspect of Christianity at every moment is somehow an assault on her faith. The horror she sees in "inclusion"—and her preposterous demand that non-Christians greet people with a religious sentiment alien to them—turns what is good about a diverse culture into some badge of shame.

Tables are especially important in public schools. They should be open to all there. Yet recent news reports from several Southern states have found a breathtaking level of "You are welcome at my table—as long as you'll pray with me" sentiments from public high school football coaches.

Mark Mariakis of the public Ridgeland High School in Georgia told the Chattanooga *Times Free Press*, "We as coaches fail if we only teach football, so we try to set an example of how a Christian man handles any situation."[20]

Another coach boasted about the players he had converted to his faith through a Bible camp, asserting, "I want to win as much as anybody, but if I don't win a single football game this year I feel successful because of those twenty-one kids who became Christians. Nothing is more important than that."[21]

Thus, in spite of numerous court decisions to the contrary, these coaches support official Christian team prayer, as did virtually every respondent to the newspaper's survey of coaches in Tennessee, Alabama, and Georgia. No fig leaves of "nonproselytizing prayers" or rotation of prayers here; just good old Christian triumphalism every Friday night.

My final example concerns a table that, while privately owned, could be big enough for lots of people—if only its owners had a more charitable vision. According to reports in the *Kansas City Star*, the Kansas City Rescue Mission has decided not to accept the offer of the Kansas City Atheist Coalition to help with distribution of two thousand Thanksgiving meals to the poor and elderly.

The Mission apparently decided to include a religious message in this year's meal boxes, and it was unclear if the atheists would go along with that. It seemed irrelevant anyway, as the Mission made it abundantly clear that it didn't want the nonbelievers' help, calling the partnership a bad fit. And that was the end of any communication.[22]

That struck me as a missed opportunity. I'll bet that there are more than two thousand poor and elderly people in the area. Wouldn't it have been more polite, more decent, and more "Christian" even, to call the atheists, tell them what neighborhoods the Christians were not covering, and give them some advice about how to serve those who might otherwise go hungry? In other words, shouldn't the Mission have at least helped the atheists set up their own table?

Alas, to those who are fearful of other beliefs, there can be only one table, one place to sit, and one seatmate to converse with. Their world begins and ends in the confines of that tiny table.

I say let a thousand tables bloom. I encourage visiting every one. After all, a person can sometimes gain a whole new perspective by occasionally switching seats.

WHO IS THE RELIGIOUS RIGHT?

To preserve the separation of church and state, you have to spend a lot of time observing, debating, and interacting with the Religious Right. The Religious Right did not appear full blown from the head of some particularly repugnant Zeus in the 1970s. It had antecedents throughout American history, as biblical literalism and/or dogmatic patriarchal teaching joined political conservatism to create a regressive social movement.

When Americans United was formed in 1948, it saw the dangers posed by the very powerful Roman Catholic hierarchy of its day in all manner of battles. Archdiocesan officials were willing to "loan out" teaching nuns to financially beleaguered public school systems who, quite predictably, added "religion" to the "reading, 'riting, and 'rithmetic" of the curriculum. These were referred to as "captive schools" and the very first lawsuit that Americans United filed was a challenge to such an arrangement in New Mexico. The new organization, however, also fought organized efforts to stop the import of controversial films like the now-classic Italian film *The Miracle*. Longshoremen American "sons of Italy" refused to unload prints from ships in the New York harbor because the principal character had generated a religious fervor based on a less-than-miraculous birth. The charge against the film was "blasphemy" in its parallel to the New Testament tale of the immaculate conception. Catholic doctrine opposing all forms of "artificial" birth control also came under our scrutiny.

In the fifties, Protestant conservatives tended to be far less visible than today, banking on a generic national religiosity to keep the nation from dipping too far into a sea of moral decay. The idea of direct partisan political involvement was nearly unthinkable, with major preachers like Billy Graham rarely commenting publicly on specific controversies in foreign or domestic policy. Even the man who would become synonymous with partisan Christianity in the seventies, the late Dr. Jerry Falwell, eschewed any political engagement during his rise to prominence as a Southern preacher.

All this changed in the early seventies, when a group of secular Republican organizers decided that it would be highly beneficial to their party to have a face of moral potency growing right out of the Protestant community. They were turned down by a number of prominent preachers. Then, Falwell suddenly shifted his position from nonengagement with politics to leading the organization known as the Moral Majority. His leadership helped dramatically to unleash the clout of other reactionary Protestants, including those who were highly offended by a Supreme Court decision that ruled that private religious schools engaged in any forms of racial discrimination could be denied precious tax exempt status. After milking that issue, Falwell soon found common cause with Catholic officials in his unswerving opposition to abortion, largely legalized in 1973 in the historic case of *Roe v. Wade*, argued at the Supreme Court by Texas lawyer Sarah Weddington, who later became a member of the Board of Trustees of Americans United.

Falwell was an indefatigable presence on radio and television, clearly enamored of his personal magnetism and somewhat less concerned with local organizing. Into the organizational vacuum, however, came Pat Robertson, creator of the Christian Broadcasting Network and himself a Presidential candidate in 1988. After a rather stunning victory in the Iowa Republican caucuses that year—and then a precipitous tumble in later contests—Robertson ended his executive aspirations and gave his impressive fundraising mailing list to Ralph Reed, a young conservative activist, who used it to create the powerful Christian Coalition.

I attended almost all of the yearly Christian Coalition confabs in Washington. What follows are a few reminiscences of those trips as chronicled in my monthly columns for *Church and State* magazine.

Uneasy Rider: Car Sick on the "Road to Victory" (1995)[23]

I spent the greater part of an early September weekend observing the Christian Coalition's "Road to Victory" Conference here in Washington. It was the Coalition's fifth conference, which means next year there will have been more "Roads" than there are sequels to "Rocky."

A reporter called me the day after the event and asked me to "sum it up." I replied, "Any conference where Pat Buchanan gives one of the more moderate speeches is a pretty extreme event." I expected to hear some pretty harsh rhetoric from the parade of speakers who addressed the gathering. What I did not expect, however, was the disturbing, mean-spirited nature of the response of so many of the attendees. Let me give you a few examples.

When Texas senator Phil Gramm addressed the group, he got a luke-warm response to the first half of his speech, which was devoted to "family friendly" changes to the tax code and other economic issues. (There was a little burst of energy when he called for a flat tax.) But when he shifted gears to social issues, the room came alive. Gramm promised to make sure crime is dealt with harshly and promised to use capital punishment "regularly." For this, he got whoops and cheers, a standing ovation, and the kind of response usually reserved for the words of heroes. People of goodwill can have differing moral beliefs regarding the propriety of the death penalty, but it was embarrassing to see religious people seem so happy about the grisly prospect of more death.

Now, you probably didn't see much of the crowd's response in the considerable network news coverage of the event. The only people I spoke to after the event who commented on the crowd were C-SPAN viewers who had been glued to the coverage provided there. The "Big News" outlets focused almost exclusively on the parade of Republican presidential candidates coming to pay homage to Pat Robertson's political power and legislative agenda.

Every Republican candidate was invited, with the notable exception of Sen. Arlen Specter of Pennsylvania. Specter has been critical of the Coalition's stranglehold on the GOP, and it was clear they didn't want to hear from a voice that might challenge their bogus rewriting of American history and constitutional law.

Indeed, I can't recall any of the candidates taking issue with *anything* on the Robertson agenda. No one had anything good to say about separation of church and state; no one suggested healing divisiveness and intolerance in the nation. There was only pandering to the pet peeves of the Robertson crowd.

Why do presidential candidates feel compelled to uncritically pay obeisance to an organization founded by a man who believes mainstream Protestants represent the "spirit of the Anti-Christ" and alleges that George Bush and Jimmy Carter may have "unknowingly and unwittingly" formed an alliance with Lucifer to create a "new world order"? The only justification is the perceived clout of Robertson's organization. During the conference, he noted claims that the Coalition is in control of eighteen state Republican parties and has significant influence in thirteen others. Robertson made it clear he is going for all fifty states.

Another low point of the event had to be Ralph Reed's request that delegates sign a pledge card. It contains such commitments as, "walk and talk in the manner of love, for God is love" and "refrain the violence of fist, tongue or heart." In fact, it was based on a pledge card the Rev. Dr. Martin Luther King asked members of the Southern Christian Leadership Conference to sign. Another proviso: "Remember always that the movement seeks justice and reconciliation—not victory." How ironic that such a pledge would be taken at a so-called "Road to Victory" conference.

"ROAD TO VICTORY" 1996: WHERE'S THE EXIT RAMP?[24]

I don't exactly go "undercover" to the Christian Coalition conferences anymore. People overhear me in the halls giving interviews to the media or just recognize me in sessions and often have plenty to tell me.

In general, they are trying to "convert" me, or at least "correct" me, by showing me the error of my ways. Sometimes things get nasty, but in general these are relatively civil exchanges. For example, a gentleman from Fairfax, Virginia, introduced me to one of his friends and said he admired my ability to articulate "those off-the-wall ideas of yours." (I think this is safely characterized as being "damned by faint praise.") Many people tell me they listen to the monthly two-hour religious liberty debates I have on Christian radio with former Rutherford Institute attorney Craig Parshall, or they tell me how much fun it was to listen to the old radio show I did with Pat Buchanan.

Speaker David Melton also predicted that we would "lose our religious freedom within ten years" if current trends continue. He then told the tragic tale of Miss North Dakota, who has already faced "religious persecution" (his words) because at one of the one hundred public schools in the state where she spoke she was not allowed to sing a Christian hymn during her presentation to students. My question, of course, is why a guest speaker was allowed to evangelize at the other ninety-nine public schools? Even if one agrees that she should be allowed to sing religious songs at a public school assembly with mandatory attendance—and I don't—does it honestly rise to the level of "persecution" if she is prevented from doing so?

Mr. Melton should read a history book to learn about real religious persecution. I direct him to the sections dealing with how Christians were treated in the Roman Empire before Constantine the Great or Henry the VIII's reign of terror against Catholics in sixteenth-century England.

Not-So-Undercover at the
Christian Coalition "Road to Victory" (1998)[25]

It turns out I am one of the bigger "photo opportunities" at the annual "Road to Victory" Conference of Pat Robertson's Christian Coalition. Many attendees wanted a picture of me to take home. Some took them surreptitiously, but more often they asked for a posed shot. Why? Maybe to prove they survived a real-life demonic encounter.

One camera-wielding woman from Bucks County, PA, said she wanted to show the snapshot to her friends. She then proceeded to give me directions to her house in case I'd ever like to stop in for lunch.

Lest you think I am getting a swelled head over this, I have to admit that a few people did mistake me for a certain flat-tax-loving presidential candidate. One fellow had his friend take a photo with his brand-new, full digital camera. After the shot, he gushed, "I loved it the night you hosted *Saturday Night Live!*" (I still can't believe this guy confused me with Steve Forbes.)

Finally, after two days of listening to a variety of screeds against most of what I believe in, I had one final encounter with a "fan." After one session, I spied a middle-aged woman barreling down the hall toward me. She rushed up and breathlessly demanded to know, "Why do you come to our events?" My response may not have been perfectly polite, but it was honest: "Because I get renewed energy with which to fight you."

The Religious Right spent millions of dollars in the final weeks of Campaign '98? What did it get them? Embarrassingly little, it seemed to me on the Wednesday morning after the election. But I wanted to hear their take on it, so I got up early that morning to go over to the National Press Club in Washington to listen to Family Research Council head Gary Bauer and Randy Tate, executive director of the Christian Coalition, "spin" the previous night's results. When I saw Bauer before his event and said I was there to hear him explain the election, he quipped, "I think I'm in trouble already."

Half an hour later, I ran into Tate who, apparently forgetting that he has referred to me as a "thug" and a "so-called minister" over the past weeks, eagerly invited me to sit down and listen to his press conference.

At each event, I had the distinct feeling I was listening to an analysis of an election on some planet other than Earth. Bauer and Tate claimed that many GOP candidates lost because they were not clear enough on the "pro-family" agenda and therefore failed to excite the conservative Christian voters, who stayed home.

It just doesn't wash. If running on the Religious Right's issues will help a candidate win, then why did Pennsylvania's Republican pro-choice governor Tom Ridge get so many crossover Democratic votes that he was easily reelected, while in Iowa Republican Jim Lightfoot, who campaigned on the theme, "It's all about life," lost dramatically?

Why did the two incumbent governors most clearly allied with the Religious Right agenda, Fob James of Alabama and David Beasley of South Carolina, lose their jobs? Opined Tate, "Some agenda beats no agenda every time." In truth, voters heard Gov. James talk about prayer in school, the Ten Commandments in courthouses, and creation science in the science classroom ad nauseam and decided they'd had enough.

Tate and his Christian Coalition colleagues might have been a little less eager to have me sit in if they had known that I would be holding an impromptu press conference right in the hallway outside their press room. My message to the media was pretty straightforward. A significant portion of the electorate did send a message to the Religious Right and its political sycophants: "Sit down and be quiet." Too close an identification with far-right causes may be the kiss of death in closely contested elections.

Back in 1998, the Religious Right threatened to defeat House members who voted against Rep. Ernest Istook's so-called "Religious Freedom Amendment?"[26] Well, of the 203 members who voted against that amendment, two were not reelected—and one was defeated by someone more committed to church-state separation.

My Chat with Pat: Exchanging Views with Brother Robertson (1999)[27]

You just never know whom you will run into in a Washington restaurant. The Thursday before the annual Christian Coalition "Road to Victory" Conference, I noticed Pat Robertson having dinner across the way from where I was chowing down. Since I saw him, I was relatively sure he saw me. After dessert, I thought I should go visiting, and even before I reached his table, he was rising to greet me, thanking me for coming to his event.

I noted that I wanted to "swell the crowd" and then mentioned that my mother actually is a viewer of the 700 Club, his daily syndicated television "news" and "information" show.

"Smart lady," he responded.

Not wanting him to get too excited, I noted that Mom "doesn't understand why Pat Robertson says those nasty things about me." He chortled that maybe she could come and visit him and they'd straighten things out.

The rest of the Christian Coalition conference went about as I expected. Republican presidential hopefuls showed up to woo the crowd, although no "straw poll" of favorites was taken. The display area had booths hawking expected wares, ranging from antipornography computer software to anti-abortion bumper stickers.

This year, Y2K fears brought out some new dealers. Chesapeake, Virginia, meteorologist Jonathan Cash was there with his book, The Age of the Antichrist. ("It's fiction," his wife said to me, which was helpful assurance that I hadn't missed something really big on CNN.) A gold-coin-dealer-turned-survival-food-vendor gave me a brown bag of turkey chili with a self-heating chemical around the food so that a simple pull of a string would activate a boil-up of the stew. (The cost for a family of four for a year is roughly $12,000, which may explain why he did not receive a single order for the product during the convention.)

As usual, I walked around the Coalition conference chatting with journalists and television reporters who were looking for "another side" of the event. Immediately after Robertson's opening address, I remarked to some news media representatives that it was "the most pro-Republican speech I have ever heard him give" and that he seemed "more interested in the G-O-P than G-O-D." That line got picked up in many places. Even Robertson saw it.

I know he saw it because he sent me a lengthy letter on the topic, cast as an "explanation to your mother." Robertson juxtaposed my comments with coverage of his speech by major media outlets. For example, he said, the Washington Post "listed line by line criticism of Congress" and CNN "played repeatedly my comments criticizing the Republican Congress." He added that "roughly 40 percent of my remarks dealt with . . . world poverty, disease, hunger, and the disparate allocation of the world's wealth . . ." and 20 to 25 percent was about school vouchers.

Now, here is where it gets a little nasty. He concluded the epistle: "Barry, what you need to tell your mother is that, unfortunately, when you were a little boy, she didn't teach you to tell the truth, and this is the reason Pat Robertson says unkind things about you from time-to-time."

It is one thing to call me a liar; it is something else to insult my mother's child rearing. So, naturally, I had to correct him by return mail.

I began pointing out that I wasn't giving a word-count analysis of his speech to reporters; I was telling them about its partisan tone. Here is a man who in past addresses has made the admittedly laughable claim that his is a "non-partisan" operation and who in press conferences has carefully labeled his voter-turnout campaigns as an effort to spur "pro-family" voters to the polls. By contrast, at this year's "Road to Victory," he blatantly stated, "We are back. If we aren't in the field this coming election, the Republicans are going to lose. I don't think there is any question about it. We will be the margin of victory in the key races."

I concluded my letter by noting that twice on his TV program he has quoted me as saying, "If your church is on fire, the municipal fire department is not allowed to put out the fire because of the separation of church and state." I neither said nor believe this ridiculous statement.

Since Brother Robertson is so intrigued by "truthfulness," I asked him to apologize on air for that fabricated quote. I'll let you know if I hear back. [Note: It is now 2015 and he has not yet corrected the record.]

By 1997, the Christian Coalition, minus Ralph Reed, was a shadow of its former self, allowing a new "superstar" Religious Right enterprise to emerge. This was the Family Research Council, headed by Tony Perkins. Perkins had been a local Louisiana politician most infamous for once allowing his campaign to buy a mailing list from notorious racist David Duke. This group replaced the Coalition in orchestrating Washington conferences, this time under the title "Value Voters Summits." Of course, I had to attend these as well:

"THE ENEMY" WITHIN: MY STRANGE TREK TO THE VALUES VOTER SUMMIT (2006)[28]

I had a pang of nostalgia as I walked into the hotel hosting the recent "Values Voter Summit" in Washington and picked up my official delegate credentials at the registration booth.

This conference was sponsored primarily by Tony Perkins's FRC Action, but it brought back memories of my many similar visits to Christian Coalition conclaves held during its heyday.

One thing the Christian Coalition and its speakers never did was give much attention to their opponents. Although the ACLU or Planned Parenthood might get a fleeting reference, Pat Robertson, Ralph Reed, and other luminaries usually did not give their ideological adversaries the pleasure of being singled out by name.

Organizers of the Values Voter Summit felt differently. One of the first sessions was a dialogue featuring Perkins, James Dobson of Focus on the Family, and Alan Sears, chief lawyer for the Alliance Defense Fund. They began with general statements about how pastors needed to get involved in the political system. Dobson said he had some hesitancy about jumping into politics this year because he didn't think the Republicans had done enough on "pro-family" issues, but then quickly explained he changed his mind "because the alternative is terrible."

That sure sounded like a clarion call to pull the Republican lever, touch the Republican part of the electronic screen, or check off the Republicans on your absentee ballot for all offices from city dogcatcher to US senator.

Although the session was long on rhetoric and I may have been nodding off, I came to full consciousness when I heard an attack on Americans United and me personally. As Dobson, Perkins and Sears were telling it, AU is trying to intimidate pastors and scare them into silence.

This was a reference to about 117,000 letters AU sent to religious leaders in eleven states, warning them about the Religious Right's efforts to politicize churches by offering them biased voter guides. Summit speakers were not keen on these letters. One even recommended using them to line bird cages.

But then Dobson surprised me. He told the crowds that he knew I had registered for the event and said he'd like to meet with me. He even called me a "nice guy."

After such an invitation, I had no choice but to find a security officer and say, "I'm the guy Dr. Dobson said he wanted to see." As arrangements for me to go backstage were being made, a gaggle of conference attendees had spotted me and many were pulling out their camera-equipped cell phones and were clicking away. It was a kind of rock star moment: The fans (or in this case, the non-fans) wanted proof they were there at some possibly historic event.

I met with Dobson, his wife Shirley (head of the National Day of Prayer Task Force), and Perkins around a circular table. We examined specific "voter guides" put out in the past by some of FOF's associated state groups. I had complained about misleading questions, inflammatory rhetoric, and the obvious (to me and any literate person) fact that these were designed to get voters to go GOP.

Dobson disagreed. He insisted they were all fairly written questions and said the guides were good for church distribution. It was a largely amiable forty minutes, but I left confident there would be no fall bonfires with the voter guides crackling on the fire.

The next day, during a panel on religion and politics, the Rev. Herb Lusk (whom we once reported to the IRS for his pulpit endorsement of George W. Bush during the 2000 GOP convention) had another take on me. Rising from his seat and pounding on the podium he said: "The enemy is out there. I know that name is Barry. But we won't mention his name today or ever again. We know who our enemy is. The more you call the enemy's name, the larger he becomes."

Right-Wing Reunion: What I Saw at the "Values Voter" Summit (2007)[29]

The 2007 gathering was exceptional for me just for the sheer number of past adversaries (and occasional allies) I bumped into. For the first time in a decade, I chatted with Don Wildmon of the American Family Association, a procensorship advocate I first locked horns with when I worked for the ACLU. We agreed that we were both aging and both "men of principle," although each of us views the other's principles as derived from a different Constitution and perhaps alternative universes.

Former education secretary William Bennett advocated jailing reporters who publish information deemed classified by our leaders. If Bennett had his way, the *Pentagon Papers* would never have seen the light of day, and Watergate would still be just the name of a hotel. More than one speaker advocated impeaching federal judges for the "crime" of handing down decisions the far right does not like.

Listening to these folks outline their plans for our country, it seemed like one of my press comments may have been literally true: "This may be the biggest collection of theocrats in one room since the Salem Witch Trials."

The most dangerous idea I heard in the last weekend, though, was one expressed by a few members of the press: The Religious Right is probably dead. Those of us who know about the Religious Right's finances, organizing ability, grassroots presence, and other resources know that obituary was issued prematurely at other times in history.

If we want to stay the course to stop advocates of theocracy, we'll need to do more than whistle past a nonexistent graveyard.

FAITH, FREEDOM, AND FRONT-ROW SEATS: I'M A "VALUES VOTER," BUT NOT THE KIND I MET AT THESE EVENTS (2010)[30]

What goes around comes around. Last year I had to miss the big Religious Right conclave in Washington held each September because I was attending my son's wedding. In penance, I had to attend two Religious Right gatherings this year.

One weekend it was Ralph Reed's Faith & Freedom Coalition's first conference and strategy briefing; the next, the Family Research Council's Values Voter Summit.

They both started out in somewhat odd ways. At Reed's event, the first speaker was Tucker Carlson, whose checkered TV career has sprawled over four networks.

Arriving early, I had taken a chair in the front row to get the best possible view. Carlson recognized me as soon as he walked out. He said, "Barry Lynn! Holy smokes! Folks, I'm sorry, my mind is blank. The great Barry Lynn! I'm amazed you're here."

This led the audience to applaud, apparently thinking he had said "Barry Goldwater" or something. Tucker quickly joked, "No, you don't need to clap, I wouldn't clap," then went on to say I was actually a nice fellow whom he enjoyed debating on television.

The following Friday, I got to the Values Voter Summit pretty early. When I asked one of the security folks when the conference ballroom would be opened, he replied, "Are you Barry Lynn?" I acknowledged that I was (my name badge even proved it), and he asked me to stand away from the doors with him.

I thought maybe I was getting special access. Nope. When the doors did open for the gathering crowd, another security guard blocked me from entering! I had to slip in another door just a few feet away. I even managed to snag another front-row seat.

These two weekends were a lot like events I used to attend nearly twenty years ago when TV preacher Pat Robertson's Christian Coalition held conferences in Washington, DC.

For example, people still wanted to take pictures with me, to prove to the folks back home that even though their trip to the nation's capital didn't lead to a photo op with Sarah Palin or Glenn Beck, they did get a snapshot or video with one of Satan's imps.

One woman even brought her twelve-year-old son over to me and said, "Now if you ever see Mr. Lynn on television, don't believe a word he says." I responded with: "Listen to your mother." She missed the irony.

OK, they don't like me much. I can live with that. But what really bothers me about these events—dripping with appeals to recapture America, defend the Constitution, and stop overregulation of American life—is the bizarre spin they give on what "values" they are trying to recapture. They talk about "freedom" and "liberty" and "the Constitution" but ignore any reference to things that most of us really care about.

US Senate candidate Christine O'Donnell of Delaware warned of overregulation of water flow in toilets and demands by some municipalities for "greener" light bulbs. Several speakers ominously prophesied that military hospitals soon might be required to pay for sex-change operations.

Are these the concerns that keep you up at night?

Both of these events featured strong efforts to link the demands of the old Religious Right (prayer in the public schools, school vouchers, anti-gay policies, restrictions on reproductive choice) with the economic principles of the Tea Party crowd.

These movements are not synonymous, but there is enough overlap to be concerned that their goal of seizing power across the political spectrum might be achieved. There are pure libertarian strains in the Tea Party that certainly hate what they call "big government" but are also appalled at the prospect of "big religion"—a powerful sectarian movement that will try to regulate them from birth to death.

The message from the two weekends was: Let's take control and we'll sort out our differences later. As I told National Public Radio's Ari Shapiro, "What we see today is that people in the Religious Right are saying, you need us, and you need our issues. And in the next fifty days or so, you really need us."

Whether this marriage of convenience between these two ideological strains is long-lasting or short-lived remains to be seen.

Always On Their Mind: Values Voter Summiteers Fixate on Americans United (2012)[31]

You could have gotten the impression that everybody was talking about Americans United during the recent Values Voters Summit in Washington, DC.

Literally seconds after I sat down for the opening session on my yearly pilgrimage to this major Religious Right gathering, I heard a fellow behind me making chitchat with the woman next to him. He was talking about "some group" that was trying to "intimidate pastors" by telling them they can't endorse candidates from the pulpit. [More on illegal electioneering in the next chapter.]

Since I had just sat down and hadn't turned around, I don't think he said this because he recognized me. I'll just have to assume it was the world's worst pickup line.

On Saturday, when AU's Rob Boston was covering the day's events, he attended a workshop on pulpit politicking organized by the Rev. Rick Scarborough. The Vision America president told the crowd, "I keep waiting for my friend Barry Lynn of Americans United for Separation of Church and State to pop in. He usually comments on what I have to say."

I have debated Rick on numerous occasions, and he actually showed a video of a media appearance we did some years back. Again, I would have come if I had been invited—and I don't hide my identity. I sign up; I wear a suit for the occasional "alternative" viewpoint television interview; I got spoken to (almost always politely) by attendees.

This year, FRC President Tony Perkins even mentioned me in a speech to a National Press Club luncheon two days before the Summit. AU's Legislative Department tuned in on C-SPAN, and one of them yelled to me, "Tony Perkins just gave you a shout-out, and it wasn't even snarky!"

Indeed, Perkins noted that I always go to his event. He recalled that one year I said the Summit is "not a gathering of GOP consultants looking for their next contract" but mainly attended by "people new to the political process who want to participate in their country's affairs." Perkins said he agreed with me there.

Chapter 5

RELIGIOUS RIGHT TACTICS

From Initiatives to License Plates to Church Rehab to Taking Over the Military and the Courts . . . (and to Sending People to Death Row, for Good Measure)

S o much of the coverage of the Religious Right focuses on what it is doing in national political circles. Its yearly conferences and straw polls emphasize its proximity to power and its ties to those in office seeking higher office and its work to get Congress to pass the kind of legislation it wants.

It is a mistake, though, to think that this movement was ever, or is now, just about Washington. Indeed, the Christian Coalition's Ralph Reed said in the seventies, "I would rather have a thousand school-board members than one president and no school-board members."[1]

Sometimes state and local politicians are more malleable than Congress and more open to considering and then actually adopting bizarre proposals. This is one of the reasons it is so important to observe city councils, school boards, and other similar entities. Sometimes mere publicity vitiates local chicanery.

Religious Right advocates often use the potentially dangerous "state initiative" process to confuse voters and pass legislation that even relatively conservative state legislatures are reluctant to adopt. In 2012, three states, for example, considered amending their state constitutions through initiatives: two failed (North Dakota and Florida), one succeeded but has not generated much activity (Missouri). All are described in a column I did a few months before those 2012 elections.

Prophet Pat?: Buchanan Predicted the Current Wave of Odious Initiatives[2]

It has been nearly twenty years since I did a nearly daily three-hour radio show for NBC with conservative pundit Pat Buchanan. It was done in the format of *Crossfire* but without quite the intensity, since yelling for three hours is, well, six times more difficult than doing it for thirty minutes.

As you may correctly assume, our worldviews were worlds, if not universes, apart. I remember only one or two issues that we agreed on.

One day, after the 1993 election, I came into the studio aglow with the final results of a referendum to permit use of California taxpayer funds for an ill-conceived (aren't they all?) school voucher program. This is a subject we had discussed with some frequency on the show.

Ironically, Buchanan had been an arch opponent of vouchers and then had a sudden and supportive change of heart. I did love to find old anti-voucher quotes of his to throw back at him, of course.

That afternoon, though, he congratulated me—and all opponents—on our anti-voucher victory, but then added, somewhat ominously, "someday conservatives will learn to fight on lots of fronts at the same time, and then we'll 'initiatize' you guys to death." (I don't think he thought that was a real verb.)

Buchanan explained that if people had to spend money in the same year fighting school vouchers, school prayer, and reproductive rights limitations, in addition to other "liberal" nonreligious controversies, we'd have to raise a vastly greater amount of money and use up far more energy.

Pat eventually went off to run for president (like the California voucher initiative, without success). In this election cycle, though, it seems like his initiative campaign idea may be taking off.

Who knows, it could have been a few listeners from nineteen years ago who are now in a position to do something about Buchanan's strategy. People still come up to me occasionally who first heard of me from that radio show. You just never know.

Whatever the genesis, some pretty terrible ideas are floating around the initiative world these days. One has been resolved already in North Dakota. It was called "Measure 3" (which sounds like the title of a bad science fiction movie) and was claimed to protect "religious liberty"—something, of course, already protected by both the North Dakota and US constitutions. It stated without nuance or equivocation that the state could not burden in any way any conscientiously held religious belief of an individual or an organization absent a compelling government interest, such as public safety or the civil rights of others.

This vaguely worded mess—opposed by all five major newspapers in the state—would lead to endless litigation about religiously motivated child neglect, violence against domestic partners, or even marriage with minors.

Next up is an ominous proposal in Missouri to amend the state constitution to protect prayer in public places and make other changes to educational practice. Obviously, school children can pray in a nondisruptive manner right now if school officials don't set the time, place, manner, or content of that prayer. So this is more about creating a so-called "right" to pray in public government meetings in an orchestrated fashion.

And let's not forget that another provision actually provides students with a right to not participate in assignments that violate their religious beliefs. I can already hear: "Mr. Geometry Teacher, I refuse to take any tests because according to 1 Kings 7:23, pi is equal to 3, but you claim in an unbiblical fashion that is it an infinite number starting with 3.1415. . . ."

With this on the plate, an eight-hundred-pound gorilla is on the threshold of the initiative movement also, a behemoth in Florida. Proposed Amendment 8 would completely eliminate the current (most recently affirmed in 1968) existing constitutional proviso prohibiting use of state tax dollars "directly or indirectly in aid of any church, sect, or religious denomination or in aid of any sectarian institution."

The language it would add is clearly designed to support any and all Florida voucher plans and lead to widespread funding of religious social services, even those that allow the open display of religious icons and scripture, discriminate in hiring employees, and refuse service to beneficiaries who don't see eye-to-eye with the service provider on religious rules or rituals.

I know that some of you might like the theory of "initiatives" where the voters speak. In all of these cases, however, the very title of the proposals is misleading and the prose of the actual amendments turgid and lawyerly (but I repeat myself).

If initiatives remain the trend, maybe we'll have to start putting up some of our own: "Only sound science will be taught in the state of 'fill in the blank.'" Or "No state funds may be given to any pervasively sectarian institution or to any church where the pastor has more than one mansion and one Rolls Royce."

You get the picture. Maybe a few of those Pat Buchanan-era radio listeners I still run into who liked my side of the argument should get started drafting now.

ACTS OF GOD—REACTION: GIVE US YOUR MONEY

I get more horrified negative reactions from "progressive" people over the question of the funding for rebuilding "historic" church property than anything else I've worked on. Perhaps it is that progressives are often, in the very best sense, "conservatives"—wanting to protect and preserve the valuable cultural contributions made by our ancestors.

My involvement in this concern began during the George W. Bush years when the Secretary of the Interior started giving out historic preservation grants to churches—notably one that is in a wealthy city with (I thought) a strong charitable spirit.

HISTORIC MISTAKE: OLD NORTH CHURCH AND OUR TAX DOLLARS[3]

Years ago when I was younger and had fewer gray hairs, I taught school in Boston. One of my courses examined Boston's history. On Wednesday afternoons I'd take the students on a tour of interesting sites. I was always surprised that many of the young people who had lived in Boston their entire lives had never visited some of these places.

One stop was, of course, Old North Church, site of the famous lanterns hung for Paul Revere—an event so eloquently dramatized in the poem by Henry Wadsworth Longfellow. I don't remember that the windows of the structure had any problems at that time, thirty years ago, but they apparently do now.

Indeed, the Bush administration has just given the church a grant of $317,000 to fix them.

One day last month, Secretary of the Interior Gale Norton left her post in Washington long enough to go to Boston with "Faith Czar" James Towey to announce the grant with great fanfare. Who could possibly oppose this restoration of American heritage? The next day she got the answer in almost every newspaper in the country: Americans United for Separation of Church and State.

It bothers me that the administration now wants to fund, not only religious ministries, but also houses of worship that retain active congregations. Old North Church has a worshiping congregation of Episcopalians that meets twice every Sunday, with Bible studies and choir practices several nights during the week. It is impossible for me to figure out how fixing the windows (and doing whatever other repairs it might need in the future) cannot be viewed as giving tax dollars to the promotion of religion.

The more I learned about the church, the more I dug in my heels. This site gets five hundred thousand visitors each year. Has anyone thought of asking them for a donation to fix the leaks? Massachusetts has thousands of businesses, large and small, which presumably want to protect the history of the commonwealth. Did anyone ask them for financial help? Apparently not, which is why the congregation turned to Uncle Sam.

The Rev. Stephen Ayres, the vicar of the church, said at a news conference that he is aware of the potential problem of having churches accept money from the government.

"Many are concerned," he said, "that religious institutions may lose their moral and prophetic voice if we become too dependent on government support. We must always ask ourselves whether receiving government grants will compromise our vocation to remind our representatives of God's concern for peace and for the care of the poor and marginalized."[4]

Yes, that's what will happen. Nevertheless, he took the money anyway.

I understand that some folks would like to make an exception in the case of "historic" religious buildings, but the slope is very slippery from Old North Church down. Every church has a history of some kind, and if some church official wants to preserve the pew where William Howard Taft sat or the site of the baptism of Supreme Court Justice Antonin Scalia, I'm sure he or she would get an open ear (and possibly, a hand) in Washington.

I'm a strong believer that churches and other religious entities should have the right to resist forced "landmarking" that ends up restricting their power to control their internal building decisions. However, when you accept that status, it should not come with a guarantee of financial support so long as you have parishioners who can contribute to repairs themselves. The US Treasury is simply not a church building fund.

The *Atlanta Journal Constitution*'s well-respected columnist Tom Teepen wrote that if this historic rebuilding was the only "faith-based initiative" of the Bush administration, even he might overlook the constitutional issue. But he noted this is just part of a bigger agenda to fund religion with tax dollars.

I made exactly that point to Barbara Bradley Hagerty of National Public Radio: "This is part and parcel of an overall plan by the Bush administration that apparently believes that every social problem, and now every architectural problem, should be solved by giving money to religious institutions."[5]

Indeed, the Department of Housing and Urban Development has announced plans to fund places of worship that provide social services in their communities. If your church basement is used for a meals program for the hungry 20 percent of the time, you would be entitled to 20 percent funding of the ceiling tiles. This would create ridiculous entanglement problems between church and state. How would we know what percentage of time the facility was actually being used for each purpose? Should we move those spy cameras that are in many big cities to photograph people going through red lights into the vestibules of the sanctuaries of churches with government grants?

The Supreme Court got it right in a 1973 case, *PEARL v. Nyquist*, when it said bluntly: "If the State may not erect buildings in which religious activities are to take place, it may not maintain such buildings or renovate them when they fall into disrepair."

I love Old North Church, just like I enjoy the wilderness places still left in America. I give voluntarily to help preserve these places. However, I also revere the Constitution. Let's preserve it.

So, when George W. Bush wanted to give money to fix Old North Church, there was no outcry from Congress, then controlled by a Republican majority. However, just a year later, "repairs" to religious facilities ginned up a fever where Republican conservatives got so intoxicated with "church/state separation" fervor that they invited me to be their star witness at a hearing to explore how to stop rebuilding California missions—a major "mission" of Senator Barbara Boxer, whom they wanted to embarrass.

Senator Boxer was not happy to see me there. She sat in the back of the hearing room, passing notes to Democratic staffers and glaring at me. But the law is the law and this is part of what I told the Subcommittee on National Parks in 2004.

There is no doubt that California's twenty-one missions, which run along a six-hundred-mile stretch of highway from San Diego to Sonoma are historically significant and contribute greatly to the rich historical, cultural and architectural heritage of California and the American West.[6] Although we recognize that preservation of these historic buildings is important, we strongly believe that the preservation of America's constitutional rights is vital. In short, the California Missions Preservation Act would violate the First Amendment by forcing taxpayers nationwide to pay for church repairs, even repairs and restoration of facilities with active congregations. I urge you today, for the sake of preserving religious liberty, to ensure that federal funds are not used to build or repair houses of worship. Instead, it is up to religious organizations and individuals to voluntarily support preservation of the California missions.

Background

The twenty-one missions comprising California's historic mission trail were founded between 1769 and 1823. Largely reconstructed after the tests of time, weather, and earthquakes, nineteen of the twenty-one missions are owned by the Roman Catholic Church, operate as active parishes, and have regularly scheduled religious services.

Under S. 1306, federal funds would be provided to pay for "efforts to restore and repair the California missions, and to preserve associated artworks and artifacts." The bill would authorize the Secretary of the Interior, under section 101(e)(4) of the National Historic Preservation Act, 16 USC § 470a(e)(4), to grant $10,000,000 in federal funds over a five-year period to support the California Missions Foundation, a charitable corporation dedicated to funding the restoration and repair of the California missions and the preservation of the Spanish colonial and mission-era artworks and artifacts of the California missions. It also would require the California Missions Foundation to match federal grant funds and to provide annual reports to the Secretary regarding the preservation efforts taken with funds provided under the bill. Americans United recognizes that the bill includes some language purportedly protective of religious liberty. Specifically, the bill states that the Secretary of the Interior "shall ensure that the purpose of a grant under this section is secular, does not promote religion, and seeks to protect those qualities that are historically significant."

Similarly, the National Historic Preservation Act, to which the bill refers, provides that "[g]rants may be made . . . for the preservation, stabilization, restoration or rehabilitation of religious properties . . . provided that the purpose of the grant is secular, does not promote religion, and seeks to protect those qualities that are historically significant." 16 USC § 470a(e)(4).

These protections are steps in the right direction, but they are insufficient as a practical matter to meet the requirements of the Constitution. Time after time, the Supreme Court has required that no government funds be used to maintain, restore, or make capital improvements to physical structures that are used as houses of worship, even if religious services are infrequent. Because most, if not all, of the missions remain active houses of worship, in addition to serving as cultural and historic institutions, it is impossible for the government to fund the California missions without violating the Constitution.

The illegality of the proposal to fund the California missions is exacerbated when one considers the issue of government directly funding religious icons. Because one of the objectives of the California Missions Foundation is to preserve the "Spanish colonial and mission-era artworks and artifacts of the California missions," and because the bill specifically authorizes federal funds to be used to "preserve the artworks and artifacts associated with the California missions," the Secretary would be empowered to provide government money specifically to maintain or restore religious artifacts and icons associated with devotional and worship activities at the missions, a result that would be clearly unconstitutional.

Providing Federal Funds to the California Missions Would Be Unconstitutional

Three Supreme Court decisions make clear that it is unconstitutional to allow federal grants for the repair of preservation of structures devoted to worship or religious instruction, and all three of these decisions remain binding law on the federal government. In *Tilton v. Richardson*, 403 US 672 (1971), the Court laid the framework for the current constitutional requirements regarding construction, upkeep, and maintenance of religious institutions' physical facilities. *Tilton* involved a challenge to the constitutionality of a federal law under which federal funds were used by secular and religious institutions of higher education for the construction of libraries and other campus buildings. Although the law allowed money to go to religious institutions, it also contained a proviso that expressly forbade funds from being spent on buildings that would be used for worship or sectarian instruction. The Court upheld the program, but it unanimously held that the proviso was constitutionally necessary and unanimously invalidated part of the statute that would have allowed religious schools to convert the federally-funded facilities for worship or sectarian instruction after twenty years had passed. No building that was built with federal funds can ever be used for worship or sectarian instruction—that is *Tilton*'s clear holding. (403 US at 692.)

In two subsequent cases decided two years later, the Supreme Court clearly reaffirmed the principle that the First Amendment prohibits the government from subsidizing the construction or repair of buildings used as houses of worship. In *Hunt v. McNair*, 413 US 734 (1973), the Supreme Court upheld the South Carolina Educational Facilities Authority Act, which established an "Educational Facilities Authority," through which educational facilities could borrow money for use in their facilities at favorable interest rates. However, the Act required each lease agreement to contain a clause forbidding religious use in such facilities and allowing inspections to enforce that requirement. (413 US at 744.) The Court upheld the Act, including the condition that government-funded physical structures could never be used for religious worship or instruction.

Finally, in *Committee for Public Education v. Nyquist*, 413 US 756 (1973), the Supreme Court struck down New York's program of providing grants to nonpublic schools for use of maintenance and repair of "school facilities and equipment to ensure health, welfare, and safety of enrolled students." (413 US at 762.) The Court summarized its previous holdings as "simply recogniz[ing] that sectarian schools perform secular, educational functions as well as religious functions, and that some forms of aid may be channeled to the secular without providing direct aid to the sectarian. But the channel is a narrow one." (Id. at 775.) The Court then held that "[i]f the State may not erect buildings in which religious activities are to take place, it may not maintain such buildings or renovate them when they fall into disrepair." (Id. at 777.) In other words, government funding for either the construction or maintenance and repair of physical structures is unconstitutional unless there is no possibility that the structures will be used for sectarian worship or instruction. Otherwise the government would be subsidizing religious activity.

All three of these cases firmly establish that it is constitutionally impermissible for the government to provide aid for the construction, repair, or maintenance of any buildings that are, or might be, used for religious purposes. The rule set down by the Supreme Court in these three cases—which requires that publicly financed buildings be used only for purely secular purposes—remains controlling law and has never been undermined or seriously questioned in any subsequent Supreme Court decision regarding direct governmental aid to religious institutions. Thus, under *Tilton, McNair,* and *Nyquist,* it would be unconstitutional for the federal government to provide funds to any of the California missions in which religious services take place.

These decisions are in keeping with a lengthy and valuable tradition in America: the idea that maintenance of houses of worship belongs to con-gregants, not to taxpayers. The idea of compelled support for religion was repellent to our Founding Fathers. Time and again one sees in their writings and public pronouncements a concern that support for religion come through voluntary channels.

Founders like Thomas Jefferson and James Madison did not hold this view because they were hostile to religion. Rather, they believed that it was morally wrong to force anyone to support religious worship, religious education, or houses of worship against his or her will. As Madison observed in his famous "Memorial and Remonstrance Against Religious Assessments," "The same authority which can force a citizen to contribute three pence only of his property for the support of any one [religious] establishment may force him to conform to any other establishment in all cases whatsoever."[7]

Madison, widely considered the Father of the Constitution, believed the federal government should stay out of the business of funding religion. As president, he vetoed a bill giving a Baptist church a small amount of federal land in Mississippi, asserting in his veto message to Congress that the measure "comprises a principle and precedent for the appropriation of funds of the United States for the use and support of religious societies, contrary to the article of the Constitution which declares that 'Congress shall make no law respecting a religious establishment.'"[8]

Denying taxpayer aid for the rebuilding, refurbishing, and maintenance of the California missions is neither a radical step nor is it an example of animus toward religion. Instead, it is wholly in line with our nation's past practices and our wise tradition of requiring religious groups to rely on voluntary support given by willing donors, not tax funds coerced by the state.

When some of this money was appropriated, Americans United looked for a way to take our argument into the Federal courts. We found Erik and Sonia Doe, non-Catholics who wanted to get married at a Catholic parish that was supposed to be granted federal funds for restoration. They were denied this opportunity and AU filed suit. Ultimately AU dismissed the suit because the money was authorized but not appropriated. That means that Congress "authorized" the provision of the funds, but Congress never passed an appropriations bill that actually doled out the money.

Then, early in the Obama administration, it became clear that the President was not about to shift the government's view on shelling out tax dollars to reconstruct, renovate, and shellac religious structures, including one right in downtown Washington.

DON'T PASS ME THE PLATE FOR YOUR CHURCH'S UPKEEP[9]

I'm a minister, so it's no surprise that I'm fond of church architecture. From gothic brownstones and simple wooden country churches to gleaming marble temples and modernistic structures of glass and steel, I continue to be amazed at the variety of edifices people have constructed to serve as houses of worship.

I'm also amazed that in this country we have paid for these structures, perhaps numbering in the tens of thousands all over the land, with the private donations of the faithful. It's a testament to how seriously Americans take religion.

At least that used to be the case. Lately, I've noticed a disturbing trend: Churches deemed "historic" are seeking taxpayer funds for repair and upkeep.

Earlier this month, the US Department of the Interior announced dozens of grants to historic structures under its "Save America's Treasures" program. Scanning the list, I was surprised to see three churches on the list.

Among them is the Washington National Cathedral in Washington, DC. I drive by this structure often. It is an amazing building that soars above the din and distractions of daily political life in the nation's capital. Over the years, I have attended many events there.

Despite its name, the cathedral obviously isn't owned by the government. Public events often take place there, and political leaders are a fixture. But the cathedral is an Episcopal church and belongs to the local diocese. It's not a museum; it is a living, active church where people regularly attend worship services.

Despite this, the church is receiving $700,000 in tax money to pay for foundation repairs and to fix stained-glass windows, doors, and metalwork. I'm disappointed. Many people who have learned of the structural problems have contributed for repairs in recent years. I'm actually going to send them a few dollars myself, voluntarily, but I shouldn't be forced to support any house of worship against my will, and neither should anyone else.

The fact that the cathedral is historic or that it plays an important role in public life is irrelevant. In this country, churches are expected to pay their own way. The men and women occupying the pews pay for building construction and upkeep. Anything else is a religion tax.

The fact is, many American churches are historic. Are we going to put them all on the taxpayers' bill?

We seem to be moving in that direction. Also on the Interior Department list for a $700,000 public grant is St. Mark's Church in Philadelphia. Built in 1847, it's a fine example of gothic architecture. But there are churches just as old and just as interesting looking all over the East, Midwest, and South. If they are in need of repairs—and I'm sure some of them are—members of the congregation ought to pay for that.

The third church, Trinity Church in Buffalo, is receiving nearly $200,000 in tax money for various repairs. The Interior Department points out that the church was designed by "noted American architect Bertram Goodhue." Yes, the church has interesting features. Is that all it takes to trump the First Amendment principle that no one can be compelled to support religion?

Two hundred years ago this month, a bill landed on the desk of President James Madison that would have officially incorporated an Episcopal church in the District of Columbia. Although the bill didn't offer any tax funds, it did outline how the church was to be organized and what steps were to be taken if the minister resigned. It also authorized the congregation to help the disadvantaged and to offer schooling to poor children.

Madison vetoed the bill. He wrote to Congress, "[T]he bill exceeds the rightful authority to which governments are limited, by the essential distinction between civil and religious functions and violates, in particular, the article of the Constitution of the United States, which declares, that 'Congress shall make no law respecting a religious establishment.'"[10]

Madison knew that government exceeds it authority when it acts to support religion. The offense is all the worse when that support takes the form of your tax dollars. The tab for building, repairing, and maintaining an active church should always be paid by its members. The fact that the church is old, looks interesting, or was designed by a noted architect does not relieve the congregants of this fundamental responsibility.

Old North Church is of great interest to residents of Boston and Northeast Coast tenants; the missions of California are revered by Californians who often did an art project on them when they were in junior high school, and DC's residents all know of the Washington Cathedral and were very unhappy when it suffered falling bricks and mortar during DC's only modern earthquake. Nevertheless, these are all at their root somewhat provincial concerns.

Not so with the nationally calamitous Hurricane Sandy! News coverage of this cataclysmic 2012 storm became a very compelling concern for people throughout the nation. So after Bruce Springsteen and dozens of other musicians held a nationally broadcast telethon for relief, Congress dipped its toes once again into the muddy waters of "Acts of God" and came up with feet covered with tax dollars. Once again, though, we had to express our constitutional concerns.

Americans United (along with a handful of other groups, including the ACLU and the Religious Action Center for Reform Judaism) is still embroiled in a lobbying effort to prevent the use of funds from the Federal Emergency Management Agency (FEMA) to rebuild churches, synagogues, mosques, and other religious real estate damaged during last October's Hurricane Sandy.[11]

The House of Representatives passed a bill in mid-February 2013 to explicitly allow direct reconstruction grants on a lopsided 354–72 vote (66 Democrats and 6 Republicans in the minority), but the Senate has yet to consider the matter. It was a "feel good" vote for most members; the persistent images of ruined homes, businesses, and lives on the Atlantic Coast shore do cry out for doing something.

There were no House hearings on this matter, a fact noted by the New York Times in its editorial opposing this funding. Frankly, a record on this would probably have given far more members reasons to object.

On the one hand, religious institutions in the affected areas can still receive federal disaster loans (which have to be repaid) and are eligible for other grants if they utilize 50 percent or more of their facilities for the provision of "essential services of a governmental nature"—such as feeding the hungry or sheltering the homeless. Therefore, these entities are not being left out in the cold.

On the other hand, neither is it accurate to suggest that, on a practical level, they are being treated in a discriminatory fashion. Churches are already tax exempt, unlike private homes and businesses, and therefore will find it easier to attract charitable gifts than the local surf shop will. Under the Religious Land Use and Institutionalized Persons Act, they are also given more leverage than other agencies to gain zoning exceptions for relocating their facilities. Religious and nonreligious buildings and their owners start off in slightly different legal positions.

And, then, of course, there is the Constitution. It has always been assumed that one thing government at any level cannot do is build your church, your temple, or your mosque. There would be no greater example of the forbidden practice of picking favorites in America's religious debates than to pay to dig out basements, buy bricks and mortar, put up walls, and raise a roof for any such buildings.

Back in the 1970s, a series of never-repudiated Supreme Court cases made that emphatically clear, even holding in one case that a religious college needed to guarantee that if it got public funds to construct a new campus building, it would never convert it to any spiritual use. Although the Supreme Court has allowed some kinds of funds to flow to religious schools (that it should not have), there is no hint that it wants to change the rock-solid construction rules.

Logically, if you can't build the First Baptist Church, you can't rebuild it either after a fire, flood, earthquake, or Hurricane Sandy.

But, hold on, say some, this is an emergency. One of the coauthors of the first book I wrote back in 1995 (*The Right to Religious Liberty*) sent a letter to the editor of the *Times*, disputing its position.

"Disaster relief is an expression of social solidarity with victims," he said, commenting further that restoring houses of worship is a recognition that they are, like other structures, "essential to functioning communities." This sentiment is well stated; its implications are quite different.

Sacred spaces are deemed "sacred" by believers in specific ideas. Some religious groups see community outreach to all as essential to their mission; others see it as secondary or even a nuisance in the general soul-saving mission they are on. I'd prefer that governments not be invited into the debate over what houses of worship are best for a community or which help a city "function"—an entanglement that curdles the blood of many theistic and nontheistic civil libertarians.

Indeed, in America's other most recent hurricane catastrophe, 2005's Hurricane Katrina, even George W. Bush did not approve reconstruction grants for places of worship.

I used to spend summers on some of the New Jersey beaches that barely exist anymore. I even went to churches there. I have never vacationed in Kansas. There are many churches there, including the notorious Westboro Baptist Church of the Rev. Fred Phelps, the group that pickets the funerals of Iraq War veterans and applauds when gay activists die.

Even if I could get over my money flowing to a little Jersey church's rebuilding fund, I'm never going to foot the bill for Phelps's edifice if it gets blown away by a tornado.

The federal government, though, can't draw such distinctions. It needs to be all in or all out; I'm voting for keeping it far away.

This funding was not appropriated, in spite of passing out of the House with that vote of 354–72. The Senate never took up this bill nor moved on their own and the initiative quietly passed away.

"RELIGION IN THE MILITARY"

My friend "Mikey" Weinstein and I are both First Amendment enthusiasts and have both been the subject of imprecatory prayers by former Navy chaplain—and recently elected Colorado state representative Gorden Klingenschmidt. Mikey runs the Military Religious Freedom Foundation (MRFF). Occasionally, however, I am asked to wade into the military arena with letters, columns, or presentations to armed service. Here is what I said during a debate with American Center for Law and Justice chief counsel Jay Sekulow before a gathering at Maxwell Air Force base in Montgomery, Alabama, back in 2010.

In my view, Defense Department policy regarding religion should start with two premises. One, it should permit the full and free expression of religious and, yes, antireligious, views by individual service members to the maximum extent possible consistent with real, not imagined, concerns for order and discipline. Second, policy should avoid giving even the appearance of official favoritism to any one religion or any religion at all.

Sounds simple. And, if this was a hippie commune in the sixties (not that I was ever in one) where there was no chain of command and no governing structures at all, we'd have very few problems adopting such a policy. However, I have noticed not a single love bead since I arrived last night, and I know that the United States military is a different creature.

It presents several thorny problems in guaranteeing what the First Amendment is about: both the free exercise of religion and the promise that governments and their official representatives will be strictly neutral on matters of religion: not hostile, not promotional, simply neutral. In the military, command influence is essential, usually appropriate, and rarely raising constitutional issues. Also in the military are a distinct noncommand slot for chaplains, persons who hold a truly unique "military occupational specialty." Chaplains are not self-appointed gurus who speak to God while consuming amounts of mushrooms (again, a reference to the sixties, which many of you know only by looking at your parents' old records in the garage); no, chaplains are certified by their denominations as trained in certain worldviews, but are then funded by American taxpayers.

I don't believe that having chaplains in the military violates the separation of church and state; indeed, I think you can make a strong case that when sending men and women to foreign lands to support asserted American interests we have an obligation to accommodate the spiritual needs of those far from their religious homes. The chaplaincy does that.

Here is where Jay and I differ a lot. I think chaplains are here to serve the needs of servicemembers who ask for assistance—persons struggling with personal, professional, or philosophical problems they want addressed from a religious viewpoint. They are not hired to be roving missionaries to all persons with whom they come in contact. This is difficult because it seems a human trait to want to tell others about any good news you have, whether that is the Gospel of Jesus Christ or the announcement of your engagement (opposite sex only, of course, in this institution). Bluntly, chaplains need to recognize and appreciate the need to refrain from religious evangelism as a part of their assignment.

Chaplains do serve one other major function: a public one, which is often called "solemnization" of ceremonies. There are two thousand different religions practiced in this country—and about twenty million Americans are nonbelievers, freethinkers, atheists. They are all represented in the military—yes, even in foxholes. We can't afford to hire one chaplain from each (and a few secular counselors to boot) in every command. Therefore, it is neither irrational, nor unconstitutional, to tell a chaplain speaking or offering an invocation at a family event on base or at any official public event that he or she should attempt to respect the diversity of those in attendance by not suggesting that there is only way to God (his or hers) or by speaking in a "nonsectarian manner"—a concept many courts have embraced. Even as a minister myself, I should note that religious thanksgiving and requests in prayer are not the only way an occasion can be made "solemn"—even silence can do that sometimes.

The other place where Jay and I have some significant differences is with the issue of what commanders may do or say about religion without exercising undue command influence; that is, inappropriate efforts to impose their ideas on those in their command. No one is suggesting that commanders have their mouths shut with duct tape if the subject of religion comes up. However, it is foolish, even dangerous, to fail to recognize that the men and women who serve under you are not going to be influenced by what you say and how you say it. If you had no capacity to lead, you wouldn't be here this morning.

So, under most circumstances, if you start to tell those in your command, for example, "I was born again after hearing the Reverend Billy Graham at a big revival in Atlanta," you are probably going to be heard us suggesting next time Graham's son is in town, you'd be real happy to see them there. In addition, that might well be read as a comment that "getting right with God" is getting right with your commander and that couldn't hurt your chances at advancement. This happens with high school football coaches whose religious comments suggest that playing time is going to be correlated with participation in team prayer or other activities and every player knows the more time you are on the field the more time college scouts have to watch you excel. Think of how much more important it is when the stakes are your whole career in the service of your country.

I notice that former chaplain Gordon Klingenschmidt contributed a chapter to your textbook. Mr. Klingenschmidt and I don't exactly have a rosy relationship: In fact, he launched an "imprecatory" prayer campaign against me about a year ago, urging people to pray for my death. I'm not losing any sleep over that, but I am deeply troubled by his crusade to try to convince Congress and the American people generally that there is widespread anti-Christian animus developing in the military. I see no evidence of that whatsoever. And, although Jay is right to be clear that Christians do need to have their legitimate rights protected, Christianity is still the religion of choice for a vast majority of armed services personnel. Majorities tend to do pretty well—even without lawyers. I am much more troubled by the claims we get in our office about what can only be described as a "Christian nationalism," an effort by some in military circles to denigrate the service of those who are not Christian, or who are not even religious. There is a real difference in my view between God and country—Christianity has not cornered the market on faith. When we lapse into a sense that what we do is a holy enterprise and that our military policy represents God's will as well as that of the Pentagon, we may find ourselves in a heap of trouble. When we act like the nonbeliever or the Muslim is less trustworthy or less committed than the Christian soldier, sailor, or airman, we risk abandoning our very American commitment to equality under the law and the strength that comes from our original national motto: "Out of many, one."

We were also engaged in efforts to stifle the advance of General William Boykin—now a mouthpiece for the Family Research Council. He was not a fan of our efforts.

Another person we have been following for some time, Lt. Gen. William Boykin of the US Army, hit the news in a big way. Earlier this year, we had successfully gotten the Army to scale back a special event Boykin was planning to hold for Baptist preachers at Fort Bragg in North Carolina.

Boykin had quite a treat lined up for the pastors. They were going to stay overnight on the base, see things there that the public is generally not permitted to visit, and enjoy "informal time" with the general. AU's complaint put the kibosh on much of that.

We had no reason to believe we would cross paths with the general again. But unbeknownst to us, Boykin was quietly approved by the Senate this summer as undersecretary of defense for intelligence, a key role in the US effort against terrorism. While looking into Boykin's background, a journalist working for the Los Angeles Times and NBC News discovered videotapes of the general addressing various church groups, while in uniform, on the topic of religion and warfare.

His comments were incredibly inappropriate. Boykin told the First Baptist Church in Broken Arrow, Oklahoma, that Osama bin Laden is not the real enemy and "the enemy that has come against our nation is a spiritual enemy. His name is Satan." Later, in Sandy, Oregon, Boykin announced that Muslim terrorists hate us so much "because we're a Christian nation . . ." He also told a Daytona, Florida, audience that he was able to capture a notorious terrorist in Somalia because the man was a Muslim and "I knew that my God was a real God, and his was an idol."

Gen. Boykin has all the right in the world to believe whatever he wants about the validity of his faith and that of others. Technically, he may not have violated the Uniform Code of Military Justice even when his in-uniform comments directly conflicted with Bush's persistent efforts not to characterize Middle East conflict as pitting Christians against Muslims. However, the actions were unconscionable, divisive, and downright dangerous. His words appeared in newspapers around the Arab world within days as living embodiments of the claims of bin Laden and other extremists that the United States is indeed fighting a literal "holy war" against Islam.

We urged Secretary of Defense Donald Rumsfeld to immediately transfer Boykin. Rumsfeld declined to take my advice, as Religious Right leaders circled the wagons around Boykin's "free speech" rights as if they were suddenly the world's greatest civil libertarians.

Our military leaders are supposed to preserve the peace and, failing that, to win wars. It is not their job to evangelize the American people nor to orchestrate a crusade against people of different religious traditions. Yes, the general has attempted to "clarify" his comments, but it is too late. His disdain for faiths other than his own has been recorded for posterity, including in the terrorist training camps of those who are trying to convince a new generation that the United States is on a campaign to "Christianize" the entire world with the military there to back up the effort.

After repeated incidents to which the military turned a blind eye, including the times when Boykin asserted that military leaders are so disgusted with President Barack Obama that many want to "take out" the president, when he said that Muslims shouldn't be allowed to build any more mosques in America, and when he once called America's efforts to combat international terrorism a "holy war," the Army finally took notice in 2013.

According to the *Washington Post*, military officials "quietly" issued a "scathing reprimand following a criminal investigation that concluded [Boykin] had wrongfully released classified information. . . ."[12]

Reported the paper, "According to the Jan. 23, 2013, memorandum, the Army determined that Boykin's 2008 book, *Never Surrender: A Soldier's Journey to the Crossroads of Faith and Freedom*, disclosed 'classified information concerning cover methods, counterterrorism/counter-proliferation operations, operational deployments, infiltration methods, pictures, and tactics, techniques and procedures that may compromise ongoing operations.'"[13]

A memo signed by Gen. Lloyd J. Austin III, who at the time was the Army's vice chief of staff, accused Boykin of "unprofessional behavior" that reflected "poorly on your character." Austin's memo further stated that Boykin's actions are "prejudicial to good order and discipline in the armed forces." Boykin was finally relieved of his position.

But General Boykin may have lost the ferocity of his anti-AU animosity.

SCALING THE SUMMIT: WHAT I LEARNED AT THIS YEAR'S FAR-RIGHT SHINDIG[14]

The day was not a total waste. Just before lunch, Oliver North made a somewhat engaging presentation about people who serve in the military. We used to do a radio show together, but I had not seen him in several years so I decided to stop by and say hello at the book-signing table. This turned out to be a little awkward because the Family Research Council's William G. "Jerry" Boykin was signing his book at the same table.

Anyway, North was happy to see me, and we chatted about cable television, the death penalty, and how we're aging. I told him that I thought one of the perks of being on radio with him years ago was that I would get a free copy of all of his future books. He noted that he had actually sold out at the Summit.

Boykin observed us speaking and jumped in, joking with North that I'm great for his fundraising. People observing this began pulling out their smartphones to snap pictures of us all together—me sandwiched between the colonel and the general. Many of them told me they'd send me a snapshot; not one did—but I feel confident that the NSA could find it.

THE JUDICIARY

The federal judiciary consists of ninety-four trial-level courts; thirteen appeals courts, and (of course) the Supreme Court. It is a prime target for Religious Right activists; for "our side," with the exception of the Alliance for Justice, not so much. When George W. Bush nominated John G. Roberts for Chief Justice in 2005, most groups from our team were silent for weeks, examining his record ad nauseam.

However, a few of us, including indefatigable feminists like Ellie Smeal (Feminist Majority Foundation), Sammie Moshenberg (National Council of Jewish Women) and Kim Gandy (then president of the National Organization for Women) held weekly planning sessions in an effort to light a fire under our brother and sister organizations to oppose his nomination.

Roberts was approved by the Senate in a 78 to 22 vote. Just one year later, Samuel Alito was nominated as an associate justice. Although somewhat-more controversial, he too was elevated to the highest court by a vote of 58 to 42.

Honestly, I don't believe that President Obama really understood the importance of getting into judicial battles quickly. Here is an excerpt from a speech made to Van Jones's Rebuild the Dream conference in the summer of 2012.

I'm a minister and a lawyer. So, indeed, I can forgive you this afternoon, go sleep on it tonight, and still sue you in the morning. Today, though, all I want to do is share one nightmarish trajectory and one of my own modest American dreams.

Let's just look at the area of my greatest professional interest: separation of church and state. We have had some very bad decisions lately. There was a 5–4 decision challenging an Arizona tax credit scheme where a resident could pay some of what he or she would otherwise owe in state taxes to a "charity," which would then dole out scholarships to mainly religious schools and claim it as a "tax credit." A five-member majority found that Arizona taxpayers did not have "standing" to even enter the courthouse door to challenge the program. See, the bare majority claimed this was not really an expenditure of tax money because the money that would have been paid in taxes hadn't physically reached the treasury. What? In the majority's view, it had reached the bank account of the charity instead: thus not technically "government" spending. In a stinging dissent, Justice Kagan noted quite accurately that "form is prevailing over substance, and differences that make no difference determine access to the Judiciary." Pretty dull stuff, right? Let's look at what is really going on. We all should know what the Right's agenda is here: privatize education, kill public schools, and transfer the teaching of the young to private entities. As the late Jerry Falwell once said, "I hope to live to see the day when there are no public schools because Christians will have taken them over."

And then, in the most recent church/state case, the Court unanimously held that any person designated as a "minister" by a religious employer would not be able to go to the EEOC (and thus never get into federal court either) to claim an adverse employment decision was based on possible racial, gender, or other discriminatory bias. Unanimous. I halfway "joked" to a reporter that this meant that the custodian of any religious body could now be designated as "minister of dirt" to avoid legal liability. But in fact the corporate entity was given the right to determine which employees would be placed in a category that prevents them from having access to federal remediation.

But the eight-hundred-pound gorilla case is coming down the road. Just three weeks ago, a number of Catholic entities and employers simultaneously filed twenty-three lawsuits challenging the yet-unwritten rules for insurance coverage of contraceptive services mandated under the Affordable Care Act These lawsuits were premature and read more like press releases than legal documents, but this issue will eventually ripen. Here is the claim: Religious corporations have a kind of "collective conscience" that trumps the conscientious medical and moral decisions of employees and students. So, for example, Catholic University asserts it doesn't want to cover birth control for students because it is a core belief of the Catholic Church that birth control is bad. If an individual student feels differently from an ethical standard, tough luck: That conscience is not worth protecting. The Conference of Catholic Bishops apparently thinks that the intrauterine device is at least as significant as the Resurrection in its theology, even though, by the way, the first papal letter condemning contraception wasn't written until 1931.

But, it is not just Catholic corporate interests that are to be protected. Some of the folks named as plaintiffs in these lawsuits are just employers in secular companies who don't want to cover contraception. As the general counsel for the Bishops asserted in an interview with USA Today: "If I quit my job tomorrow and opened a Taco Bell, I want the right to decide what will be covered in my health insurance plan." See where this goes? I am a Jehovah's Witness; I run a company selling widgets; I'm not covering surgery in my healthcare plan because so many of them require blood transfusions that I think are immoral. The Supreme Court, whatever its makeup, is very likely going to see just these claims made in the not terribly distant future. Under the claim of "religious freedom"—the cover for a gigantic new fictional creature called "corporate conscience"—the rights of workers could be given short shrift once again. [More on this in chapter 8.]

This is my take on one area of constitutional law and corporate decision making. But let me spend a few minutes on a broader issue.

We progressives repeatedly claim there is not just an already-too-frequent substantive constitutional philosophy crisis, but a structural crisis as well, an emergency of unfilled benches at the appellate court level: twelve vacancies, a considerably higher number than at this point in 2004 or 2008. So, last week, Senator Mitch McConnell announced invocation of the so-called "Thurmond Rule," a largely fictional claim that in presidential-election years the party whose President is in office is supposed to sit on its hands and await the outcome in November. This is named for Senator Strom Thurmond, arch-segregationist to the end; Strom Thurmond, who never saw a wasteful weapons system he didn't want to fund; Strom Thurmond, who attempted to get John Lennon deported; Senator Strom Thurmond, who has no moral standing to be invoked for one blessed thing. If we truly believe that this is a real emergency because these vacancies are denying the opportunity for Americans to be heard when their fundamental rights and liberties are in jeopardy, then we should insist that the Senate not allow the Thurmond rule to be the last word. You deal with a real crisis immediately and aggressively; you know, you don't just fly over a dying and drowning city in Air Force One.

I was happy last March when a deal was cut to confirm fourteen judges in a seven-week period. I was glad that the obviously qualified Judge Andrew Hurwitz was confirmed for the Ninth Circuit last week. But progressives should insist that this process not stop! For example, there are already four appeals court judges who have had affirmative votes by the Judiciary Committee; last week two obviously qualified nominations were made for vacancies on the DC Circuit. Well, let's suggest that the Senate start moving them to the floor right away. Let the obstructionist Republicans protest; let cloture petitions be filed to end debate; let the obstructionist Republicans protest again;

then—here's the good part—keep filing cloture petitions and don't move on to other business; then, we can let the obstructionist Republicans protest live, and in person from cots if necessary, in marathon sessions for hours and days on end—*Mr. Smith Goes To Washington* style—and when a quorum is not physically present, find the Senators and get them to the floor. That's my kind of affirmative response to a filibuster threat. In poker, it's called "calling a bluff." And let America see right on C-SPAN what happens when bizarre ideological complaints about the President prevent good and decent men and women from filling the jobs that need to be filled to make the courts actually work! Those viewers won't see and hear substantive arguments about judicial philosophy because obstructionists are incapable of making them, they will notice one minority party wasting the time and money of the taxpayers, and, I predict, they will be royally ticked off.

Some may say, but this will mean the Senate won't get other important work done. Like what? We know from the Equal Pay Act debacle from two weeks ago that obstructionists won't let important legislation move anyway. Should the Senate take up some of the cockamamie legislation the House has sent over? Maybe that bill to "reaffirm 'In God We Trust'" as our national motto, one of John Boehner's pet projects from a few months ago?

And finally, as the Senate "yap fest" that I imagine drones on, the real supporters of a judiciary by and for the people can make some righteous and ringing speeches proclaiming what the courts and the Constitution are all about. The Constitution—the Bill of Rights in particular—was filled with "majestic generalities" precisely so that federal courts could breathe life into them as the reality of America changed. As my friend Professor Erwin Chemerinsky puts it so clearly, "There always has been a living Constitution and hopefully always will be. The opposite of a living Constitution is a dead Constitution and no society can be governed under that." [15] How true. The promise of anyone seeking to be on the federal bench, the Supreme Court in particular, must again be—not to serve as Chief Justice Roberts's "referee" but to do what is necessary to serve that one great overarching value of American democracy: to serve as a constraint on the otherwise overarching tyranny of the majority (and their political allies) for us and future generations. Thank you.

Things have gotten a bit better since 2013. A few more appellate judges have been confirmed. However, as Congress adjourned in December 2014, thirty-four district court judicial nominations were languishing in either the Judiciary Committee or the Senate floor. (Another fifty-six district and seven circuit-court vacancies had not been the subject of any Administration nomination.)

According to a recent study by the *New York Times*,[16] for the first time in more than a decade judges appointed by Democratic presidents considerably outnumber judges appointed by Republican presidents. Democratic appointees who hear cases full time now hold a majority of seats on nine of the thirteen United States Courts of Appeals. When Mr. Obama took office, only one of those courts had more full-time judges nominated by a Democrat.

The Democrats' advantage has grown since late last year, when the majority stripped Republicans of their ability to filibuster the president's district and appellate nominees. I had mixed feelings about this, concerned about the precedent it set when next a Republican gets to the White House (or even when Republicans control the Senate). With this change, it is a national embarrassment that the Senate adjourned with *any* nominees pending at all.

TAKIN' IT TO THE SUPREME COURT

Sometimes we get to go to the Supreme Court. We may file an amicus (friend of the court) brief or be heard directly. That can be fun. Sometimes.

It is true, but unfortunate, that major media tends to ignore judicial decisions—unless they happen to be announced by the US Supreme Court. Some years ago, the three "original networks"—ABC, NBC, and CBS—even got rid of their Supreme Court correspondents—Tim O'Brien, Carl Stern, and Fred Graham, respectively. One network official was quoted as noting, "What is the point? Everything will be a 5–4 decision."

He was not correct and the public suffered for the absence of these three well-trained reporters. The coverage of the Arizona "standing" case and *Hossana-Tabor* (the afore-mentioned "ministerial exception" case), discussed in my summer 2013 speech above, was spotty and one of the last major decisions of the Rehnquist court went relatively unnoticed. (NBC's Pete Williams, CNN's Bill Mears, and NPR's Nina Totenberg have, however, fought to retain solid electronic coverage.)

THE HIGH COURT AND DAVEY: HANDING A BIG VICTORY TO THE OPTIMISTS' CLUB[17]

Sometimes, "guarded" optimists like me get more than they hoped for. I was planning to take Feb. 25 off from work, but shortly after ten that morning I got a call at home from AU communications director Joe Conn, who said the Supreme Court had just ruled in *Locke v. Davey*, a case questioning whether Washington State had to fund scholarships for ministerial students. Our side had won.

The news got better. It was a 7–2 decision, and Chief Justice William H. Rehnquist authored the opinion. This had now become staggering news. The chief justice is rarely a defender of separation of church and state.

So much for my day off! I did a few interviews for newspapers with early deadlines, like the *Christian Science Monitor*, and radio networks looking for sound bites to put on the air at eleven and then got suited up for the ABC and NBC evening news broadcasts, as well as NPR's *All Things Considered*. (I realize that you couldn't see that suit on NPR, but I can assure you the purple-and-grey tie was very nice.)

It was interesting to listen to those on the losing side trying to "spin" their argument. Religious Right and pro-voucher groups had a lot riding on this case. Last year, Jay Sekulow, Pat Robertson's top legal strategist who argued the case at the high court, issued a fund-raising appeal labeling Davey one of the "MOST IMPORTANT RELIGION CASES OF OUR TIME." Sekulow claimed that if the taxpayers were required to pay for Davey's religious training, "religious freedom will be protected like never before."

But having lost, the right wing suddenly tried to argue that the case was merely an insignificant footnote that really had no implications beyond one state not paying for one student's theological education. TV preacher Jerry Falwell appeared with me that night on CNBC and attempted to pose as a legal scholar, insisting that "there is no separation of church and state." He noted that aside from leaving a "bad impression," this "cloudy" decision had no real significance and "changes nothing."

The Religious Right and its pro-voucher allies had to play it this way, because the truth is almost too much for them to bear. If the high court had bought the Sekulow-Falwell-Bush administration position in this case, every state would have been forced to pay for any religious service or program that had a secular counterpart. In other words, if a state pays for public education, it would have to pay for religious schooling as well.

This would have taken the bad decision of two years ago permitting vouchers for religious institutions under some circumstances and greatly expanded it, forcing states to include religious schools in any subsidy program. That would have been a constitutional catastrophe of biblical proportions. It did not happen. The right wing lost, and it lost badly.

There is a bizarre footnote to this day. During the CNBC show, before I had even opened my mouth, Falwell referred to me as a "Christ hater." I'm used to him saying ugly things about me, but even I was shocked a few minutes later by an astonishingly bizarre statement Falwell made about a total stranger. The host suddenly turned the topic to Mel Gibson's movie *The Passion of the Christ* and told both of us that a news report had just come in that a woman in Wichita, KS, had died of a heart attack while viewing the film. Falwell instantly retorted, "That lady would have died if she was at a water fountain in the park." I literally heard broadcast staffers in the room next to the studio gasp in shock over the remark.

Although Falwell and I clearly have different theological views, one would think that a purely pastoral concern would lead any minister to express sympathy instead of making some rude and dismissive comment about any person's death. For the record, the dead woman, Peggy Lee Scott, was in fact a daughter, a wife, a mother, and a grandmother who worked for several local radio stations. Whatever point Falwell was trying to make was aptly characterized by one viewer as "a cheap shot" from a man who seems to be "commenting from the gutter."

It was also designed, as this was the emphasis found in briefs like those of the Becket Fund for Religious Liberty, to have the Supreme Court invalidate often inaptly-named "Blaine amendments" to state constitutions. These are provisions in thirty-seven state constitutions that explicitly deny the use of tax dollars to religious ministries, missions, schools, and clergy. The hope of the antiseparationists, who are only federalists when it suits them, was to have the Court declare that all state constitutions that afford greater protection of the public treasury from the hands of religious supplicants than the First Amendment as interpreted does, would effectively be nullified.

My friend Michael Newdow successfully challenged the use of the words "under God" in a Ninth Circuit case in 2004. Regrettably, although he was an eloquent oral advocate at the Supreme Court—with an unassailable bottom line argument—he was held to have lacked standing, since he lacked custody of his daughter, who attended public school. He filed again in 2005 in the United States District Court for the Eastern District of California on behalf of three unnamed parents and their children. Based on the previous ruling by the Ninth Circuit, the trial judge ruled that the pledge is unconstitutional when recited in public schools.

On March 11, 2010, a different panel of the United States Court of Appeals for the Ninth Circuit upheld the words "under God" in the Pledge of Allegiance in the case of *Newdow v. Rio Linda Union School District*, stating that "the School District's Policy of having teachers lead students in the daily recitation of the Pledge, and allowing those who do not wish to participate to refuse to do so with impunity, do not violate the Establishment Clause."[18]

It is somewhat rare that a direct Americans United case gets to the Supreme Court, but in 2014, a challenge to legislative prayer in Greece, New York, made its way there.

Here is a little presentation I gave to the students at Rutgers's Law School just weeks before the ultimate Supreme Court decision in 2014.

Marsh v. Chambers, upholding the constitutionality of the regular prayers of a chaplain hired by the Nebraska legislature, may well be the most poorly reasoned decision regarding religion in modern Supreme Court jurisprudence. Applying no traditionally recognizable "test" of constitutionality, it ultimately upholds a religious ritual using public funds, affirming the continuance of the practice solely on its history.

In my view, flawed as *Marsh* may be, its reasoning is readily distinguishable from the issues raised in the controversy in *Galloway v. Town of Greece*. Our two plaintiffs, Susan Galloway and Linda Stephens, challenged monthly town council prayers—which were almost always given by Christian ministers. Ms. Galloway is Jewish; Ms. Stephens, an avowed atheist.

Here is what I consider the relevant background of this case: Prior to 1999, the Greece Town Council started its business meetings with a moment of silence, a nod to dignifying the occasion of action by a legislative body. Upon the election of a new board chair, John Auberger, however, the "opening" policy changed to one in which a prayer was offered by a local member of the clergy, invited from persons representing institutions listed on a vaguely and erratically constructed "clergy list" garnered by city employees from publicly available sources.

Actual attendance at town council meetings is sparse. Residents who do attend largely fall into one of several categories: certain city employees whose jobs require attendance, newly appointed police officers sworn in on these occasions, citizens being awarded various city awards, high school students who are visiting the body to fulfill part of a civics graduation requirement, and residents who are seeking a change in public policy or a "benefit" that the council has the authority to provide. Our plaintiffs fell into that last category.

When our clients went to a council meeting, they were confronted with a religious activity they found wholly inappropriate for such a venue: A prayer was given by the selected minister from behind a podium containing the town of Greece seal, who faces the audience, not the seated members of the council. In the eighteen months before the record in this case closed, 85 percent of those prayers specifically mentioned "Jesus," the "Holy Spirit," "Your son," or "Christ." Indeed many were clearly based on Christian doctrinal beliefs, including the Resurrection, Pentecost, or the Ascension of Christ into heaven. Some asked for very concrete affirmative conduct on the part of the audience, including standing, "joining," or bowing one's head. Others assumed that all of those present were Christian (for example, referring to "us as Christian people" or proclaiming "our Christian faith"). Finally, after the lawsuit was filed, a few prayers even made veiled references to the Council being "God fearing" and implying that certain other people were not, including in the view of one prayer-giver, certain unspecified "ignorant" minorities. Some of these prayer offerers were officially referred to as the "Chaplain of the Month."

Over the course of this protracted litigation, there were four exceptions to the overarching theological direction I've just noted. A Wiccan priestess offered one invocation, a Baha'i leader spoke once, and—although the council apparently found it impossible to find a rabbi—a Jewish person who knew some Jewish prayers twice offered one. None of these figures were accorded the title of "Chaplain." Curiously, these four "exceptional" offerings were all done in 2008, the year in which the litigation began. After 2008, and until the record closed, the speakers were, once again, all Christians. Throughout much of this litigation, the town claimed in various media appearances and in court filings that it would be willing to have anyone from the town appear. However, this sentiment was never actually announced to the residents, much less formally adopted as policy by the board.

Our clients' claims were rejected at trial, but on appeal to the Second Circuit, the lower court was reversed in a unanimous decision. The central and persuasive finding in that decision was an assessment of the "totality of the circumstances," concluding that the manner of the prayer's presentation and its consistent basic content appeared "to affiliate the town with a particular creed." The decision referred to the "steady drumbeat of often specifically sectarian Christian prayers." The Second Circuit did not hold that "the town cannot open its public meetings with a prayer or invocation," noting that the *Marsh* decision allows legislative prayers under some circumstances. The town council appealed and the Supreme Court—frankly, to my surprise—granted certiorari on May 20, 2013. The case was argued on November 6, 2013, just a few months ago.

In the judgment of the Americans United legal team, the Second Circuit reached the right decision under the facts, but did not do so with the strongest possible analysis, particularly in distinguishing the Greece circumstances from those in *Marsh*. Here are some of the differences we pointed out in our brief and oral argument to the Supreme Court.

First, in Nebraska, as during invocations for the United States Congress, the prayer is directed to the members of the body. The trial court in *Marsh* referred to this as "an internal act." It should be noted that in Washington very few members are actually present to hear these prayers, but some of those not present claim to watch the prayer on the television feed sent to their offices. The public that is in attendance are sitting in a gallery watching events; they are not asked or expected to participate. Indeed, certain efforts to embellish or critique the invocation get you ejected and sometimes arrested. A small group of Christians found themselves in just that circumstance in July 2007, when they vocally chastised the first Hindu asked to give the Senate prayer, labeling him "wicked" and "an abomination."

This difference is also significant as a matter of law because the people in the gallery are not there to plead a case or argue a position to the legislators. (At Congressional hearings, where advocates for positions do appear, there is never any offering of a prayer or other religious activity, and witnesses can even choose to "affirm" rather than "swear" to tell the truth, which to many suggests a religiously based promise.)

Under the state and federal seating schema, legislators are not in a position to observe the audience and, thus, notice which people are "appropriately" observing the religious event on the floor. In Greece, however, the Council is viewing the audience and failure to participate fully will be observed and indeed could be used as a strike against doing what that audience member pleads for a few minutes later, a detrimental start to achieving the very goal she or he is seeking. There is no lawyer or advocate for any person appearing before a legislative, judicial, or executive branch body who would not recommend that persons "go along" with any formalistic practice whether they like it or not. In its simplest form, this is what causes me to label the Greece practice inherently "coercive," tending to make people operate in a manner that they would otherwise not choose to do but for the pressure to conform and the fear of reprisal for failing to do so. The Second Circuit characterized this as putting attendees in the awkward position of "either participating in prayers invoking beliefs they did not share or appearing to show disrespect for the invocation."

There is no way to escape this pressure, other than to forfeit one's right to attend the board meeting. As the Supreme Court, in one of its rulings prohibiting prayers at high school graduation put it, no citizen should be required to "take unilateral and private action to avoid compromising religious scruples."[19] Coercion could be "subtle and indirect" it continued, a recognition that coercion of course does not occur only through the mechanisms of gunpoint or threatening imprisonment. The Court even labeled prayer over the public address system in a high school football stadium as having the effect for children and adults in the bleachers of the "improper effect of coercing those present to participate in an act of religious worship,"[20] correctly identifying prayer as a participatory event. Significant social science research, analyzed in our brief to the Supreme Court, buttresses the claim of real coercion just from a sense of needing to go along with majority sentiments and practice.

We come now to the second major distinction between Greece's practice and the activity in the Nebraska legislature. The long-serving Presbyterian chaplain there thirty-four years ago had, at the request of a Jewish legislator, removed references to Jesus from his prayers, making generic references to a deity but eliminating most Christian theological references. He did not try to proselytize non-Christian members of the body. This fact is noted repeatedly by the majority in *Marsh*. They believed that the prayers could be accurately labeled "nonsectarian"; indeed, they wrote that the prayers there had not been "exploited to proselytize or advance any one"[21] faith. As I have noted earlier, the prayers in Greece are anything but that.

The construct of a "nonsectarian" prayer is admittedly an odd one for some of us, particularly those of us who actually engage in that practice. Normally, a prayer is directed to a specific entity, envisioned in a certain way—from bearded man in flowing robes to spiritual energy field—and for the purpose of thanks for a perceived "blessing" or a request for help for the future. This is not what a majority of the Supreme Court's members seem to mean, however. A definition that seemingly does not bother most members of the current court is one I'd submit would be seen as "strange" (to be polite) by virtually any religion scholar in the world. Here is a version of that definition written by Justice Antonin Scalia: A sectarian prayer is one "specifying details upon which men and women who believe in a benevolent, omnipotent Creator and Ruler of the world are known to differ (for example, the divinity of Christ)."[22]

For many, once you announce support for one God, as opposed to multiple ones or none at all, you are making a profound and profoundly sectarian statement. Adding to that such characteristics as being all-powerful, all good, the basis for creation, and active in ongoing human history makes any characterization of such "god" as nonsectarian patently ridiculous.

Some of the *amici* in Greece did make this point, but as the attorneys for our clients, we felt a need to walk on the decrepit porch that had been erected. Even by Justice Scalia's flawed definition, however, the Greece prayers are overwhelmingly sectarian, taking positions precisely on such core claims as "the divinity of Jesus."

If *Marsh* stands for the proposition that legislative prayers must be nonsectarian, and a number of justices led by Justice Kennedy have found constitutional problems with "coercive" prayers, the prayer mechanism used by the Town Council in Greece fails on both counts.

The oral argument in Greece did not add much to the written record in the case. It was a time in which I understood why Justice Clarence Thomas never asks questions. There were, as I wrote in a *Washington Post* article, so many red herrings present that they would turn a cerulean blue sea, purple.

The biggest school of those herrings involved a ceaseless effort to figure out how to avoid the so-called "censorship" by government of the prayers of those visiting chaplains. Somehow, chaplains asked to provide a prayer in other legislative venues do not seem to be troubled by this. Thirty-seven states have guidelines for chaplains and/or guest prayer-givers about their expected conduct and expression. Written instructions for guest preachers in the United States House of Representatives clearly remind them that the body consists of "Members of many faith traditions." Although Senate guidelines are apparently orally given, they seem to match those of the House, and one review of recent Senate prayers revealed that only 5 percent even mention Jesus.

Remember that there is no constitutional "right" for the clergy to pray at any legislative event. Legislatures are not mandated to allow spiritual sentiments to be expressed. When prayers occur it is only because of an act of delegated governmental authority by that legislature. Surely that body can therefore set parameters and expect compliance. When Chairman Auberger in his deposition was asked whether he would permit a prayer imploring "our white Lord Jesus to grant peace to the white residents of Greece but not the blacks or the Jews or homosexuals or other perverts," he noted that he would. I'd submit this "do whatever you want" is a breathtakingly preposterous position to adopt, flying in the face of standard procedures for citizen involvement in governmental matters and commonsense sensitivities.

As one example, the House of Representatives guidelines are quite specific. Prayers are limited to 150 words, must be entirely in English, and may not make "any intimations pertaining to foreign or domestic policy." The Obama administration, it should be noted, took the side of the Greece town council in this case, articulating the fear that to require a more stringent effort to address the lopsided nature of Greece invocations would cast doubt on the legitimacy of the congressional prayers. The government's brief suggests this is important. Honestly, though, does President Obama believe that prayers in the John Boehner-controlled House help move quality legislation forward or quell the partisan vitriol spilled on a near daily basis? I might even suggest to any nontheists in attendance that if you want one more quiver in your argument that prayer is entirely ineffectual, just ask believers how much it has produced recently in that deliberative body.

Perhaps the greatest postargument concern raised by some civil libertarians who were critiquing the performance of our chosen oral advocate, Professor Douglas Laycock of the University of Virginia Law School, was that he somehow "threw atheists under the bus" in his time before the

Court. He conceded that under the definition of "nonsectarian" used by the Court, polytheists and atheists would not be happy with a result that simply allowed a Scalia-like definition to guide future prayer policies. When Justice Samuel Alito noted, "I don't think it's possible to compose anything that you could call a prayer that would be acceptable to all these groups," Laycock responded "You can't treat everyone equally without getting rid of prayer altogether."[23] I have known Professor Laycock for decades and don't always agree with him. Nevertheless, I cannot imagine him being upset were the Court to throw up its hands in despair, apologize for past judicial error, and overturn *Marsh* precisely to protect the consciences and concerns Justice Alito mentioned. Indeed, in a 1986 law review article he called the *Marsh* decision "wholly unprincipled and indefensible."[24]

I wish I believed that every politician in a legislature that supports prayer before the business session was doing so out of some deep personal conviction to which he or she subscribed on a twenty-four-hour-a-day basis. Regrettably, I have known too many politicians to give that view any credibility. Religion, along with patriotism, has sometimes come to be the last bastion of scoundrels. The truly devout need not leave their religious views out of their hearts or minds. Justice Scalia, at the oral argument, made a serious mistake in dealing with that premise, however. He said, "When local government officials attend their business meetings, they do so as citizens, take their beliefs with them, and their religious practices, and that includes their habit of 'invoking the Deity' just as they do at home before eating meals."

Surely, there must be a legally cognizable difference between a council member saying grace over his barbecue in the backyard and offering a prayer in an official business capacity. If every government employee has the unfettered right to use public time to promote religion, teachers could pray in homeroom with their third graders, football coaches could insist that players get in a circle and praise Jesus before entering the field, and IRS agents could tell someone they are auditing about how only belief in Jesus makes you a moral person just before inquiring about the claimed donation to B'nai B'rith or the Church of Scientology.

No, those who share a faith with others in a legislative body can meet in one of their offices and engage in the specific spiritual activity of their choice before getting to the public's business of potholes, cable television rates, and green buildings. Those who are Christian may even turn in their Bibles to Matthew 6:6 and find out about a man named Jesus who recommended that the politicos of his day "go into a closet and pray privately" so as not to appear to be praying in public as hypocrites. Not a sermon; just a suggestion.

In May of 2014, the Supreme Court rejected the reasoning I articulated above and in a 5–4 decision upheld this prayer practice in *Greece*. However, the majority opinion was written by Justice Anthony Kennedy—the swing vote on virtually every controversial matter. Kennedy allowed for significant wiggle room, indicating that governments "maintain . . . a policy of non-discrimination," the prayer be delivered principally at "lawmakers themselves" and not directed at participation by the public, not single out and denigrate "non-believers or religious minorities," and divorce invocations from policy-making.[25]

Americans United started a project called "Operation Inclusion" two days after the decision. We urged Americans to try to get local governments to remove *all* invocations, but that if that maneuver failed, to insist that representatives who are members of minority faiths and atheists be allowed to get in the queue. This has led to some impressive results, including a Wiccan priest giving an invocation in Huntsville, Alabama, for a spirit of peace and community (he was initially denied the opportunity but AU volunteered to represent him) and atheist invocations in Glendale, Arizona; Sioux Falls, South Dakota; Largo, Florida; and, ironically, Greece, New York, itself.

All of this prompted the evangelical magazine *Charisma* to pose the question: "Did the Supreme Court win backfire on Christians?" Only time will tell.

When the Religious Right "triumphs" in a case before the United States Supreme Court—as it did most recently in the recent Hobby Lobby (discussed later) and Greece cases, it is easy to get depressed. These cases did have a direct negative effect on huge numbers of people, marginalizing them as second-class citizens undeserving of the same treatment the Christian majority receives.

There is also a kind of despondency I hear from people in, say, New York City, where the Right is weaker than most places, about the conditions under which people need to live in, say, Baton Rouge, Louisiana, even if they never plan to visit the state, much less live there. Those New Yorkers hear about schoolbooks promoting creationism or legislation to impose new strictures on the provision of abortion services and are horrified in principle.

But there is one horrific incident that went well beyond depression or despondency. It is the story of what happened to three then-young, now-approaching-middle-aged, men who ran afoul of religious conventions in the small town of West Memphis, Arkansas. I did frequent interviews on my radio show with the defense team for the "West Memphis 3." There was finally a resolution of their case in 2013. The good news: None of them was erroneously executed. The bad news: They all spent eighteen years and seventy-eight days in prison.

West of Fairness and Justice: New Documentary Showcases Dangers of Religious Hysteria[26]

I admit it: I slipped out of work early one day in late January. It wouldn't be honest to say I had a "medical" appointment; my fear of dentists knocks that reason out, and of course there was no "continuing legal education" seminar that just called out to be attended.

No, the plain truth is that I just went to the movies. If you read this column regularly, you know I am a film buff. The documentary I went to see that day hits so close to home that I didn't even feel I was missing work.

The film is very sad. It is about three young men who spent eighteen years in prison for murders they did not commit. Here's the church-state angle: The major reason they were convicted was that a jury had been tainted by a so-called "expert witness" whose fundamentalist-inspired views made a mockery of the idea of a fair trial.

The film is titled *West of Memphis*, and it was mainly produced by Peter Jackson of *Lord of the Rings* and *The Hobbit* fame.

Some background: On May 6, 1993, the bodies of three eight-year-old boys were found in a drainage ditch in West Memphis, Arkansas. They had been horribly mutilated and tied up with shoe laces.

Three teenagers from the community, Damien Echols, Jessie Misskelley Jr., and Jason Baldwin, were arrested, put on trial, and convicted in 1994. However, on August 19, 2011, the three—including Echols, who had been on death row—were released from prison after a deal was cut with state officials.

I have been troubled by this case for more than a decade since reading the first account of it, *Devil's Knot*, by Arkansas reporter and civil liberties activist Mara Leveritt. I became so engrossed by Leveritt's book during a long plane trip that I didn't even realize we had landed and people were departing until a flight attendant asked me if there was something wrong.

I watched three HBO documentaries about this matter and interviewed a woman who left her job to work on the case (and eventually married Damien Echols) on my *Culture Shocks* radio show on several occasions.

There were a large number of judicial errors made in this case, but I keep returning to the original trial of Echols and Baldwin. There was no DNA evidence, fiber evidence, or eyewitness evidence linking these men to the crimes. So how did they get drawn into it?

A man named Dale W. Griffis was the key. Griffis, who liked to be referred to as "Dr. Griffis," was a consultant with a degree from an unaccredited institution in California that is widely regarded as a diploma mill specializing in "distance learning." In the 1990s, Griffis was a familiar figure promoting his seminars to police departments on the topic of "Satanic crimes."

At the trial, the defense tried to have him disqualified as an expert witness because of his lack of anything but "a mail-order PhD." But the judge allowed him to present, asserting that Griffis's "experience" in life allowed him to function as an expert on "the occult."

Griffis testified that a series of factors led him to conclude that this was an "occult" crime: It had been committed on the night of a full moon, there was sexual mutilation, blood had been extracted from the victims, and, of course, all three of the children were eight years old, supposedly a "witches' number."

I hope you get the point. Indeed, so much of everything Griffis said turned out to be just plain wrong.

The judge also allowed into evidence that Echols wore black clothing and had Stephen King novels in his room and had once gotten a book from the library on Wicca.

That was it. That was all it took for the convictions in the absence of any other data. But an atmosphere had been generated in the courtroom that made the motive clear to the jurors (at least one of whom still believes it today): A pact with the devil had led to the murders.

There have been times when I spoke about this case to AU chapters or other groups. There were always other issues I addressed in the same speeches or presentations. Every one of those issues was and remains important. But it is somehow particularly horrifying to think that three innocent people spent eighteen years in an Arkansas prison for a crime almost no one—including the parents of the murdered children—now believes they committed. (*West of Memphis* points a sharp finger at a much more likely suspect.)

This happened because a judge let a crank testify about a case he knew little about and who had a background only in creating a level of hysteria that would have been right in place in Salem, Massachusetts, in 1692.

I encourage you to see this film. It will help you understand how bad things can get when a whiff of theocracy leads people to turn against anyone who is unconventional or has no religious beliefs—and how a reckless combination of church and state can obscure the truth.

Chapter 6

WHEN GOVERNMENT OFFICIALS PRAY, GET OUT THE TV CAMERAS; WHEN THEY PUT UP THE TEN COMMANDMENTS, DON'T EXPECT THEM TO FOLLOW THEM

I recently spoke to a women's group in Montgomery County, Maryland. The last question related to politicians who want to appear pious. When I answered the question and then said, "You almost get the sense that every word processing program in Washington automatically adds to speeches on any topic—from pipelines to defense—the phrase . . ." And before I could finish the sentence, there were numerous vocalizations of "God Bless America." Yes, they got it right.

But of course, the Religious Right loves when government officials pray.

WHO NEEDS A NATIONAL DAY OF PRAYER?[1]

A federal judge on April 15 ruled that the National Day of Prayer (NDP) is unconstitutional—and the Religious Right is up in arms.

"This is a concerted effort by a small but determined number of people who have tried to prohibit all references to the Creator in the public square, whether it be the Ten Commandments, the Pledge of Allegiance, or the simple act of corporate prayer—this is unconscionable for a free society," Shirley Dobson, wife of radio counselor James Dobson and chair of the National Day of Prayer Task Force, asserted.[2]

Jay Sekulow, chief counsel of TV preacher Pat Robertson's American Center for Law and Justice, which represented thirty-one members of Congress in a friend-of-the-court brief defending the National Day of Prayer, also chimed in.

"It is unfortunate that this court failed to understand that a day set aside for prayer for the country represents a time-honored tradition that embraces the First Amendment, not violates it," he moaned.[3]

Give it a rest. The court made the right call. Here's why.

Government is supposed to be neutral on religion. It has no business telling people how, when, or where to pray—or even if they ought to pray. Government does lots of things well, but meddling in our private religious lives is not among them.

As a Christian minister, I can't understand why some clergy ever thought the National Day of Prayer was a good idea. Furthermore, the National Day of Prayer has always been soaked in the kind of offensive "God and country" rhetoric that many of us find nauseating. It was first proposed in the 1950s to show those "godless Commies" a thing or two. In 1988, Congress codified it as the first Thursday in May. Congressionally mandated prayer in a country that separates church and state? I don't think so.

The NDP is not just an acknowledgment that Americans pray. It actively promotes religious practice. The government is, in fact, urging you to pray. That's simply not government's job.

In recent years, the NDP events have been taken over by aggressive Religious Right groups—like Focus on the Family, founded by Shirley Dobson's husband—which have used it in a highly offensive way and drenched it in fallacious, right-wing "Christian nation" pseudohistory. Worse, they've sponsored "Christians only" prayer events that exclude millions of Americans. (And by "Christians" they mean fundamentalists. Progressive Christians like me got nowhere near the microphone.)

In some communities, people got so fed up with the exclusive nature of NDP events that they started sponsoring rival get-togethers that were more inclusive. So we had dueling prayer showdowns! Nice way to bring everybody together, right?

Let's keep this simple: We separate religion and government in this country. That means the state has no business setting aside special days for prayer or other religious observances.

Thomas Jefferson knew that. He refused to issue prayer proclamations during his presidency. James Madison issued a few under pressure from Congress but later in his life wrote an essay saying he wished he hadn't.

Andrew Jackson followed Jefferson's lead and refused to issue such proclamations entirely.

I know enough about the subject to realize that for prayer to be meaningful it has to come from the heart, be freely chosen, and not be an engine
of state policy. Prayers pushed by the government aren't worth saying.

You want to pray on May 6? More power to you. I'll let you in on a little
secret: You don't, and never did, need the government to give you a nudge.

In 2010, I did join a few influential religious leaders to call on organizers
of the National Prayer Breakfast, members of Congress attending, and the
president to use the opportunity to send a clear, unified message against the
horrendous Ugandan "Anti-Homosexuality Bill." (The National Prayer Breakfast
is not organized by any government officials, but plenty of them attend.) This
"unofficial" event merely adds insult to the injury of the National Day of Prayer,
particularly given who organizes this annual event.

In addition to Rev. Harry Knox, then with the Human Rights Campaign, the
Rev. Elder Darlene Garne from Metropolitan Community Church, and Bishop
Gene Robinson, the first openly gay bishop in the Episcopal Church, we were
joined by "Moses," a gay Ugandan man seeking asylum in the United States. At
the press event, he said, "It breaks my heart that I have to leave my family and
loved ones to seek asylum in this country simply because I am gay. Even as I
speak, gay people are being persecuted as a result of this proposed law against
gay people. I can only imagine how bad it will be if the bill is actually passed."

My statements called on President Obama to take the lead on human rights
for everyone, everywhere, regardless of sexual orientation or gender identity.

Speaking at the breakfast in 2010, Hillary Clinton condemned Uganda's
notorious Anti-Homosexuality Bill, saying that the United States was "standing up
for gays and lesbians who deserve to be treated as full human beings" and noted
that she had personally informed Uganda's president, Yoweri Museveni, of "our
strongest concerns about a law being considered in the Parliament of Uganda."[4]

Obama would later echo those sentiments at the same Prayer Breakfast:
"We may disagree about gay marriage, but surely we can agree that it is unconscionable to target gays and lesbians for who they are—whether it's here in the
United States or, as Hillary mentioned, more extremely in odious laws that are
being proposed most recently in Uganda."[5]

National Prayer Breakfasts are, of course, organized by the Fellowship Foundation (which is maybe better known by its other name "The Family"), a shadowy far-right group whose members campaigned for the passage of Uganda's bill.

Museveni passed the bill despite Clinton's urging, only for it to be struck down in 2014 by the country's high court on a technicality. Parliamentarians swiftly reintroduced the bill; as of printing, it had not yet passed.

WHY I'M NOT GOING TO THE NATIONAL PRAYER BREAKFAST[6]

Let's see, where will I be eating breakfast Thursday? I've seen some really mouth-watering ads for a new dish at Denny's (or maybe it was the International House of Pancakes) that involves hash browns covered with lots of cheese and meat and maybe some pancakes, too. But I can't eat that. I've been sticking to my postholiday diet for four weeks, dropping pounds and lowering my blood sugar. I can't go back to cholesterol, fats, and carbs.

There is another possibility: I could hightail over to the National Prayer Breakfast and eat with a bevy of Washington luminaries, including many members of Congress of both parties and the president. One drawback is that I'd have to be invited, and it looks like my invite got lost in the mail. The other is that the tickets are pricey, which would severely cut into my monthly budget for renting DVDs.

But the most important reason I don't plan to go is the company I'd be keeping. I don't mean the politicians who attend to pray and be seen (or is it be seen praying)? I'm talking about the sponsors.

This sixtieth-anniversary eggs-and-muffin extravaganza is sponsored by an Arlington-based organization called the Fellowship, but more commonly known as the Family. One adjective used to describe the group is "shadowy," but that doesn't begin to tell the story.

Journalist Jeff Sharlet has doggedly researched the Family and written two books on the topic.[7] The Family was founded in 1935 by Abraham Vereide, a Norwegian clergyman living in Seattle. Vereide formed the organization with a small group of businessmen who seemed untroubled by some of the extreme movements then sweeping Europe.

According to Sharlet's books, the group believes that God's covenant with the Jews has been broken and that Family acolytes are the new chosen, destined to remake the world in Jesus's honor.

Sharlet says the Family uses the National Prayer Breakfast to advance its goals in part by guiding the powerful attendees (and potentially future power brokers) to smaller, more frequent prayer meetings. At these events, the rich and powerful are told they can "meet Jesus man to man," Sharlet writes.

But the Family isn't just peddling theology. There's a political angle, too. The Family has big dreams that transcend winning an election or passing some bill about a hot-button social issue. It wants to reshape the entire world's "worldview" in accordance with its understanding of the Bible, according to Sharlet.

Group leaders aren't big on going on CNN or even Fox News to discuss their agenda or methods, but annoying facts keep slipping out. As recently as 2009, the *New York Times* reported that an obscure Ugandan legislator, who had participated in a set of homophobic workshops put on by American evangelicals, introduced a bill that initially called for the death penalty for gay people in the country, later modified to offer extensive imprisonment and a chance while there to perhaps be "cured" of your gayness. Several researchers uncovered links between Family members and the legislator, although the Family claimed they hadn't intended the legislation to be so draconian.

And, then, there were the sex scandals. In 2009, then-senator John Ensign admitted to having an affair with the wife of a top aide while living at the C Street house, a structure on Capitol Hill that is owned by the Family. He later resigned. Ex-South Carolina governor Mark Sanford seems to have gotten advice from other politicians living on C Street after his much-publicized flight to Argentina with the love of his life who just didn't happen to be his wife. But the Family doesn't comment on such matters.

The National Prayer Breakfast is a privately sponsored event, so it's not a constitutional issue when members of the government attend. It is a common-sense issue. What possible message does it send?

A 2010 Gallup Poll found that 83 percent of Americans believe that God answers at least some of their prayers. Since there is only one professed nontheist in Congress, I'd expect to find the same percentage there. The thing is, there is already a taxpayer-funded chaplain in each chamber who prays every morning. Members of Congress have plenty of opportunities to pray.

But I understand that sometime people want to pray in a group. Fine.

But why should members of Congress let those prayers be organized by people who have been accused of thinking gays are sinners, any woman who has an abortion is a murderer, and Muslims are members of a "false" religion?

Anyone who takes prayer seriously should avoid, not embrace, these folks. Why not have the courage to stand up for your faith by witnessing with those who share it, not blithely participate in an act of worship that offends your own deepest understandings of divine purpose?

Here's my offer: If politicians must go to a prayer breakfast, come with me to a Denny's or IHOP in Maryland. I'm a minister. I can lead a prayer; more importantly I can listen to you pray and not presume it is always the same as what is on my mind.

Maybe we could have a respectful chat about any differences over the meal. Just as I'm giving up those carbs, fats, and cholesterol, you can give up the secrecy of the Family and embrace transparency. Drop the divisiveness of the Family's theology and embrace some commonalities of all decent people. Skip the high-ticket prices and by-invitation-only nature of the Family's feast and break bread in a place with a menu that your constituents can afford.

It's just a thought.

In 2013, Maryland pediatric neurosurgeon (and potential 2016 Republican presidential candidate) Ben Carson gave the "keynote address" at this event, where he pontificated at great length about how bad Obamacare was and how pro-life he was. It was particularly obnoxious because President Obama had to listen to this twenty minute screed sitting on the dais. Carson claims in his 2014 autobiography that the White House demanded that he apologize.[8] He did not.

CHAPLAINS IN CONGRESS

The chaplains in Congress are expensive and wholly unnecessary—although courts have been unwilling to engage in any serious analytical tests of their constitutionality. Briefly, in 1995, new congressional leadership considered abolition.

CONGRESSIONAL CHAPLAINS: A WASTE OF TAXPAYER MONEY[9]

Over the years I've spent in Washington, I've met many pastors whose churches are within blocks of the US Capitol. Many of these places of worship are home to members of Congress when business or bad weather keeps them here over a weekend and away from their families and constituents.

Many of these ministers have expressed an interest in a more active ministry to elected officials, wondering how they could be more available for counseling and other spiritual duties. Denominational officials with offices near Capitol Hill, who spend most of their time advocating their faith group's positions on issues, also wrestle with how to serve as occasional ministers and counselors to Congress. No one I've talked to about this ever expressed any desire to charge for their spiritual services.

On the other hand, two ministers work right in the Capitol, and they are richly rewarded. They are the House and Senate chaplains. The Senate chaplain, Richard C. Halverson, who plans to retire soon after fourteen years, makes $115,700 annually. His House counterpart, James Ford, pulls in even more—$123,000.

The Supreme Court in the case of *Marsh v. Chambers* overlooked the fact that even some of those who crafted the Constitution had serious doubts about tax-supported clergy. James Madison, for example, wrote that such employment was a "palpable violation of equal rights as well as Constitutional principles" and a "national establishment" of religion.[10] He suggested that if Congress wanted chaplains to discharge religious duties, members should pay for them from their own pockets. "How just would it be in its principle!" he proclaimed.

Indeed, one of Madison's concerns—inequality of faith representation by the chaplains—has been a problem for more than two hundred years. All of the Senate chaplains but one have been Protestant males. (A Catholic priest served briefly in the mid-nineteenth century.) [The current chaplain, in 2015, is Barry Black, a Seventh Day Adventist.] There have been numerous unsuccessful calls for the appointment of a woman to replace the Senate's Halverson, with active lobbying for specific candidates. [The House appointed its only Catholic chaplains in 2000 and 2011.] All of this appears a little unseemly to me. No single pastor can be expected to seriously understand the nuances (or sometimes even the central tenants) of the diverse collection of politicians in today's multicultural nation.

The prayers uttered each morning are rarely memorable (except for a prayer for O. J. Simpson, which barely mentioned the victims of the horrendous crimes he was charged with committing, that drew fire from dozens of C-SPAN viewers). This may be one of the reasons virtually no members are in attendance at morning prayer.

The new and self-proclaimed fiscally responsible leadership of Congress has a wonderful opportunity to apply Madisonian principles to the present day. Halverson's position could be left unfilled. Ford could go back to the pastorate or some other line of work.

This is not a pipe dream. Rep. Jim Nussle, an Iowa Republican who heads the transition team to Republican rule back in 1995, indicated in a recent press interview that he would explore using volunteer chaplains of rotating denominations to fill Ford's slot. This practice has historical precedent. The House had no chaplain from 1855 to 1861, and members of the District of Columbia clergy officiated at the prayer that opened each day's legislative session.

Roll Call, a Capitol Hill newspaper, recently ran an article that quoted from a pre-Civil War era report of the House Judiciary Committee, which had been asked to study the constitutional appropriateness of Congress's chaplains. The committee decided chaplains passed muster since "there never was a deliberative body that so eminently needed the fervent prayers of righteousness as the Congress of the United States." That's a pretty clever line. However, accepting the undisputed premise—Congress needs help—doesn't lead necessarily to a paid chaplain.

We have ministers who are eager to give more of their time *gratis* to the spiritual aid of members of Congress. Moreover, much talk circulates these days about cutting the fat on Capitol Hill, making it less like a country club and more like the average American work place. We stand at a moment when all the stars could be heading toward a constitutional convergence. The result: elimination of an expensive throwback to another era. Who knows, maybe the $288,000 saved—and did I neglect to mention that the Senate chaplain has a $50,000-per-year assistant?—could be directed to save some of the school lunches that may be cut.

Speaker Newt Gingrich eventually told the *New York Times* that the chaplains would stay because it would send the wrong message to eliminate them. Of course, for Mr. Gingrich, it is all about the appearance.

RELIGIOUS DISPLAYS

So, once politicians succeed or fail at having prayers before their legislative gatherings—or create Christian prayer days—what is next? It is, of course, insistence about the public display of religious icons, sayings, Scriptures, or other such items.

A NEW COMMANDMENT FOR POLITICIANS: THOU SHALT NOT BE A HYPOCRITE[11]

US Rep. Robert Aderholt of Alabama has been preparing to introduce "The Ten Commandments Defense Act" to "allow the states . . . to display the Ten Commandments" in public buildings.[12]

Aderholt alleges the action is permitted under his peculiar interpretation of the Tenth Amendment. Apparently he has not noticed that this kind of legal argument has never prevailed about any constitutional prohibition—against an establishment of religion or censoring a free press or any other portion of the Bill of Rights.

He asserts that on the issue of state versus federal jurisdiction "you could go both ways on that issue." No, not really. Maybe on the "Planet of the Apes" (I don't know what their Constitution looks like), but not here in the United States.

The ever-inventive Judge Roy Moore, also of Alabama and now its elected chief justice of the Supreme Court, is also itching for a new fight over the Ten Commandments. You may recall that he fought a long legal battle over a hand-carved Decalogue displayed behind his judicial bench a few years ago. Moore has now unilaterally decided to place a two-and-a-half ton monument in the rotunda of the Alabama Judicial Building, which contains a version of the Commandments along with other symbols of what he views as our suppressed Christian heritage.

In his speech announcing this placement, Moore insisted, "It is axiomatic that to restore morality we must first recognize the source from which all morality springs."[13]

Far from axiomatic, his assertion that nonbelievers cannot possibly be moral actors is an affront to millions of Americans. Moreover, the notion that without government approval, specific religious texts will have less persuasive power is the height of insult to adherents to the Commandments who have managed to learn about them without being informed by Moore and other second-rate politicians.

It is my "prophetic" view that he will soon face a legal action that will challenge this sneer at the foundations of our Constitution, and unfortunately give Moore martyr status for another run for public office.

And, of course, Chief Justice Moore was sued by Americans United, the Southern Poverty Law Center, and the Alabama affiliate of the ACLU. Here is a summary of what happened: (More details appear in my earlier book, *Piety and Politics*.)

JUDGING ROY: WHY THE COURT RULED AGAINST MOORE'S MONUMENT[14]

I arrived at the Americans United office on November 18 knowing it was going to be a busy day.

A federal judge in Montgomery, Alabama, had announced that he would issue a ruling in AU's lawsuit against Alabama Supreme Court Chief Justice Roy Moore, who last year erected a 2,350-pound granite monument engraved with the Ten Commandments in the lobby of the Alabama Judicial Building.

US District Judge Myron Thompson didn't waste any time. At ten a.m. on the dot (nine a.m. in Alabama), the decision began sliding through our fax machine.

Americans United Legal Director Ayesha Khan had worked on the case with Morris Dees of the Southern Poverty Law Center and attorneys with the American Civil Liberties Union of Alabama. We all agreed that the trial had gone well and believed Judge Thompson would rule our way. Sure enough, the decision was a clear victory for our side and a strong affirmation of the importance of church-state separation.

Cable talk shows wanted to discuss the case that evening. On CNN's *Crossfire*, conservative host Tucker Carlson asked me to look at a large photo. He said, "Not only are the Ten Commandments in a courtroom in Alabama, this picture right here of Moses, with the actual tablet, do you know where that is from?"

Of course I knew where it was from—the US Supreme Court building. I've seen it a thousand times there.

I told Carlson that. He replied, "Why aren't you picking on it?" My comeback was simple, "Well, could you read the third [commandment] there, please?"

Carlson's reply was rather lame: "I don't have my contacts in."

The most powerful contacts in the world wouldn't have made it possible for Carlson to read the third commandment, because none of the wording is included in the artistic rendering. Moses is depicted cradling two tablets on a frieze that also includes historical lawgivers like Hammurabi, Solomon, Confucius, Muhammad, Napoleon, and the Roman emperor Augustus. The display represents the evolution of the law over the centuries. It's not intended to promote religion.

I tried to explain the difference to Carlson. "Judge Moore's monument is a monument to intolerance," I said. "It's the promotion of his own version of what the Ten Commandments ought to read. . . . But it is nothing like that phrase which you can't even read."

Carlson still didn't get it. "I want to get the Lynn standard here," he said. "So it is OK to have the Ten Commandments . . . so long as you can't read the lettering."

I tried again. The frieze, I pointed out, "also has Confucius . . . because that's a piece of a series of pictures of famous law-givers. It's nothing like the promotion by a right-wing judge of his particular religious viewpoint." The "Lynn test," as Carlson put it, contains many other factors, but frankly, the audience seemed convinced that at least for starters there was some kind of difference between a part of a sculpted frieze with literally no words on it and a multiton monolith placed as the centerpiece of a state's major judicial center.

Despite rumors that Moore has his eye on a US Senate seat, I don't think his actions are about political posturing. I believe Moore is a "true believer" in his faith. In fact, I'm so convinced of this that I told Sam Donaldson the next day that I thought Moore should resign from the court and find a new job. Moore's zeal and doctrinal certainty make him a poor fit for the bench, but they'd serve him well in another position—say, a pulpit.

Days after the decision to have the monument removed, Moore announced his intention to disobey the court's order. Adding insult to injury, large rallies in support of Moore and the Ten Commandments monument began forming in front of the judicial building, featuring speakers such as Alan Keyes, the Reverend Jerry Falwell, and Moore himself. Several hundred to over a thousand protesters remained in Alabama through the end of August as a show of support for Moore's monument.

The Eleventh Circuit agreed with the trial court; the Supreme Court refused to hear the case; and Judge Moore was thrown off the court by a unanimous decision of his all-Republican colleagues. Bizarrely, since we neglected to seek to have him permanently disbarred, he was reelected to the court in 2012 where he continues to promote weird ideas about courts and the Constitution (as discussed later in the book).

The United States Supreme Court waited three years to take on two cases with variations on the theme.

Church-state cases before the Supreme Court always precipitate a whirlwind of activity at Americans United.[15] This was particularly true in early March when two back-to-back arguments about placement of the Ten Commandments on government property were argued, one from Texas and the other from Kentucky.

I was up early to tape a debate for MSNBC with Jay Sekulow, chief counsel of the American Center for Law and Justice. It was then just a two-floor elevator ride down to the studios of C-SPAN. There I did a forty-five-minute discussion on Washington Journal with Kelly Shackleford, an attorney with a Texas-based group called the Liberty Legal Institute.

Shackleford's main argument was that if the court rules that the six-foot-high granite display on the grounds of the Texas state capitol is unconstitutional, then thousands of these monoliths will have to be "bulldozed" off public land. I explained that, given the number of churches in America, these structures could simply and reverentially be relocated to appropriate private spaces.[16]

Apparently my comments were not reassuring, because Shackleford used the bulldozer image another five times during the show. Several callers to the program made particularly offensive references to minority religious groups.

The oral arguments were up next. Arriving at the court, I spotted demonstrators on both sides and was pleased to see a healthy number of Americans United members were among them, some being interviewed by the media.

The arguments were simultaneously enlightening and scary. Duke University Law School professor Erwin Chemerinsky began to set out the argument in the Texas case (representing the plaintiff, who is a homeless former attorney), but after just a few sentences, as is so often the case, Justice Antonin Scalia interrupted with a harangue disguised as a question.

Scalia has an extremely narrow view of religious freedom, but he seemed particularly antagonistic that morning—perhaps hitting a new low. According to Scalia, government-sponsored Commandments displays are only intended to reinforce the idea that our government flows from God. He has a simple remedy for those who might be offended: "Turn your eyes away if it's such a big deal to you."[17]

Thankfully, many of the other justices asked more thoughtful questions that indicated they were taking the issue more seriously. Justice Ruth Bader Ginsberg challenged an assertion by Mat Staver of the conservative Liberty Counsel that the Ten Commandments aren't really that religious, firing back, "Have you read the first four commandments and could you say that?"[18]

From the court, I headed over to the offices of the Fox News Channel to discuss the arguments. To my surprise, I encountered former Alabama Chief Justice Roy Moore in the greenroom. Despite AU's long legal tangle with him over his display of his two-and-a-half-ton granite Ten Commandments in the state judicial building, I had never met the man face to face. We had a civil, albeit chilly, conversation. I commented that I had "followed your career"; he responded, "I've noticed."

The result of these cases was a "split decision."

I know it wasn't a circus because there were no elephants or acrobats.[19] The scene outside the Supreme Court on June 27, however, was as colorful and chaotic as any I have ever seen there.

I was at the court to respond to the expected decisions on the posting of the Ten Commandments on public property. For the same reason, the Rev. Rob Schenck of the National Clergy Council had set up a podium for prayer and distribution of Commandments pamphlets and, a few feet away, American Atheists president Ellen Johnson had a speaking platform from which to question the validity of the Decalogue.

Under Chief Justice William H. Rehnquist, the court always convenes promptly at ten. We "waiters" were standing in the sun on a hot, humid day that would cloud over and threaten torrential downpours every ten minutes or so. In front of us was a bank of a dozen television cameras and even more microphones. Rev. Schenck was at the mikes, a cell phone at each ear to get updates about the decisions.

I was accompanied by several AU staff members. At about 10:15, Communications Director Joe Conn got a call reporting that the decision involving the Commandments case from McCreary County, Kentucky, had been announced inside; a 5–4 majority had ruled the courthouse poster display unconstitutional.

Another fifteen minutes or so went by. We learned that Justice Antonin Scalia was inside reading parts of his "withering dissent." Scalia has never seen a Christian religious display he didn't think the government should erect, so his outrage was predictable. He may have been auditioning for chief justice in the event of Rehnquist's retirement.

As dark clouds rolled in, secularists and religious people alike joked about the omen-like significance were the heavens to open. I remarked that I understood that it rains on the just and the unjust, so nobody should read anything into any deluge.

A few more minutes passed, and another call came through: The court had approved the display of a 1960s-era Commandments monument outside the Texas statehouse, calling it historical and uncontroversial and declaring that it did not primarily promote religion. We had a split decision.

Rev. Schenck and a few other Religious Right figures made statements to the news media, followed by the AA's Johnson. I held back for a bit, trying to skim the decisions brought out to me by one of our staff members who had been inside the court.

It was soon clear that this "split" had broken in our favor. We would have to live with many of the Commandments monuments that had been put up as props for the Cecil B. DeMille's 1956 biblical movie epic. But these rulings would in no way permit the display of the Decalogue in public schools and would not allow the kind of display attempted by former Alabama Chief Justice Roy Moore with his multiton monolith in the state judicial building.

I was pleasantly surprised that evening to see that Jon Stewart's *The Daily Show* had an item on these cases, including a brief clip of me saying "Unfortunately, the Court has not set forth a clean rule: You shall not festoon government property with religious symbols." Stewart deadpanned: "If Mr. Lynn got his way, a major Washington renovation would have to be scrapped." Then an altered image of the Washington Monument with a crossbeam attached, turning it into a mega-cross, appeared on the screen.[20]

And then there is the "war on Christmas" . . .

"Why bother?"[21]

That was the reaction of a few of my friends, including a number of Americans United supporters, after seeing me on television or quoted in their local papers rebutting the idea that there is a "war on Christmas."

I can understand the sentiment, but this issue is far from trivial. Religious Right efforts to make 2005 the year of the "war on Christmas" got under way long before Halloween. The Rev. Jerry Falwell announced that he was mobilizing more than seven hundred lawyers in a battle to "save Christmas" in mid-October. About the same time, Fox News Channel host John Gibson published a book titled The War on Christmas.

I knew it was going to be a long holiday period. My first thought was to ignore the whole thing. Fox News was calling us to do three different shows on the same day, and I did not want to feed their conspiracy theories.

But the stories just kept coming and soon began appearing in the legitimate media as well. Falwell was being quoted all over the place, and reporters seemed to be accepting his wild claims that the season was being captured by the spirit of "political correctness" run amok, leaving the dark hint that soon children would not realize there was a holiday to celebrate at all!

Some of what Falwell was complaining about struck me as picayune. He seemed obsessed with greetings used by store clerks, for example, and he threw a fit after a Boston city government press release referred to the arrival of a "holiday tree." The mayor hadn't approved such a designation and immediately informed Falwell of that fact. (We do not know the current location of the writer of the press release, but I'll bet it is colder than Boston.)

Soon hard-to-swallow stories were flying left and right. Public schools were being accused of banning the colors green and red, forbidding students from saying "Merry Christmas," and changing the words of well-known Christmas carols to strike out religious references. To most of the readers of this column, this all sounds pretty unlikely. But, frankly, I became convinced that if these accusations went uncontested, they would become "true" just by dint of repetition. I knew Americans United had to fight back to correct the record.

I accepted an offer from www.beliefnet.com to do a back and forth e-mail dialogue with Gibson so that I could deal with some of his claims point by point. AU also issued an open letter to Falwell, reminding him (and the public) that generating a phony controversy around Christmas, heralded by Christians as a "season of peace," makes a mockery of real faith.

Most importantly, AU investigated the Religious Right's most common examples of the "war on Christmas." Guess what? They're bogus! Two schools accused of banning red and green did no such thing. Another school was accused of rewriting "Silent Night." In reality, it was putting on an eighteen-year-old play that changes the words of familiar Christmas carols to fit the play's secular theme of homelessness.

How do these crazy stories get started? Some people just believe what they want to believe heedless of the facts. I was discussing this issue on *The Michael Medved Show* when a caller insisted that a Chicago television station had cut out Linus's reading from the New Testament when it aired *A Charlie Brown Christmas*.

I was skeptical. During a commercial break, Medved's staff received two calls from people who had seen the same broadcast and noted that the Linus scene hadn't been cut. Michael is a conservative, but he immediately put the myth to rest. I wish every conservative was that forthright in correcting untruths.

The stakes are really much higher than whether someone does or does not think calling an evergreen a "Christmas tree" or a "holiday tree" is a big deal. For me, it is about the need to tell the truth. If government actions violate someone's constitutional rights, we have to say so. However, as people struggle to deal with the multiplicity of religious and philosophical viewpoints in America, it is also important not to permit false and pernicious stories to circulate unfettered by analysis and criticism.

In 2012, Gretchen Carlson, Fox News commentator said, "We're not nuts, are we? There is a war on Christmas!"[22] If Fox had invited me to respond, I would have responded: "You're not nuts, Gretchen, just listening to your network's own words too often."

And there are political types who try to put out pro-Christian license plates.

Perhaps the most frustrating argument I hear against the separation of church and state boils down to this: We need the government to "recognize" the value of religion—usually this means Christianity—in our city, county, state, or nation.[23] It's never adequately explained why those of us who are religious would need this. Can't we appreciate what we believe on our own?

This issue arose anew in December 2008 after Americans United won a preliminary ruling from a federal court in South Carolina stalling (and soon, we hope, permanently preventing) distribution of special "I Believe" license plates.

Lest anyone think the belief is generic, let me remind you that these tags feature a cross and a stained glass window—symbols not common in, say, the Hindu or Islamic traditions. It's clearly a "Christian" license plate.

Immediately after the grant of an order stopping the release of these plates, the blogosphere was ablaze (or, more appropriately, befogged) with comments about how this "censorship" would prevent the free expression of Christian beliefs.

Really? Since when do South Carolinians need a boost from government to express their faith?

In fact, long before South Carolina legislators decided to design this plate and then pass a bill authorizing its production and marketing, Christians there were perfectly capable of expressing their religiosity—even with their cars. Some put bumper stickers on their vehicles expressing religious views ("In the event of Rapture, this car will stop") and attached fish symbols to their trunks. The drivers were communicating their views and if other drivers didn't like it, too bad. That's free expression.

However, when state legislators decided to appropriate a few Christian symbols for their political purpose (never too unhealthy to pander to the state majority in a turmoil-filled election year), they crossed a forbidden line. They were now promoting Christianity over all other faiths.

Indeed, some legislators happily admitted they wouldn't promote Islamic, Wiccan, or Buddhist plates. The argument seems to be: no Muslim plates because we don't want to look like we are supporting that faith, but a Christian plate is great—although in court we'll say that isn't a sign of support. When you combine hypocrisy with bad constitutional law, little wonder you buy yourself a lawsuit!

So we were (as predicted) successful in the lawsuit against South Carolina's ill-advised and unconstitutional license plate promotion. No appeal was taken up by the state. Things have not gone so well when the issue is crosses on public lands.

As I was sitting next to Religious Right attorney Jay Sekulow in the Supreme Court bar section listening to arguments in the *Salazar v. Buono*[24] case, I couldn't help passing him a few notes.[25]

Salazar involved the sale of one acre—out of 1.6 million desert acres— in the Mojave Preserve to the Veterans of Foreign Wars to maintain a cross that purportedly represents all veterans.

When I am listening to an argument, I tend to jot down thoughts that I will express later to the assembled press. Some of what was happening that day struck me as so strange, I'd jot it down and nudge Jay to take a look at it.

Like what?

At one point in the argument, Solicitor General Elena Kagan suggested that the government could put up a sign indicating that there was a "private" cross a few miles up the road.[26]

"Since when," I wondered, "does the government put up signs for private property owners?"

I made a quick sketch of a road sign reading, "Private Cross 1 mile; Wall Drug 1,000 miles; South of the Border 2,500 miles." For non-road travelers, Wall Drug in South Dakota and South of the Border, the tacky Mexican-themed rest stop between Virginia and North Carolina, are probably the most well-advertised destinations along the highway system, but are advertised on private billboards.

One of the other odd comments was Justice Antonin Scalia's assertion that a cross obviously honored all veterans regardless of religion. He asked ACLU attorney Peter Eliasberg whether he'd prefer "some conglomeration of a cross, a star of David and, you know, a Muslim half-moon and star"?

Perhaps Scalia had slept through a comparative religion class at Georgetown University and was thus unfamiliar with Islamic iconography. I wrote Jay: "Well, at least he got Muslims half right." (Half of a half moon is closer to the crescent moon and star that serves as an Islamic symbol.)

I listened to the rest of the largely arcane discussion about "standing" and whether Congress can dissolve a court-ordered permanent injunction. It was then outside to the bank of media microphones.

I made a few comments, all in simple declarative sentences, because the press is not interested in hearing a lengthy historical/constitutional lecture.

I then noticed he *Washington Post*'s Dana Milbank in the crowd. For non-*Post* readers, Dana is a very clever writer who takes a dim view of public figures, often quoting their pontifications and skewering their conclusions.

I decided to use a punchy little analogy that I was sure would grab his attention.

I said, "If the government gets its way in this case, what's next? Would we sell two steps of the Supreme Court to some group that wants to put up a Jesus in the manger scene year round?"

Sure enough, the next day that quote appeared in Milbank's column, along with one from a Religious Right advocate. Dana, of course, scoffed at both comments as "equally absurd."

The Court ruled that the cross could stay, but the matter was sent back to the trial court. Eleven days after the decision, the cross was stolen. It was never recovered. Nobody I knew had anything to do with its disappearance. A "replica" was erected shortly thereafter.

The Religious Right likes to claim that sectarian war memorials on public grounds are just fine, as if a Christian cross can really represent our diverse armed forces. The forty-three-foot tall, twenty-ton Mount Soledad cross statue in California is among the most famous of these memorials, and it's also one of the most controversial. Built in 1954 on public property, then rededicated as a war memorial in the 1990s, it's been the target of lawsuits from Americans United and other civil liberties groups. Its fate is still uncertain after the Supreme Court decided the case should go back to an appeals court.

There is a provision in the December 2015 National Defense Authorization Bill that permits a land transfer to the Mount Soledad Memorial Association at the structure's appraised value. At this writing, lawyers for Vietnam Veteran Steve Trunk, the plaintiff in this case, notes that they "proved the point" of no government ownership of this cross and will see if the transfer terms will be acceptable to his client.

Officials in Boone County, Missouri recently agreed to cover an ichthus on a war memorial that stood on public ground. The memorial's supporters claimed that the ichthus represented the personal beliefs of fallen soldiers, but since it doesn't stand on private property it violates the First Amendment. Similarly, in January 2015, the city of Grand Haven, Michigan, agreed to stop displaying a cross and to permanently convert it into an anchor. Also in January 2015, the city of King, North Carolina, agreed to take down a Christian flag and replace the cross in a statue with a secular grave marker.

Chapter 7

DOES THE RELIGIOUS RIGHT HATE EVERYBODY? ANSWER: YES

O K, technically, the Religious Right doesn't hate everybody. They actually like people who are just like themselves. Too much deviation, however, can rapidly move you from the "like" to the "hate" category. Indeed, a persistent problem in Christendom is the vast array of sectarian differences that have led to the ever-increasing number of sects and denominations that constitute American Christianity today.

Anyone reading this book from the "Religious Right" universe would also beg to differ with my conclusion. They might even state the platitude, "We hate the sin, but not the sinner." People sometimes write to me or come up to me after a speech and politely inform me, "I am praying for you." I actually don't question the integrity of all such comments, but certainly it is hard to be convinced of the sincerity of those beliefs as articulated by most such commenters.

In the pages that follow I take a look at the varieties of people the Religious Right doesn't care for. These include: Wiccans, Muslims, women, atheists, members of the LGBTQ community, and dying people.

MINORITY RELIGIOUS GROUPS

All non-Christians, and of course all humanists and atheists, are *persona non grata* in heaven, according to a very widely held rightwing belief. But there may be a special place in "the other place" for those who characterize themselves as pagans or Wiccans. I've represented their interests since 1985 and on July 4, 2007, was asked to speak at a rally for Pagan Rights in Washington, DC.

Here is some of what I said:

I was recently surfing the Internet to look at some of the latest information on pagan websites, and I noticed that some of those pages discuss the various unpleasant things people say about you because they do not understand you or disagree with what you believe in. So I feel like I'm in good company because I think some of the same people are writing to me. I recently got this note: "Barry Lynn is a disgusting punk. I almost puked every time I saw him. I no longer see him because I got rid of cable." Well, one less viewer for the Fox News Channel.

I must confess that I didn't know much about modern paganism or Wicca until one afternoon in September of 1985. I was about to leave my office at the American Civil Liberties Union, on the way to my dentist for completion of a root canal, when I got a call from a staff member of one of the best religious liberties advocates in the Senate at the time. She said, "I just wanted to tell you that Senator Jesse Helms just put some language in the bill to fund the Internal Revenue Service that the tax agency will be prohibited from granting or maintaining a tax exemption for any group 'which has as its primary purpose the promotion of witchcraft.'" She went on to say that "witchcraft" was defined as the "purported use of power derived from evil spirits, sorcery, or supernatural powers with malicious intent." Her question: should my boss have objected to that? Politely, I answered, "Yes! Of course!"

I had one more thing to do as I delayed my dental appointment: call the news wire services and tell them about this, and how I as a civil libertarian was outraged by any government effort to give more or less favorable tax treatment to any group based on the nature of its religious beliefs. That night Hurricane Gloria struck Washington. (I know you had nothing to do with it: I've been told about the rule of three.) Roads were flooded and I didn't get into work until about one o'clock the next day. When I arrived I had over fifty of those pink "While You Were Out" message slips from all over the country from people whose names were totally unfamiliar to me. As I called them back, I found they were all wiccans or pagans or neo-Pagans who had seen that comment of mine in the morning paper and they were all (a) unhappy with what Senator Helms had done and (b) eager to do something about it. Over the course of the next six weeks (and in this pre-email era) thousands of pagans got organized, wrote letters to Congress, appeared on television shows, and, if you will, corrected the record: "witches" do not cast evil spells, or routinely wear pointed black hats (unless it was fashionably appropriate), or even worship Satan. They did talk about all the damage this amendment would cause if it resulted in tax liabilities for places of worship and celebration and for sacred sites and lands.

Well, when the House of Representatives own tax committee took up the issue, its members had been sufficiently well informed that they literally laughed the Helms amendment out of the bill—all this just one day prior to Halloween. (Goddesses, too, may work in mysterious ways!) What a terrific organizing effort, too, to educate people about and to protect the constitutional right to worship. And, of course, we didn't need to set up a federal commission to determine which spirits were "evil" and which were "good."

I am a big music fan. Every once in a while I hear a song that just blows me away. I felt that way the first time I heard the late singer-songwriter Steve Goodman perform his great train song "City of New Orleans." I had the same reaction to a song with which many of you are probably familiar: Dar Williams's "The Christians and the Pagans," about a family reconciliation over a Christmas/Solstice dinner. The last verse goes: "So the Christians and the Pagans sat together at the table/ Finding faith and common good the best that they were able/ Lighting trees in darkness/ Learning new ways from the old and/ making sense of history and drawing worth out of the cold."[1]

To make sense out of the religious history of America we need to understand the basic impulse behind the First Amendment's protection of religious freedom. It was the widespread (but not universally held) belief of the Founders that keeping a decent distance between the institutions of government and those of religion would ultimately help each one. Has it worked? Well, I can't think of any better model on the planet. The United States has close to two thousand different identifiable religions and twenty million nonbelievers, freethinkers, and humanists. We have lived, worked, played, and studied side by side to make the rich mosaic that is the American experience. No sugarcoating, though, is permissible. We also rioted in the 1870s over which version of the Christian Bible should be read in Philadelphia schools; we forced the children of Jehovah's Witnesses to recite the Pledge of Allegiance in West Virginia schools, even though for them this was an act of idolatry; we destroyed mosques and killed innocent Muslims and Sikhs in the pursuit of unfocused retribution after the 9/11 attacks; we failed to stand against anti-Semitism in our own immigration policies during Hitler's sweep through Europe. But, in the main, we have worked to make real the promise of George Washington when he wrote that in America we would give "to bigotry no sanction."

Many of you find, however, that it is still common to have to fight for your dignity and liberty. That is frequently the case for new religions, or in your case, old religions with dramatic growth spurts. To go back to Dar Williams's song, though, from the cold chill of persecution there is still worth to be drawn. We saw the tremendous organizing efforts derived from the Helms amendment that are bearing even more fruit now than twenty years ago. There are other examples of gaining awareness when you see the abuse of power in the actions and comments of those in power.

Near the end of 2003, the then-head of President Bush's Office of Faith-Based Initiatives Jim Towey was asked if "pagan faith-based groups" should be given consideration as recipients of federal funding. He gave this nasty response: "I haven't run into a pagan faith-based group yet, much less a pagan group that cares for the poor. . . . Helping the poor is tough work and only those with loving hearts seem drawn to it."[2] Apparently, Mr. Towey was still suffering from "childhood post-traumatic Hansel and Gretel syndrome." Many of you let him know directly, and through a well-done article in the Washington Post,[3] that you possess the same heart he claims. Pagan Pride groups alone have contributed seventy-four thousand pounds of food and $51,000 in donations to homeless shelters recently. Chicago pagans fund a battered women's shelter and Massachusetts pagans give thousands to help children with AIDS. Unlike the nearly exclusively Christian recipients of these government funds, most pagans actually appear quite properly skeptical of the entanglement of government and religion in the President's plan. I suspect that if you got any funds you would not use them to promote your faith (or criticize that of others) and you wouldn't be making hiring decisions or decisions about who to help based on some religious litmus test. Sadly, that is the practice of some of the actual recipients, as many people learned after the Towey incident.

A bedrock principle of religious freedom is that freedom is achieved only if it is achieved for all. Too frequently, though, politicians and even judges simply insist on setting one standard for the religions they understand or believe in and a lower one for ones they find "troubling."

Why is it that witch Cynthia Simpson (whom Americans United helped represent) was told by a federal appeals court that the Chesterfield County (Virginia) Board of Supervisors could bar her from getting into a rotation of clergy to open their meetings with an invocation. The court said it was just a matter of choice by the Board, a matter of discretion not to be overruled by the judicial branch. Upon what basis, though, was that "choice" made. We can't know the soul of others with precision, but we can listen to the words of some of those board members. One said to call Wicca a religion was "a mockery. It is not any religion I would subscribe to." A second said, "I hope she's a good witch like Glenda."[4] These are what we might call clues to the source of Ms. Simpson's rejection: they add up to ugly prejudice that has no place in America.

Or consider another judge, Marion Indiana family law judge Cole Bradford. He granted a pagan couple a divorce decree in 2004, but then added a provision a year later that stated that the couple's nine-year-old son could not be exposed to any "nonmainstream religions." The good news is that an appeals court has now thrown out that condition as an unconstitutional impediment to the right of parents to decide the religious upbringing of their children. But I remember how upset this boy's father, Thomas Jones, sounded when I interviewed him on my radio show and he told me how painful it was for him to engage in Yule or Ostara rituals down-stairs in his house while his son was relegated by court order to spend that celebratory time alone upstairs in his bedroom. What could conceivably have motivated that judge to create such obvious additional pain for this family? These judicial decisions, though, I hope have made more pagans interested in the need to ensure that judges understand the importance of a respect for the Constitution and the First Amendment rights of all by giving careful scrutiny to those appointed to our courts. Groups like Americans United monitor federal judges and alert our allies about ones for whom the First Amendment is treated as a first draft of little consequence.

Even on this day that many of us remember those who serve the nation in many capacities, including the military, we are sadly reminded that some of those who send our sons and daughters to war do not respect the faith that was carried into battle. Remember when former Georgia Congressman Bob Barr said that Fort Hood, Texas should not even be accommodating the desire of Wiccans to meet together on base for discussion and worship. In his buffoonish stereotyping, Barr asked, "What's next? Will armored divisions be forced to travel with sacrificial animals for Satanic rituals?" At that time, George W. Bush said he agreed with Barr's concern. One wonders if some of that hostility is still behind the Veterans Administration's continued refusal to provide a pentacle symbol on headstones in veterans' cemeteries for those Wiccans who have died in service to their country. You'll hear more of this from Roberta Stewart about her struggle to have the spiritual symbol of meaning to her and her husband placed on a memorial plaque after his death in Afghanistan.

We learn even from the bad experiences in life; from the challenges to individual rights and freedoms we encounter. What is critical is that all of us understand that the same Constitution was designed to protect us all. If the day ever comes that paganism and Wicca are officially treated as second-class faiths, their believers and practitioners second-class citizens, real religious liberty will have died in the United States. Together, I know that we can prevent the sun from rising on such a day in America.

The story of Roberta Stewart mentioned in that July 4th speech was about to become an Americans United lawsuit. Here is how I characterized the conflict between the United States government and Ms. Stewart and other widows from the Korean War, the Vietnam War, and our multiple engagements in the Middle East:

WICCANS AND THE VA: THE CASE FOR DECENCY AND COMMON SENSE[5]

Some things should be easy. Some injustices ought to be resolved under notions of common sense and basic decency.

That is the case with a request from Roberta Stewart of Fernley, Nevada. Roberta's husband, Sgt. Patrick Stewart, was killed in action when his helicopter was shot down on September 25, 2005, over Afghanistan. Sgt. Stewart had served with the military in a variety of capacities for sixteen years. He had returned to the Middle East in 2005 after serving earlier in Operation Desert Storm, and he was a decorated soldier.

His widow, following his wishes, wanted to put a symbol of his religion on a military memorial plaque in Nevada that commemorates local veterans. She was told that it was not presently an option.

At this point, some readers might be thinking that the powers and bureaucrats that be were just deciding not to raise any religious issues on these markers. The Department of Veterans Affairs, which is responsible for such decisions, however, crossed that river a long time ago. Thirty-eight icons and symbols have been approved by the VA for use on government-provided headstones, markers, and plaques. If you are a Christian or a Jew or a Muslim or a Buddhist or a Hindu or a follower of Eckankar, there is a symbol for you. Indeed, if you are a secular humanist or an atheist, there is a symbol for you, too.

Sgt. Stewart, however, was a Wiccan, who, along with his wife Roberta, followed a nature-centered spirituality, and the VA has not approved any symbol for that belief system.

It is not as though the VA hasn't had time to think about this. Indeed, there have been Wiccan applications pending for recognizing the pentacle, an interlaced five-pointed star inside a circle, since 1997.

New symbols for six other groups, including Sikhs, Soka Gakkai, and Izumo Taishakyo Mission of Hawaii, were added, but the Wiccan applications lay dormant—so dormant that the VA didn't turn them down, it just ignored them.

Enter Roberta Stewart. Her situation came to a head when she was told that she could only have a plaque for her husband at the Nevada military memorial without a pentacle. She refused, and there is currently only a blank spot on the Wall of Heroes where Patrick's plaque should be.

I met Roberta on Independence Day at a religious rights rally near the VA headquarters and the White House. A crowd of pagans, Wiccans, and those of other faith perspectives had gathered to hear speakers discuss the need for the "free exercise of religion" to include all religions and those who choose no belief in spirituality.

When I talked with Roberta, it was clear that this was a matter of justice for her husband and for other Wiccan military personnel past and future. It is reported that Wicca is one of the fastest-growing religions in the United States, so this is neither a small nor theoretical problem.

Roberta and the senior minister of her church, Circle Sanctuary, the Rev. Selena Fox, came to my house that afternoon. We met the following day in the AU office to discuss their imminent meetings with congressional staff and with the undersecretary for memorial affairs at the VA.

From the VA, they heard again that their requests were not being "turned down," but that this time the agency was concerned that the current regulations may have been improperly adopted in 2005. The VA is looking into that. The VA apparently looks into everything for a very long time these days. On the other hand, the veterans they serve reported for duty immediately.

After several more weeks of inertia, Ms. Stewart and the Rev. Fox decided to have AU represent them in the pursuit of their goal of fair and equal treatment. We will work with Congress; we will work with VA regulators and officials; we will appeal within the VA; we will file a lawsuit if necessary.

But why should it come to this? Even most of the Religious Right is on board (or at least silent with no opposition). No one is claiming, as Senator Helms had, that Wiccans are in league with Satan. No one is arguing that Wiccans want special treatment. No one is running for reelection on a "No Pentacle" platform.

Why should Roberta Stewart pass the anniversary of her husband's death with an empty space on a wall in Nevada?

I was asked to return to the 2008 Pagan Rights rally—that year, right across from the White House—to report on the success of our legal effort on behalf of the so-called "Wiccan widows."

Last year I chronicled some of the legal problems of Wiccans and pagans over the past twenty-five years since I first worked with some of you to preserve your organizations' tax-exempt status after Senator Jesse Helms nearly had it revoked for all "practitioners of witchcraft," something he had learned about while watching a special on television. This was sad proof of just how dangerous television can really be. But at least there may be a silver lining about television these days; more people at Halloween will now dress up like Paris Hilton and Ann Coulter if they really want to scare people and fewer will paint their face green and wear a pointed black hat. This year the Rally has moved closer to the heart of the beast and at the same time we have in large part resolved the principal legal question that was the subject of so much of last year's rally: achieving a legal victory against this Administration's virulent refusal to grant Wiccan veterans the pentacle as an emblem of honor. We who believe in religious freedom for all may be on a roll.

The President [Bush] and his attorney general, Alberto Gonzales, have started up something called "The First Freedom Project" to highlight all the great work they are doing to protect religious freedom in America. (I have the list here somewhere.) To suggest that this administration supports real religious liberty is like calling the Guantanamo prison "a gated timeshare community in the Northern Caribbean." This is the administration that fought against the grant of the pentacle as an emblem of honor. This was the administration that we found in our work on behalf of Roberta Stewart and many others was blocking the pentacle because it remembered that back when George W. Bush was governor of Texas (we refer to that period as the "good old days") he did not want pagans to even meet for worship at the Fort Hood army base because he didn't think "witchcraft was a real religion."

Why this hostility to what you do and how you worship on the part of the President and his top people? What causes it? Could it be the undue influence of repetitive readings of Hansel and Gretel at Barbara Bush's knee? Possibly. In the 1950s there was a widely syndicated newspaper comic strip one December that featured Rudolf the Red-Nosed Reindeer battling to save Christmas from the grasp of an evil witch who had planned to suck up all the toys from Santa's workshop with a vacuum cleaner. Maybe that image has not been deleted from the President's memory. But I'm not buying that because he seems to delete so many other things from his same memory: ranging from the message in that daily intelligence briefing he got in August 2001 about a group called al-Qaeda and its interest in using airliners to attack America on to the fact that he placed his hand on his Bible to take the oath of office twice and swore to uphold the Constitution and the Bill of Rights and not shred it article by article and amendment by amendment. Did he read any of the coverage about the Pentacle Quest and the men and women who sacrificed their lives for this country? The answer is almost certainly no. I'm not trying to be insulting. He has said he doesn't read the newspapers, and in his most recent interview on the subject he said he still didn't read them but his aides will bring them in and if he sees an interesting headline he'll "look" at it—not read, "look."

I love working with you: I have been fortunate enough to work on some important issues in my life so far. But there was something about the Pentacle Quest that was different. Something about the potency of the spiritual commitment behind it on the part of the folks we represented.

When we announced the settlement in April, Roberta Stewart and Selena Fox joined me and the legal staff at Americans United (the legal staff who did all the heavy lifting from our end) at a news conference at the National Press Club. We went back to my office so that we could tape my own syndicated radio show for later in the day and so that Roberta and Selena could do other media appearances. And as Selena was about to go on the air with National Public Radio, one of the lawyers brought her a copy of the official Veterans' Administration regulation form that had, one day earlier, depicted thirty-eight emblems of honor; it had been changed that morning to include the 39th. Selena Fox is rarely speechless, but as she looked at the symbol at first she said nothing and then I would swear that a light came out of her body. It was the closest thing this Christian has ever seen to something we call "transfiguration." That's what a combination of joy and justice will do to you!

But we need to get the VA to understand that the pentacle is not the only emblem of interest to this diverse community you all represent. There are probably more kinds of pagans and Wiccans than there are kinds of Baptists; it's just that you are probably nicer to each other than some of those Baptists are to each other. Those other groups amongst you deserve their emblems too. And when we look at folks on active duty today, the growing diversity of service membership deserves a recognition that spiritual assistance cannot be granted solely to members of the groups with the largest number of adherents at the moment. Pagan chaplaincy programs for those far from home and in harm's way need to be established now.

See, the essence of America is that we have no second-class citizens, we have no second-class soldiers, and we have no second-class religions. A battle for the rights of one group is ultimately a struggle for all groups in this county. In a nutshell, until pagans are treated no differently than Presbyterians or Pentecostals, none of us should count ourselves as free.

The basic privileges that Wiccans are continually refused—like being able to express their faith even at a final resting place—illustrates one of the greatest problems I fight every day: inconsistency. In a country in which the rule of law guarantees that everybody is entitled to equal treatment, religious differences are still enough to bend the rules. But, then again, being different has warranted poor treatment since the country's inception. Just ask the Catholics and Jews of yesteryear. History reminds us that questioning an individual's religion (or, if one were to look at *Burwell v. Hobby Lobby Stores, Inc.*, even that of a company) is sacrilege until it comes to the nonbelievers and nontraditional faiths. The face of the unknown might change—what was once a Quaker is now a Wiccan—but at least the Religious Right is consistent in its despicable treatment of those who are different.

But this ire is not reserved just for Wiccans—but other religious minorities as well.

Islam has been a particular target of hostility, of course, since 9/11.

Sadly, there were two kinds of responses that showed a few Americans at their worst. First, there have been acts of cruelty and violence directed against religious minorities. The Ohio mosque in which the parents of an Americans United staff member worship had its stained glass windows demolished by rock-throwers. In Arizona, a Sikh was shot to death outside his gas station in an incident law enforcement officials attributed solely to the killer's ignorant belief that the owner was a Muslim, and his morally reprehensible collateral view that such identification marked him as a target of vengeance. In a third incident, an Arab-American Christian was assaulted.

The other sad note was the instantly well-known and deeply disturbing dialogue between Pat Robertson and Jerry Falwell. Before Falwell was even introduced on that broadcast, Robertson noted that the Supreme Court's doctrine on separation of church and state—in his words—"has essentially stuck its finger in God's eye and said we're going to legislate you out of the schools. . . . We have insulted God at the highest levels of our government. And then we say, 'Why does this happen?'"[6] Only later on the broadcast did Falwell make his grotesque remarks about how civil rights groups, feminists, gay people, and pagans have so enraged God that God has "lifted the curtain" of protection and allowed the terrorists to—in his words—"give us probably what we deserve."

In all the years I've spent following these men's careers and debating them in the media, I have heard many strange things from them but never such a set of abominable political or theological statements. Not since segregationist preachers in the 1950's used the words of Genesis that "God separated the light from the darkness" to justify Jim Crow laws has the true meaning of the Gospel been so defaced.

There are a few curious footnotes to this story. First, even before the Falwell-Robertson exchange, the very first telephone call for me at the office the day after the attack was a woman who claimed I was personally responsible for the acts of terrorism because, she said, since I do not want to allow praise to God every moment of the day God has turned on the nation. I have heard variants on this for many years; the assertion that prayer should be allowed in school at all times so that teachers or students can lead prayers whenever they feel like it. What I didn't anticipate were the number of writers and callers who said to me, "Jerry Falwell should never have backed down." Falwell had made some vague statements about how he wished he had not named specific groups in his causation explanation. This fallout just indicates that not only can leaders of these Religious Right groups be extremists, the local folks they have unleashed can be even worse. Here is some of what happened around the country after the 9/11 attacks:

We have seen a great upsurge in what sociologists call "civil religion" and judges often refer to as "ceremonial deism," that uneasy merger of religious imagery and patriotic fervor.[7] Much of this, like the President's declaration of his third national day of prayer since his inauguration are beyond the scope of judicial review, but sometimes they do offend by their exclusionary nature. Thomas Jefferson refused to declare any national days of prayer or fasting even during the darkest days of his Presidency. I got an email from a woman who works at the Department of Housing and Urban Development after she got a letter from Secretary Mel Martinez offering employees prayer sessions and extra leave for "healing through prayer." She did not object to the thoughtfulness of his acts, just the thoughtlessness of not recognizing that some did not turn to religion at all in times of crisis. She wrote, "We all need to heal, to regain strength, and to come together with others in community, even those of us who do not pray and do not believe in anything to pray to. There was no recognition of our needs—there never is." It's a good thing that President Bush invited Jews, Muslims, and even a Hindu to the White House, but why in over eight weeks has he not been able to make a single reference to the millions of decent Americans who deal with calamity in ways that do not involve religion? It's not so hard.

Even more direct violations of the Constitution have already occurred. Some schools have been turning to mandatory assemblies in which outside ministers or the principal lead children in prayer in direct violation of Supreme Court rulings. After one such event in a Texas middle school the governor announced he would run for reelection on a platform of returning government promoted prayer to schools. Some of these practices have now stopped as more sober members of the community realized that the First Amendment was not suspended on 9/11, and that this was not the time to make any young person feel like a second-class citizen in his or her own school. Such recognition has not always come. You may have seen the reports of a controversy in Northern California at an elementary school that had posted a "God Bless America" banner on the marquee over the school's front door. One mother kept her child out of class because she was uncomfortable with the school's embrace of a religious concept that her daughter was not taught at home. Perhaps some of you find that trivial. However, as the incident escalated and the principal released the name of the objecting parent to the media, the mother became fearful for her daughter's physical safety if she returned to school. She has not returned. For me, the bottom line is that no American should have to fear their next-door neighbor more than they fear Osama bin Laden. Somehow, that community must work this out.

Misunderstanding has already turned to vindictiveness in other places. In Ringgold, Georgia, a newly erected city council display includes a framed Ten Commandments, a framed Lord's Prayer, and an empty picture frame. The last, according to sponsor Bill McMillon is "for those who believe in nothing." Ho. Ho. Ho. When the Associated Press asked if this imagery wouldn't offend non-Christians, particularly Muslims, he answered that "We don't have any of them around here." Well, with that kind of a welcome mat out, don't expect the next town doctor, or teacher, or firefighter to be a Muslim.

The Ringgold story has the seeds of a happy ending, however.[8] Last June, Americans United and the Georgia affiliate of the American Civil Liberties Union sued to have the display removed. One of our plaintiffs chose to remain anonymous, fearful of his safety. The other plaintiff was a very vocal longtime resident, Thomas J. Odom.

Odom, a Vietnam veteran, had to look at the display every time he attended his Rotary Club meeting with other local businesspeople at city hall. His view, he told the Chattanooga Times Free Press, "goes back to when I became an officer in the Army. I swore allegiance to defend the Constitution." Our local counsel for Odom, Georgia K. Lord, explained that her client felt the need to fight for our constitutional rights when his local officials decided to promote one religious tradition over others.

In mid-August, the city council hastily called an "emergency" meeting to discuss the trio of plaques. Shortly thereafter, the display was quietly removed. Council members and other city officials, who were proud and boastful when the religious display went up, were suddenly shy. In fact, they refused to discuss the decision to remove the plaques.

We can safely assume that the lawsuit was the prime mover here. That's why I noted earlier that the Ringgold case contains the "seeds" of the best outcome. Vital and effective as lawsuits are, they don't always change the hearts or minds of the losing side.

After over a decade of remembrances of 9/11, American Muslims still face heightened scrutiny in some quarters.

Post 9/11, of course, the Religious Right (and a few nontheists to boot) also found Islam to be a horrifying example of religion-gone-amok. All religions are entitled to First Amendment protection; that includes Islam. But for some, that truth is hard to swallow. As the Muslim community grows apace in the United States, Muslim Americans are seeking to build houses of worship in their neighborhoods. They are not always welcomed.

In 2010, plans to build a Muslim community center on land near the site of the 9/11 attacks in New York City raised the ire of conservative pundits. This construction was repeatedly referred to as the "Ground Zero Mosque"—but it was neither at Ground Zero nor was it a mosque. Now, Muslims had every right to build on that land. I appeared on outlets like Fox News to explain exactly why: It's a religious liberty matter. There's no legal reason to prevent them from building a community center simply because of its relative proximity to the site of great tragedy. But the Religious Right accused them of attempting to recruit terrorists—a grave allegation they could never substantiate. After severe public backlash, the plans were scrapped. (Admittedly, this may also have been a result of a lack of funding, however.)

Muslims in Murfreesboro, Tennessee, encountered similar problems while trying to build a worship space for their own growing community. Although country commissioners approved the building, infuriated residents filed suit after suit to stop its construction. They argued that the mosque would be used to implement sharia law, and, incredibly, that Islam wasn't even a religion. Someone even set the construction site on fire. But that didn't deter Murfreesboro's Muslims, and in 2012 they finally opened their new building. Of course, they shouldn't have had to deal with that legal battle at all—a battle in which Tennessee's lieutenant governor took the position that Islam is not a "real" religion.

The Constitution is very clear that all religions have the right to worship freely, and that includes the construction of worship spaces. But opponents of Islam frequently try to use zoning laws to discriminate against members of the faith.

In Kennesaw, Georgia, city council members approved a zoning permit for a church, but rejected one for a mosque. The argument: Muslims wanted to build the mosque in a local storefront, which violated zoning laws. But that's exactly where a local Pentecostal congregation had sought to build a church in July 2014, and the city council rushed to grant them an exemption. Protests may have influenced the decision, too. Local residents vociferously opposed the mosque, relying on the same tired arguments we've heard before about our Muslim neighbors. The storefront space would be used for terrorist purposes. Sharia law would come to Georgia, and thus end democratic rule.

But we can't base legal decisions on our fears. Kennesaw Muslims have indicated through their attorney that they may sue the city; they'll probably win if they do. It's high time people accepted that Muslims have the right to build mosques, and that the law that permits them to do so is the same law that protects their own rights, too.

In 2000, Congress passed the "Religious Land Use and Institutionalized Persons Act" (RLUIPA), to require that the federal government actually provide a "compelling interest" to avoid accommodating religious claims regarding zoning or the conditions of imprisonment.

Some secularists opposed this as granting yet another "special privilege" to theists. Although there is a compelling case for this position, there is also a way in which a parallel "privilege" was expanded to sincere nontheists by court action. Under the Military Selective Service Act, only religiously motivated "conscientious objectors" could be awarded that status. In 1970, however, an atheist named Elliot A. Welsh II successfully argued to the Supreme Court that his "opposition to war in any form" was based on secular principles that in his mind "were at the level of traditional religious doctrine."[9] Ironically, a Roman Catholic claimant failed when he suggested that his opposition to the Vietnam War was based on his conclusion that it was "unjust." The Court rejected this effort to expand opposition to all wars to selective opposition to some wars, even though that is a generally recognized position of the Catholic Church and other religious bodies. Couldn't this be viewed as a "special privilege" for members of "historic peace churches" like the Amish, Mennonites, and the Church of the Brethren.

I do find it disturbing, however, when "liberals" accede too quickly to exemptions they know or believe are unique to American Muslims. Americans United was virtually the only group that opposed the actions of several high schools in California that gave as a homework assignment the memorization of the prayers of the Quran. Imagine the outcry if any school insisted that all students memorize the Lord's Prayer or the Twenty-third Psalm and then claimed that it was purely for "cultural" and not "religious" purposes.

Similarly, Americans United strongly opposed the reconstruction of bathrooms at the University of Michigan at Dearborn to accommodate foot washing by Muslim students, something, it turned out, that had not even been requested by any student followers of Islam. Permanent alternations of architecture at a state-run facility seemed much more of an accommodation that the Constitution requires.

ATHEISTS

Recent polls suggest that far more parents are supportive of their children marrying a person who is of a different race than are happy about a child being joined in matrimony with an "atheist." Similarly, poll takers find little support for politicians who openly declare they are nonbelievers in divinity. This may be why so few candidates ever suggest they are atheists. For many years the only atheist in Congress—or at least the only openly avowed atheist—was California Representative Fortney "Pete" Stark.

I was approached in early 2014 by David Silverman and Amanda Knief of American Atheists about doing a plenary address at their convention scheduled for Easter weekend in Salt Lake City, Utah. They even made it clear that the presentation would be scheduled for Saturday so I could go to church on Sunday.

I agreed; the speech printed below was well received. I did fail to get to church the next day, though, as I had to fly home for someone's seventieth birthday party.

Thanks for inviting me here. I am unique at this gathering. It is not because I am wearing a suit: This is an obviously fashion conscious crowd. It is not because I am a theist, because you know there are "hidden theists" among you, all trying to figure out what the secret "atheist agenda for America" is, since similar people spent years trying to locate the secret "gay agenda" at national conferences. (They found the answer: We want to be viewed as first-class citizens.) No, I am unique in my possession of this: this stuffed monkey in a devil costume, a representation of the two things Christian fundamentalists fear the most: "Satan" and "evolution."

In the course of the next twenty-five minutes, I will offer a few bits of unrequested advice about how to grow the atheist movement, this a tactic used so that you like me more. For example: Ask Darren Aronofsky to make more Bible-themed epics like *Noah*—a film in which giant things that look like Transformers toys made out of clay help Noah nail the Ark together. I'd suggest you work on a movie where these same "giants in the earth" extract Jonah from the gullet of a big fish, and a second where these creatures seek unsuccessfully to help Mary and Joseph locate an open inn in Bethlehem.

Reporters have been calling me this past week—"what are you going to say?" I will not be discussing the existence of the divine nor pondering such questions as whether there is purpose to the universe or why something exists rather than nothing. Exciting and important as these matters are, the resolution of them might take us another two millennia. I am here to urge us to deal with something all believers in secular government—theists and atheists—need to work on right now: saving the heart and "soul" (metaphorically speaking, of course) of the First Amendment: The demand that government be rigorously neutral on matters of religion; that it not pick winners and losers among religions or between religious belief and nonbelief; that it not expand one cent of tax funds in support of any religious institution's doctrine or dogma, ministry or mission. What could be simpler than that?

Sadly, it isn't. So today in 2014 we can be just as sure as we are that we don't know where Malaysian Airlines Flight 370 is that we do know there are powerful, well-connected politico-religious forces trying to upend the very idea of the separation of church and state and the freedom to believe, doubt, or detest according to your own beliefs. The "religious freedom" promoted by Bill O'Reilly, Sarah Palin, the Conference of Catholic Bishops, the Religious Right of Ken Ham and Tony Perkins is a fraud and a scam; it is antithetical to true freedom of conscience and belief.

See, far from an assault on religion generally or Christianity specifically, we have a dizzying level of spiritual supply in America—two thousand different faiths and twenty-five million freethinkers, atheists, humanists who make up this American intellectual landscape. Christian majorities have nothing serious to worry about: It is only you and members of minority religious groups that find your liberties in jeopardy. I said that to a Congressional committee not long ago, headed by Arizona Republican congressman Trent Franks. It really didn't go over too well with him because he had begun the hearing asserting that "religious freedom" was in serious jeopardy and reminding the rather large audience that the nation was founded on that principle, harkening back to the fact that Christopher Columbus himself was exercising his "religious freedom" when he "set sail from Spain to find the new world." I actually recall that he was looking for India at the time—but I have come to expect nothing short of breathtaking confusion from Mr. Franks.

Right now in 2014 America, we face problems from two directions. Are there any physicists here? That figures. Be gentle with me here because I'm going to use an analogy from physics that may not be completely scientifically accurate. I'm going to call one front the danger from momentum and the other a danger from inertia, as in the "object at rest tends to stay at rest" variety.

Momentum to destroy the wall of separation comes via the continued presence of a powerful political force we call (when we are being polite) the "Religious Right," which constitutes about 20 percent of the American electorate. This is a movement of theocrats, seeking to write public policy along their own narrow sectarian lines. I have a book on my desk called *Politics According to the Bible*, which in its 619 pages gives a purported answer to every conceivable political issue. It doesn't just tell you that US policy should prohibit abortion and disallow same-sex marriage, but drills down to explain what the Bible, properly understood, tells us should be the next fighter aircraft to be purchased by the Air Force (the F-22 Raptor, in case you are taking notes). Did you all forget Romans 13:4?

Many of the people who think this way are also yammering about an alleged loss of "religious liberty." To make this case, they need to dramatically alter the meaning of those two words. Confucius once remarked (allegedly) that "when words lose their meaning the universe crumbles." If true, this ceiling is at risk right now.

In an egregious example of altering the meaning of "religious liberty," they believe that even for-profit corporations, whose bosses oppose contraception, can refuse to cover it in their employees' health insurance plans because of the corporation's "religious liberty." This was the topic of a Supreme Court argument I listened to about ten days ago at the US Supreme Court.

The far right says corporations have free speech rights identified in the recent Citizens United case, so they must have religious liberty rights too, a kind of "corporate conscience." One of the companies making this claim is the national arts and crafts chain Hobby Lobby; another is a Mennonite-owned furniture company called Conestoga Wood. Whatever you think of Citizens United, speaking is a major thing corporations do—it is called advertising and it is why they spend 1.5 million dollars to have Danica Patrick in a bikini for a Super Bowl ad. Corporations engaging in "religion" are harder to find. If I ever see a make-it-yourself garden gnome next to me in a pew at church or open up a wooden cabinet and have it ask me to join in a chorus of "Nearer My God To Thee," maybe I'll consider that companies have legally cognizable religious freedom claims. Until then, this is just a way to claim that the religious convictions of the head of the company control the moral decision-making of the dozens or thousands of women who work for these firms.

When you consider the ramifications of this thinking, it is staggering. Just in the healthcare world alone, if a Catholic employer says no coverage of birth control, surely a Scientologist business owner can refuse coverage for psychiatry and the Jehovah's Witness employer can reject surgical coverage because so much surgery ends up requiring whole blood products, use of which is forbidden in their faith. But these medical corollaries are just the tip of the iceberg. Once you jump over this cliff of business "religion rights," there is no easy way to turn back.

For example, I was on the Laura Ingraham radio show a month ago to discuss a lawsuit in Colorado. Two men went to a bake shop to order a cake. Somehow it arose that the two men were themselves the happy couple and that the cake was to be used as a post-wedding celebration. This was not strictly speaking a "wedding cake," because Colorado may have pot now, but it doesn't have marriage equality. The couple was getting married in Massachusetts and then some days later returning for a party in Colorado. The owner of the bakery refused to take the order for his cake masterpiece—and actually the name of his company is "Masterpiece Bakery." Owner Jack Phillips said he couldn't make this cake because of his Christian religious objections to same-sex weddings. This guy is a real piece of work. The Colorado ACLU represented the couple and in the course of seeking evidence found that Mr. Phillips has a wide range of curious beliefs. He will not bake Halloween cakes; he did once agree, however, to making a cake for a "wedding" of two dogs, but claimed that if he had baked the gay couple's post-wedding cake would be like baking a "pedophile cake" (whatever that is). A lower-level Colorado court has just ruled that when you are in the business of serving the public, you have to serve everyone. The judge rejected the idea that Mr. Phillips's cakes are "expressive behavior" protected under the free speech clause. There is a kind of surface appeal to this argument for civil libertarians, but the service offered is making a cake based on the wish of your customer not the creative spirit within you the proprietor. The court even noted that the bakery had the right to put into its ads or on its walls that it didn't approve of marriage equality. Nevertheless it had to serve all the people who wanted the publicly available service. Just last week the Supreme Court rejected an appeal in a New Mexico case involving a similar refusal to photograph a same-gender commitment ceremony. But someday a case like these will get to that august body.

So, here we have cases about cakes and contraception that could still eventually lead to what I consider a bizarre outcome: religious claims trump any and all laws some corporate owner doesn't agree with. Why not just let companies refuse to go along with civil rights laws based on religious objections. Some of us heard preachers in the early sixties actually argue that the words in book of Genesis, "God separated the light from the darkness," should be interpreted to reject school integration. And how about the Equal Pay Act? Why pay those women as much as men, because the "man is head of the house just as Christ is head of the Church," thus hubby has more responsibility on his shoulders. Legislation allowing this kind of trumping the civil law with religious claims—allowing denial of services to non-Christians or LGBT travelers nearly was enacted in Arizona (Gov. Brewer there perhaps both read the Constitution and some columns suggesting that the NFL would be moving the Super Bowl out of Phoenix next year in deciding that she'd veto the bill. OK, she was probably more concerned with football than the First Amendment). [There will be more discussion of this kind of legislative battle in the next chapter.]

Also, we have now begun a wide range of case involvement at religiously connected hospitals and universities that are already exempt from having to cover contraception, in my view a completely unnecessary accommodation this administration doled up to such entities. All a place like Notre Dame needs to do is sign a statement refusing to cover contraception and the government will then get a third party to cover it for free. We represent the only actual women involved in any of these cases, and Notre Dame has told them that the university refuses to sign a refusal letter because even that would "trigger" a response that would lead to the sinful birth control option. So refusing to say you won't do something is the moral equivalent of doing it. Maybe in one of Michio Kaku's alternate multiverses, but that is from a legal viewpoint what is technically referred to in the Latin as de minimis" and, in the equally technical language of common sense, as "batshit crazy."

But there are a few things happening that give me solace about the Religious Right's future—or perhaps its lack of one. First, sometimes when it comes up with bizarre ideas, like a North Carolina proposal a year ago to allow each county to "align" itself with a particular religion (and we all know that there would be so many atheist and Scientology counties), a few comedic comments by Jon Stewart or Rachel Maddow are often enough to laugh it off the legislative landscape. Second, its own primary polling organization, the Barna Group, finds that it is losing its grip on its own children. A growing percentage of fundamentalist children now accept the evidence for evolution, and the percentage of young evangelicals supporting marriage equality is now 64 percent. Those are not exactly pro-growth trajectories for extremism.

Remember the flap in 2012 when Republican presidential candidate Rick Santorum said he wasn't worried about cuts to higher education loans because when you send your kid to college she becomes an atheist.[10] I remember ridiculing that on the Ed Show a couple times, but it turns out that there is a kernel of truth in what he said. Many young people who go to religious private high schools or to one of the one-third of public schools that don't teach evolution, then hear about it in college and start to accept the evidence for it, rejecting at least the Bible literalism that requires belief in a six-thousand-year-old universe. Similarly, if they have been told growing up about the "Gay Agenda," which includes a virtual kidnapping of straight people into the so-called "homosexual lifestyle," they find halfway through the semester that one of the people on their dorm floor is "gay" and never once has tried to seduce him in the shower. See, reality-based experience and education can go a long way to terminating utter nonsense. But we aren't out of the cold, dark woods yet.

A more insidious threat comes from what writer Michael Lewis might call "moral inertia," that "so long as it serves the narrow self-interests of everyone inside it, no one on the inside would ever seek to change it, no matter how corrupt or sinister it became. . . ."[11] Let me just give you a few examples from Washington.

Let's start with money for religious groups. George W. Bush began a program referred to as the Faith-Based Initiative, an effort to get more grants and contracts to religious providers of secular services, from mentoring to feeding the hungry, based on the largely mythological claim—akin to the existence of "weapons of mass destruction" in Iraq—that there was widespread discrimination in giving government funds to religious groups. At the time, Catholic Charities alone appeared to be getting over five hundred million dollars in aid and the Salvation Army, literally a Christian denomination with strong homophobic tendencies, was getting eighty-nine million dollars for work in New York alone. He did recognize that you couldn't force people to participate in religious services to get help (although plenty of groups still try), but he did allow groups to get subsidies even where they refused to hire persons in those subsidized programs who had different religious beliefs. You could literally hang up a sign in a Baptist homeless shelter seeking staff: "No Jews or Atheists Need Apply," as if humanists tucked in bedsheets differently than did those Baptists. This reversed executive orders from the Truman administration barring such religious discrimination in hiring with taxpayer dollars.

And then what about tax laws? Churches and other charities are given a 501(c)(3) exemption (and churches just that status automatically without having to file any documents) and can engage in absolutely no endorsement or opposition to any candidate for public office. So over the past few years we have reported about thirty really egregious cases of pulpit politicking for or against candidates—not allowing people to get on the church bus to the polling place unless you agreed to vote Republican, telling people that voting for Barack Obama was like voting for both Hitler and Stalin at the same time. But those complaints have now languished for years. Why? A judge in 2010 ruled that the IRS needed to rewrite a simple regulation to have a slightly more senior official sign off on investigations of this kind of activity. This administration has been sitting on such a change for four and a half years. Two monkeys in a locked room with a typewriter would have typed the right fix through random key pecking in about a month, but this administration has been unable to publish a rewrite in close to four and a half years.

President Barack Obama needs to fix these things. And if he did what was right, the public would support him. In the most recent polls, close to two-thirds of us do not believe that churches should be able to endorse candidates, and nearly as many believe that if a religious group receives federal funds it should not be able to discriminate in its hiring with that money. So, we have already prevailed in the world of public opinion: To do what the public agrees is correct policy is hardly something even a marginally progressive President should be worried about doing.

There is a final policy the administration has pursued that always comes up during Q and A, which we aren't having today, so I'll go out on a limb here pretending to be a psychic and say I'll bet you are shocked if you know this and will be shocked if you don't. Americans United represents two women in Greece, New York, a suburb of Rochester, who are trying to stop the almost exclusively Christian prayers given by a town council-selected minister before their monthly meetings. Our clients felt uncomfortable about this practice because the few people who show up at these meetings usually want to ask the council for something: A change in cable TV access policy, a business special exemption, a new stoplight, assistance for a handicapped child, or the dozens of other things that come up in relatively small cities. Since our clients did not want to participate in Christian prayers, they felt (we thought quite reasonably) that an outlier—someone who doesn't bow her head or stand or recite words when asked by the minister—would be noticed and might find her requests rejected. The council of course said, "We would never do that."

The Obama administration said, "We side with the town council." Why if this kind of prayer practice is illegal, maybe the prayers of the chaplains in the House and Senate would also be illegal. For a range of strategic reasons, we so narrowly crafted the relief we wanted in this case that such a result wouldn't have been possible—at least because of this case. But so what if it did? Legislative prayers are a terrible idea and unnecessary as a part of the business of any government. Like with *Noah*, here is another piece of gratuitous advice directed to all nontheists in particular in this room—if you wanted to make the case that prayer doesn't work, all you have to look at is how much "good stuff" gets done in Congress after it prays every day it is in session.

I am convinced that with vigilance we will prevail in these battles. I don't mean that all those cable TV preachers will start sending money *to* us, but I mean that governments will not make religion a test of patriotism nor will it pick up the financial pieces the faithful are unwilling to donate themselves to the collection plate. We are winning the hearts and minds of the people on the issues I've mentioned. Six months ago we saw the first-ever public opinion poll where a majority of Americans oppose school vouchers.

There are plenty of judges hanging around who are on the wrong side of these issues and will be there for the next decade or so. There may be some bad Supreme Court decisions that will need to be reversed. There are entrenched legislators who fear any change in their antiquated viewpoints. However, there are new generations abornin' and they don't think much of the hate gospel, the big government/big church coalition, "religious rights" for furniture companies, and other lousy ideas that makes a mockery of individual freedom. They are the people upon whom we should focus a lot of attention. They are the future and they appear to be "getting the message" of separation a far sight easier than many of us older folks did.

Here's my final thought—a final bit of advice to my nontheistic brothers and sisters. You have come a long way from the days when an atheist book would not be printed by most private publishers and mailing atheist pamphlets was a federal crime. You have come a long way since atheists like Herb Silverman had to sue just to run for an office in a state that barred nonbelievers from holding public office. You have come a long way from the days when Phil Donahue was pilloried for having Madelyn Murray O'Hare on his syndicated show (she was his most frequent guest) to now when David Silverman regularly eviscerates Bill O'Reilly on his own program.

Sometimes I hear critics say "well what good did atheists ever do for anybody." Well, you were leaders in many cities in the struggle to end segregation, but that was an era when a Baptist preacher would seek a rabbi or a priest to join him on a civil rights march but wouldn't even consider linking up with a known atheist. You were not to blame for that. You were some of the earliest advocates for the availability of contraceptives to give men and women the ability to take medical, moral, and economic control of their lives. You are today asking some of the most challenging questions of the "faithful" and being self-critical about the stain of sexism and racism in when it arises in the culture. It is a pleasure to work with you and your sister organizations on the preservation of the very principles that will allow all of us to act and be seen as first-class citizens in all places in every part of this country—no matter what we think this weekend does or doesn't mean.

WOMEN

Women may hold up 51 percent of the sky, but the Religious Right and the Catholic hierarchy barely see them as co-equals to men. Even the leadership of the fundamentalist Concerned Women for America has primarily been male. The Roman Catholic Church does not ordain women, does not allow women to vote on local ecclesiastical matters, and does not take much interest in women once they stop being fetuses. I am frequently asked to address the religious roots of these conclusions and regularly do so at reproductive justice events, including this "opening statement" in a debate I had with Christian apologist John Rankin at the University of Richmond in March of 2009:

One of the reasons I like having these debates with John is because they don't come with presuppositions. They are open ended; they stake out the differences we have clearly because they let both of us answer a fundamental question. Tonight's is basic: "Women, Choice, and Abortion: What Are the Issues?" To me, there are indeed three big issues.

First is the relevance of the Constitution to the resolution of the reproductive choice debate. Second, of what relevance is Holy Scripture (including the Christian Bible) in the debate? Third, what would the ramifications be if we created a legal regimen that protected fetal life like the lives of everyone in this audience?

I realize that, statistically speaking, if this were a random group of citizens, at least a third of you believe that every abortion is a murder of a human being and that the Holocaust of Hitler's Germany pales in comparison to the number of deaths of fetuses through abortion. For those of you with different views, though, it is incredibly important that you not cede any ethical high ground to "anti-choice" advocates, no matter what rhetoric they use. Indeed, as I said to the million people on the Mall at the March for Women's Lives in 2004, it is the pro-choice movement that is on the sacred space, a place where every child is a wanted child. Every woman facing a moral decision about her reproductive choice must be guaranteed the right to make a choice without fear that it will be trumped by what her husband thinks, her boyfriend thinks, the Virginia legislature thinks, or the Congress of the United States thinks. Indeed, there are those who believe that abortion should be a crime even in the case of rape—and that the rapist effectively should have a vote in the matter.

Let's look at issue number one. The Supreme Court really only started thinking about the scope of individual rights in the 1930s; it wasn't until 1965 that it actually ruled on the merits about whether married couples could use contraceptives in the state of Connecticut. Seven justices said that the Constitution's Fourteenth Amendment in fact was designed to take an expansive view of "liberty": it guaranteed "a freedom from all substantial arbitrary impositions and purposeless restraints." In plain terms, the Court said "let's apply some commonsense here; where would a state think it had acquired the right to tell a married couple they couldn't use a condom to limit the size of their family." Six years later, the Court said there really isn't any difference between married and unmarried couples when it comes to what it called "the right . . . to be free from unwarranted governmental intrusions into matters so fundamentally affecting a person as the decision whether to bear or begat a child." I'm curious about whether John agrees with that reasoning; many anti-choice advocates do not and indeed there is now a renewed national movement to prevent access to contraceptives. Many erroneously claim that most methods of birth control are really "abortifacients," that is that they induce abortion by preventing the implantation of fertilized eggs in the uterine wall. Others, like R. Albert Mohler, Jr., president of Southern Baptist Theological Seminary, argues against what he calls the "contraceptive mentality," which he calls "an insidious attack upon God's glory in creation, and the Creator's gift of procreation to the married couple."[12]

On the other hand, some folks actually agree with the court about contraceptives—but see something radically different when it comes to abortion, the subject of the decision in Roe v. Wade, because of the claim that there is then more than one "person" involved. *Roe*, of course, eliminated laws against abortion that existed in about thirty states. The Court used the completely legitimate argument that in intimate personal matters, privacy prevailed over the majority wishes of legislators, at least up to the point of "viability" (assessed by the court at that time to be not earlier than twenty-four to twenty-eight weeks of gestation.) We'll get back to that "two persons" argument in a few minutes.

Although *Roe* was correctly decided, I wish the Court had also used another basis for invalidating antiabortion law, enshrining the right of women to make moral choices on issues of reproductive choice on the basis of the separation of church and state.

The reason we are here tonight—and the reason that the average year brings over fifty new state laws restricting reproductive choice—is because powerful religious groups want to claim divine truth for their anti-choice position. If you go to women's clinics that provide abortions you will very frequently find picketers; they are waving Bibles—not the constitutions of their states and not medical journals. This is a battle over theology, bringing me to issue two: the value of Scripture in resolving issues of legal rights. In my view, it is without relevance.

Indeed, anti-choice forces have built an entire movement based on an issue that is not even mentioned in the very book, the sacred text from which they claim to draw their moral teachings. There is no reference to abortion in the Bible: none. The closest we get is a description, found in the book of Exodus, of the penalties in early Jewish law for killing a woman and for causing a woman to have a miscarriage. It was greater for the former. What is important is that this demonstrates that abortion was not viewed as the same as murder because, if it had been, the penalties would have been identical. The topic is also not addressed in the Christian New Testament.

In the absence of any concrete references, advocates turn to obscure poetic references like one in Jeremiah where God reportedly notes, "Before I formed you in the belly, I knew you." Clearly, this passage is merely a reflection of the belief that God is the creative force in all the universe. Taken literally, of course, it suggests that God had knowledge you were coming even before you had been conceived, before the merger of sperm and egg. That then sounds like an argument for immediate intercourse than a proscription of abortion.

Religious antiabortion advocates are on a form of interpretational quicksand to which even the earliest Fathers of the Church, the progenitors of Catholicism today, did not subscribe. Many of the early Christian leaders, for example, did not even believe the termination of pregnancy posed any moral question until the point of ensoulment, generally traced to thirty days after conception for a male and sixty days after conception for a female. The difference at the time was clearly linked to sexist views of male superiority: "my soul is older and wiser than yours."

Any of you absolutely have the right to believe that "life begins at conception" or "life starts at ensoulment," and to make all your personal decisions based on such beliefs. However, such views should not have any legal significance at all because this nation is regulated by the commonly shared values articulated in the Constitution, not the spiritual allegations of any religious body.

As I said, I wish the Supreme Court itself had been forthright about this. Justice John Paul Stevens wrote a concurring opinion in a 1989 case that spelled this out very well. The state of Missouri had passed restrictions on public employees performing abortions and had written into the statute's preamble that the reason for such a prohibition was that "the life of each human being begins at conception."[13] Stevens noted that such a definition was "an unequivocal endorsement of a religious tenet by some but by no means all Christian faiths" and thus "serves no identifiable secular purpose." He continued that the legislature "may not inject its endorsement of a particular tradition into this debate."[14] Admittedly, Justice Stevens's view was a minority one that day, but one case's dissent can easily become another day's enlightened majority decision.

As promised, I want to turn to what difference it makes that there is a "second entity" involved when a fertilized egg becomes part of the debate. Here is where John and others sometimes claim that there really is a "nonreligious" basis for the anti-choice vision. Fertilized eggs (zygotes) and fetuses are (with rare exceptions generally not yet tested in courts) not currently considered to have legal rights aside from the mother's interest. Just knowing what to call these "entities" is difficult. Some of the people on my side of the debate refer to them as "potential life"—but that is wrong because they are clearly "living," they are not minerals or plastics. But similarly, when people on both sides of the debate refer to them as "unborn babies," they are wrong also. Babies are "persons" given legal status generally by the very act of birth.

Most of the arguments for treating them identically to persons are pure sophistry, reflecting a disdain for science and evidence. At its rawest, people argue that the appearance of fetuses on sonograms proves they are people. Even Christopher Hitchens, one of the very rare nonreligious opponents of abortion makes this loopy claim. If it looks like a person it is a person, though, is not far removed from one early theological claim that because of the shape of sperm (which of course wasn't even known at the time), sperm contained a "homunculus"—a little human that gradually developed in the womb. Left alone, this would generate a male child; if injured, it would become a female child—another resounding affirmation of the negative view of women at the time.

And, of course, the argument gets corrupted even further. Fetuses feel pain, claim anti-choice advocates, because you can see, on a sonogram, fetuses moving away from needles. A great deal of medical research has been done on this issue, nearly uniformly warning that this conclusion is inaccurate. In perhaps the most comprehensive recent survey of medical literature, published in a 2005 edition of the Journal of the American Medical Association, the authors conclude that any fetal awareness of "pain" requires a conscious awareness of the noxious stimulus and that this rests on certain structural connections in the brain that do not exist until twenty-eight to thirty weeks.

Now, recall that at this point, Roe actually permits states to severely restrict abortions, and many do. However, this is not the same thing as passing bans on so-called "partial birth abortions," all of which have been ruled unconstitutional because they would all have the effect of restricting reproductive rights long before that fetus is in the birth canal.

My third "issue" is what would happen if John and his friends achieved their goal of limiting or eliminating abortions—if compulsory pregnancy became the rule of the day. Very bad things would happen.

Women would go to jail for murder. I have heard people claim that only doctors would go to prison, because women would be seen as "victims" of those physicians. Once again, this is a demeaning view of women based on the assumption that they couldn't possibly be making a genuine ethical choice. In fact, pre-Roe literature is replete with stories of how physicians were literally being pleaded with by women to do that which the law generally did not allow: terminate a pregnancy that the woman had decided was wrong for her at that time for reasons related to health, economics, or family dysfunction.

Medical research would be impeded, as it was for the past eight years, by prohibitions on such techniques as embryonic stem cell research. The reason then-president George W. Bush said that new lines of cells could not be created from existing frozen embryos (regardless of the wishes of the donors) was that this would lead to the destruction of persons. It is bizarre to me that any rational person could argue that these embryos, which will never be implanted anywhere and will eventually be destroyed as medical waste, should not be utilized for research on the crippling and fatal diseases of those whose "personhood" is not in doubt at all.

In addition, the economic status of women, which has gradually been creeping toward, although nowhere near, parity with males would be severely stifled. Forced pregnancy will make dire economic times worse not only because of the cost of raising more children, but because of lost opportunities for good jobs at good wages. The availability of abortions has allowed many young women to continue their educations in universities and graduate schools, something barred by early pregnancy. This is not to be trivialized as an example of selfishness over the needs of others. Indeed, it is women who have historically been the caregivers, the nurturers, the peacemakers—that's why their ethical compass must be the guide to their own life decisions.

And, yes, of course in a world where abortion was criminalized, women would once again die. Politicians love to say they want to make abortion "safe, legal, and rare," but the truth is that it is unlikely to ever be rare. Indeed, in a world where information is restricted and contraception availability limited, there will be more persons seeking abortions or trying to do them themselves. Even today, the ignorance spread by the anti-choice movement is responsible for many unwanted pregnancies and later-term abortions. (We can talk about that later, too, if you want.) I wonder how many people saw the film *Revolutionary Road* and didn't realize that the book upon which it was based was written pre-Roe (by twelve years) and that the homemade abortion effort that kills the wife in the book was a commonplace occurrence with a sadly commonplace conclusion. That is not a world to which I want my children and grandchildren subjected.

There might have been some lightheartedness during the debate in May of 2009, but there was nothing funny about what happened a month later.

The Assassination of Dr. Tiller: Do Religious Right Extremists Share Some of the Blame?[15]

Americans United's field director, Beth Corbin, called me on my cell phone minutes after the news was reported that Dr. George Tiller had been assassinated while serving as an usher at Reformation Lutheran Church, the church in Wichita that he attended most Sundays.

I pulled the car over, and we talked about the terrible tragedy this represented for his family, his friends, and his patients. I had met Dr. Tiller just once, but he seemed to be unstintingly dedicated to both his patients' choices and the preservation of the constitutional basis for guaranteeing that those intimate moral choices could be made by individuals, not by legislatures and sectarian lobbying groups.

I returned home and scoured the internet for information. I was struck by how many accounts referred to the murder of an "abortion doctor." It would have been more accurate to call Tiller a "doctor who performs abortions," a nod to the idea that he was a physician who met specific needs that his patients had.

Within hours, Scott Roeder was arrested for the crime. Although some at the church had seen him around the area previously, Roeder was not a "leader" of any "right-to-life" group locally or nationally. He did only occasional postings on right-wing websites.

I was curious about the response of the anti-choice movement. Most groups issued denials of any connection to Roeder and wailed about how a "pro-life" movement could never take a life, even the life of the provider of abortions. Frankly, I thought those denials and denunciations rang a little hollow, because the rhetoric used by most of those groups is so demonizing to pro-choice advocates and is filled with statements that refer to abortion as morally indistinguishable from murder.

Over the next few days, some of the most visible anti-choice activists stopped even the semblance of distancing themselves from the crime. Randall Terry, the founder of Operation Rescue, held a press event in Washington within twenty-four hours of the killing, during which he insisted that he would never stop using language that he felt was accurate.

"George Tiller was a mass murderer," Terry said. "We grieve for him that he did not have time to properly prepare his soul to face God."[16] That was clearly the only reason for his "grief." Not to be outdone, Pastor Wiley Drake (the same clergyman who has been praying "imprecatory prayers" for my demise for over a decade) asserted directly on his daily radio show, "I am glad George Tiller is dead," referring to Tiller as a "brutal, murdering monster" who was "far greater in his atrocities than Adolf Hitler."[17]

When talk show host Alan Colmes asked Drake a few days later whether he prayed for Tiller's murder, Drake "clarified" that he prayed that God get rid of him in some way. (Incredibly, Drake then announced that he was also praying daily for the death of President Barack Obama.[18])

Those of us who support the First Amendment vigorously, including the provision of freedom of speech, do so because we understand that words do matter, do have meaning and power and influence. This is all the more reason to choose our words carefully.

I made this point to the annual convention of the American Humanist Association in June, when I was honored to receive its Religious Liberty Award. I noted Drake's claim that prayer had done in Dr. Tiller, remarking, "No, Pastor Drake, it was not prayers that killed him; it was a man who listened to the rantings of people like you who provided him with the amoral framework to justify his actions."[19]

Many Religious Right groups had been highly offended several months back when the Department of Homeland Security issued a memo suggesting that law enforcement agencies needed to be concerned about domestic, as well as foreign, "terrorism" and specifically noted that persons allied with the anti-choice and anti-immigrant movements could be in that category.

About a week after Tiller's shooting, Roeder called the Associated Press from his jail cell and told them there was a "plan" to have other people do what he did. If there is a plan or, given the possible lack of veracity with which Roeder speaks, even might be a plan, this seems like a pretty concrete thing to investigate in the "anti-choice" world.

This doesn't mean that every leader of an anti-abortion group should be hauled into the nearest FBI office for interrogation. It doesn't mean that government infiltrators have to head to every rally against reproductive freedom. It just means that prudent investigative steps need to be taken.

Just one day after I expressed sentiments like these on my Beliefnet. com blog, an eighty-eight-year-old man long associated with anti-Semitic hate groups walked into the Holocaust Memorial Museum in Washington firing a weapon, killing a security guard before being shot himself by other security personnel. He had told people that he blamed the Jews for electing Obama, also claiming that Jews were not "God's Chosen." Presumably, he thought he was a person in that elite category.

Those of us who support church-state separation, diversity, and reproductive freedom have many opponents. I support their right to speak out against our views. But violence is never acceptable. Anyone who engages in it must expect to face the full force of the law.

Not satisfied with lowering women to second-class "person bearer" status, the Religious Right decided to go further. Enter the mindset of "your employer gets to decide about your birth control." Here is what I said at a 2013 session at the annual conference of the Feminist Majority Foundation, held in Washington, DC. [You can find more about the Hobby Lobby case in the next chapter.]

The hierarchy of the Roman Catholic Church today has no moral authority whatsoever to speak on the rights of women or the nature of human sexuality. Its authority has been abdicated on pillars of bad constitutional interpretation, junk science, and a framework of patriarchy right out of the twelfth century. In other words, if I may borrow a word I just learned last week from Rick Santorum in his response to a *New York Times* reporter—this is "bullshit."

The battle being waged against coverage of contraception in healthcare plans is not about "religious liberty." That claim is fraudulent. Contrary to a Baptist "moral theologian" at one Congressional hearing—having a fundamentalist university simply inform women employees or students about how to obtain no co-pay birth control is not "a rape of the soul."[20] Contrary to the Catholic Bishop's top lobbying official, Bishop William Lori, it is also not comparable to forcing an Orthodox Jew to eat pork.[21] Have these men no decency and no moral perspective? The central message of the Christian Church is about the significance of Jesus as Christ; it is not and never has been about IUDs, or Norplant, or frankly even about abortion.

Now, religious liberty does means something very important in America. It means that government cannot tell churches what to believe; it means that we try to accommodate religious observance that doesn't significantly affect the rights of others; it does mean government can't play favorites among religions or even between theists and atheists; it means that persons of faith can proselytize, evangelize, even condemn those who don't believe so long as they do it on their own dime. But now the definition is being twisted and we are told to believe that it means, "We in the institutional church have the right to get as much money from the government as our well-heeled lobbyists can squeeze out of it and we as a corporate entity demand that we be allowed to ignore any and all rules, regulations, or civil rights laws that we don't like." Well, this construction cannot be allowed to stand. With this interpretation, the church ends up setting the rules: Anything that violates some claimed tenet of some faith, no matter how trivial it may be, becomes a justification for exemption from laws that apply to the rest of us; any adverse effect this has on anybody else is just a cost of doing the church's business.

I'm not going to explain all the convoluted changes these insurance regulations have gone through because I think it is morally wrong to put people into a coma before lunch. The bottom line is this: The Obama administration initially wanted big religiously affiliated hospitals and universities (not the church on the corner) to cover birth control for their students and employees who chose to use it. And why not? First, these corporations employ hundreds or even thousands of people who have no connection to the religious orientation of their employer. Second, these corporations get hundreds of millions of tax dollars through state and federal programs. Third, these corporations hold themselves out as performing a public function in their community. No Catholic hospital advertises, "Come to St. Joseph's and learn about Jesus"; they promote that they are going to treat and try to cure your cancer. This is the trifecta of reasons that they should not be allowed to ignore the rules that apply to everybody else. Then the administration started to try to be conciliatory and, if final regulations ever actually come out—and if the world doesn't end on December 21 at the end of the Mayan calendar—I predict this is what they will say: Big religious institutions just have to give employees a piece of paper that tells them how to get birth control coverage from some insurance company outside the institution.

And you know what? The Conference of Catholic Bishops and the Family Research Council will again scream from the rooftops, "This is an impingement on freedom." Even a simple administrative act like handing out a form will be treated as complicity in a sin comparable to murder, theft, or adultery. And we know already something else they will say, because they are saying it already: "We demand that every single Catholic or fundamentalist business owner has a right to overrule the conscience of his employees."

Anthony Picarello, general counsel of the Conference of Catholic Bishops told *USA Today* that, as a good Catholic, if he quit his current job and decided to open a Taco Bell—not too likely, I suspect—he would want the right to deny women employees insurance coverage for birth control, sterilization, and anything else he found immoral.[22] Of course, we all know that women who garner the munificent wages of the fast food industry will have plenty of disposable income for paying for their own family planning. And under this standard, would an employer who is a member of the Jehovah's Witnesses be able to refuse coverage for surgeries under the theory that many require blood transfusions, which the church opposes? You can't run a comprehensive healthcare system in America—a compelling governmental interest—if every employer can opt out of providing other people coverage they desperately want whenever a single tenet of the faith is impinged upon in some tangential way.

I testified in November at a Judiciary Committee hearing alongside the aforementioned Bishop William Lori. He was all upset that a grant to the Catholic Conference to stop sex trafficking had not been renewed, and he suggested anti-Catholic bias as the reason. I suggested it was something else—the church's unwillingness to provide comprehensive services to the girls and young women being sold. I've spoken to some of the brave people who sometimes literally drag women from the very brothels in which they have just been forced to provide sex. Neither the church nor any of its one hundred subgrantees would provide Plan B contraceptives,[23] wouldn't even admit there is an option for abortion, and won't tell these abuse survivors where they can go for a full range of information—all because these steps would again violate the "conscience" of the Roman Catholic Church.

Well, they went to court and, a few days ago, they lost. You don't get grants and contracts when you can't or won't do the work required. The judge in the case ruled that it would violate the principle of separation of church and state if a religious organization could "impose religiously based restrictions on the expenditure of taxpayer funds"; that this would "implicitly endorse the religious beliefs of the Catholic Church."[24]

We are hoping that soon courts will start to undermine the premise of the George W. Bush/Barack Obama "faith-based initiative," which still allows funds to go to bigoted religious groups that refuse to hire people outside of their own faith for the very programs funded by federal taxpayers. We are, of course, happy that no court has accepted the preposterous claim in some clergy sex abuse of children cases that the church should be allowed to use canon law—principles of church doctrine— in civil or criminal cases involving priest who abuse children. But the church keeps trying, doesn't it?

The day before the Darrell Issa hearing, I thought that I would be testifying along with Sandra Fluke: The two of us obviously more than capable of debunking all of the then-sixteen witnesses on the other side. When, at four in the afternoon, I was told that Issa had not considered Sandra "qualified" to speak, I was immediately faxed my invitation to appear, which I promptly tore up. The next day, Issa explained how although he never agreed with me I was "well respected" and that maybe I would actually show up in spite of me not responding to his letter calling me as a witness. Of course he wanted me there because he wanted to try to embarrass the Democrats who objected to the gender bias of the other witnesses. Issa declared, "I note that Barry Lynn is not a female."[25] That's true, but Barry Lynn is a feminist. We feminists stick together. We feminists do not play games with women's health; we feminists do not let the patriarchal rulers of religious mega-corporations tell us or our partners or our daughters what choices to make on the most intimate moral decisions of our lives. And, as I think the nation has been learning again over the past four weeks, we do not go quietly into the night. We organize, we petition, we growl, and we go on to win. [More about the Darrell Issa hearing in chapter 8.]

LGBTQ COMMUNITY

Honestly, the Religious Right is so upset by the LGBTQ community and its regular legislative and judicial successes that it can barely contain itself. Former dean of Jerry Falwell's Liberty University's law school Mat Staver recently said that marriage equality "is something that I believe is the beginning of the end of Western civilization."[26] And Mr. Staver and his colleagues have been unhappy for a long time.

Here is an after-dinner speech I gave in 2007 to Michigan's highly respected Triangle Foundation—supporters of LGBTQ rights.

Thanks for that kind introduction. Yes, both a minister and a lawyer: a man who can forgive you one day and go on to sue you the next day. Look,

I don't have too much time tonight, so I will have to eliminate any further attempts at humor. I'm really glad to be here and I'm only able to be here because it is still September. Starting October 1, I will be spending the next eighty-six days in a relentless "war against Christmas"—kicking over Nativity scenes, telling big box retail stores to insist their employees shout "Happy Holidays" to shoppers instead of "Merry Christmas," and of course looking for elves to run over on my way to work. You'll be able to see reports that discuss all this on Bill O'Reilly's show on the Fox News Channel. Maybe Bill will even have me back on again—and he can again tell me in one sentence both how I am one of his favorite guests and later refer to me as a "paranoid crazy." I'd like to thank the Triangle Foundation for mentioning his characterization of me in the press release for this event.

Actually, I'm glad to be here for another reason. I'm under a curse. That's right. Last month, Americans United filed a complaint with the Internal Revenue Service against the pastor of the Buena Park Baptist Church out in California, a man with a name some would consider more appropriate for the Cartoon Network than real life, Wiley Drake. We said he violated the tax exempt status of his church by endorsing the Presidential candidacy of former Arkansas Governor Mike Huckabee both on his official church sta-tionery and on his daily radio show run out of his church basement. He was upset. So he asked all his supporters to pray "imprecatory prayers" against the two gentlemen from my communications department listed on our press release on the matter and yours truly. "Imprecatory prayers" are basically requests for God to do unpleasant things to people. In case his folks didn't know what to say, he had a few suggestions, including "may his wife be a widow and his children fatherless. Let his children be continually vagabonds upon the earth, let them seek their bread also out of their desolate places." Apparently, the pastor didn't realize my son is employed at Google and my daughter is at the University of Virginia Law School. I'm hoping they take me with them to the desolate corners of the fancy French restaurants they will be scouring for baguettes!

I love my kids; I hope I taught them a few things along the road. Par-enting is pretty great. Americans United's legislative director and his partner just adopted their second child last month—men can do that in the District of Columbia. I hope I'm still around to see the day when gender becomes irrelevant in adoptions throughout America. I'll tell you one of the best ways to determine if a parent is a good one, and it has nothing to do with gender: good parents give their kids gifts like this cuddly SpongeBob SquarePants—bad parents give their children this hard plastic Ann Coulter talking action figure.

Ann is a trip isn't she. She's not really fond of the LGBTQ community. Actually, there are a lot of groups and people she doesn't care for. She wrote an obituary following Jerry Falwell's death last April in which she said she agreed with everything the man ever said except . . . Quoting Ms. Coulter: "actually there is one small item I think Falwell got wrong regarding his statement after 9/11 that 'the pagans, and the abortionists, and the feminists, and the gays and lesbians. . . . I point my finger in their face and say 'You helped this happen.' I disagreed with that statement because Falwell neglected to specifically include Teddy Kennedy and 'the Reverend' Barry Lynn."[27] I'm proud to be in the company of every one of the groups she and the late Dr. Falwell included in that outrageous remark. And I'm proud to be aligned with Senator Edward Kennedy, who was the lead sponsor of the hate crimes bill passed three days ago helping protect those against whom violence is directed because of race or gender or gender identity or sexual orientation. It's about time. The Senator said, "At a time when our ideals are under attack by terrorists in other lands, it is more important than ever to demonstrate that we practice what we preach, and that we are doing all we can to root out the bigotry and prejudice in our own country that lead to violence here at home."[28]

This legislation is an important step; it does not trample on the right of any American to speak, even using hateful rhetoric, but it makes it clear that some acts of hate have a goal far more pernicious than the random act of violence—these are the acts that are designed to serve as a warning for an entire community that all of its members have been targeted for the worst kind of vengeance simply because they exist.

Here's one problem: Hate crimes legislation only gets us so far. It doesn't have the capacity to stop hate itself. That is the far greater task. I don't really mind the stuff the Religious Right says about me: After all, it provides fodder for after-dinner speeches. But when it comes to their attacks on whole groups of folks, there is something much worse going on. There really is a whole "anti-GLBT hate industry" in this country. It is a campaign of marginalization; it is a campaign of fear-mongering; it is a campaign to make you invisible. This movement wants to say, as President Ahmadinejad did at Columbia University, there are no gay people in my country. In the

United States this effort is primarily generated by the Religious Right, but it is enabled by the deafening silence of too many in the religious center, and even the "religious left."

I understand that Frank Kameny is an advisory board member of the Triangle Foundation. I've known Frank a long time, and I had a chance to interview him on my radio show a few days before he was honored by the Smithsonian with a display of his papers and his memorabilia about the beginnings of the gay rights movement. Frank, along with Del Martin and Phyllis Lyon, founders of the Daughters of Bilitis, were demanding equality at a time when same-gender relationships were often referred to as "the love that dare not speak its name." You speak it now. But on the other side is a "hate that cannot stop speaking, indeed screaming, its vitriol."

This hate machine operates on many levels, and the operators are a mix of bigots and blowhards and beguilers. The groups and individuals in this movement often operate in all three dimensions, in large measure depending on their primary audience at the moment. One outlier, of course, is Fred Phelps of Westboro Baptist Church in Topeka, Kansas. He and most of his family are the creators of the "God Hates America.com" and "God Hates Fags.com" websites. They scream their homophobic denunciations at funerals of persons who have died of AIDS. Lately they have gone to many funerals of gay and straight GI s killed in Iraq, shouting from the sidewalk, "Thank God for Improvised Explosive Devices," to try to make their "point" that a nation that tolerates homosexuality in any way deserves destruction. When Dr. Jerry Falwell died, Fred Phelps put up a video in which he assured viewers that "Falwell split Hell wide open the instant he died" because he was a "fag enabler": that means he occasionally talked with members of the gay and lesbian community. One of the many sad things about Phelps is that he usually makes people with equally bigoted views sound more rea- sonable as they condemn his tactics but never truly challenge his assump- tions. In fact, they thrive on the same assumptions that members of the GLBT community are and should forever be second-class citizens in their own country.

The bigotry, though, sometimes takes an oratorical backseat when the blowhards of the hate industry appear, for example, on talk shows on cable television. But they are so self-righteous as they pontificate. Peter Sprigg of the Family Research Council says things like it is "foolishly naïve to think that 'liberated' homosexuals will settle down into faithful, monogamous, childrearing relationships." Bob Knight, long associated with Concerned Women for America (don't go there) is always seeking connections between "leftist" groups. He once famously asserted, "If you look at the footage from Operation Rescue, um, vigils outside abortion clinics, you will see that the anti-Operation Rescue demonstrators invariably have a pink triangle on and they are usually pretty big heavyset women who look like they've been over working October Fest for the last six years."[29] Last weekend, Bob was down in Florida at this big gay-bashing conference and claimed that gay journalists were frauds who ought to sell their material to the *Weekly World News*, joking that they might have some "gay alien" stories.[30] And then there is Peter Lababara, who runs this new outfit called Americans for Truth about Homosexuality. His website has a list of issues along the left side including the provocative "Public Sex in Your Neighborhood?" For your protection, I clicked on it, then clicked on Michigan, and found that nothing is happening in your entire state. I have known these guys for decades. What motivates a person to spend his entire career trying to stop the wheels of justice and human understanding?

So we have chatted about the overt bigots and the blustery bloviators, who are the beguilers in this industry of hate? The most important ones are those who claim either scientific or religious scholarship to prove that the GLBT community is sick and/or going to hell. They lure people in the middle into thinking that there is only one set of facts on these matters. Their so-called "scientific" tests are always coming up with some new alleged proof that homosexuality can be reversed through some kind of "reparative therapy." Writers like Wayne Besen have looked into this phony and expensive cottage industry and found it filled with loopy science. But, you know anything labeled "scientific" can fool some of the people. I can't stand here and say that no one has temporarily, or even permanently, changed the locus of their sexual interest, but I can tell you this much: if there were conventions for "ex-straights" organizations, they would be a lot bigger than any "ex-gay" convention.

And, of course, they have the Bible scholars (who always assert that you don't need the Bible to reach the conclusion that hate crimes bills or equal-employment measures are bad, but of course really don't mean that because they always fall back on allegedly Christian views). One of my favorites is Professor Robert Gagnon at the Pittsburgh Theological Seminary. He is so anti-gay that he has written, and I quote, ". . . faithful polyamorous arrangements—whether a traditional polygamous bond or non-traditional 'threesomes' . . . are not as severe a violation of God's sexual norms as are homosexual unions."[31] What seminary class did I miss where Jesus took that view? I recently asked Gagnon whether if the threesome had two men in it, would it be still be considered better than a loving gay union of two men? I don't think he understood the question.

Almost all of these folks have a legislative agenda. It is a very dangerous one. At the top of the list is still the proposed amendment to the United States Constitution often referred to as the Federal Marriage Amendment. It would define marriage in all states as the relationship between one man and one woman. It would be the first time that we constitutionalized bigotry. It would also violate the principle of the separation of church and state. During the unsuccessful effort to pass this in the last Congress, we knew that it was all about religion from the very rhetoric its supporters used. President Bush called it necessary to preserve a "sacred" institution; then-majority-leader (and long-distance psychic diagnostician of Mrs. Terri Schiavo) Dr. Bill Frist insisted that the Senate's failure to pass this meant the "sacrament" of marriage was jeopardized, another religious referent. I am proud of the fact that the denomination in which I was ordained, the United Church of Christ, allows its ministers to perform same-sex marriages, and I'm glad that Unitarian ministers and Reform rabbis can do the same. Unfortunately, with an amended Constitution, the very relationships we do sanctify with our rituals are considered meaningless in the eyes of the state. But opposite-gender rituals performed by other faiths pass muster. That is not equal protection of the law. That is religious preferentialism. That the Constitution today forbids. And if state and federal courts were populated with people of wisdom and courage not one of the state anti-same-sex marriage amendments would stand up to the federal Constitutional mandate.

If federal courts respected fundamental values as much as they respect federalism when it serves their purpose, the idiotically named Defense of Marriage Act would have been declared unconstitutional long ago.

The Right is so concerned that someday this will happen that they have even argued that federal courts should not be permitted to hear cases challenging anti-gay restrictions like the Defense of Marriage Act and actually got a majority of the House of Representatives back in 2004 to pass what is called a "court stripping bill" on the subject, denying federal courts the right to hear any cases on this topic.

The Right is still arguing with a straight face that if gay people get married, it will hurt the 50 percent of straight marriages that manage to hang together. I have been married for thirty-seven years, as it happens, to the same woman. If the two gay men up the street are allowed to be married in the state of Maryland, does James Dobson actually believe that I will be catapulted into paroxysm of newfound lust, terminating my longstanding relationship. That might not even happen if Nicole Kidman moved into my neighborhood. (Sorry, that was a joke, and I said there would be no more funny stuff.)

Although it appears from the current level of publicity that the next Presidential election is occurring next week, it is actually over thirteen months away. The Right is still hoping, indeed there is an imprecatory prayer circle praying, that one of the remaining liberal members of the Court be forced to step down—or simply die. They don't just want Chief Justice Roberts and Justice Alito to push the narrow, crabbed anti-vision of the Constitution to which the Right subscribes; they want another guaranteed vote on the Court. Should anyone else leave the Court, the majority in the Senate should not hold hearings, should not dance around the nominees qualifications; they should just say, "This President does not deserve one more lifetime appointment to the Court." No more rhetoric about "rolling the dice" in the hopes of a fair nominee; this isn't a monopoly game, this is the future of the rights of the people at stake.

And then there is the President's much-discussed "faith-based initiative": a way, as it turns out, to funnel a modest amount of money to churches that might learn to be friendlier to Republicans if they got a few grants. One of the many constitutional problems with this program is that it allows the recipients of the funds to discriminate in hiring people to fill the slots paid for by all of us, the taxpayers. In a case Americans United is doing with the Gay and Lesbian Rights Project of the ACLU, a woman who worked as a counselor at the taxpayer-subsidized Kentucky Baptist Home for Children was fired after the following events occurred: A photographer took a picture of our client and her partner at an AIDS march. A year later, the picture was exhibited at a county fair. The woman's supervisor saw the picture and recognized our client. The next morning, the supervisor confronted her: "Are you a lesbian?" "Yes." "You are fired!" Ironically, the courts have ruled that she has no cause of action for the firing, but we are now investigating whether such a pervasively religious organization should have gotten tax monies in the first place.

The people with this machinery and this agenda are dangerous people in whatever guise they appear. Adding to the problem is just how well-heeled they are. The group called the Traditional Values Coalition, which labeled this week's anti-hate-crimes bill "The She-Male Enabling Pro-Homosexual Drag Queen" bill, raked in about 6.5 million dollars last year;[32] the Family Research Council made 10.8 million.[33] James Dobson's Focus on the Family groups hauled in a whopping 157 million dollars.[34]

For years, Pat Robertson's Christian Coalition had an annual convention in Washington with a "bookstore" that sold a book written by George Grant called *Legislating Immorality*. It called for the execution of all gay people but was discrete enough to qualify in a footnote that in our judicial system we would have to give them a trial first. As we know because of Matthew Shepherd and Brandon Teena and countless others whose names we don't know, some people in America do not read the footnotes. See, you can't peddle hate literature out of the back of your bookstore and then take no moral responsibility for the actions of others who act on those prejudices. Last year, Dr. James Dobson and his supporters had a Values Voters Conference in DC. They were excited when prominent African American pastor Wellington Boone said, "Blacks who are oppressed had not broken any laws of nature or of nature's God. . . . Sodomites are people who willfully break the laws of God and the laws of the land. . . . You tell me a gay has a right to get on some of [those civil rights]? Get out of here! . . . Back in the days when I was a kid, we see guys that don't stand strong on principle, we call them 'faggots.'"[35] I presume Pastor Boone now knows exactly what that word originally mean—a bundle of sticks, specially used in the thirteenth century to burn, while still alive, heretics and sexual minorities. Just sheer naked bigotry from a man whose forbearers themselves had to fight the lynchings that had come to replace the killing fires. Words have power; the First Amendment gives people the right to use them—it gives us the power to condemn them and expect that others will challenge them as well. For Christians there to allow this insulting speech to go unchallenged was a disgrace; an example of the immorality of silence.

Now, I've referred to this group I've been discussing as a "hate industry." You know, though, that this is a good old capitalist country. It means industries have to compete to stay alive. There is a "respect industry" out there too. It is selling its ideas every time an elected official stands up for GLBT concerns; every time a local pastor denounces an attack on a gay man and also denounces the immoral thinking that allowed the attacker to justify his crime; every time a family is open and affirming about their gay son or lesbian daughter and is proud to discuss his or her work; every time a union passes a resolution in support of passage of legislation to end job discrimination; every time somebody writes a letter to the editor acknowledging that something they have learned by finding out a friend or colleague is gay has changed their outlook on the necessity for equal rights under the law; every time a parent says to his son who has just called another kid at school a "fag" that that expression is intolerable and then explains why.

See, I remain an optimist about the long haul. I share the Rev. Dr. Martin Luther King's frequent observation that "the arc of change is long, but it tends toward justice." We have all come a long way in the last half of the twentieth century. The twenty-first is only moving in one direction. Unless we leave the field, unless we stop the struggle, we are going to prevail.

Two days of rallies outside the Supreme Court were held as the justices were discussing the fate of the Defense of Marriage Act (DOMA). The Human Rights Campaign asked me to do a short speech on the steps of the Supreme Court in March of 2013:

I am a minister in the United Church of Christ and a member of the Supreme Court bar. Long ago, I gave up thinking I had the gift of prophecy generally, and I've also given up trying to predict specifically what the justices behind us will do.

Two groups of Americans have been gathering here for the past two days. I know quite a few people in both camps. Those who are anti-marriage-equality are not all haters and bigots. But—they are all wrong. Their time is past and they know it; polls demonstrate that they cannot even convince their own children they are right. Their ethical analyses and their purportedly moral viewpoints will soon be relegated to the dustbin of human history.

I oppose the agenda of the Religious Right every day at Americans United for Separation of Church and State because I know that America is not a theocracy; it is not a place where the law reflects some powerful group's narrow and crabbed view of what any holy scripture allegedly says. It is why we have fought for a separation of church and state—and why we need to get that correct each day. We would not have DOMA or Proposition

8 if it were not for the powerful, wealthy sectarian forces that stand behind the rubric of marriage inequality and who treat some to a second-class citizenship our Constitution abhors.

American history is an interesting thing. Taking the long view, it is crafted by ordinary people like us more than by presidents or senators or Supreme Court justices. And sometimes sooner, sometimes later, we the people tend to get it right. And we—the second camp—are getting it right today: We are standing up for something so fundamental, so real, so remarkably simple that these marble steps cry that we haven't seen it sooner.

I have been married to my spouse, Joanne, for forty-two years; we have two great children, one girl, one boy; we are just what one anti-equality speaker on the radio yesterday said was the dream American family. I know how good that feels. Yesterday, I was in tears listening to the dreams of other families, dreams that cannot yet be fulfilled for them because of the very law being debated today inside that building. You shouldn't need a theological or a legal degree to recognize one simple equation. All people who are willing to accept the rights and responsibilities of a long-term commitment deserve equal treatment under our Constitution no matter what job they do, no matter in what state they live, no matter who they love. A simple equation of simple justice!

As I said, I don't know what this Supreme Court will do in June. I don't know whether our side will win or lose or get a mixed message or perhaps get no definitive answers at all. This I do know: If decisions don't go our way, we will find every other venue in which to make our arguments, and we will return to this court one day. Even if we prevail on the arguments of the past two days, our job will not be over. Decisions of this court are not self-executing. We will need to be vigilant that every family is accorded whatever rights this Court grants them. Just like *Brown v. Board of Education*, we will need to be sure that every state, every community puts the principle into practice, so that no one is left behind.

And we will do that because we have always done that. We do not stop litigating, we do not stop marching, we do not stop debating, we do not stop organizing until we win equal rights for every family, everywhere, forever.

DOMA was declared unconstitutional on June 26, 2013. It has been cited as a cornerstone for rejected state laws and initiatives that sought to define marriage solely as a relationship between one man and one woman. As of this writing, four of the thirteen circuit courts have had an opportunity to examine these laws and have found them to be unconstitutional violations of the principle of equal protection under the law. As of this writing, the Supreme Court has been asked to consider the Sixth Circuit's outlier decision upholding a narrow definition of marriage. There is a widespread belief on all sides of this debate that on or about June 30, 2015 "marriage equality" will be the law everywhere in America.

DEATH AND DYING

The Religious Right doesn't always wait to bother people once they're buried six feet under. (See the last section on the Wiccans' difficulty with the Department of Veteran Affairs.) Recently, the Religious Right has decided that it can also impress its perception of the world onto people who are lying on their deathbeds. As you are about to read below, in a speech that I gave at the 2009 Compassion and Choices Conference in Washington, DC, the Religious Right is also ready to tell you how to end your life (that is, let "nature's God" take its course).

Thanks for inviting me here. I'm not sure how many of you even know who I am. I am one of those people better known by my enemies than by my friends. How do I know this? Last week, a group associated with the late Jerry Falwell's Liberty University announced that they were soon issuing a group of trading cards—like baseball cards—of dangerous "liberals," and simultaneously launching an "adopt-a-liberal" prayer campaign, trying to get them to become fundamentalist conservatives. They announced the first eleven names—Barack Obama, Arnold Schwarzenegger, and eight other government officials—and, then, me. I was honored. I did have to send out a brief press release of my own, though, because I wanted to make it clear that if anybody wanted to "adopt" me, they should know in advance (a kind of advance directive) that I don't rake leaves and I stay up really late.

I have some bad news for you. The so-called "Religious Right" is not in favor of "choices" (compassionate or otherwise) at the end of life. Here is the more comforting news: You are not alone. The Religious Right is not in favor of real choice about much of anything from the moment of conception until the moment of death, or pretty much at any moment in between. They have all the answers and, if you don't accept them voluntarily, they will be happy to try to enlist the power of government to force you to accept them.

I think that a lot of folks didn't even realize that the Religious Right saw end-of-life decisions as big moral/social policy matters to butt into—until, of course, the spring of 2005 when it launched one of the most reprehensible campaigns in its sordid history. Why mince words about it?

This movement turned a little known decades-long tragedy into its latest sideshow. I won't remind you of all the details, but I want to highlight a few of the facts of those days to show you what we are up against. Ms. Terri Schiavo had been in a persistent vegetative state for a decade. Her husband, Michael, was her legal guardian under Florida law and, after heroic efforts himself to find medical help, reluctantly concluded that withdrawal of life sustaining treatment was necessary. After years, Florida's highest court agreed—and that is when the Right stepped in, people who did not know him, had not known his wife, but only knew that Ms. Schiavo's parents did not approve of Michael's informed decision, and decided to launch a campaign to "save" her.

I never expected to get directly involved in this matter, but things don't always go as planned. In March of 2005, the then House Majority Leader Tom DeLay called his congressional colleagues back from vacation on a Sunday night to pass legislation to undo Florida's final legal pronouncement before Michael could actually have nutrition and hydration removed.

This bill was an attempt to start all the proceedings over again in federal court, a so-called de novo review of all the issues that had been reviewed endlessly for eight years by twenty state and federal judicial panels. The bill noted, additionally, that none of the earlier evidence regarding her medical condition, her own wishes on this matter, or the qualifications of her husband as guardian were to be considered.

A few hours after the lopsided vote (and a dishearteningly limited opposition to it by the bleary-eyed returnees), I was listening to a most extraordinary tape recording. It was of Tom DeLay, two days earlier, speaking to a lobbying outfit called the Family Research Council. Listen to why he was so eager to get into the Schiavo fray.

He bemoaned: "One thing that God has brought us is Terri Schiavo, to help elevate the visibility of what is going on in America. This is exactly the issue that is going on in America, of attacks against the conservative movement, against me, and against many others."[36] DeLay added that "the other side" was leading the attack with a goal "to defeat the conservative movement."

Why was he comparing himself to Ms. Schiavo? As you probably recall, he was under fire for allegedly funneling illegal corporate contributions into Texas state government races, an offense for which he was indicted[37] (and then the conviction was overturned)—and still could be indicted for further misconduct even though he is now a dancer and not a congressman.[38]

The *New York Times* was keenly interested in this matter—and in fact featured the tape on its front page for two days. Since I was credited with releasing the tape, the cable shows were eager to hear me. Although usually I lack reluctance to appear on these broadcasts—I didn't want to show up and do what every other guest seemed to be doing—I didn't want to appear to have miraculously earned a medical degree. It was bad enough that actual doctor-then-senator Bill Frist had developed the power of long-distance "diagnosis," declaring that Ms. Schiavo's case was not hopeless, even though his examination was from six hundred miles away.

I did these shows because there were some other points to be made, points relevant to today and into the future.

First, the same "activists" who demanded that Ms. Schiavo be kept on artificial support forever were precisely the same cast of characters that are involved in every other control effort. They were the same people who screech outside of women's medical centers, the same people who we had battled legally in Alabama when a state judge (now former judge) put up a two-and-a-half ton granite monument of the Ten Commandments in the new courthouse and refused to take it down even after ordered to do so by several federal courts; they are the same people who turn their churches in election cycles into veritable campaign headquarters for their favorite right-wing candidates and then compare the IRS to Nazis when it warns them that such partisanship can cost them their tax exemption.

Second, these people are blatant hypocrites. In general they don't want federal courts to do much of anything. In the same session of Congress in which the Schiavo debacle occurred, they had tried to remove federal jurisdiction—including Supreme Court jurisdiction—on all kinds of issues: abortion rights, the words of the Pledge of Allegiance, some applications of the "equal protection" guarantee. Here, they demanded that the federal courts get involved in what is quintessentially a matter of state law: family law, including guardianship. They want certain results; they don't give a hoot about how they reach them.

For two weeks, courts had to review the constitutionality of the new legislation. There must be "finality": you can't litigate forever. And eventually that is what happened. Judge Stanley F. Birch Jr. of the Eleventh Circuit Court of Appeals wrote, "When the fervor of political passions moves the executive and legislative branches to act in a way inimical to basic constitutional principles, it is the duty of the judiciary to intervene. . . . [T]he [other] branches of our government have acted in a manner demonstrably at odds with our Founding Fathers' blueprint for the governance of a free people— our Constitution."[39] When hours later, the Supreme Court rejected any need to hear an appeal, the nightmare was ended.

In the course of these weeks, Michael Schiavo allowed Terri's parents and a cast of rotating advisors and loudmouths to visit her hospital room every day, even though he had no legal responsibility to do so. He knew that they would leave, hold another press conference, and make the vilest comments about him again and again. I don't know if his tolerance of this routine is "saintly," but it sure showed more class than I've seen from most of the Religious Right over the years.

The Religious Right lied during the event and after it. After an appearance on *Nancy Grace*, one of the "religious advisors" for Schiavo's parents came running up to me from another studio, yelling at me for defending Michael's position. The Rev. Patrick Mahoney said that Michael had ordered the hospital window shades closed so Terri would be trapped in darkness—while knowing full well that the shades were drawn because "his side" had hired photographers with telephoto lenses to try to get a shot of anything they could skew and claim showed how "alive" Ms. Schiavo was. In other words, they wanted more footage like the overused, underexplained old snippet, which they falsely claimed showed her "following" the motion of a balloon.

When this whole disgraceful episode was over, CBS news did a poll and found out that 80 percent of Americans thought the government should never have gotten involved in the Schiavo case.[40] Eighty percent is incredibly high; I don't think you could get 80 percent of us to answer "yes" to the question, "Does the Sun appear to rise in the East?"

The final reaction took a significant number of arrows out of the quiver for the Right, but, sadly, reinforced weapons have again arrived on the scene. The "debate" (and I use that term advisedly) about healthcare now occurring here has been thoroughly corrupted by all manner of nonsense, but one highly damaging distraction has been false statements about end-of-life issues, tainted with the phrase "death panels." Once again, the movement most responsible for all this turns out to be the Religious Right: its front persons not merely soon-to-be-bestselling author Sarah Palin but a popular Bush appointee as head of the faith-based initiative office, Jim Towey (now the president of a small college in Pennsylvania).

Frankly, if only Sarah Palin was involved, there would not have been such a fuss. She said on her Facebook page, "The America I know and love is not one in which my parents or my baby with Downs Syndrome will have to stand in front of Obama's 'death panel' so his bureaucrats can decide, based on a subjective judgment of their 'level of productivity,' whether they are worthy of healthcare. Such a system is downright evil."[41] And whatever alternative universe has a guy named Obama with such a system would be an evil place. That is, of course, not our universe.

But we have to remember that outlandish statements only die if they are not repeated. CNN, in its crawl across the bottom of the screen, had a one-sentence statement about Palin's belief in "death panels" for over twenty-four hours. You saw it far more frequently than the news story the network did about it, which gave little credence to the idea.

The Palin statement merely built on other claims that had been made by conservative news outlets virtually from the time that the president announced that he wanted healthcare reform to be a major legislative priority in his first year in office. The *Washington Times* had earlier invoked references to euthanasia programs in Nazi Germany.[42] Commentators like Glenn Beck (who in most other cultures would be shouting his nuttiness to people in public parks) said the Obama plan was: "sometimes for the common good, you just have to say, 'Hey, Grandpa, you've had a good life'—and so you have to go."[43]

On August 18, Jim Towey threw gasoline on this illusory fire with an op-ed in the *Wall Street Journal* headlined "The Death Book for Veterans." This was a screed against a book used by the Veterans Administration's National Center for Ethics in Health Care called *Your Life, Your Choices*, first published in 1997 and used until well-known ethical scholar George W. Bush decided it was not any good. Most of you know Towey's criticism: that it had scenarios designed, in his words, to "steer vulnerable individuals to conclude for themselves that life is not worth living."[44] He claimed that raising issues like financial burdens and being in a wheelchair were a "push poll" for "predetermined conclusions." Towey, of course, then noted that he had written a twelve-page document that was much better.

I have known Towey for thirty years. I first met him when he was a legislative assistant to Oregon Senator Mark Hatfield. Hatfield was a very progressive Republican I worked with on many issues, but we just had to disagree on abortion rights. Towey went on to be Mother Theresa's lawyer and then an assistant to Florida governor Jeb Bush. He ended up running the White House Office of Faith-Based Initiatives after its first director quit in disgust, telling *Esquire* magazine, "What you've got is everything—and I mean everything—being run by the political arm. It's the reign of the Mayberry Machiavellis."[45]

By the time he got back to Washington, he was certainly a different fellow than when I first knew him. He turned the office into a massive partisan political machine.

The evidence for this political manipulation was all confirmed when Towey's second-in-command, David Kuo, wrote a book about the office. Kuo told of how Karl Rove became interested in the possible political impact of suggesting that pastors could get money, even though he knew most of them wouldn't get a dime. (Rove referred to the evangelicals who had to get invited to the White House for photo ops as "the nuts.") Oh, and on Florida as one example of the partisan intent, Kuo wrote: "More than a dozen conferences with more than 20,000 faith and community leaders were held . . . in every significant battleground state, including one in Miami ten days before the 2004 election. The political power was incalculable."[46]

I give you this background because Towey's credibility should have been severely stained by his faith-based funding shenanigans. It wasn't tainted enough, because hundreds of other papers and blogs reprinted the audacious misstatements of the original *Wall Street Journal* piece.

As you know, this was all about the mere facts that Congress had included modest Medicare funding for voluntary "end-of-life consultations" with physicians and, separately, a council to help conduct research on comparative effectiveness of medical interventions, with a prohibition that any council recommendations cannot "be construed as mandates or clinical guidelines for payment, coverage, or treatment."[47]

One might say, well, all the Right was doing was warning against the possibility that someone other than yourself would be making decisions about the end of your life. Perhaps these same people would take a more libertarian bent when it comes to making up your own mind on these matters. Perhaps they embrace many of the ideas that have long been of concern to members of this organization—durable powers of attorney for health-care and "living wills"; perhaps even "physician assistance in dying." No such luck. Listen to some of the rhetoric about "physician assisted suicide"; that would be—your dying. The most powerful Religious Right lobby now is something called the Family Research Council, an offshoot of James Dobson's Focus on the Family. In their most sophisticated arguments, they espouse the old tired arguments about not being able to draw any lines, that this is not a "private" decision at all, that this will lead depressed people to kill themselves and aren't we all depressed.

But the bigger issue is the one they talk about when they are talking to supporters: God decides when and how you die, not you. So you are not just having a debate with a local evangelical preacher when you are debating this issue in your communities—you are debating God. It is theo-logically clear to these folks that God decides that you get bone cancer, that you die in an airliner crash, that you are shot in a bar, but *never* would God decide that you leaving this planet surrounded by friends and caregivers after saying goodbye to those you love is the time or place to do it.

Luckily, in this country we do have a "separation of church and state." It doesn't stop people like those in the FRC from making arguments about what the law should say on moral matters. It does, however, prohibit gov-ernments from passing laws that rely primarily on references to somebody's interpretation of some group's "holy scripture."

A recent pew survey[48] showed that two-thirds of Americans say there are at least some situations in which a patient should be allowed to die. At the same time, a growing share of Americans also believe individuals have a moral right to end their own lives. Meanwhile, the public remains closely divided on the issue of physician-assisted suicide: 47 percent approve and 49 percent disapprove of laws that would allow a physician to prescribe lethal doses of drugs that a terminally ill patient could use to terminate his life.

As of this writing, only Vermont, Oregon, and Washington have statutory protection for this right to choose. Montana's Supreme Court recognized this right in 2009 and New Mexico's courts seem to be moving in this direction. In

2012, a Massachusetts ballot initiative failed 51 to 49 percent, with 80 percent of the funds to defeat it emanating from the Catholic Church or wealthy individuals allied with the church. The California Senate has already passed an End of Life Option act, with a hearing scheduled in the appropriations committee. And New Jersey's Assembly passed The Aid in Dying for the Terminally Ill Act, which also has state Senate support.

Just as the Religious Right continues to survive, it seems that this issue is not going away soon. From cradle to grave, the Religious Right is concerned about every choice you make.

Chapter 8

THE BIG WALL-BANGERS (AKA THE BIGGEST THREATS TO CHURCH-STATE SEPARATION)— FAITH-BASED FUNDING AND RELIGIOUSLY MOTIVATED REFUSALS

FAITH-BASED INITIATIVES

Two enormously important issues have arisen in the past fifteen years that swamp the concerns many of us have about the state of "church and state separation."

One is the notion of providing financial and other support for "faith-based" programs in religious settings—the so-called "faith-based initiative." Although first implemented by President Bill Clinton (who sought to have its most unconstitutional provisions corrected after signing the first "charitable choice" bill late in his Presidency), it flourished under the Presidency of George W. Bush and then, unexpectedly, increased under the tenure of Barack Obama. As a candidate, Obama said that he would eliminate the most onerous proviso—allowing federally funded charities to discriminate in hiring along religious lines, giving preference to co-religionists. He did not stop this, however, relying on input from his first Faith-Based and Community Services czar, Joshua DuBois, and the threats made by World Vision and Catholic Charities to get out of the privately funded aid programs they had set up and for which they then sought government funding.

After President George W. Bush announced his Faith-Based Initiative during the third week of his presidency, it got a huge amount of attention. Much of that attention supported the initiative, but there was some criticism as well. Americans United did much of that criticizing, but surprisingly, we were joined by such "principled conservatives" as syndicated columnist Cal Thomas and the Cato Institute's Michael Tanner.

President Bush's efforts to get Congress to enact his version of the Faith-Based Initiative floundered for over two years. The Republican-controlled House, led by Texas congressman Tom DeLay, passed a bill, but the Democratic-controlled Senate let it lie on Congressional hearing room floors.

Bush's first Faith-Based Office director, University of Pennsylvania professor John DiIulio, managed to last for most of its first two years but then wrote a scathing critique of the program and left Washington to return to Penn. He was replaced by Florida-based Jim Towey.

The president eventually decided to bypass Congress and implement his "vision" of the program by executive orders. The essential features of his plan had not changed over those two years; neither had his justification or false claims about how beleaguered charities had been in the past.

I sorted through many speeches I did after the President unilaterally implemented his Faith-Based Program. What follows is a speech from 2003 to the Pew Forum in Washington. You may notice that the stinging critiques of the program then are still the ones I'm making today—evidence to follow.

Two years ago, when President Bush announced the Faith-Based Initiative, I said to some interviewer that it was the worst idea since they took King Kong from Skull Island and brought him to New York. I would now like to apologize to the Kong family; the president's idea is much worse. Now that I got that cheap laugh, I'd like to prove it was justified. Even though the president's program has never actually passed Congress and is being implemented in a kind of "stealth" atmosphere, virtually everything that has happened with it demonstrates unfortunate intended or unintended consequences of any government-funded religious programs.

All the particular problems find their genesis in a fundamental design flaw—the belief that you can protect Constitutional principles simply by assenting that public funds may go to religious groups so long as they were not used for "religious worship, instruction, or proselytization." As often phrased by administration officials, tax dollars will be used to "buy bread, not Bibles."[1] This conveniently ignores that when the government does fund some loaves of bread for the church-based hunger program it just frees up more church funds to buy scriptures or raise the pastor's salary. On the flipside, it is not possible for most religious groups to just turn off the religious element of what they are doing when a federal dollar floats by, but turn the spiritual spigot back on when it is a voluntarily contributed dollar. In practical effect in most cases, grants to or contracts with religious groups do aid, do promote, do foster religion with tax dollars, violating a core principle of the First Amendment. In the process, those funds promote the theological assumptions, spiritual messages, and biases of the recipient. What do we see two-and-a-half years later?

The first major problem is that the administration has made every effort to legitimize the funding of invidious job discrimination. In every set of proposed regulations, and in the president's December executive order, there is clear language that permits a recipient to hire persons to run taxpayer-funded programs solely on the basis of their religious affiliation or beliefs. This means that a Roman Catholic provider can refuse to hire, or can fire at will, a pregnant single mother; it effectively permits a fundamentalist Christian church from putting the words "NO MUSLIMS NEED APPLY" on the top of its employment form. The president asserts this is designed to protect the integrity of the religious identity of the organization. Of course, private religious groups can make such employment decisions with privately solicited funds. However, the constitutional and moral calculus changes when tax dollars enter the equation. It is wrong to create a system where you can be taxed to help pay for a job you cannot get even if you are eminently qualified for the position. I have never found that a Methodist ladles out stew in a soup kitchen differently from a Hindu, nor do Baptists change the bedsheets in a homeless shelter using a different methodology than a nonbeliever. The administration has poisoned the employment pool, aiding and abetting state officials who want to dole out tax dollars to discriminating organizations. For example, the Lambda Legal Defense Fund represents Alan Yorker, a psychotherapist who wanted to work at the Methodist Home for Children in Georgia. The Home functions as a residential foster care facility and is 40 percent funded by state taxpayers. When Mr. Yorker arrived at his job interview, he was asked to fill out an information form, and he placed the name of his rabbi and synagogue in the spaces labeled "Pastor" and "Church." When the Home's administrator reviewed it—oops—she said we don't hire Jews.[2] Another employee had been informed that the Home's practice was to "throw in the trash" resumes with "Jewish sounding names."[3] This is morally wrong. If you get government money you have to be open to hiring the best qualified person, without regard to religious opinion.

We have a similar complaint in our own suit against Iowa and the Prison Fellowship, where funds go to a prison ministry program that hires— and indeed only accepts as volunteers—evangelical Christians, but which gets virtually all of the funding for such "rehab" programs in that facility.

Second, there is growing doubt about who will in fact be getting these funds. When George Bush was campaigning for the presidency he said that groups promoting hate would not be eligible, specifically mentioning the Nation of Islam.[4] White House official Stephen Goldsmith, has said that Wiccans could not get funding because they were not "humane" enough to provide services like child care.[5] In America, we can personally have all kinds of biases based on our theological differences. We know that just by listening to Jerry Falwell, who has opined that Mohammed was a "terrorist" and "a virulent man of war." I once had to remind him, for the record, that there were a lot of people who thought Jerry was pretty hateful himself. But I cringe at the very idea that governments will put together lists of acceptable and unacceptable religions on the basis of the passion of their rhetoric or the idiosyncratic nature of their beliefs. Government seals of approval for faith serve as an exemplar of how little this administration understands about the First Amendment.

The flip side of this is that groups that are being courted by politicians could become the beneficiaries of government largess. Sadly, we don't need to speculate about this anymore: it happens. Last September, Secretary of Health and Human Services Tommy Thompson announced twenty-one grants out of the Compassion Capital Fund, a program that was set up solely for the purpose of funding "technical assistance" programs so that small charities could learn how to apply for public and private grants. Over five hundred grant applications for all kind of programs were received. Imagine my surprise when I discovered that one of the "winners" was the Reverend Pat Robertson's Operation Blessing, the beneficiary of over a half million dollars.[6] Could it be true that the most controversial TV preacher in America, who said that Americans had caused the World Trade Center attack and that Hindus are devil worshippers, was being funded? That Pat Robertson, who has a billion dollar endowment for his university alone, was getting one of these twenty-one grants? Operation Blessing is a tad controversial in its own right because it was caught diverting its medical missionary planes in Africa in order to pick up equipment for Pat's diamond mining company in Zaire.[7] Only a quick "refund" prevented a criminal prosecution in the state of Virginia. Anyway, half of this money will be used for his own program, and the rest will be distributed to other groups, ostensibly for "training." However, there is no real oversight of sub-grantees, so it will be hard to figure out where it goes or how it is used. But, here's my hunch: no Hindus will get any.

I don't want to beat up on Brother Robertson excessively, but this grant illustrates another curious point about the insidious nature of this initiative. When first announced, it was not only Barry Lynn who opposed it; so did Pat Robertson. He warned that any group that took federal funds would end up finding it to be a—his word—"narcotic."[8] He doesn't say that anymore. It is difficult for a religious institution to be on Caesar's dole and still speak critically of Caesar. How loud will the prophetic witness be if the prophet's microphones are purchased by the state?

A third trend is that the Faith-Based Initiative is becoming a perfect example of how governments try to palm off on private groups the problems they can't or won't fix themselves? I used to predict that this plan would amount to just dumping the poor on the church steps one day, dumping a small bag of money there the next day, and then praying the two find each other. That is now precisely what is happening. From the outset, the president's program itself contained infinitesimal additional funding, if any at all, for those in need. He seems to want to pit the current providers against a raft of new faith-based providers for the crumbs from an increasingly small slice of federal funding pie for human needs. In the first year of his Presidency, George Bush did things like "zero out" an entire program for inner city development.[9]

And nothing has changed in the current budget. About four hundred thousand people may be kicked off the low-income fuel-subsidy program, which primarily helps people to heat their homes in the winter. Now, think about this: If it is too cold to stay in your apartment because you have lost your heating subsidy, why should we be impressed if a small percentage of the newly homeless will be taken in by a federally funded faith-based homeless shelter? That is not compassion; that is just plain stupid.

Fourth, the blatantly political and partisan nature of this whole effort is abundantly clear. It was clear even before the first Faith-Based Director John Dilulio issued his scathing critique of the White House "Mayberry Machiavellis"—his phrase—in *Esquire* magazine. The administration has been setting up how-to seminars to lure people, particularly African American pastors, into hearing about this "faith money," as one speaker puts it, and believing they will actually get some of it.[10] The locations of these efforts, though, made for a very suspicious pattern in advance of the recent elections. They were overwhelmingly being held in congressional districts deemed pivotal in the Republican effort to retain control of the House, or in states like Florida with highly competitive gubernatorial elections. In South Carolina, the event was actually cosponsored by the state Republican Party—the invitation to the Democratic Party there apparently lost in the mail.[11] This is the worst kind of politicizing of the church. This administration knows, though, that the church can be tempted just like anyone else and sometimes give in. Whenever I made this allegation during the last electoral cycle, Jim Towey and his staff would deny it. You know where Mr. Towey spent Election Night 2002 according to the *Miami Herald*? Watching the returns with Gov. Jeb Bush and his family![12]

Fifth, the administration is already paving the way for implicit and explicit restrictions on the content of religious programs that will be eligible for funding. For example, several grants have now gone to Christian groups for "strengthening marriage." For most religious groups, marriage is a sacrament. When the government funds a program that teaches that divorce is never acceptable in the eyes of God, doesn't this in fact give government blessing to certain theological beliefs? It is absolutely inevitable that grants will eventually be awarded after a review process that includes consideration of the theologies that undergird the potential recipients' programs.

This is already occurring in other programs involving intimate personal matters. Funding for community- and school-based sex education may only go to organizations that teach "abstinence only before marriage," not merely that abstinence is preferable. One program in Louisiana has been successfully challenged in federal court because tax dollars are paying for a blatantly fundamentalist curriculum.[13] If we go one step further and restrict the content of a program run by a faith-based group, you are effectively giving preferential treatment and funding to some theological viewpoints over others.

It is not only "liberals" who worry about this. Columnist Joseph Farah complained recently that some "faith-based money" might end up going through the Department of Energy to religious groups that have left-wing environmental views.[14] After all, many denominational structures actually believe in "global warming"; the National Council of Churches actually got behind that "What Would Jesus Drive?" campaign challenging the auto industry's apparent belief in the God-given right of every man, woman, and driving-age child on the planet to own an SUV.[15] Ladies and Gentlemen, we cannot allow a system that makes funding decisions in part based on parallels between an administration's secular policy goals and a religious group's theological and ethical understanding. That is the road we are traveling.

We now know that the president wants to help more persons who are substance-addicted by giving them vouchers so they can go to any treatment program they want,[16] including those that believe that addiction is "sin," pure and simple, and reject even a medical component to their programs. The Louisiana-based group he praised in his State of the Union address is in that category.[17] Again, we cannot fund religious conversions, even if that had a temporary side benefit of stopping a person from substance abuse. The successful court challenge of one of the Wisconsin Faith Works programs makes that clear.[18] Of course, we don't know whether these untested programs even have that secondary effect, but to this administration that doesn't appear to matter very much. How does a homeless street addict know where to go with her voucher to get real help? Will *U.S. News and World Report* do an issue on best addiction programs like they now do one on best graduate schools? Many of us have worked with persons with addiction challenges at some time in our careers. These are frequently people for whom the very idea of "choosing" services is an absurd proposition. Of course, this is the same administration that believes if we just privatized Social Security my eighty-eight-year-old mother could go back to picking stocks to pay for her nursing home care.

Last month, the nation learned that the administration would be allowing federal housing department dollars to be used for the partial construction of houses of worship. Here's the theory: If you want to build an annex to the church, which contains a Sunday school room and a counseling center, a portion of the walls, mortar, and roofing tiles equivalent to the space used for secular purposes will be eligible for taxpayer funding. Now think about this. First, in 1971 the Supreme Court ruled that church-related colleges couldn't even get construction grants for mixed-use, religious and secular, campus buildings. It went further by upholding a requirement that any college that accepted the funds for secular purposes had to guarantee that the building would be used secularly in perpetuity. If the Constitution doesn't permit campus construction, what is the administration thinking when it comes up with building grants for mosques, temples, churches, and synagogues? In America, we build our places of worship and mission with our own dimes and dollars, not those of our neighbors who choose some other path to enlightenment and/or salvation. Just a final practical note: How do we monitor the percentage of "religious" use? Perhaps we could divert those red-light-runner spy cams to the vestibule. Maybe even bring in the currently unemployed Enron auditors.

Sixth, and finally, we have mounting evidence that significant damage is being done to current ecumenical efforts and other community initiatives:

As one example, in a public display of animosity, two African American leaders in Louisville, Kentucky, had a difference of opinion about the value of the Faith-Based Initiative. In letters and news articles, one labeled the other a "hustler" and a "Judas," while the other responded that his critic was "discombobulated," had not read the Bible, and was actually a "Judas" himself. So much for harmony among the peoples of God.

In a second incident, a homeless shelter for veterans west of Boston was told that its federal grant was being cut from previous years so substantially that almost fifty percent of the beds would be eliminated. Their lost funds were now to go to several "faith-based" shelters in Utah and North Carolina. A veteran's activist told the *Boston Globe* bluntly that this meant more people in Massachusetts would be out in the cold and, quote, "more people will die."[19] This is what happens when you look at the wrong problem in the first place: The problem in America is the needs of human beings crying for help, not the false claim, the lie, that "faith based organizations" have not had a level playing field, so we should make up for it by punishing secular groups. The Salvation Army—a religious denomination—would barely exist if it wasn't for the tax dollars of the American people.

This whole program is so tempting though, in spite of what I have just said. However, notwithstanding the State of the Union address where the President spoke of funding everything from AIDS projects in Africa to hydrogen-powered cars, we know that the public is never going to support the level of taxation necessary to accomplish that and everything else. Therefore, we must keep private philanthropy alive and well. I remain concerned that one unintended consequence of the Faith-Based Initiative will actually be a reduction in voluntary faith community giving to others. If Uncle Sam is paying for the Presbyterian Wednesday night dinner for the homeless in your church, won't a few of your parishioners think about skimping on that pledge for next year? But how do you get it back when Uncle Sam likes the Methodist program across the street more than yours next year, and you lose that grant you got this year?

OK, I admit it. I don't like the Faith-Based Initiative. In fact, it should crawl back in a hole before it does any more damage to the integrity of our civil rights laws, the First Amendment, or the faith communities of America. It is about time sensible people reject the idea that the president's "armies of compassion" can get their marching orders from the church but expect their rations from the taxpayers.

In 2003, the White House Office of Faith-Based and Community Initiatives issued the report entitled, "Protecting the Civil Rights and Religious Liberty of Faith-Based Organizations: Why Religious Hiring Must Be Preserved," outlining the administration's Faith-Based Initiative and again setting out its ill-conceived arguments as to why it allows organizations to discriminate with government funds. In that same year, then president Bush issued Executive Order 13279, which provided for hiring discrimination in religious institutions, even if they are receiving government contracts. This was a drastic departure from existing law and overrode an executive order issued by Lyndon B. Johnson, which required all federal contractors, including faith-based organizations, to hire without regard to religion.

In 2007, the Office of Legal Counsel (OLC) for the Department of Justice issued a memo asserting that faith-based organizations have a right under the Religious Freedom Restoration Act (RFRA), to engage in employment discrimination with federal funds. The memo concluded that RFRA could be "reasonably construed" to allow a faith-based organization providing social services to be exempt from statutory restrictions on religious hiring, even if the statute contained an explicit antidiscrimination provision.

So, this was where we left it at the end of the George W. Bush administration. But candidate Barack Obama had expressed a deep sense of concern about the hiring discrimination issue on the campaign trail in the summer of 2008 and we went into high gear at Americans United to try to flesh out how to implement his apparent interest in "fixing" the system—although we had scant hope that he would terminate it. By February of 2009, however, it was sickeningly clear that few if any changes would be made—but there was still the tantalizing possibility that some other issues might get resolved later by the Department of Justice.

Faith-Based Folly: Obama's Executive Order Leaves Much to Be Desired[20]

Thursday, February 5, 2009, was not an ordinary day at Americans United. It was a day that could have been an historic and positive one for the separation of church and state. Indeed, it started by having the president of the United States affirming his strong support for that very concept at the National Prayer Breakfast, a private event held at a Washington, DC, hotel.

Unfortunately, not long after saying that, Barack Obama announced he would soon be signing an executive order creating a kind of refurbished White House office on faith-based initiatives, to replace the one originally created by George W. Bush.

Even with changes, I thought the office would be deeply problematic because it is so difficult to monitor the actual use of funds and figure out when a "spiritual" activity was being funded by private dollars and when by taxpayer dollars. However, candidate Obama sure seemed to be moving in several positive directions.

In the days leading up to the February announcement, we heard many rumors and reports, often in conflict, about exactly what rules Obama would establish in his executive order. AU Director of Legislative Affairs Aaron Schuham and his staff had many visits and calls with Obama staffers to lay out our case.

All we could do was wait. I began to get suspicious that things weren't going well when National Public Radio contacted me for comment. An official with the evangelical Christian organization World Vision claimed that Obama had indicated that he would not repeal a Bush executive order allowing religious groups to take tax funds and still discriminate on religious grounds when hiring.

Obama signed his executive order several hours after the Prayer Breakfast, in a private ceremony with no reporters present. The release of the order was delayed by several hours, but it was finally made public at about two in the afternoon.

What a shocking disappointment!

Here was an order setting up a faith-based office and a council of "advisors" (mostly clergy), with no roadmap for what they were supposed to do. There was no sentence that said that this council must work strictly within the confines of the First Amendment and in concert with the civil rights principles of our nation.

Worse, not one of the Bush-era executive orders was overturned, including the one giving religious groups a "right" to take public funds and still discriminate when hiring staff. It read as if the twenty-six-year-old Pentecostal minister who was named executive director of the faith-based office was just supposed to make up whatever rules he wanted.

It made it pretty hard to figure out how to even respond to the press— not usually one of my problems. Did Obama break his promise from Ohio? I noted that it was, at least, a "promise unfulfilled." Did this mean that a Christian group receiving funds for food distribution could say they would hire no Jewish or atheist truck drivers to deliver the produce?

Well, yes, since the old regulations were still in place. Could proselytism occur in these programs? I said I hoped not—but nothing in this order prohibited it.

The order did state that some of these issues might be submitted to the US Justice Department for review. What would happen there, reporters wanted to know. I could only say what I wished would happen—a ruling that hiring bias with tax funds is always wrong.

This was a real nightmare. And we didn't have to have it. The solution to these legal questions should be apparent. As US Rep. Bobby Scott of Virginia put it to me, "You are either against religious discrimination or you are for it." How could Obama answer any way but "against"?

I think Obama has fallen prey to bad advice. The president seemed convinced that religious charities cannot function without the authority to hire people who are "like them," even to do the most menial tasks. That's the same bogus reason that people have always given to justify discrimination: people like eating in lunchrooms with members of the same race; business passengers are "more comfortable" seeing stewardesses in skirts than male flight attendants.

In the case of government programs, however, are we taxpayers supposed to concur with such use of our dollars? Not at all.

A lesbian plaintiff in an ongoing AU-sponsored lawsuit challenging faith-based abuses put it well.

"If a group can discriminate against me because of my orientation," she said, "I can't even get a job I helped pay for with my taxes."

Sadly, that is precisely what will happen if the president doesn't get this right, and get it right soon.

So, the gamesmanship of the Obama administration's faith-based office continued.

New "faith czar" Joshua DuBois held a number of meetings to garner support for the idea in principle and announce the twenty-five-member "advisory council" for the presidential initiative. He also noted that there would be "task forces" set up to assist the advisory council and that I would be on one of them, dealing with the "constitutional and legal basis for the office." This was a lengthy and unsuccessful process.

In 2010, I wrote a scathing piece about all this for the *Huffington Post*. This led to a blistering phone call from Joshua DuBois that evening while my wife was driving me home in her Prius (now you know what a tree-hugger I really am).

FAITH, HOPE, AND CHARITY: WHY PRESIDENT OBAMA'S "FAITH-BASED" AGENDA MUST CHANGE[21]

I am not a member of the president's twenty-five-member Advisory Council on Faith-Based and Neighborhood Partnerships, the body Obama formed one year ago to examine these issues. But I did serve on a task force offering the Council advice on a range of questions.

During our deliberations, I often found myself on the other side from conservative religious activists, who resisted even the most benign and reasonable rules that would safeguard the rights of taxpayers and the disadvantaged as well as help preserve the constitutional separation of church and state.

For example, I argued that all public funds that go to a house of worship to operate social services should be handled by a separately incorporated nonprofit—or at least be kept in a separate bank account so we can keep track of how the money is spent. A 2006 report by the Government Accountability Office examined faith-based offices in several federal agencies and found a lack of oversight of these programs.[22]

I also urged that publicly funded social services should not take place in a space where sectarian symbols or signs might make some disadvantaged people feel unwelcome. (Think of the homeless gay man who thinks of a large cross in a space providing dinner as the same icon wielded by Pastor Fred Phelps the last time he was in town to tell gays that they would be heading to hell.)

Conservative religious representatives on the Council disagreed. They want sectarian groups to have access to plenty of government money with very little (if any) meaningful accountability. That's the status quo; they like it.

Worse yet, some of the Council members appointed by President Obama are powerful religious lobbyists whose denominations and groups benefit handsomely from government funds. They include representatives from the US Conference of Catholic Bishops, Catholic Charities, the Union of Orthodox Jewish Congregations, and the evangelical charity World Vision.

Government databases indicate that Catholic Charities (including its various affiliates) has taken at least $521 million over the last ten years. The Catholic bishops' conference has corralled $304.8 million over the same period, and World Vision has taken in $405.9 million. Orthodox Union-affiliated synagogues and Jewish schools have also benefited from millions in federal grants, though government reporting methods make the precise figure impossible to ascertain.

Wouldn't this be a conflict of interest by any ethical standard?

But, aside from the Council, other faith-based policies in the Obama administration are just as problematic. When Americans United urged the Department of Justice (DOJ) to discontinue Bush-era funding for four fundamentalist groups that openly discriminate and proselytize, DOJ attorneys brushed aside the request. These organizations, they assured AU, had been told not to violate the law.

The DOJ, so far, has even refused to overturn a Bush-era memo that gives faith-based charities a sweeping "religious liberty" right to engage in employment bias in all federally funded programs.

Don't think this doesn't matter in the real world or that it's all a theoretical spat among policy wonks obsessed with arcane Beltway regulations. The *Global Post* recently ran a troubling story about World Vision, which received $281 million in government grants in 2008 —yet offers full-time employment only to Christians who fit the group's creed.[23]

The story makes it clear that people in other countries are being denied jobs in US-funded programs because World Vision is discriminatory. As Torrey Olsen, World Vision's Senior Director for Christian Engagement, put it, "We do want to be witnesses to Jesus Christ by life, word, deed and sign."[24] Fabiano Franz, another World Vision official, added, "We're very clear from the beginning about hiring Christians. It's not a surprise, so it's not discrimination."[25]

Why is government—which is supported by taxpayers of many faiths and none —subsidizing such bias and evangelistic activity?

Dissatisfaction with Obama's inaction on this issue is widespread. On February 4, 2010, twenty-five national religious and public-policy organizations sent a letter to Obama, urging him to fix the faith-based initiative. The groups range from the American Association of University Women, the Human Rights Campaign, and the National Association for the Advancement of Colored People to the American Jewish Committee, the Baptist Joint Committee for Religious Liberty, and the United Methodist Church, General Board of Church and Society.

These groups have grown impatient with Obama, as have I, for leaving the odious Bush faith-based scheme in place substantially unchanged.

Our persistent efforts to convince the President to alter his faith-based initiative have, to date, largely failed.

IT'S TIME FOR OBAMA TO FIX THE FAITH-BASED INITIATIVE[26]

The White House is now pondering recommendations offered by its Advisory Council on Faith-Based and Neighborhood Partnerships. I've written here before about inappropriate financial self-interest on the part of numerous members of that Council. However, what were the overall merits and demerits of the final report presented to President Barack Obama in the Oval Office on March 9?

Many of the issues the Council tackled resulted in consensus recommendations that I support. First, the Council urged strengthening the rules requiring the separation of religion from government-funded programs. Any federally funded program must be separated in time or space from any religious activity in a facility. People being served have a right to refuse to attend any religious activity occurring there. The Council also asks the President to adopt separation rules that would be applied to all federally funded programs and to vast numbers of sub-grantees as well.

Second, the Council unanimously urged the President to strengthen protections for social-service beneficiaries. The recommendations state that beneficiaries who attend publicly funded programs operated by faith-based organizations must have a right to an alternative religious or secular provider and must be informed of this right when they first enter the program.

Third, the Council urged the President to increase transparency and monitoring. Council members admitted that "it has not been easy for us to locate and access information" and documents.[27] Imagine, then, how difficult it would be for an average citizen to find grant applications or documents. Thus, the Council requested that government agencies be required to post information, including the identification of recipient groups, on the internet. The Council acknowledged that the government has a "constitutional obligation to monitor and enforce church-state standards" in federally funded programs.[28]

Posting information about who received grants and how the money will be used would make it easier for civil liberties activists to get a heads-up on grants that seem constitutionally or otherwise legally suspect. For example, a US Government Accountability Office investigation indicated that many religiously oriented groups that got grants and contracts during the last administration flagrantly ignored prohibitions on using funds to promote their religious beliefs.[29] (Some were reportedly surprised to learn they had any restrictions.) We have found groups using public funds to purchase Bibles and Jesus keychains, and some faith-based ministries take public funding for "secular" efforts while proudly proclaiming on their internet sites that they are Christ-focused 24/7.

To my disappointment, however, the Council failed to reach consensus on two major issues. By only a one-vote margin, the Council recommended that houses of worship that seek to receive federal funds must form separately incorporated entities to use them. (This could include setting up a tax-exempt 501(c)(3) charity or other appropriate structure.) This is necessary to protect the autonomy and integrity of the religious institution as well as ensure that federal funds are not used for religious purposes.

Opponents claimed this would be too burdensome. Curiously, however, no evidence was actually offered that any groups would decline federal aid if required to set up a secular arm.

Most troubling is that sixteen Council members asserted that "the administration should neither require nor encourage the removal of religious symbols where services subsidized by Federal grant or contract funds are provided."[30] In the view of most scholars, the Constitution forbids government to send religious messages to beneficiaries participating in publicly funded programs through signs, symbols, or iconography. Only nine members of the Council, however, supported a standard mandating that such religious messages be removed, at least where "feasible."

Why is this such a big deal?

Frankly, the whole point of separating evangelism from secular services, such as serving meals and providing job training, is that rock-solid First Amendment doctrine forbids government entities to advance religion. What is a more potent promotion of any religious system than having the central symbols of that faith (a Christian cross, for example, or religious statements like "Jesus said, 'I am the Way, the Truth and the Life'") on the walls of a soup kitchen or counseling center?

Many religious groups promote the idea that a single encounter with the core message of the faith can lead to spiritual conversion. Is someone seeking shelter going to have the courage to report that this faith-saturated environment makes her or his children feel unwelcome and very uncomfortable? And, in most parts of the country, how long will it take to even locate some alternative provider? In reality, her real choice may be whether to face the symbols of a faith not her own or go cold and hungry.

The Council report and the process for faith-based reform are now back in the president's hands. There should be no more studying, and no more delays. I hope that President Obama will act expeditiously to fulfill his campaign promises to place the faith-based office on sound footing.

This means accepting the Council's good recommendations (which were agreed to by every Council member from the past president of the Southern Baptist Convention to the religious outreach director of the Human Rights Campaign) and toughening the ones I've addressed here.

We've seen lately that executive orders—even on contentious issues—can literally be written overnight. That's all it would take here.

I really don't want to get too deeply "into the weeds" here. But the bottom line is that the Advisory Council report mentioned above, with its twelve unanimous recommendations and its above-noted deficiencies was the basis for a number of what could loosely be called "procedural next steps." An interagency working group was supposed to examine this document and come up with a report within 120 days. It eventually, and somewhat belatedly, reported back in April of 2012. Sixteen months later, the Office of Management and Budget (OMB) issued a memo advising agencies to develop regulations and guidance on how to implement the president's program that were "consistent with the Working Group's model guidance."[31] The director of the president's Faith-Based Office has been meeting with members of each agency to draft and promulgate new regulations. Public comments will then be accepted so that agencies can consider editing their regulations. After public comment, the agencies will issue final rules. It should be noted that the president will leave office in January of 2016.

Obviously, faith-based-hiring changes have also not occurred to date. The Department of Justice still relies on the Bush-era OLC memo that allows religious organizations to engage in "preferential" (I call it "discriminatory") hiring with taxpayer dollars. Lest there be any mistake about that, an FAQ (frequently asked questions) document for the Department of Justice issued in 2014 regarding implementation of the Violence Against Women Act—which specifically prohibits religious discrimination—allowed the same kind of "preferential" hiring mentioned in the OLC memo.[32]

FAITH-BASED PROCRASTINATION: RELIGIOUS JOB BIAS IN TAXPAYER-FUNDED PROGRAMS[33]

No American should be denied a taxpayer-funded job because of what he or she believes about religion. Yet that's exactly what is happening today under the "faith-based" initiative. It's wrong, and it is time for it to stop.

The idea of awarding tax aid to religious groups to run various secular programs for people in need is not new. As a strict advocate of separation of church and state, I'm not a huge fan of the idea, but courts have permitted such public aid under certain conditions.

What is new is the insistence that religious groups can take tax aid and still engage in overt discrimination on religious grounds when hiring staff. This concept was aggressively promoted by the administration of President George W. Bush. It was a bad idea then, and it hasn't improved with age.

However, Joshua DuBois, executive director of the White House Office of Faith-Based and Neighborhood Partnerships, at a recent Brookings Institution gathering, did note that the pesky hiring issue was officially "entirely unresolved."

I'd call this a "close but no cigar" assessment of what is actually going on. I have no doubt that the administration didn't want to resolve the hiring issue in the midst of a campaign where every opponent of the president had declared him the lead general in some completely nonexistent "war on religion."

For several years, though, Obama administration officials have said that any discriminatory hiring in federally funded programs would be assessed on a "case-by-case" basis—although they didn't disclose what standards were to be used to make or break the "case." Standardless reviews are usually referred to as "doing whatever you want," not a well-known constitutional or administrative law standard.

At the Brookings event, DuBois acknowledged that "the policy is as it was before."[34] This has meant that a religious grant-seeker could simply assert—you might say "self-certify"—that it believed its religious practice would be "burdened" by not being allowed to take government funds and discriminate with them.

The Justice Department has acknowledged it affirmatively permitted nine grantees to use religion to discriminate in 2009 alone. There is no information on how many more of these waivers have been granted by other agencies or whether anyone's "self-certified" assessment had been rejected.

Many people have heard that it is a burden to have to hire openly and without regard to some particular attribute. It's an old argument. Airlines used to say they didn't want to hire men as flight attendants because the then-overwhelmingly male business travelers felt more "comfortable" with service from pretty young women in skirts.

Comfort level in these instances has long been rejected as a legally permissible standard. Yet some religious voices of today make spiritual camaraderie a basis for using taxpayer dollars from all to hire only from a pool of those just like them. Under the faith-based initiative, this is elevated to some kind of constitutional rights claim instead of being relegated to the dustbin of invidious discrimination.

Our country first committed itself to the principle that no one should be disqualified from government-funded jobs because of his or her religion in 1941, when President Franklin D. Roosevelt signed an executive order ending such discrimination.

Subsequent presidents—Republican and Democrat alike—recommitted themselves to this principle over the next several decades. As President John F. Kennedy explained, "[I]t is the plain and positive obligation of the United States government to promote and ensure equal opportunity for all qualified persons, without regard to race, creed, color, or national origin, employed or seeking employment . . . on government contracts."[35]

After this longstanding national commitment to nondiscrimination was repudiated by the Bush administration, I was heartened in 2008, when, as a presidential candidate, Obama promised to return to our old principles.

"If you get a federal grant," he said during a speech in Ohio, "you can't use that grant money to proselytize to the people you help and you can't discriminate against them—or against the people you hire—on the basis of their religion."

Fulfilling that commitment should not be so hard. It would be a simple acknowledgment that Bush had been wrong in his failure to adhere to a decades-old commitment to a civil rights framework that didn't allow religious discrimination either.

Much was made at Brookings of the work the current White House faith-based office does to encourage interfaith dialogue and programs in the United States and around the world. There was even a hint that this might help national security—and, yes, it might.

But it could also backfire. Is US prestige overseas enhanced when we give tens of millions of dollars to groups like World Vision, an evangelical outfit active around the globe—even in predominately Hindu or Muslim nations— that requires employees to sign a Trinitarian Christian statement of faith?

More to the point, how can any administration make a case, with a straight face, that our national values are respected when some religious employers can receive taxpayer money even as they figuratively or literally post signs reading, "Help Wanted. No Jews, Muslims, or Hindus Need Apply?"

Organizations—religious or otherwise—that take government money must abide by certain rules. That some religious groups don't want to follow the rules does not mean their religious freedom rights have been violated; they aren't entitled to these funds, nor are they required to take them. The organization can continue to do their work and discriminate with their own money.

The government should not fund efforts to use religion to discriminate. We must protect the religious freedom of our government employees and stand for the principle of nondiscrimination.

In July 2014, President Obama signed an executive order barring federal contractors from discriminating in hiring on the basis of sexual orientation or gender identity. Even though when the order was initially proposed, some religious groups immediately called for an exemption for "faith-based" organizations. Americans United joined with ninety-eight religious, civil rights, women's, LGBT, secular, and other groups in a letter urging Obama to reject those demands.

The President ultimately agreed with us. This executive order makes no exemption for religious groups, which we hailed as a step in the right direction.

Still hanging out there like a pernicious hangnail is the option that faith-based groups that accept federal contracts be allowed to prefer members of their own faith in hiring—under that executive order that dates from the George W. Bush presidency. Of course, it may be very difficult to figure out if "religious" preference is not merely a cover for anti-LGBT bigotry.

RELIGIOUS REFUSALS: "WE DON'T HAVE TO OBEY THE CIVIL LAW BECAUSE . . ."

Religious groups have consistently sought exemptions from laws of general applicability. Indeed, they have sought to be excluded from the requirements of licensing daycare providers, zoning regulations, and nondiscriminatory hiring. They also have asked for tax exemptions relating to everything from property tax and tax-exempt bond financing to sales tax on religious publications.

Are all of these "special privileges" necessary? Almost certainly not. Indeed, very few "exemptions" have been reviewed by federal courts and, in some instances, special treatment has been ruled unconstitutional.

In 1982, an Amish employer famously sued the US government, claiming that he should not have to pay Social Security taxes for his employees of any religious background because individual Amish do not contribute to, nor benefit from, the Social Security program. The Supreme Court disagreed, stating that the Social Security tax for employees was not an infringement upon the employer's rights.[36]

But in 2014, a new and sweeping construct hit the news—related specifically to the Affordable Care Act (aka "Obamacare") and its coverage of insurance for contraceptives.

Silent Witness: House Panel Can't Handle the Truth from Sandra Fluke—or Me[37]

I was once, literally, a footnote to history. In an important Supreme Court decision involving the military draft, Justice William Brennan (sadly, in dissent, as he so often was) cited some of my testimony on this topic to a House of Representatives committee.

Well, I am now a metaphorical footnote to a matter that could be of even greater consequence. On February 16, Democrats on the House Oversight and Government Reform Committee asked whether I would consider testifying on a hearing about "religious freedom" that the Republican majority had convened.

The hearing was really about the controversy over the Obama administration's decision to require religiously affiliated institutions to contract with insurance companies that would offer birth control at no cost to those employees who want it. Even though the policy doesn't require religious groups to pay for contraceptives directly, some clergy claim it violates their right of conscience.

I've testified at a lot of congressional hearings over the years. This one struck me as particularly strange. The Democrats requested two witnesses, while the Republican majority was planning on at least eight. Originally, the Republican witnesses were all men.

I was happy to learn that my co-witness would be a woman named Sandra Fluke, a third-year student at my alma mater, Georgetown Law Center, who had been speaking out against Georgetown's policy, which has the effect of denying contraceptive coverage even for women who need it for life-threatening medical reasons.

US Rep. Darrell Issa (R-CA), chair of the committee, decided that Fluke would not be allowed to testify. Around four in the afternoon the day before the hearing, Issa told the Democrats that Fluke was not "qualified" to appear as a witness and that they could have one witness only—me.

The morning of the hearing, Issa stated that I was "clearly qualified," although he pointed out that he doesn't agree with me. He also noted that I'm not a woman. (He didn't have to tell me that.)

I rejected his offer to be the only witness for the Democrats because, frankly, I wanted a woman to testify and believed that if there was to be one witness on our side, it should be Fluke. She had a compelling story to tell, and I thought the nation should hear it. The hearing went on with no witness debunking the phony "religious freedom" claims of the Catholic hierarchy and other conservatives.

The rest is history. The male-dominated, one-sided hearing was a disaster for the GOP, and Fluke later offered her testimony to a separate hearing held by the Democrats. The articulate and poised Fluke was already attracting a lot of media attention before talk-radio bloviator Rush Limbaugh decided to launch an ignorant and vile personal attack on her. That also backfired, leading Limbaugh to offer an insincere apology in a desperate (and unsuccessful) attempt to stop dozens of advertisers from fleeing his show like the proverbial rats on a sinking ship.

The only downside to being a footnote in this saga is that I never got the opportunity to tell Congress why it should reject the religious freedom claims being made in this case. I did submit written testimony to Issa's committee, but it would have been nice to say it in person.

If current political and legal trends continue, more and more Americans may find that their healthcare hinges not on what their doctors think is best for them but what their bosses believe about religion.

This curious state of affairs stems from a deliberate attempt to redefine religious freedom in America. You read that right—religious liberty. A freedom that has historically been interpreted as an individual right of self-determination is being twisted into a means of controlling others and meddling in their most personal affairs.

Religious Liberty and the Coming Corporate Theocracy[38]

Later this month, the US Supreme Court will hear oral arguments in a pair of cases concerning Americans' access to birth control. Specifically, the high court will decide whether an employer who has a sincere religious objection to contraceptives can refuse to provide them to employees, even though the Affordable Care Act mandates otherwise.

Birth control is widely used in this country, so how did we get to this point where access to it may be imperiled for millions of Americans under a strange theory of "religious liberty"?

To answer that question, we have to go all the way back to 1990. That's the year the Supreme Court handed down a decision in a case called *Employment Division v. Smith*. The reaction to that ruling is a tale of good intentions gone awry.

The Smith case dealt with two Native American drug counselors who were fired from their jobs because they had used peyote, a kind of hallucinogenic cactus, in religious rituals. The two argued that they had a right, under the First Amendment's "free exercise" of religion guarantee, to engage in this activity and should not have been punished for it.

The Supreme Court disagreed. Furthermore, the court said religious groups and individuals must abide by generally applicable laws that are on their face neutral—that is, not aimed at specific religious practices. Justice Antonin Scalia warned that allowing people to pick and choose which laws they would follow on the basis of religion "would be courting anarchy."

Some people thought this went too far. After all, some things religious people want to do are rather harmless and pose no threat to society, such as wearing religious garb or certain types of head coverings (yarmulkes and turbans, for example).

Many organizations from across the political spectrum came together to seek federal legislation that would remedy this problem. After a few years of squabbling, they worked with legislators to produce the Religious Freedom Restoration Act (RFRA). President Bill Clinton signed it into law in 1993.

RFRA requires governments to demonstrate a "compelling state interest" before infringing in a "substantial" way on anyone's religious liberty, as well as prove that it has employed the "least restrictive" means available to achieve its policy goal.

Most of the advocates for this bill didn't actually want to commit to whether this new law would have protected the drug counselors who got in trouble. Instead people bemoaned that under the high court's more restrictive definition of religious liberty, Muslim firefighters were being denied the right to wear beards in some jurisdictions and historic preservation laws were being used to tell churches they couldn't modify their architecture because of the "historical value" of the original edifice. The purpose of RFRA was to address these types of problems. It was never intended to do the things people are now saying it does, such as give secular for-profit corporations the right to meddle in the private medical choices of their employees.

RFRA was declared unconstitutional insofar as it affected state laws in 1997, but it still applies to the federal government. This is the statute that is being cited by the owners of secular businesses, like the craft store chain Hobby Lobby and Conestoga Wood Corporation, which don't want to provide their employees with certain types of contraceptives.

The heads of these companies have religious objections to using certain artificial birth control, and they argue that those personal views should be transferred to their corporate entity. Essentially, they assert that for-profit companies that are not even remotely engaged in religious activities can nevertheless claim a kind of "corporate conscience" that trumps the individual moral decision-making of their employees.

Many people thought it absurd when the Supreme Court gave a broad panoply of "free speech rights" to corporations in the Citizens United case in 2010. But corporations do "speak"—that's how they spend $1.5 million dollars on sixty-second commercials during the Super Bowl.

But to assert that corporations also have religious freedom rights is to stretch credulity to the breaking point. Who has ever noticed a corporation sitting next to them in a church pew? Does a corporation-made wooden chair robustly sing "Nearer My God to Thee" during Sunday services? Probably not.

Scalia warned of anarchy. I don't often agree with the combative justice, but he was right about that. If the Supreme Court interprets RFRA broadly, it could issue a decision allowing secular businesses to lay claim to the religious freedom rights meant for individuals. If not anarchy, that would certainly spawn a generous amount of chaos.

Let's start with some modest steps down the slippery slope. A business run by a Scientologist could claim exemption from covering mental health counseling from Scientology's nemesis, the psychiatric profession. How about Jehovah's Witness-owned corporations bowing out of coverage for surgeries because so many of them require use of whole blood products prohibited for use by members of that church?

More examples: Some Christians adhere to the doctrine that "For a husband is the head of his wife as Christ is the head of the church" (Ephesians 5:23). Let's say your boss takes this literally. Can he reject the thesis of the Equal Pay Act because that would deny him the ability to pay men—more likely to be or become husbands in charge of the family—more than women?

How about those fundamentalists who adhere to prohibitions against eating pork and shellfish found in the Book of Leviticus? Can they demand that employees sign agreements that even off the job site they will limit themselves to red meat and poultry?

It is very difficult to imagine how courts could draw the line between failing to provide contraceptive services (viewed as a mandated service in the Affordable Care Act) and running their companies along their other biblically complicit strictures.

But it gets even worse. Much ink was spilled commenting on a recent bill in Arizona that many say would have given religious fundamentalists who own businesses the right to deny services to LGBTQ people. Gov. Jan Brewer vetoed the measure, but versions of it have appeared in other states.

The justifiable fear by non-Christian religious minorities, nontheists, and members of the LGBTQ community was that this would create a gigantic loophole in local public accommodation statutes so that a hotel owner, restaurant owner, etc. could refuse to allow certain members of the public to eat at Joe's Diner or stay at the Honeymoon Haven Hotel. It would have been a backdoor to a kind of "Jim Crow 2.0," allowing discrimination based on religious beliefs.

Lest one believe this result "unthinkable," remember that in the 1960s some fundamentalist pastors in the Deep South preached separation of the races as a God-ordained plan. (After all, Genesis 1:4 says God separated the light from the dark.)

Arizona's bill died, but some state legislators are holding off until they see the result in the Hobby Lobby case. If the justices uphold the demanded exemption from contraceptive coverage, state politicos will find it dazzlingly simple to justify allowing all businesses to make judgments on religious beliefs, doctrinal or idiosyncratic. Religion will then trump all but the most gigantic of governmental interests.

So, anarchy could be coming to your neighborhood soon—and it will all start with birth control restrictions. On second thought, it could be worse than anarchy. If giant corporations win the right to void participation in all laws with which they disagree merely by adopting a religious patina, the result will be something worse.

In these times when it is so difficult to determine where governmental power and corporate potency separate, maybe an exercise in corporate theology would lead to something other than anarchy—a thing called "theocracy."

So what happened in the Hobby Lobby case? Here is how I described it to a Unitarian Fellowship in Ann Arbor, Michigan, in the fall of 2014:

From the very beginning of this contraception battle, the Obama administration never wanted to require churches, seminaries, and other pervasively religious institutions of any size to cover birth control drugs. Subsequently, religiously affiliated entities like Catholic hospitals or evangelical colleges—where official dogma opposes birth control—were also exempted from having to cover contraception if they merely signed and mailed in a 737-word form in which they declared their moral opposition to such coverage. In those cases, the federal government guaranteed that women affected by their institution's "opt out" would be given free coverage from some other entity. Finally, though, for-profit secular companies headed by persons with personal religious objections to some or all birth control methods had to obey the law and provide coverage. That's the way the system was established.

Hobby Lobby is a national arts and crafts chain, whose website advertises such spiritual items as pink flamingo wind chimes and do-it-yourself garden gnome cross-stitch kits, and Conestoga Wood, a wood products and furniture company in Pennsylvania. They said: We don't want anything to do with funding some forms of contraception because we think it is immoral and in fact we think that most birth control is just another form of abortion. Hobby Lobby won its case making that argument in one federal appeals court; Conestoga Wood lost in another—this "conflict in the circuits" (as we lawyers like to put it) virtually invited the Supreme Court to resolve the matter.

The Supreme Court was asked to interpret a federal law called the Religious Freedom Restoration Act. The ACLU, for which I worked at the time, supported it; instrumentalities of the United Church of Christ supported it; and extremely conservative groups like Concerned Women for America supported it. This was a "kumbaya" moment. All of its authors thought it guaranteed that certain personal religious observances and activities could not be prohibited by governments: that a Jewish military chaplain could wear a yarmulke and that a Native American religious group could ingest an otherwise-prohibited hallucinogenic tea in important faith rituals.

But now, the companies that want these birth control exemptions insist that the statute be read to give them the right to say "no" to laws they don't happen to like—and, effectively, the collateral right to impose their own religious beliefs on others. This stretches the law beyond its intended purpose. I told the *Washington Post* recently that if, during the three years of drafting and moving this legislature to Bill Clinton's desk, anyone had said this law was about a crafts store telling its thousands of women employees they couldn't get insurance coverage for contraception, this coalition of support would "have exploded like a ripe watermelon hit by a shotgun blast."[39]

But the Supreme Court did. It ruled that under Religious Freedom Restoration Act, even some (we'll see later if it is "all") for-profit corporations could use their owners' religious beliefs to refuse to provide otherwise-required insurance coverage for methods of contraception.

Within this decision are the seeds of a huge problem for all kinds of people. The dissenting justices, including unsurprisingly all three women on the Court, had warned of a kind of "parade of horribles"[40] that could come—and in fact all the evidence is that the march has started. If a closely held corporation can deny one health-related benefit, why not others? What about companies that already exist who do not believe in the concept of "equal pay"? Here is their argument from Christian scripture: "Jesus is the head of the church; the husband is the head of the family; because the husband has more responsibility in a patriarchal culture, they must get paid more." And on and on it goes.

Some interesting issues arise from the decision itself about truth and sincerity. The "truth or falsity" of religious beliefs is not supposed to be an issue that is resolved by the courts, and I believe that is a good idea (some of you may not), but the Supreme Court said back in the 1940s that "sincerity of belief" is something that courts could explore. They did that in regard to the postal service charging something called the "I Am" movement with mail fraud for raising funds based on a belief about visiting saints in multiple layers of heaven, which the founders of the group didn't even believe was true.[41]

In Hobby Lobby, the argument used was that requiring coverage of four specific methods of contraception (out of twenty) violated its "conscience" because those four were abortion-inducing. That is more certainly "junk science," because the generally accepted view of how IUDs and "morning-after" pills work is that they prevent fertilization of egg by sperm, thus no "conception" in the first place. But you could argue that even if it is bad science, it is still a "religious" belief. No one ever questioned the sincerity of the claim—but in my judgment the administration should have.

If you want to be "purer than Caesar's wife" then you really need to avoid touching that which you think is immoral or sinful. By that test, Hobby Lobby is, in my view, insincere. It won't offer contraceptive choice to employees but it does allow a range of retirement plan investment choices to those same employees and some of the vehicles you can choose include investing in the very same pharmaceutical companies that make the contraceptives Hobby Lobby won't cover. And, before there was an Affordable Care Act, the company used to cover the very same contraceptives with which it now disapproves, claiming it wasn't aware that these forms of contraception were abortifacients—even though this was a widely promoted claim by evangelical fundamentalists for decades earlier. Then there is the small problem that they purchase hundreds of millions of dollars' worth of goods made in China, which still essentially has a forced-abortion policy after the birth of your first child. And then, finally, it is completely clear that if you make the most effective forms of contraception unavailable, it will lead to about 30 percent more unplanned pregnancies, and half of them will end in abortion. So if you are genuinely worried about abortion, you, Hobby Lobby, will have a lot of explaining to do.

But by now most of you know that medical issues are just the tip of the iceberg. There is absolutely nothing in the majority opinion of the Court that suggests that religious claims will be summarily dismissed when someone wants to have veto power over some federal law they don't want to follow, unless it is a claim about not paying taxes or engaging in race discrimination. Everything else is on the table, although Justice Kennedy wrote a separate opinion suggesting that he personally would be more cautious in supporting broad religious vetoes. How cautious? We don't know. What about motel chains that might decide not to rent rooms to same-gender couples—or unmarried couples (strike that: there would be very few rentals in that case)?

So what to do? Everything's possible. There is already a bill called "Not My Boss's Business," which seeks to get around the Supreme Court decision. It was filibustered in the summer of 2014 and the 56 to 43 vote was insufficient to stop debate through a procedure called "invoking cloture," which requires sixty votes. Even if the bill had passed the Senate, House Speaker John Boehner—or "Mr. Weepy" as he is sometimes called—would have never allowed the House to vote on it.[42]

But whatever the fate of a piece of legislation, there are other avenues to express opposition. A clergy member of the United Church of Christ out in Tulsa, Oklahoma (home base of Hobby Lobby), has started handing out condoms at their flagship store's parking lot.[43] Other guerilla theater is going on it some stores themselves, including customers rearranging displays so that they read "I want my birth control."[44]

There are now roughly twenty-three states that have their own RFRAs. A major national fervor arose over the meaning of Indiana's version in mid-2015. Indiana's RFRA was clearly designed (per the statements of its sponsors) to restrict LGBT rights. Marriage equality is the law in Indiana, thanks to a federal court ruling, and some legislators wanted to find a way to make sure that florists, bakers, photographers, hoteliers, etc. would not have to serve same-sex couples.[45]

As originally written, the Indiana RFRA would have had the effect of nullifying laws that prohibit discrimination against LGBT residents, which exists in a handful of Indiana cities and counties. The so-called "fix" of the bill was a very modest baby step in the right direction—but it still allows discriminatory treatment in the many Hoosier state communities that don't have such ordinances.

When all is said and done, the difference between the purpose of the federal RFRA and this new wave of bills is enormous. The new bills seek to deliberately hurt people; they are occurring in anticipation of a looming Supreme Court decision that many analysts believe will extend marriage equality nationwide.

In the midst of this entire outcry came the owners of Memories Pizza in Walkerton, Indiana. They told the media that they would serve gays in their pizzeria but would not cater a same-sex wedding. Under the "fix" signed into law by Governor Mike Pence, they are still allowed to act like bigots because there is no law protecting LGBT people from discrimination in Walkerton.

As most of you know, I've been to both law school and seminary. Even this specialized training fails to tell me by what stretch of the imagination one can justify serving two slices of pepperoni pizza to a couple but not providing two hundred slices for their wedding.

If someone does have an idiosyncratic religious reason for treating these events differently, in my view it would be so trivial a piece of moral detritus that it doesn't deserve public recognition or approval.

CANON LAW/ABUSE BY PRIESTS

Can things get even worse? In December 2014, attorneys for the Catholic arch-diocese of Fort Wayne-South Bend, Indiana, actually argued that civil courts had no jurisdiction to consider gender discrimination claims against churches because courts will demolish "religious freedom" if they have the right to tell religious organizations what to do. This did not fly.[46] However, I outlined some more conceivable claims for the July 2012 annual conference of SNAP (the Sur-vivors Network of those Abused by Priests).

It's always nice to be in Chicago in late July. There's only a 20 to 25 percent chance of snow. I'm honored to have been asked to come here this morning. In writing to a friend on Thursday, I mentioned that I would be here but then added how sad it felt to be speaking to a group organized around atrocities that should not have occurred in the first place, actions that were taken, then ignored, then covered up by the one institution above all others that claims to represent the highest ethical values emanating from the literal creator of the universe.

In my view, the leadership of the Catholic Church in America—with rare exception— has no moral authority to speak on matters of women's rights or human sexuality. If ever it had this authority, it has abandoned it. It abandoned it when, as an institution, much of the Church decided—in situ-ation after situation—that it was above the criminal and civil laws that the rest of us have to follow. For years, under the misleading and self-serving cloak of "religious freedom," the Church has labored to relieve itself of the legal rules that apply to everybody and instead to apply its own rules whenever it finds itself in a conflict. I'm going to talk about a number of specific examples of this behavior this morning, but they are all variations on a single theme: that most of the Catholic leadership today considers the Church to be above secular law—and they claim to "proof text" that from both the Bible and the Constitution.

You may recall news coverage from earlier this summer about the Conference of Catholic Bishops' Fortnight for Freedom. The Bishops took issue with a set of proposed regulations under the Obama Administration's Affordable Care Act, just recently upheld in part by the Supreme Court. I'm not going to explain all the convoluted changes these insurance regulations have gone through because I think it is simply wrong to put people into a coma this soon after breakfast. The bottom line is this: The Bishops were horrified that the Obama administration had proposed that all employers be required to provide health insurance to their employees, which would include coverage for contraception. There would be a religious exemption only for local churches and other religious entities like seminaries. This meant that large Catholic hospitals and educational institutions had to provide this coverage.

You may wonder why I'm spending time with this; this is, after all, not the Planned Parenthood convention. I hope by the end of these remarks you'll see that this current healthcare fight is the tip of a gigantic, Titanic-killing iceberg that threatens freedom of conscience and human dignity.

What the Conference of Catholic Bishops demands is an exception excluding any institution that has some element of Catholic ownership. On the surface, that clearly includes the big hospitals and educational institutions—but, under the Bishops' reasoning, it would also extend to any business owned by a Catholic person.

The Bishops have consistently justified this demand in terms of "religious liberty." They claim that if any Catholic business owner is required to contribute to a health insurance plan that offers contraception coverage—even to non-Catholic employees—the government will have violated his religious liberty. Not only that, the Bishops have the audacity to claim that it will violate the "freedom" of the non-Catholic men and women who are denied coverage. Think about these words, taken from the Bishops' latest official objection to the proposed regulations: "[A]s a result [of the insurance mandate], women will have less freedom, not more. They will not have the freedom to decline such coverage."[47] This is epic, Orwellian double-speak, and it conceals the true nature of the Bishops' demands.

The fact that a product is available doesn't mean anybody has to use it—I passed up a pastry just this morning. In fact, the original regulation contained a provision that any religious organization required to provide coverage could also put up a notice to their employees that said something like, "We offer birth control, but we think it is immoral to use it—and so does God."

The battle the Bishops are waging against coverage of contraception in healthcare plans is not about "religious liberty." That claim is fraudulent.

Liberty does not mean being given state sanction to force your own ideas—religious or otherwise—on other people. It does not mean being given a free pass from laws you don't like.

The French observer of eighteenth-century America Alexis De Tocqueville famously quipped that "there is hardly a political question in the United States which does not sooner or later turn into a judicial one,"[48] and indeed the Bishops are already fighting this issue in the courts as well as in the presses. They have met with only limited success.

The debate over the insurance mandate is recent and highly visible, but it is not the only area where the Church has attempted to hold itself to different standards. As I said at the beginning, this episode just shows how the Catholic leadership has abdicated legal accountability and, with it, moral authority. Before I get to their shameful behavior on human sexuality, I want to highlight some other threads in the pattern of evasion and irresponsibility.

There are whole fields of civil law from which the Church would like to be exempt, preferring to use its own internal canon law instead. They have been trying for decades to get courts to let them do this, and it may surprise you to hear that they have recently met with some success. In *Hosanna-Tabor*, a unanimous Supreme Court case decided just this January, the Conference of Catholic Bishops was part of a coalition that convinced the Court to broaden the reach of something called the "ministerial exception." This is an entirely "judge-created" encrustation on to the 1964 Civil Rights Act that otherwise would require that there could be no discrimination in hiring people for church jobs. These judges (and frankly I agree with this in principle) thought it ludicrous to force a synagogue to hire a Wiccan priestess as its new rabbi. For ministers of a church you could prefer those of the same religious persuasion. But now the "exception" has been allowed to take a much bigger bite. After January's decision, any personnel decision made by a church about any employee who performed any kind of "religious function" will be exempt from the prohibition against employment discrimination. The Bishops took an incredibly broad view of what a "religious function" was; as long as the religious employer took care to assign the employee any small "religious" task, the relationship between the church and the employee would be immune from those labor laws that otherwise bar discriminatory hiring or firing. Now, so long as a church labels the custodian's duties a "ministry of cleanliness," it is free to ignore laws against employment discrimination. So even if that custodian is really fired not because of some religious disagreement; if he is discharged for racial reasons, for example, having been declared a "minister" under some real or imagined church doctrine means he can't go to the Equal Employment Opportunity Commission or the federal courts for redress. Nine votes out of nine Supreme Court members said this.

As Law Professor Marci Hamilton—whom many of you know as a staunch protector of the rights of abused and exploited children—has pointed out, the holding in *Hosanna-Tabor* could have been much worse; the ministerial exception does not bar cases against churches—at least so far—other than for employment discrimination. But I'm sure you can see why the Bishops were so eager to win this case. The lawsuits brought by victims of sexual abuse by priests are often based on negligent supervision or hiring by a bishop. Although negligence in hiring and supervision is different from a violation of employment law, I believe the Church is building up its case to be exempted from responsibility for negligence as well. In fact, they have already made that argument in a number of state courts, with mixed success. Some state courts have granted them the exemption, but others have refused when it comes to allegations of abuse of children. For instance, courts in Maine recognize the ministerial exception as applied to negligent supervision of clergy by a bishop, but do not allow any immunity when there is a particularly sensitive individual relationship between the church and the alleged victim—such as that between a priest and a youth.

But forget the legal details—the point this morning is that the Church made the argument. Its lawyers have stood up in court, time after time, and said, with tolerably straight faces, "We are not responsible. Yes, our bishop kept on a priest he should have known was a pedophile, and, yes, he moved the priest from parish to parish, endangering children and failing to report accusations of abuse to the police. That doesn't matter; we're the Church, and the normal rules don't apply to us." Are these the actions of a Church leadership with the moral authority to lecture us on human sexuality? No.

In other areas the Church has not yet convinced the courts to throw up their hands and let the Bishops set the rules. For instance, the Church has tried to get courts to use canon law, rather than common law, to settle disputes of property ownership. They've dragged the same theory into bankruptcy court. For the most part, courts have declined these invitations.

In family law, as well, courts have resisted efforts by Catholic individuals involved in divorces to apply canon law in resolving spousal support and child custody disputes. There was an interesting case from Ohio a few years ago in which Bai MacFarlane, a Catholic divorcée, tried to get a family law court to modify her child support obligations downward. Although Mrs. MacFarlane had a mechanical engineering degree, she believed that Catholic canon law required to her to be a stay-at-home mom and home school her children. Mrs. MacFarlane argued before her family law judge, first, that she should be allowed to interrogate her ex-husband on the stand on Catholic canon law to prove that he shared her beliefs. Second, she proclaimed that her alleged obligations under canon law merited the child support increase she requested. Neither the trial judge nor the Court of Appeals of Ohio would stand for such a thing. Although Mrs. MacFarlane did have her own lawyer, she also received considerable support from her local Catholic diocese.[49]

Mrs. MacFarlane lost her case, but she went on to start an organization that advocates for "covenant marriages"—that is, marriages in which the usual no-fault divorce rules do not apply, and in which couples are held to religious standards to which they agree at the beginning of the marriage—religious standards that they expect civil courts to apply in the event of a dissolution of that marriage. Although the Conference of Catholic Bishops has not officially endorsed covenant marriage legislation, individual bishops have spoken strongly in favor of it. Three states have officially recognized covenant marriages, showing that the Church has gained at least some traction on this issue in the state legislatures. Bills have been introduced in many other states.

The Church has made significant inroads with legislatures on another issue—exemption from otherwise mandatory reporting of probable sex offenses against children when a priest learns of such abuse in the confession booth. In no less than twenty-nine states, clergy are permitted an exemption from laws requiring most service professionals to report suspected abuse or neglect of a child. Five other statutes allow the exemption but do require clergy to report when there is a high likelihood of abuse or neglect. Should we accept the Church leadership's moralizing on issues of sex when they have lobbied their way into being excused from reporting sexual abuse against children? I think you know my answer.

As you also know, it often takes decades for a survivor of sexual abuse to gain the strength and courage to speak out. Because of this, the perpetrators of the abuse can often hide behind state statutes of limitations. Many states have begun to expand the time period during which you can bring a claim of sexual abuse, but the Catholic Bishops have, predictably, opposed these moves very forcefully. In some cases, they have justified this opposition simply on the grounds that the number of suits that would result would bankrupt certain dioceses. Think about that for a minute, as a justification: "State legislature, we don't want you to expand the statute of limitations because so many people will sue us we'll go straight out of business"—and most of them are legitimate suits! Patrick Schiltz, a lawyer (now federal judge) who defended Catholic dioceses in over five hundred lawsuits, concluded that fewer than ten were based on false accusations. That's two percent. This estimate was backed up by a 2004 report that was commissioned by none other than the Conference of Catholic Bishops. Given that, I can understand why the Church would obstruct attempts to let more victims into court. But that does not make it right.

I'll just add that the Bishops' fears of a tidal wave of lawsuits are not actually unreasonable. When California passed a statute providing a one-year window in which people could bring older sex abuse suits against the church, there were over 550 claims. So, naturally, the Catholic Bishops have been active in lobbying against extensions of the statute of limitations in Massachusetts, New York, and New Jersey, and have managed to defeat "window" legislation in Ohio, Maryland, Illinois, Washington, DC, New York, and Colorado. Again, are these the actions of a Church leadership with the moral authority to lecture us on human sexuality? No.

In Colorado, Archbishop Charles Chaput led the efforts to defeat legislation that would have provided a window for sex abuse victims to bring old cases to court. He instructed his priests to raise the issue during Mass and to distribute lobbying postcards, which they did—including in the Catholic congregation attended by the Senate president, who had introduced the bill. Archbishop Chaput is also interesting because he has since been transferred to the Archdiocese of Philadelphia—the church unit in which Monsignor William Lynn has now been convicted of endangering a child by covering up for a clergy molester.[50] You have probably heard that Monsignor Lynn was, just this week, sentenced to three to six years in prison in the first case of its kind anywhere in the United States.[51] This is the pattern of leadership of the Catholic Church: Constant denial of legal responsibility, constant efforts to shield themselves from liability, constant efforts to place themselves above the law. How can these men claim to have moral authority over issues of human sexuality when they have so loudly rejected responsibility for their own misconduct? They cannot, and they do not.

Bill Donohue, the president of the Catholic League for Religious and Civil Rights, has actually argued, with a straight face, that the Church does not have a problem with sex abuse by the clergy, because, in his notorious words, "[T]hey weren't children, and they weren't raped."[52] Think about that statement. He then went on to blame the abuse on homosexuality. This is, by the way, the same man who claimed that kissing and inappropriate sexual talk is not abuse, and in the same interview called Irish accusers of Catholic priests "gold diggers." Now, in fairness to the Conference of Catholic Bishops, the Catholic League is not an official organ of the church. Thank goodness for small favors.

I want to bring this "corporate conscience" claim full circle as I close here because there is an astounding disconnect that you may have already figured out about the disparate way the Catholic Bishops understand the reach of their moral responsibility. In the case of the birth control mandate, even to refer an employee to someone else who will give her insurance coverage for a procedure or a treatment as a way to space children in a family is wrong. Church officials would have us believe such a simple act condones what they consider a sin against God. Indeed, this gossamer-thin analysis is so attenuated that a connection it is nearly invisible to most of us. But, consider the chain of events in so many of the cases that have had such a profound impact on your lives and the lives of your families as children and today. In the abuse cases, these same church officials go out of their way to explain how they were unconnected to a "sin"; how they can't be held responsible for the actions of others, even those they supervised. They have gone out of their way to nitpick reasons why they can wash the blood from their hands. They are looking for excuse after excuse after excuse to exonerate their own complicity in what traditional Catholics know is "sin" and which moral persons of any or no religious persuasion recognize as a crime against the deepest understanding of intimacy and of human sexuality and a violation of the very nature of the human spirit.

No matter how clever the lawyer, no matter how articulate the prelate, they are all apologists for what is to most of us unimaginable distortions of the very idea of liberty and freedom. If I leave you with one message, it is that many of us, from a variety of religious traditions, know that we have a moral duty to prevent these distorted claims from successfully becoming a part of American judicial philosophy.

There are several groups around the country today raising funds to stop "sharia," Islamic holy law, from being used in America. Oklahoma's residents recently passed an initiative on this matter. There are plenty of things to worry about these days—sharia is not one of them. Ironically, one of them is the effort to turn current Catholic religious doctrine into a public and legal policy that will have an effect on all Americans, whether they like it or not.

Chapter 9

RELIGION IN POLITICS

WE KNOW THAT RELIGION IS GETTING MORE POLITICAL . . .

T he law is clear and unequivocal—no charities that are tax exempt under section 501(c)(3) of the Internal Revenue Code may engage in partisan politicking. These religious, educational, and other charities may not "endorse or oppose . . . any candidate for public office." This is unlike the standard for the category of 501(c)(4) "social welfare" organizations that came to public attention in 2014 when (largely-false) claims were made that the IRS had "targeted" conservative groups for additional time-wasting scrutiny before granting them tax-exempt status in 2012. Honestly, can the IRS be blamed for scrutinizing a tad more an application for the "Texas Tea Party," since this "party" sounded more likely to be a political entity than, say, a "hookers and cocaine" party? These entities cannot have political activity as their "primary purpose." That standard is vague and clearly allows a substantial amount of outright political candidate advocacy so long as you have some other educational function.

My first "official act" at Americans United was submitting an IRS complaint against the Church at Pierce Creek for its *USA Today* advertisement instructing readers not to commit the "sin" of voting for Bill Clinton. We also set up a program called Project Fair Play to report violations of the "no politicking" with church resources rule.

By 2000, the country was awash in electoral shenanigans involving breaching the "no politicking" rule for 501(c)(3) groups. This was a part of both major parties decision that playing a "God card" or two might bring in more Christian voters (or in the case of the Democrats, perhaps more "Judeo-Christian" voters).

Campaign 2000: It's a National Contest for President, not Preacher[1]

I spent much of the week before the Democratic National Convention talking to the press about Vice President Al Gore's selection of Sen. Joseph Lieberman as his running mate. Since Americans United is strictly nonpartisan, I expressed no opinion about the wisdom of the selection. However, there was plenty to talk about as soon as Sen. Lieberman introduced himself to voters in a speech that began with a prayer, continued with a recitation from the Book of Chronicles, and contained close to thirty religious references.

Was this an "over the top" effort to interject yet more religion into a presidential campaign already oversaturated with religiosity and pandering? When I was in law school I took a course in torts and personal injury law. There is something called the "one-bite rule." The basic principle is that you're less likely to win a lawsuit against your neighbor if his dog has never bitten anyone until you. The dog was not previously known as a biter. The second person who gets a chunk of flesh removed will be in a much stronger legal position.

I took the same initial view of the senator's speech, including an hourlong interview on CNN right after he made it. Those of us inside the Beltway know Lieberman to be a sincerely devoted Orthodox Jew who says his faith is his moral compass. Most Americans, however, had never even heard of him prior to his selection as Gore's vice presidential pick. He took the opportunity of his selection speech to convey the importance of his personal religious devotion, and most Americans took it that way.

Here's the rub for me, though. After he said it and explained himself, it was time to move on. So far, he seems generally to have done so. If Lieberman or other candidates decide to begin every political pep talk with a prayer and a Bible verse or state their position and a proof text of scripture to boot, their actions will quickly proceed from being personal affirmations to political pandering. In other words, in a presidential campaign what we need is an emphasis on policy, not piety.

I'm convinced that most of us want the candidates to discuss what they see as the real solutions to the challenges that still face our nation. Repeated reliance on personal statements of faith would be seen by many as the exploitation of religion, even its cheapening by rhetorical repetition. This manipulation wouldn't benefit the political process or religion itself.

Regrettably, this campaign has already been marred by inappropriate church-state mixing. It was wrong for Gore to go to a New York church in February to receive a from-the-pulpit endorsement by the Rev. Floyd Flake, a powerful pastor. It was at least equally troubling when the Republican National Convention planners beamed into the hall via satellite the Rev. Herbert Lusk from his Philadelphia pulpit to announce that he (and apparently his entire congregation) was supporting George W. Bush. I should point out that even Pat Robertson's American Center for Law and Justice has produced a pamphlet of "dos and don'ts" for pastors that specifically recommends against political endorsements from the pulpit. Of course, it's also hard to overlook that we've been told by one of Gore's chief policy lieutenants that the Democrats are going to "take God back this time" and that Bush declared "Jesus Day" in Texas on June 10.

Project Fair Play has led to some interesting blowback over the years—from (now-former) senator and reverse-mortgage huckster Fred Thompson as well as an effort by the late senator Jesse Helms and still-incumbent senator Jeff Sessions to have me sent to federal prison for intimidating Christians and keeping them from voting.[2]

Congressional interest in our little project began in the summer of 1997. The first thrust started with a US Marshal and ended up with a meaningless report.

SUBPOENA SURPRISE: FRED THOMPSON COMES KNOCKING[3]

At first I thought it was just an office prank. AU Legal Director Steve Green came up to my office and said a federal marshal with a subpoena from the US Senate was in the lobby.

Sure.

I went downstairs expecting to find a man in a gorilla suit with a bouquet of balloons as a belated birthday gift. I told Steve to have somebody bring a camera.

But there in the lobby stood a man who looked like a stereotypical US marshal in a movie where the government serves notice on an organized crime lord. He flashed a badge—and it soon became apparent that he was a real marshal and he had a real subpoena from Sen. Fred Thompson (who played stereotypical political roles in movies before getting elected to the Senate in 1994). Thompson is chairman of the powerful Government Affairs Committee, investigating campaign irregularities and foreign money contributions in the 1996 election.

The first thought that popped into my head was, "What is this guy doing here? Did he come into the wrong building?" I don't even look like a gangster, a wealthy influence peddler, or a Hong Kong businessman. But the subpoena had Americans United's name on it. I signed for it and went into our conference room for a quick read.

It is an extraordinary document. It demanded that by August 22, 1997, Americans United deliver every piece of paper we produced during 1995 and 1996 that related to our involvement in election campaigns. That's easy—there aren't any.

But the subpoena also demanded all our documents about "publicly debated issues." Here's where things get tricky. I can understand why the committee might have an interest in political involvement by nonprofit groups. By law, Americans United and other nonprofits are not permitted to intervene in partisan elections. But we have not done that—or even anything close to it.

But this business about "publicly debated" issues throws me. Americans United has every right, as an issue-based organization, to generate this type of information. It's why we exist. We are lawfully permitted to alert our members and the public to legislation posing a danger to church-state separation. We are permitted to advocate for church-state separation. However, internal documents about issue strategies, correspondence with individual AU members or members of Congress, or materials never released publicly should not be open to the prying eyes of a Senate committee.

Over the next few days, I got a quick legal education in the Kafkaesque world of congressional subpoenas. The bottom line: You have far fewer rights than you would in a court of law. It is exceedingly difficult to meaningfully challenge the breadth of your subpoena or claim any privileges—such as a lawyer-client privilege—to withhold documents.

If the committee wants something and you don't give it up or answer the committee's questions, you can be held in contempt of Congress. Only as you are packing your toothbrush for the federal penitentiary can you then file a lawsuit and make your case before a federal judge.

As for rules to determine who is called to give evidence to these committees, they are equally nonexistent. Forget "probable cause" that a crime has been committed, or "reasonable suspicion" of unlawful activity—statements familiar to viewers of Court TV and police movies. The Senate committee counsel freely admits they have absolutely no evidence to suggest that AU has done anything improper and that they "don't know what we're looking for until we see it."

Essentially, this is a world-class fishing expedition.

SEN. THOMPSON AND CO. DIDN'T COME OUT AS EXPECTED[4]

My son Nick and I went to see the movie *US Marshals* recently. It's a sequel to *The Fugitive*.

Watching the movie, I was reminded of my own brush with a US marshal last summer. The Senate Committee on Governmental Affairs demanded AU turn over various documentation relating to our internal governance, activities, and other matters.

The committee wanted to see any documents we had relating to political activity. At that point, we consulted with the well-known Washington, DC, law firm of McKenna and Cuneo, which provided us with excellent *pro bono* services.

After due reflection, we turned over a package of documents. I have to say, this was not the stuff of which headlines are made. Most of the letters were from me to political candidates, explaining that Americans United is nonpartisan and thus unable to assist getting anyone elected to public office anywhere.

The committee also requested "any and all correspondence with the Internal Revenue Service." This we complied with eagerly because it gave us the opportunity to send Senator Thompson all of our Project Fair Play letters reporting instances of religious groups and houses of worship abusing their tax-exempt status by intervening in partisan campaigns. I believed the committee would welcome this material, since it provided examples of the very type of wrong-doing it was allegedly eager to ferret out.

After our first filing to the committee, we heard absolutely nothing. There were no requests for more back-up material, no calls to clarity issues, and certainly no invitation to appear at the televised hearing to discuss our evidence. Then, abruptly, Senator Thompson announced on October 31 that he was shutting down the entire investigation. A few weeks later, our boxes of material were returned to us.

Last month, Thompson issued a report on his findings. In the short section on nonprofits, an astonishingly reckless charge appears—that all of the subpoenaed groups "were allegedly involved in a variety of questionable campaign practices."[5] In fact, no one at any time made such an allegation about Americans United. Representatives from other groups, including Christian Coalition officials, refused to even show up when subpoenaed to give depositions, but we maintained that we would welcome the opportunity to discuss the matter.

Since we gave the committee much of what they sought, isn't it curious that they didn't want to learn more? Not if that meant taking on the Christian Coalition, I guess. After all, Senator Thompson and ultraconservative colleagues in the Senate are the ones who benefit the most from the group's activities.

But the Thompson Committee was not a complete waste of time. The minority report, written by Democratic staff, has a whole chapter on the Christian Coalition and its repeated abuses of election law. A large number of the citations regarding improper Coalition activities come from *Church & State* magazine.

I like history. I like accurate history even more. Even though Senator Thompson apparently didn't want the truth, the Thompson Committee's minority report at least strike some blows for truth-telling.

Things then got even stranger in the US Senate. If they can't interrogate you, why not just send you to jail? (And, by the way, not bother to tell you that you're being investigated?)

When a member of the United States Senate wants the Justice Department to investigate you, there are apparently two things he doesn't need to provide: persuasive evidence that you have done something wrong and notification to you.[6]

I was more than a bit surprised a few weeks ago when I learned of a letter sent by Sen. Jesse Helms (R-NC) and five of his colleagues calling on Attorney General Janet Reno to launch a criminal investigation of Americans United for possibly violating a federal statute prohibiting intimidation of people seeking to exercise their right to vote.

I came to know about this only because a reporter called to ask about it. Someone in Sen. Paul Coverdell's office had faxed him—probably by accident—a copy of the Helms letter.

We put two and two together and came up with the likely scenario that Christian Coalition President Pat Robertson, after a meeting in June with the Senate leadership, had prodded several senators to take action against the group he hates the most, the group that he blames in large part for the denial of his much-sought Coalition tax exemption. That group is Americans United.

How could these senators possible justify asking for a criminal probe of Americans United? They claim AU is trying to "intimidate" religious voters because of two things: Number one, I told *Congressional Quarterly* that churches are unlikely to distribute Christian Coalition voter guides because of the Coalition's well-established partisan reputation. And number two, because we have sent memos to churches advising them that handing out biased voters guides could get them in trouble with the IRS. That's it.

Normally, government agencies begin investigations after they have evidence of "probable cause" of a crime or at least "reasonable suspicion" that one has been committed. It's hard to believe that six senators would become convinced of a need for this type of probe on the basis of this flimsy "evidence"—unless they had been persuaded to do it by a little bird (or a major campaign contributor).

The evidence against AU may be nonexistent, but the Department of Justice told reporters that an investigation had been started by the Public Integrity section of the Criminal Division.

During a recent appearance on CNN's *Crossfire*, I was asked about this matter by cohost Robert Novak. I called the Helms missive what it is—a witch hunt. We chose to release the letter, along with our evidence of Robertson's involvement and a demand for apologies from all six senators, chiefly because we felt wronged. We also wanted to demonstrate how simple it is for real intimidation to come from powerful government officials—undeterred by such mundane matters as the truth—when they are motivated by sycophantic desires to keep good relations with powerful supporters.

The irony does not escape me that it is the Christian Coalition that has played fast and loose with the tax and election laws for years, while AU does only genuinely nonpartisan public education. Curiously, one sentence in the senators' letter is particularly chilling: They want Janet Reno to look into whether "injunctions" against Americans United might be appropriate (along with the fines and prison time provided in the statute they claim we violated).

Injunctions are court orders to stop us from doing things in the future, presumably publishing *Church & State* articles, posting material on the Internet, and sending out legal memoranda to religious groups telling them what they can and cannot do in the realm of voter education. This is very serious stuff.

Many reporters have recently asked me why Pat Robertson has such an interest in stopping AU. That's simple: He knows Americans United is effective. We have blown the whistle on his political shenanigans, his efforts to raid the public treasury, and his blistering insults about people whose religion differs from his own.

But this misadventure by the Senate had a positive end result—our vindication!

THE HELMS WITCH HUNT: A HAPPY ENDING TO AN UNHAPPY EPISODE[7]

Put away all those recipes involving how to bake cakes with files in them. It looks like the Americans United staff will not be going to a federal penitentiary after all, in spite of Pat Robertson's and Jesse Helms's efforts to put us there.

The senators' letter actually began a six-month investigation by the Public Integrity Section of the Criminal Division of the Justice Department. In early January, I wrote Janet Reno suggesting that if the inquiry was over, we'd like to know what had happened; if not, we'd be happy to cooperate in providing information about our activities (something we had been happy to do in July as well). Finally, in early February, Deputy Assistant Attorney General John C. Keeney wrote me that the charges lacked merit and that the criminal statutes were designed to "reach only threats of physical or economic harm that are communicated to voters to stimulate or deter them from voting in federal elections," not our efforts to inform people of what can and cannot be done in the arena of political education by churches and other tax-exempt groups.

Americans United, of course, issued a press release properly labeling Keeney's letter a full exoneration. Our statement also called for an apology by the six senators who acted on such flimsy evidence to try to stop our own constitutionally protected activity. Although it is safe to say that the initial demand to investigate us got more press attention than the decision by Ms. Reno not to, many reporters did want to close the chapter with an exoneration story. In so doing, several made efforts to contact the six senators. They got some curious responses.

Senator Don Nickles of Oklahoma had an aide respond to the *Tulsa World*. "The aide indicated that Lynn should not be waiting by the phone," the story explained, adding that the aide said it would be "a cold day in Belize" before we got the apology. Alabama Senator Jeff Sessions sent spokesman John Cox to tell the Associated Press that he "thinks Americans United is one of the most aggressively left-wing organizations in America" and is still "offended" by our suggestions of Christian Coalition improprieties. Pardon us.

I don't think I really expected to be sent flowers or chocolates along with a letter of apology from any of the six. However, I didn't expect that they would choose the event of our vindication to send overzealous, ill-informed assistants to issue flip responses on the subject. After all, the statutes they believed we violated have serious consequences, including prison time, heavy fines, and stopping the publication of printed material.

From the beginning of our concern about illegal politicking by houses of worship, we have often suggested that church leaders sometimes get extremely arrogant in their belief that parishioners "need" their advice on which candidate to support (as opposed to real education on issues and help on genuine voter education). In a front-page story of the *Washington Post* just a few days before the South Carolina primary, religion writer Hanna Rosin suggests that the Christian Right's fervor in that state has "gone cold."[8] Near the end of the article, Rosin quotes conservative activist Cyndi Mosteller, who is not completely unhappy that the Christian Coalition fell apart there: "They have good minds and good hearts, but we will not be told by any organization who to vote for."

AT THE FALWELL FOLLIES: JERRY FINALLY 'FESSES UP ON FOX NEWS CHANNEL[9]

One of my favorite stories about politicians and religion deals with President Calvin Coolidge, who, as the story goes, was once approached by a reporter after attending a church service and asked what the sermon had been about.

"Silent Cal" replied, "sin," which led the reporter to ask, "What did the preacher say about it?"

Replied Coolidge, "He was against it."

I feel the same way about lying. I stand firmly against it. So, indulge me for another column about the continued misinformation being spread by the Rev. Jerry Falwell. Recently I wrote about some of the false claims he makes about me; now I'd like to comment on some of the false claims he makes about himself and the Internal Revenue Service.

On July 15, I wrote a letter to the IRS alleging that Falwell used the resources and website of a tax-exempt entity, Jerry Falwell Ministries, to endorse George W. Bush for president. He also linked his site to that of former presidential candidate Gary Bauer's political action committee, the misnamed Campaign for Working Families, to make it easy to give money to Bush and other GOP candidates.

These actions are violations of federal tax law. Falwell is free to endorse a candidate in his personal capacity as a minister, just like a lawyer, an auto mechanic, or an organic farmer could. But he is not permitted to use the website or publications of a tax-exempt group to further partisan ends. Also, tax-exempt groups cannot use their resources to promote political action committees that seek to elect certain candidates to public office.

A day after my letter was delivered to the IRS, CNBC's *Capital Report* invited Falwell and me to debate the issue. Falwell made a convoluted argument, insisting that his website is owned by a non-tax-exempt group and therefore has the right to promote Bush. The whole thing sounded like one of those "hide the pea under the shell" games you wouldn't play at a backwoods carnival.

I responded that listeners would perhaps not want to take tax advice from Falwell, since in 1993 his *Old-Time Gospel Hour* (OTGH) had admitted to violations of federal tax law. The television ministry lost its tax exemption for politicking in 1986 and 1987 and was forced to pay $50,000 in back taxes.

Falwell went absolutely ballistic. He said I was lying. He announced that his church in Lynchburg, Virginia, had never lost its tax exemption. That's true, but irrelevant. As I pointed out on the air, it was the *Old-Time Gospel Hour* that ran afoul of federal tax law, not his church.

Falwell continued to deny that any of his organizations had ever lost their exemptions even for a minute. Remember, I put a premium on truth-telling. Before going on the air, I had reviewed media coverage from 1993 and dug up an old *New York Times* story about the incident. I was right, he was wrong, and no manner of bullying and screaming was going to change that. Yet two weeks later, Falwell repeated the same denials in a debate with AU's Rob Boston on Fox New Channel's *The Big Story with John Gibson*.

Not long after that, we obtained a copy of the public statement the IRS required Falwell to issue in the aftermath of the federal agency's audit. Dated Feb. 17, 1993, and signed by Falwell, the document could not be clearer. It reads in part, "OTGH agrees to the two-year revocation of tax-exempt status, based on the IRS finding that it engaged in political activity, and the payment of $50,000 for tax deficiencies."

On August 8, I got a golden opportunity to use the statement during another debate with Falwell on Fox News Channel. I took the document with me and literally held it up to the camera when Falwell started his denial rant again. The host told him to be quiet long enough for me to explain the significance of the statement.

And, proving that three is still a charm, Falwell was finally forced to concede the truth—but belittled it by saying he had agreed to pay back taxes only to avoid increasing legal fees to fight the ongoing audit. So much for principle.

There was a brief effort to repeal this IRS provision in 2002. The hearing on the topic had as its high point Congressman John Lewis's rebuttal to the Religious Right's claims about what Dr. Martin Luther King would have thought of the IRS.

The House Ways and Means Committee meets in just about the nicest hearing room on Capitol Hill.[10] I'd never testified in this lavish venue before my recent appearance to discuss what is very wrong about two bills that would allow churches to engage in partisan politicking.

The room in the Longworth Office Building is so huge because usually it's overflowing with supplicants for tax breaks in the continual epic writing of the Internal Revenue Code. The room was less full when the Subcommittee on Oversight held a hearing May 14 on Rep. Walter Jones's "House of Worship Political Speech Protection Act" and Rep. Phil Crane's "Bright-Line Act."

That's too bad. What we discussed that day is, in many ways, far more important than whether widget production gets preferred tax treatment or whether the alternative minimum tax is abolished. Even changing a few words in the law that applies to nonprofits and electioneering could have dramatically negative effects on both the integrity of religious institutions and the already-suspect honor of the campaign-finance system.

Much of the day, I felt like the bills' advocates were literally talking about life on some other planet or astral plane. To hear the proponents of these measures talk, houses of worship aren't allowed to utter a peep about political matters. Proponents before the committee, like TV preacher D. James Kennedy and Colby May of Pat Robertson's American Center for Law and Justice, refused to acknowledge that tax laws currently permit virtually unlimited advocacy of moral positions. Pastors can speak out on issues all they want; they simply cannot endorse or oppose a candidate for public office.

Do Kennedy and Colby know nothing about recent history? Don't they read the newspapers? Houses of worship led the fight for civil rights and advocated for an end to the Vietnam War. Conservative churches successfully lobbied for "abstinence-only" sex education in many public schools and oppose legal abortion.

There's a crucial distinction between speaking out on the issues of moral justice and pushing for a particular candidate. Rep. John Lewis, who is one of America's most prominent civil rights leaders, made this crystal clear. Lewis was responding to Walter Fauntroy, a Baptist minister in Washington, DC, who had invoked Martin Luther King in explaining why he believes churches must have the right to endorse candidates.

Lewis was not persuaded. "I knew Martin Luther King; he was a friend of mine," Lewis said. "He never, to my knowledge, endorsed a political candidate."[11] It was a clear message that moral persuasion on matters of justice can be just as effective as political power-mongering.

Kennedy's Coral Ridge Ministries has actually sent out fundraising letters that depict ministers with gags over their mouths and the IRS shuttering churches. Even allowing for a little hyperbole to pay the bills, this is simply fear-mongering and hysteria.

The fact is, only one church in modern history has actually lost its tax exemption for electioneering. The Church at Pierce Creek in New York blatantly violated the law in 1992 by placing a $44,000 ad in *USA Today* advocating the defeat of Bill Clinton. The church's pastor, who told reporters that he didn't care what the IRS or the courts thought, is still in business under a different corporate name.

Mr. May claimed that "conservative" churches are held to a tighter standard, noting that Pastor Floyd Flake received just a warning from the IRS after he endorsed Al Gore from the pulpit in 2000.

But May overlooked a few relevant facts. The pastor of the Church at Pierce Creek repeatedly said that he would continue to do whatever he felt like doing, while Flake acknowledged that he made a mistake and promised not to violate the law again. Despite the IRS's reputation for ferocity, the agency will in fact give any pastor a second chance. Pierce Creek's pastor turned it down and essentially dared the IRS to use the ultimate sanction.

Walter Jones and company did get a vote on this proposal under a House procedure known as a "suspension of the rules," which usually occurs on Monday afternoons after debate on legislation that is not deemed controversial and is expected to pass easily. Jones must have been a bit aghast when his proposal barely got a majority vote. It hasn't been brought to the floor again!

The failure to have another vote is a bit surprising, given all the press this issue gets during an election cycle. There is even a well-funded effort by the Arizona-based Alliance Defending Freedom (ADF) (formerly the Alliance Defense Fund) called "Pulpit Freedom Sunday" that urges pastors to deliberately violate the tax code so that the provision can be tested in court. The ADF primarily makes this simple prohibition appear wildly complex and designed to virtually strap tape over the mouth of the preacher who has a thought about a social or political issue.

IT's REAL SIMPLE: FEDERAL TAX LAW FORBIDS CHURCHES TO ENDORSE POLITICAL CANDIDATES[12]

As I was checking out at the grocery store the other night, I spotted a magazine called *Real Simple*, a publication with the subhead "Life Made Easier."

What struck me was that it was 276 pages long. Perhaps it is just me, but life would start being easier if magazines like this were, say, 76 pages long. It is full of advertising for products I didn't even know existed. (Who knew you could buy shoes with an air-circulation system built inside or that you could now add "black cherry streusel" flavoring to your coffee?)

It also included articles on how to recycle everything you ever use; how to spend a day with the family picking apples; how to winterize your garden; how to buy new desk chairs; how to avoid over-cleansing, over-exfoliating, or over-moisturizing your skin; and even how to find out if your house is haunted. About two hundred pages in, you also learn "10 Ways to Be Happier." How about starting by buying a few apples at the store and ceasing to worry about whether your home is haunted until a ghost trips you down the stairs? Just a thought: simplify.

This magazine did make me think about how some lawyers have a habit of taking all kinds of simple things and encrusting them with layers of linguistic and technical mumbo jumbo combined with a complete suspension of common sense.

I don't mean to knock lawyers too much. I am one, after all. But this tendency was apparent among Religious Right lawyers as AU labored prior to the election to stop illegal partisan politicking by churches and other religious charities.

The Internal Revenue Service says tax-exempt groups "are absolutely prohibited from directly or indirectly participating in, or intervening in, any political campaign on behalf of (or in opposition to) any candidate for elective public office."

This doesn't suggest a huge gray area. Endorsing or opposing a candidate isn't something you do accidentally. Some do it on purpose: The Alliance Defense Fund (ADF), a Religious Right legal outfit, corralled thirty-one pastors into endorsing candidates from the pulpit on September 28. The ADF assumed somebody would report this activity to the IRS—which AU did—and then if the IRS penalized one or more churches with loss of tax exemption, fines or other actions, the ADF would swoop in and defend them in court.

A group of rabbis once asked me to speak on this topic, and one asked me how a religious leader would know if he had violated the law. I replied, "Ask yourself this question: Is what I am about to do or say with my congregation's resources done for the purpose of helping somebody get elected? If your answer is 'yes,' then don't do it." This seemed like a reasonable suggestion to the assembled leaders.

The actions of the ADF's pastors (and others we have reported) are so flagrant that there is no serious doubt about what they intended. Could anyone believe that a Catholic bishop who posted a letter on the diocese's website noting that "the present democratic candidate for President" supports abortion and opposes the very concept of human freedom and comparing him to Herod Antipas, the Roman-era ruler who ordered the beheading of John the Baptist, is doing anything but opposing Barack Obama?

Consider the New Mexico pastor who plastered two pictures on the side of his church. One is a picture of a smiling baby, with the word "McCain" beneath it; the other the remains of an aborted fetus with the word "Obama" under it. These are then capped off with the phrase "YOU WILL DECIDE."

Were these gentlemen merely trying to start a dialogue? Of course not. They were telling people whom to vote for. They were using church resources and bringing the clout of an institutional endorsement right into the partisan political battlefield.

None of this activity is "vague." It is a blatant violation of federal tax law. To be frank, we don't have to worry about vague cases. There are plenty of the belligerent, stick-in-the-eye examples to be investigated. And they should be. No matter who has won the presidential election by the time you read this, the law needs to be enforced.

Last Sunday, as many as three dozen pastors may knowingly have violated federal tax law by endorsing US Sen. John McCain from the pulpit or attacking US Sen. Barack Obama.[13]

The campaign was organized by the Alliance Defense Fund (ADF), an Arizona-based Religious Right legal group founded by a collection of TV and radio preachers in 1993. The ADF hopes that the Internal Revenue Service will strip at least one church of its tax-exempt status, enabling a team of Religious Right lawyers to launch a test case. The leaders of the Religious Right, being the masters of euphemism that they are, called this monstrosity "Pulpit Freedom Sunday."

So what's really going on here? I see the ADF gambit as part of an ongoing struggle to politicize America's houses of worship and create a powerful political machine that will work on behalf of the most reactionary right-wing conservatives—candidates who elevate divisive "culture war" issues like same-sex marriage, abortion, and religion in public life above all others.

Thankfully, forces are pushing back. Three former top IRS officials wrote to the tax agency, pointing out that it's not cool for tax attorneys to urge their clients to violate the law. In fact, it is a violation of the professional code that governs tax attorneys. The ex-IRS officials requested an investigation into the ADF's reckless ploy.

Even Jonathan Falwell, son of the late Moral Majority founder, seems wary. "I don't intend to endorse anyone," he said recently. "I don't think it's my role to be telling anyone who to vote for."[14]

All of this comes at a time when record numbers of Americans are telling pollsters that they want to see religion and politics decoupled. Put simply, Americans attend houses of worship for spiritual reasons; they are weary of political pulpits.

The IRS is aware that this massive program of deliberate law breaking is approaching. The tax agency has repeatedly stated that it intends to enforce the law and, in fact, runs a special project called the Political Activity Compliance Initiative to make sure nonprofits follow the law. Here's hoping the IRS will be watching as well.

So—why no investigations, much less tax revocations, during the Obama administration? I tried to answer this in a piece for the *Huffington Post* in 2013:

CHURCH ELECTIONEERING AND THE IRS: ANOTHER EXAMPLE OF TAX AGENCY FAILURE[15]

You might have noticed that there has been a little controversy about the Internal Revenue Service lately.

It appears that officials in a Cincinnati IRS office subjected some conservative organizations that were seeking a form of tax exemption to heightened scrutiny and additional procedures because they had words like "Tea Party" and "patriot" in their names.

For some years now, Americans United for Separation of Church and State has been urging the IRS to crack down on tax-exempt religious organizations that engage in blatant partisan electioneering. These are clear violations of the law, and yet the IRS seems to have done nothing to penalize scofflaws.

When I say clear violations of the law, I mean clear. I'm talking about religious organizations using their tax-exempt personnel and resources to intervene in elections. I'm talking about pastors standing up and telling their congregants which candidates to vote for or against, endorsing candidates in church bulletins, or taking other actions that step way over the line.

These activities are not permitted. No tax-exempt, 501(c)(3) organization—religious or nonreligious—can engage in behaviors designed to
intervene in an election by endorsing or opposing a candidate. This is so
because one of the conditions of tax exemption (which is a very lucrative
benefit) is that the groups holding it must refrain from this type of overt partisan politicking.

But some houses of worship do it anyway. They openly violate the law
and even brag about it. One Religious Right outfit, the Alliance Defending
Freedom, even sets aside a Sunday each year to encourage political
chicanery.

This is not a secret. Americans United has been pressing the IRS to put
a stop to this for years. The agency continues to drag its feet.

In 2012, we reported a church in Leakey, Texas, that put a sign on
its marquee reading, "VOTE FOR THE MORMON, NOT THE MUSLIM!
THE CAPITALIST, NOT THE COMMUNIST!" (Real subtle, huh?) In Maiden,
North Carolina, a Baptist pastor gave a sermon during which he recommended quarantining all gay people and leaving them to die out and concluded by telling congregants not to vote for Barack Obama. (He said, "I
ain't gonna vote for a baby killer and a homosexual lover. You said, 'Did
you mean to say that?' You better believe I did.")[16]

Those are just two examples. There were many others. And we don't
confine ourselves to churches that endorse Republicans. Over the years, AU
has reported houses of worship for endorsing or opposing Democrats and
third-party candidates, too.

The evidence in these cases is strong. As I said, some pastors even taunt
the IRS by openly breaking the law and boasting about it. The IRS talks a
good game about enforcing the law but does not act. Why?

Part of the problem may be due to foot-dragging at the IRS over some
internal procedures. In 2006, Americans United reported the Living Word
Christian Center in Minnesota after its pastor endorsed US Rep. Michele
Bachmann (R-MN) from the pulpit. The IRS tried to audit the church, but
the church sued, claiming that the audit had not been approved by the
specific official named in the regulations. That position had been abolished
in a reorganization plan. The church won the case in court. The IRS subsequently announced that it would develop new rules for what constitutes
a high-ranking official and conducted a formal rule-making. That was in
2009. The IRS has subsequently done nothing. Yet this would not seem to

a big deal. It's a regulatory alteration simple enough to be crafted by a few monkeys with typewriters, at random, by just letting them work in a closed room for a week. A procedural matter that could be resolved in an afternoon has been pending for five years.

This is not rocket science. As Americans United told the IRS in November of 2009, "Given the pervasiveness of church politicking violations, as well as efforts by some organizations in recent years to encourage houses of worship to blatantly violate federal law, having a clear and valid enforcement regime is absolutely essential for the ongoing protection of religious liberty."[17]

But, wait, you may say, didn't the advocacy group Freedom From Religion Foundation (FFRF) get some kind of victory in a direct challenge to the IRS. Not exactly.

The Freedom From Religion Foundation sued the Internal Revenue Service for failing to enforce electioneering restrictions against churches and religious organizations, calling it a violation of the Establishment Clause of the First Amendment and of FFRF's equal-protection rights. FFRF filed the lawsuit November 14, 2012, in the US District Court for the Western District of Wisconsin.

The lawsuit claimed that the IRS had a policy of nonenforcement of the electioneering restrictions against churches and religious organizations, which it needed to correct. The IRS countered, stating that, since 2010, the agency has flagged churches involved with political intervention, including churches that submitted materials as part of Pulpit Freedom Sunday. Also, an IRS review committee determined that ninety-nine churches were marked for "high-priority examination." The IRS has still done nothing to actually "examine" them however.

On August 1, 2014, US District Judge Lynn S. Adelman issued an order granting the joint motion for dismissal between FFRF and the IRS. Adelman's decision and order agreed that FFRF may voluntarily dismiss its lawsuit "without prejudice," meaning FFRF can renew the lawsuit if the IRS reverts to its previous inaction.

And so we wait. Much as progressives criticize the *Citizens United* decision allowing virtually unlimited corporate spending in elections, ignoring the significance of church politicking could easily be more damaging to the electoral process.

BUT ARE POLITICIANS GETTING MORE "RELIGIOUS"?

Probably not, but you wouldn't know it by listening to them.

In *Piety and Politics*, I describe how the "God card" had been played up through the 2004 election cycle. Things have not gotten much better since. The media itself has become enamored with the religion of presidential candidates, generally unwilling to accept "no comment" as an appropriate response in a nation that, according to Article III of our Constitution is to have "no religious test" for public office. On the broader issues of the relationships of political figures and religious groups, the media itself has to shoulder some of the blame for exacerbating the problem.

The Bush-Cheney ticket was reelected in 2004, and there was a strong effort to mobilize the same Christian voters in 2006 midterm elections. Things didn't go as planned and Democrats had resounding victories in both the House and the Senate. Democrats took control of 233 seats in the House and 52 in the Senate. The marriage of fundamentalism in religion and politics seemed to have hit a bump in the road.

Just over six weeks ago, the Rev. Jerry Falwell told a group of pastors at a breakfast in Washington, DC, that they should have no worries about a Democratic takeover of Congress.[18] Falwell assured the crowd that the Republicans would remain in power.

As he put it, "I think the Lord's going to take care of that."

Religious conservatives had been convinced up until Election Day that the powerful machine they had built would defend enough incumbents to preserve their access to power from the White House to Capitol Hill. This year, instead of merely taking marching orders from national groups like Focus on the Family or the latest Falwell incarnation of the Moral Majority, Religious Right activists in places like Ohio ran grassroots-oriented campaigns to enlist local pastors to promote favored candidates.

I told the *New York Times* back in 2005 that this ground-level strategy was particularly dangerous for those of us who disagree with the goals of the Religious Right.[19] Leaders of one group even used my comment on some of their literature to buttress what they were doing.

During the run-up to Election Day, AU continued to challenge church-based politicking. As part of the promotional tour for my book *Piety & Politics*, I had a chance to debate Ohio Religious Right leader Russell Johnson and several of his colleagues at a forum in Columbus in early October. Pastor Johnson led efforts to keep Republican gubernatorial candidate Kenneth Blackwell visible in evangelical churches and promote the reelection of US Sen. Mike DeWine. At the forum, Johnson was upbeat about his program of energizing the conservative base.

Johnson assured me that his church was not going to break tax laws—even though several complaints had been filed against his operation earlier this year by fellow clergy in the state. Undaunted, his group never missed a beat, working right until November 7.

The election results must have come as a shock: Democrat Ted Strickland beat Blackwell in a blowout, 60 percent to 37 percent. The GOP's DeWine was knocked out by US Rep. Sherrod Brown by twelve points.

The Religious Right lost some other champions as well, including two senators on its short list for the 2008 Republican presidential nomination: Virginia's George Allen and Pennsylvania's Rick Santorum. Ernest Istook, who as a congressman constantly advocated a constitutional amendment to bring government-supported prayer back to public schools, garnered only 33 percent of the vote as he attempted to become Oklahoma's governor. US Rep. John Hostettler of Indiana, author of the bill in the House of Representatives to deny successful litigant lawyers any attorney fees or costs in certain church-state cases, lost his seat, as did Kentucky's Anne Northup, accused of exploiting the "faith-based" initiative to get pastors to convince congregants to support Republicans.

Does this mean the Religious Right is now a toothless tiger? Sadly, no. Although I am not a hunter, I understand tigers who feel threatened just fight harder. Indeed, on November 8 many in the Religious Right began arguing that the GOP had lost because it hadn't placated religious conservatives enough! In other words, if the Republicans had supported even more extreme measures, they would have won reelection.

Sadly, any lessons about mixing religion and politics were soon lost in the massive run-up to the 2008 elections. The distinction between honest answers and religious politicking was at risk of being completely erased—on all sides.

GOD-TALK AND POLITICIANS: WHEN DOES HONESTY TURN INTO PLAIN OLD PANDERING?[20]

The *New York Times* cited "faith consultant" Mara Vanderslice, who argues that candidates should not use the phrase "separation of church and state" because of its negative connotations for religious voters.[21] Oddly, in our *First Freedom First* polling and focus group work done with the Interfaith Alliance Foundation, the phrase went over very positively with the great majority of our samples.

I never suggest that a person's faith is all for show. My point is that, important as religion may actually be to many of these candidates, I honestly think most voters want to know what politicians will do to fix problems more than what metaphysical values or scriptural references, if any, could be used to justify those solutions.

Once you start talking about your faith, you also need to be prepared for journalists to ask just the kind of questions Soledad O'Brien raised in that recent televised presidential debate on CNN on religion: What do you pray about?— to Senator Clinton; What is your greatest sin?—to Senator Edwards.[22]

Reporters can ask anything they want, but candidates also should be able to say the question is inappropriate (as Mitt Romney did on *60 Minutes* regarding whether he engaged in premarital sex). But if you talk a lot about the topic of religion, and then answer more questions, don't be surprised if you eventually get asked, "Do you really believe in the Virgin Birth?"

This reached an early point of nonlucidity when presumptive 2008 Republican presidential candidate Mitt Romney decided to address how his Mormon background would and would not affect his governance were he to be elected President. It worked for John F. Kennedy in 1960; the results were far less certain for Romney in 2007. As it turned out, of course, Romney's star fell and John McCain joined with Sarah Palin as the Republican "dream team."

ROMNEY, RELIGION, AND JOHN F. KENNEDY: TWO SPEECHES, TWO DIFFERENT VIEWPOINTS[23]

I was disappointed in Mitt Romney's statement today on the role of religion in politics. It was billed in the press as Romney's version of the famous John F. Kennedy speech to the Houston Ministerial Association back in 1960.

But the two addresses were not very similar. Kennedy said, "I believe in an America where the separation of church and state is absolute. . . . I believe in an America that is officially neither Catholic, Protestant, nor Jewish—where no public official either requests or accepts instructions on public policy from the Pope, the National Council of Churches, or any other ecclesiastical source—where no religious body seeks to impose its will directly or indirectly upon the general populace or the public acts of its officials"[24]

Romney took a different tack. While he affirmed religious liberty in principle, he said we are in danger of taking church-state separation too far and that we are at risk of establishing a religion of secularism. He is mistaken. The founders of our Constitution clearly meant for religion and government to be completely separate. That's the only way we can have real religious freedom in our incredibly diverse society.

I was particularly outraged that Romney thinks that the Constitution is somehow based on faith and that judges should rule accordingly. That's a gross misunderstanding of the framework of our constitutional system. Judges should make their decisions based on civil and constitutional law, not religious concepts.

I think it is telling that Romney quoted John Adams instead of Thomas Jefferson or James Madison. Jefferson and Madison are the towering figures who gave us religious liberty and church-state separation.

I was also disappointed that Romney doesn't seem to recognize that many Americans are nonbelievers. Polls repeatedly show that millions of people have chosen to follow no spiritual path at all. Romney ought to have acknowledged that fact.

With blazing speed, Texas governor Rick Perry sought to enter the Republican Presidential primaries in 2012—with a clearly perceived need to grab the "God vote."

MY RESPONSE TO "THE RESPONSE":
WHAT I SAW (AND FELT) AT PERRY'S PRAYER FEST[25]

I don't normally jet off to Houston when the mercury is hitting 102 there, but I just couldn't pass up the opportunity to attend Texas Gov. Rick Perry's big event at Reliant Stadium called "The Response." I also participated in a counterevent the evening before and stirred up trouble in other ways.

"The Response" was initiated by the governor as a gigantic prayer rally for fundamentalist Christians. I found it strange from the start because I was unaware that the Texas governor job description included leading people to Jesus. Moreover, why did the governor need to start a prayer event rolling? Has Texas suddenly developed a dearth of preachers who could do that?

The more I learned about the August 6 event, the more troubling it became. Perry said that attendees would see people of all ages, races, and Christian denominations. This didn't sound very inclusive—although people running the event later made clear in response to a letter of mine and other criticism that they didn't want to bar anybody from attending because, after all, then people could learn about Jesus and presumably be converted. Again, I don't think this is a gubernatorial function.

Americans United, the Texas branch of the American Civil Liberties Union, the Houston AU chapter, and some local activists announced that we would put on a more inclusive and welcoming event at Mount Ararat Baptist Church. Our event, which included Humanists, Unitarians, Jews, Muslims, Hindus, Christians, and others, would share the Constitution, not only one faith tradition. A press conference to explain this event Friday morning drew fourteen television cameras. (Here in Washington only sexting scandals draw that kind of attention.)

I had an opportunity to appear on MSNBC's *Hardball with Chris Matthews* that afternoon, along with Family Research Council president Tony Perkins. Matthews's producers had created a clip highlighting outrageous statements by rally sponsors, including one pastor who claims that the Statue of Liberty is a "demonic idol."

Perkins was asked whether he agreed with this, and looking absolutely nonplussed, responded that he didn't accept everything the other participants had said in the past. He didn't add any criticism of those fringe ideas though and, frankly, I don't think he scored too many points in his favor.

On Saturday morning, it was off to the stadium. From the shuttle, I saw bands of protesters outside the arena, along with some members of the notorious Fred Phelps clan, who were in town to proclaim that the organizers of "The Response" were not homophobic enough.

Inside the facility, I did some media interviews. Sandhya Bathija from AU's Communications Department was working to round up more interviews. As I headed to one, I encountered a muscle-bound fundamentalist weight lifter who wanted to argue with me about the Constitution. This guy belongs to one of those groups that tries to sneak religion into public school assemblies. I was in no mood to argue with him (or get snapped in half), so I kept it short.

A few minutes later, a fellow strolled up to me and asked, "Did anybody force you to be here?" He seemed to think that my complaint (he had seen me on the local news) was that people were there, not that the governor had induced them to come. He was joined by others who were perfectly affable, even though I had a distinct feeling that upon returning to their seats they would be tweeting that they had just come across a demon in the foyer.

Notwithstanding some good gospel bluegrass from Ricky Skaggs, I couldn't take it any longer. It wasn't because of the praying itself; it was what I knew was behind their calls for the nation to improve itself. They meant to stop all reproductive choice, block same-sex marriage, divert tax money to private religious schools, and fight a new crusade against Islam. That's not exactly the spiritual platform I'm on.

I ended my trip by going outside to greet the protesters (who had been placed in four different areas near the main road) and was happy to see the largely favorable response, including waves and honking, from passing vehicles. Of course, there were some ruder responses, but in America it's fine to protest even protesters.

Not everyone in Reliant Stadium was some hopeless bigot. It's just that, on balance, I enjoyed being with the folks at Mount Ararat Baptist Church and the protesters outside because they represent the true breadth of American thought.

Recall that I like top ten lists. When I use them in speeches, among other things, it gives people who may be bored some general sense of when the address will be over so they can go home and binge-watch *The Walking Dead* before going to bed.

Here is part of one I did at the John Danforth Center at Washington University in St. Louis during the heart of the 2012 presidential nomination campaign.

I enjoy Missouri, and as I was flying in this afternoon I noticed that you have a lot of open spaces here, a considerable amount of undeveloped land.

I recently noticed the same thing when I was traveling to Indiana and Tennessee and even Florida over the last few weeks. Maybe somebody should tell Newt Gingrich we may not have to colonize the moon after all! Don't worry: I'll manage to disparage every candidate in the next forty-five minutes.

During the 1992 Presidential campaign between Bill Clinton and George H. W. Bush, Clinton campaign strategist James Carville put up a sign in his candidate's Little Rock headquarters with three points on it: point #2 simply read: "The Economy, Stupid." Just like people think Humphrey Bogart said in *Casablanca*, "Play it again, Sam," although he didn't, people think Carville actually used the now popular variation "It's the Economy, Stupid." And of course, others have replaced "economy" with alternatives like "deficit," "math," and tonight "religion."

Now, sometimes, like tonight, I do speeches that are in the form of top ten lists. I do this for two reasons. One, David Letterman does top ten lists that make him popular, and somebody in an airport once mistook me for David Letterman. (Frankly, I am much more frequently mistaken for Alan Alda or 1990s Republican Presidential candidate Steve Forbes: "I love your flat tax," they say.) Second, if you know it's a top ten list, you won't find it as necessary to wonder "how the hell long is he going to speak?" You'll know by the number how close to the end I am.

I'm very worried about the future of separation of church and state: will it survive in a meaningful way? I'll tell you, there are a very large number of people throughout this country whose values, statements, and conduct appear to place them in some alternate universe governed by some constitution they apparently found while cleaning out their sock drawer. It is not the American "living" Constitution that reflects, increasingly, the search for individual freedom and justice: in other words, what the Constitution's purpose is.

So, for the next period, here are the top ten reasons I am convinced the current political climate, overtly and covertly, and in spite of being told by cable news commentators that it is about something else, is really about religion. This means I'm worried about whether we'll keep the tradition of real religious liberty alive for all Americans: the ones on the two thousand different spiritual paths people tread and the twenty to twenty-five million Americans who are nonreligious and quite comfortable about that. So, here is why this election is all about religion.

First, one party's candidates think they are chosen by God. For the first time in modern history, four people originally seeking the Republican nomination said that God had chosen them to run. OK—now we know there was a failure to communicate. Herman Cain out of the race; Michelle Bachmann out of the race; Rick Perry out of the race. The only possible God appointee still in is Rick Santorum, and Rick reminds us that God told his wife, not him, that he should run. This fact alone could be yet another confirmation that women are often better listeners than men, although in Rick's view they still shouldn't go too close to combat and should be instructed on contraception by the Catholic Bishops. By the way, this is presumably the same divine voice that told former Arkansas governor Mike Huckabee not to run and to stay on Fox News so he could afford the big mansion he's building in Blue Mountain Beach, Florida.

Second, the Bible, not the Constitution is becoming the basis for federal law. Ron Paul told a meeting in Washington last October that he didn't just get his position on abortion from the Bible (odd because the Bible doesn't even mention the topic) but that he derives all of his policies from the Bible, including his tax policy and his defense policy. Isn't he mixing up the Constitution with his Holy Scripture? It can get confusing.

But, see, we aren't supposed to be making policy based on anyone's interpretation of their holy writ; we are supposed to be using the commonly shared values found in our foundational document: the Constitution.

So now we come to reason number three that I am convinced that it's all about religion: Democrats are working hard not to get too far behind on the Jesus momentum. Apparently, the more nonconstitutional one party gets, the more the alternative starts ratcheting up its religiosity quotient. For example, in the week following the release of Gov. Rick Perry's now somewhat famous television advertisement labeling the Obama administration as antireligious—the first salvo in what has been called "The War on Religion," two curious things happened. First, HHS Secretary Kathleen Sibelius rejected the scientific findings of the FDA, which had concluded it would be a good thing to allow access by women under seventeen to over-the-counter Plan B contraceptives. Rejecting this was a huge win for the Religious Right. And that Monday morning, Joshua DuBois, the head of the President's Office of Faith-Based Initiatives, just happened to send out a color photo from the Associated Press to his enormous email list of the Presidential family walking across the street from the White House to a church. Curiously, the mere fact that this was deemed "newsworthy" just reminded a lot of people that he usually doesn't go to church. And the President went to the incredibly rightwing National Prayer Breakfast last month and gave a speech in which he more or less suggested that Jesus would like his tax reform package.

I don't want every civil libertarian among you to get too depressed. "God talk" overkill seems to be having some unexpected blowback. Just a week after Governor Perry's war on religion ad hit YouTube, it had received over seven hundred thousand "thumbs down" clicks, the third largest negative reaction to anything ever posted in the history of the website. (And, yes, he was beaten by a Justin Bieber video.) In addition, the Southern Baptist Convention recently released a poll they had done in which 16 percent of Americans said they were more likely to vote for a candidate who regularly shares his or her religious beliefs publicly, while a whopping 30 percent say such "sharing" alone would make it less likely they'd vote for that candidate.

Fourth reason: We are told by media outlets as diverse as the Fox News Channel and the *Drudge Report* (just kidding about diversity) that there is a mounting "war on religion" (well, actually, the Christian religion) in America. I testified a few months ago before the House Judiciary Committee, now chaired by Arizona congressman Trent Franks, on the state of religious freedom in the United States. Mr. Franks began the event by noting that "one Christopher Columbus was exercising his religious liberty when he went out into the oceans to find the new world and came upon America."[26] As I recall it he was looking for India, and Mr. Franks of course also failed to recall there actually were people here, they had a set of indigenous religions, and Chris and the variety of European successors did all they could to convert them or wipe them out by shooting them or spreading disease.

With that as the backdrop, little wonder that he didn't seem to accept my premise that if you are a member of the majority Christian faith still here, there is what I called "a dizzying level of religious freedom" and that the challenges to practicing you faith or asserting your lack of it arising almost exclusively from minorities in America. I gave examples, of course. Down in Murfreesboro, Tennessee, the construction of a mosque was delayed by vandalism, bomb threats, and a baseless lawsuit supported by the lieutenant governor, who thinks Islam is not a "real religion." In Johnson County, Tennessee . . . I am not trying to pick on this state; there are worse states on the separation of church and state scale; at least Tennessee doesn't have a governor who wants to have taxpayers subsidize construction of a Noah's

Ark-themed water park—that's in Kentucky. But back to Johnson County. We won a lawsuit there, where an atheist simply wanted to put up a display documenting the historical roots of church-state separation in a courthouse public forum that already displayed the Ten Commandments. One councilmember there said he was happy when anybody moved there, but if that person didn't believe in God, it'd be even better if he left town.

What even I—a man who is rarely surprised by anything said, done, or even contemplated by the Religious Right—found surprising was the bizarre set of examples of anti-Christian activities used by the other two "Republican-chosen" witnesses: Colby May, chief counsel for Pat Robertson's American Center for Law and Justice and Bishop William Lori of Connecticut, who is now head of the new official lobbying office for the Conference of Catholic Bishops.

The Robertson-ite [May] began with the tale of a sex education "assembly" in Massachusetts that he claimed was so graphic that it violated the religious freedom rights of parents in the school, presumably because it contradicted their approach to sexuality information. That approach, apparently, is the one where you say, "Don't have sex; it's ugly anyway." Now, the parents actually had the right to opt out of the whole sex education program, but they didn't get notice of the specific assembly, which was called "Hot, Sexy, and Safer." A federal court ruled that there was no constitutional violation of the parents' rights, and this case occurred in 1995. Attorney Colby May cited no other courts that followed the decision, nor any other incidents involving anything like this. I was tempted to say the case was so old that the program would now probably be called "Lukewarm, Sagging, But Still Safer."

The Bishop, on the other hand, was moaning first about same-sex marriage, which, as we all know, clearly disrupts the authenticity, stability, and historicity of "marriage" and probably makes men from Georgia go astray.

But more disturbing was his kind of radical redefinition of the meaning of "religious liberty," which presents us with proof number five: The First Amendment's protection of religion means something new this year. Religious freedom is not the freedom to worship anymore or the freedom to evangelize: it is the right to get huge amounts of tax money and then ignore any and all laws you don't like.

Lori claimed, for example, that certain Catholic Church-related charities were being denied grants because of anti-Catholicism. In fact, Catholic-related charities appear to be getting more funding in this administration than they did in the Bush Administration. Bishop Lori, though, decried the specific denial of a grant to help sex trafficking victims. Now, sex trafficking victims have by definition been sexually abused; some are rescued literally from brothels where they are being forced to "work." The Catholic charities, however, will not give them Plan B, or help pregnant victims to obtain abortions, or even counsel them about where they could get abortions. Is it any wonder that a group that will not promote a truly comprehensive program on trafficking is passed over for ones that will? This is like complaining that you didn't get a grant for afterschool mentoring in reading after you concede that the mentors are themselves illiterate.

But it actually gets worse. The Bishop also thought that there needed to be more exemptions to other federal programs so, for example, Catholic charitable institutions could take government funding for adoption and refuse to place children with gay or lesbian couples, even if the city in which they were operating had strong local or state statutes protecting access for LGBT communities. Doesn't all this sound a little like what the Right falsely claims the LGBT community wants: "special rights"?

The sixth reason I say this election is about religion is that following up on the notorious decision in the Citizens United case, there is elevated talk that even tax-exempt churches should be allowed to engage in partisan electioneering. What could possibly go wrong with having every "ministry" from the Little Brown Church in the Vale to the television megaministries of prosperity gospel pastors like Benny Hinn just endorse candidates from the pulpit, send out pledge envelopes for their favorite pol, and maybe just ship money from the collection plate to the candidate's office (money is speech you know).

Remember the first primary. It was long ago; in fact, I think dinosaurs still roamed the earth at that time. There was a change in the election count for the Iowa primary a few weeks after it had occurred and Rick Santorum won by thirty-four votes, not lost by eight. Former Senator Santorum's extraordinary showing was made possible largely because of the personal endorsements of some of Iowa's most influential evangelical pastors. What those pastors tried not to do, though, was risk violating federal tax law by endorsing or supporting a candidate with church resources. North Carolina Congressman Walter Jones has been trying to change this for years and remove the longstanding tax code's prohibition against churches endorsing or opposing any candidate for public office. Americans United has always opposed this. But this year, joined by Democrat Emmanuel Cleaver—from right in this neck of the Midwestern woods, Jones is trying to pass legislation that gives all nonprofits the right to endorse candidates, and it seems to me that then all of them can make the same contributions that Halliburton or some Super PAC can make. Well, we still oppose it. And the good news is over two-thirds of the American people in the latest poll are on our side.

This is all consistent with the best from our history. The Rev. Dr. Martin Luther King Jr. spoke in religious institutions almost every day of his adult life but never once told a congregation or gathering there for whom to vote.

Seventh clue: Some of the talk about education is downright biblical and most of the changes sought are thinly disguised efforts to subsidize private religious education. Rick Santorum has even attacked President Obama's plans to get more scholarship aid for young people to go to college as an obvious effort to "secularize" young people. Everybody running seems to be willing to deflect more money from public schools to private—overwhelmingly religious—ones. Since the 2002 decision in the Cleveland voucher case, few successful voucher programs have been implemented if they are challenged under state constitutions. This hasn't stopped the ideologues though.

Eighth, Democrats and Republicans are getting attached to the idea that "faith-based" institutions that do work in the community are obviously entitled to get government funding to do so. One real tragedy of the Obama administration's continued commitment to, and indeed expansion of, predecessor George Bush's "faith-based initiative" is that it normalizes something truly abnormal in American history. For most of our history eleemosynary organizations—charitable groups including churches and other places of work and worship—were assumed to be responsible for raising money from believers for all their activities: from paying the preacher, to fixing the church roof, to setting up programs for the homeless. But these days, the idea of "equal access" to money by religious and secular groups is becoming the norm. It is terribly mistaken.

The greed of these groups is insufferable. In many communities, Catholic Charities, the Salvation Army, and the domestic arm of World Vision suck up such a high percentage of funding that about one third of the smaller shelters, agencies, crisis centers, and training programs have gone out of business since 2008. To compound the problem, the big boys have the audacity to say, "If you make us abide by a lot of government rules or the civil rights acts, we'll stop working and the poor will be without help."

There's a moral position for you! Here's some good news: We win when we call their bluff about this. In the District of Columbia, Catholic Charities said it would move its (yes, heavily subsidized by government) social programs out of DC if the City Council passed the same-sex marriage bill. Again, this is a moral stance if I ever heard one. The Council passed the bill and Catholic Charities only got out of the adoption placement business. It turned out that it was only seeking help for thirty-four kids and those children were immediately picked up by other secular groups, and religious charities not stuck in the twelfth century.

Ninth, at the nonpresidential level (although candidates will eventually get drawn into this), we are learning that politicians love "states' rights" unless those pesky state constitutions protect religious minorities from having to shell out money for the activities of religious majorities. This is why they are trying to change them, starting down in Florida with Amendment 8 on the November ballot. Amendment 8 is an effort to literally erase the separation of church and state provision in Florida's constitution, a section mirrored in the constitutions of thirty-seven other states.

In my view, the most important decision ever written by the late Chief Justice William Rehnquist was in a case called *Locke v. Davey*. This issue was whether the state of Washington's Supreme Court was permitted to interpret its "no aid to religion" clause (not dissimilar to the one in Florida and the one in your state's constitution) in such a way as to refuse to fund the education of a seminary student in the same way that it provided scholarship assistance to law students or agriculture students. Mr. Davey said that violated the US Constitution. Rehnquist, who conceded that he wasn't a fan of the stringent no-aid provision, nevertheless ruled in a 7–2 decision that the Washington Supreme Court had the right to interpret its own constitution in a way that would give a broader "separation" between church and state than had been recognized in the First Amendment. Now, this is what I call states' rights properly understood.

And the tenth piece of evidence that religion is indeed what this election cycle is about is the nearly apocalyptic biblical approach to hating the federal courts. Here, again, is Rick Santorum: "Satan is attacking the great institutions of America, using the voices of pride, vanity, and sensuality as the root to attack all of the strong plants that had deeply rooted in the American tradition."[27] This is not merely a challenge to block even the moderate jurists President Obama has somewhat haltingly tried to appoint to the judiciary, but to challenge the very ideas of an independent judiciary. The new mantra of the Right is that we don't have three coequal branches of government, that the courts are an inferior branch that has no final authority. Some even question the principle established in *Marbury v. Madison* in 1803 that the Supreme Court can declare statutes unconstitutional. And, then, of course, the logic of these states becomes impeccably perverse when Newt Gingrich notes that judges should be accountable to the president and Congress for their rulings, arguing a few weeks ago that federal marshals should be called in to forcibly bring judges to appear at congressional hearings about decisions Congress doesn't like. This feels particularly personal to us at Americans United because he calls out by name judge Fred Biery, who granted us a temporary restraining order in a case in Texas challenging use of prayer at a high school graduation. In a speech in October, Gingrich called on Judge Biery to be "summarily dismissed." By who was not made clear, but perhaps he thinks he has that power himself already. Gingrich, particularly on matters of religion in the courts, sees the courts as, at least, figuratively—perhaps literally—"demonic."

See, we are at the end, and for the first time tonight I will admit I lied to you about something. We are not quite finished: thirty seconds to go. This lecture may have depressed some of you. Even leaders many of you like seem to have lost their way through the thicket of religious pressure groups and dubious new spins of the real meaning of the Constitution. But all is not lost. The only way we will without uncertainty lose the heart and soul of the First Amendment if we give up the fight. Hopelessness is the biggest challenge: apathy is a suicide pact with our constitutional values. The great constitutionalist, Justice Learned Hand, once said: "Liberty lies in the hearts of men and women; when it dies there, no constitution, no law, no court can save it."[28] I travel the country; people like many of you come out. Many of you defend the wall of separation against the dynamiters, the bulldozers, the well-heeled termites who would tear it down, brick by brick or board by board. Those of us in Washington couldn't help save it without all of you. For those of you who do, a big thank-you. To all: Thanks for coming out tonight.

As an aside, Pat Robertson once again seemed to have his divine communication wires scrambled about the 2012 campaign—President Obama was re-elected easily with 51 percent of the electoral vote.

Chapter 10

WHY DOES ANYBODY SPEND THEIR ADULT LIFE DOING THIS?

B ecause of the people you meet, and the places you go, the opportunities you are given, and the "alternate universes" you visit (and the awards you get if you stick to it long enough).

NICE FAMOUS PEOPLE

But, okay, one of the other things that keeps me going are the genuinely nice people you meet, including genuinely nice famous people—including comic genius Stephen Colbert, newscaster Walter Cronkite, and the actual founder of Americans United.

Here are some excerpts from columns about some of the encounters:

Several weeks ago AU Director of Development Rudy Bush and I spent a delightful few hours with Glenn and Ruth Archer.[1] Dr. Glenn Archer was the founding executive director of Americans United, then known as Protestants and Other Americans United for Separation of Church and State (POAU). I've heard he was a shoo-in to become governor of Kansas before he was lured to Washington to take a chance on running a brand-new, unfunded organization in need of the missionary zeal he could provide. He is today a still mesmerizing storyteller, with a wealth of detail about the cause to which he dedicated most of his adult life.

Dr. Archer explained to us how he attended meeting and rallies where thousands of people crowded Masonic temples, or Washington's Constitution Hall, or the largest Presbyterian church in some Midwestern town, just to learn of the latest challenge to separation. We can only imagine what rich and moving experiences these must have been! Where were VCRs and minicams when we needed them?

Dr. Archer wrote in his autobiography *The Dream Lives On*, "Circumstances may change. Discontent with institutions may grow. New and subtle arguments may be advanced to effect greater entanglement between church and state."[2] Indeed, this is a time and place different from that of the founding days—or even founding decades—of AU.

There has been a disturbing trend within many faith groups to ignore the threats to separation out there, not wishing to stir up controversy. People then to sit home and watch *Larry King Live* for political sustenance rather than go to hear the addresses of visiting scholars, luminaries, or even rabble-rousers. We get embarrassed about "passing the plate" at public meetings, preferring the lure of direct mail, telemarketing, and 800-number response lines.

But even as these emphases and styles change, the threats actually remain the same. The first legal case Dr. Archer got AU involved with was in Dixon, New Mexico, where Roman Catholic nuns, brothers, and priests were paid salaries to teach in public schools, adding a hefty dose of religious activity alongside geometry and world civilization. All this was done at a then-staggering cost of a quarter of a million dollars per year. Was this activity so different from today's actions, where the Rev. Jerry Falwell's sectarian Liberty University in Virginia gets more than one million dollars yearly in taxpayers' funds to subsidize mandatory church attendance, doctrinal teaching, and the expulsion of students who attend the "wrong" church?

The Manifesto of AU, excerpts of which were printed on the front page of the *New York Times* on January 12, 1948, cited as one goal to "give all possible aid to the citizens of any county or state who are seeking to protect their public schools from sectarian domination." That is still an important part of our mandate, and instead of efforts to require students to pray Hail Marys (one of the practices in Dixon), the "new and subtle" efforts are to interject sectarian holiday celebrations, bring youth ministers onto high school campuses, and perform daily "educational" readings from the Bible. The song remains the same.

Eleanor Roosevelt once told Glenn Archer, "The battle for church-state separation may have to be fought all over again." She has been proven correct, over and over again.

It would be nice for AU to be able to pack up its archives and retire its staff because we had won a lasting victory. The smoke on the horizon, though, suggests we shouldn't be hiring the U-Hauls to move those archives right now.

Defending Church-State Separation: It Can Be a Laughing Matter[3]

A few weeks after the media frenzy of the days leading up to the removal of Judge Roy Moore's monolith, AU's Communications Department got an unusual call. It was from a producer of *The Daily Show with Jon Stewart*, a program on the cable network Comedy Central. That's right, it's an all-humor network. The producer wanted me to come to New York for an interview.

This was not an offer to have me do a five-minute stand-up comedy act. It was just an interview about the Ten Commandments lawsuit that would be interspersed with clips from an interview with Alabama's Christian Coalition head John Giles. They wanted me to play it straight.

Everybody I know who is between twenty and thirty-five watches and loves this show and insisted that I must do it. They did concede that the editing of these interviews is sometimes creative, to say the least, and that the format is clearly that of a mock news program. Nevertheless, I must do it, I was told. They said my own children would even watch it. So I went to New York City one Tuesday to film it at the Judson Memorial Church where my friend Peter Laarman is the minister.

The filming took an astonishing three hours, while I sat in the choir loft surrounded by really hot TV lights, cameras, and other unidentifiable electronic gizmos. Some of the questions from correspondent Stephen Colbert were pretty routine, such as, "Why did Americans United get involved in this case?"[4]

Most, however, were a tad more unusual. One of my favorites was, "Did you get your ordination by responding to a computer pop-up ad?" I was happy to have the opportunity to clear up how I got ordained, since Falwell constantly accuses me of being a phony minister.

A second interesting question was, "Now, the Ten Commandments are in the Constitution, right?" When I responded in a pretty straightforward way to that one, the follow-up was, "I was just in Alabama and those folks told me they were. You might want to check your facts."

Colbert also asked how I could say that the monument removal had not cast a pall over Alabama since when visiting he "got a speeding ticket for going a mere eight miles over the speed limit, could not find a cup of coffee after 9:30 in the morning, and couldn't find a single Starbucks in the capital city at all."

Remember, this is a comedy program. I will admit that I couldn't keep a straight face even listening to some of the questions, and I could more or less see the overall direction this piece was going to take.

I was able to appreciate that spirit, knowing that humor has long had its place in the range of protective tactics that prevent people in activist battles from sinking into despair or rage.

THE MARCH FOR WOMEN'S LIVES: ONE SPEECH, TWO MINUTES, A MILLION AMENS[5]

There is something humbling about being asked to speak to one million people. Just over one hundred of us were asked to do just that, each for two minutes, by the organizers of the March for Women's Lives in Washington on April 25, 2004.

My task in the time allotted was to look at the role of Religious Right leaders in efforts to overturn the landmark *Roe v. Wade* decision and their push to restrict birth control and education on human sexuality. Whatever the "anti-choice" movement may have been in other iterations, it is now almost exclusively an effort to impose a particular religious viewpoint on all of us.

On the march route from the Washington Monument to the US Capitol there were several blocks of so-called "pro-life" demonstrators lining the streets; I did not see a single person waving a poster, screaming through a bullhorn, or wearing a t-shirt who did not make it unequivocally clear that he or she was there to make a religious statement about what God wanted.

There seemed to be a nearly instinctive understanding of the roots of the anti-choice movement in that crowd. I was introduced at about 11:30 a.m., following Sen. Hillary Rodham Clinton and folksinger Sonia (one of the few songwriters still writing very good and very political songs in the Woody Guthrie and Phil Ochs tradition). When the emcee just mentioned the name of our organization—Americans United for Separation of Church and State—there was thunderous applause for blocks. I thought about not saying anything so as not to dampen the moment, but that thought passed.

Here is the heart of what I did say: "The Religious Right is out there trying to collapse the wall of separation between church and state, to crush anyone who does not see the world the way it does. And, if they succeed, we will enter a Falwellian Dark Age where state-sponsored religion replaces responsible moral choice. We'll wake up to a nation where comprehensive sex education is censored, and we just pray that ignorance doesn't kill our children. Our country's laws could be based on Pat Robertson's messages from God, not based on the liberties secured by our Constitution.

"The Religious Right's leaders are the people who contemptibly proclaimed that pro-choice Americans caused the attacks of September 11. They are neither smart enough nor moral enough to dare impose their vision on all of America. On this Sunday morning, this is hallowed space. This is a place where every child is a wanted child. This is where every woman's moral choice trumps the will of politicians and TV preachers.

"This is where we honor the struggles of our mothers and promote the dreams of our daughters by committing ourselves to protecting women's lives—by protecting women's choices. In 2004, pessimism is death. Dr. Martin Luther King reminded us that 'the arc of change is long but it tends toward justice.' We will step off soon on this historic march to help guarantee that justice, once achieved, will never be rolled back. The only way we lose is if we quit. Will you be quitting?"

Needless to say, that final question was not treated rhetorically and there was a resounding "No" shouted back to the stage.

This was a sadly necessary, but magnificent, day. I mentioned that you approach a speech to a million people with real humility. It is also true that there is tremendous excitement in completing such a presentation and sometimes even unexpected rewards for the effort.

After the march, I went to a little restaurant in Vienna, Virginia, to unwind and hear Eric Andersen, a songwriter I've been listening to since 1963. I was alone at a prime table near the stage, and a family asked if they could join me.

"Of course," I said.

The father recognized me as an image from one of the giant TV screens that had been placed throughout the Mall. He asked me if I had addressed the march earlier.

I wasn't sure what to expect, but I said yes, I had been on the stage. I needn't have worried. He simply smiled and said, "Can I buy you a cup of coffee?"

AND THAT'S THE WAY IT IS: WALTER CRONKITE, AN ANCHOR OF TRUTH[6]

Most child-rearing experts would tell you that families should eat dinner together every night. My mother and father were great role models in every way, but did fail that dinner test (at least on weekdays). But it was my fault. As a young teenager, I insisted that I had to eat dinner on a TV tray in the living room, embedded in front of the fifteen-minute CBS evening news broadcast to watch Walter Cronkite.

I admired Cronkite from the start. Like many Americans, I stayed with his broadcast over the years, through the tumultuous '60s and '70s until his retirement in March of 1981. During my professional career, I've had the opportunity to meet many broadcast journalists, but Cronkite has not been one of them.

That changed recently. It took about five decades, but I finally got to meet Walter Cronkite in February.

It came about like this: Since leaving the anchor chair, Cronkite hasn't hesitated to speak out on the issues of the day that concern him. He's a strong advocate for church-state separation and was an early endorser of First Freedom First, the joint religious-freedom project sponsored by Americans United and the Interfaith Alliance Foundation.

When the Rev. C. Welton Gaddy, president of the Interfaith Alliance Foundation, told me that Cronkite had agreed to take part in a First Freedom First event in San Jose, California, sponsored by the Commonwealth Club, I was delighted.

Younger folks might have a hard time grasping the iconic status accorded to Cronkite and his famous "And that's the way it is" sign-off. Folks closer my age don't. Every night he was with us, reporting on the struggle for racial justice, the Vietnam War, the race to the moon, the Cuban missile crisis, and so much more. These events were utterly fascinating, even if they sometimes seemed far removed from my normal life growing up in the steel town of Bethlehem, Pennsylvania. For years, Americans routinely told pollsters that they considered Cronkite the "most trusted man in America."

Welton, Walter, and I had a chance to chat for about a half hour in an anteroom before the event began. Cronkite talked about his love of sailing and developments in the news business. However, he seemed even more interested in asking questions than in answering them.

As one example, he quizzed Welton and me on the role Mitt Romney's

Mormonism could play in voter interest in the upcoming presidential campaign; he wondered whether there were parallels with America's struggle with electing John F. Kennedy as our first Roman Catholic head of state.

There were a few other things Cronkite taught me about the news; mainly, that it is all right to have some emotional connection to what you were reporting. Who can forget his effort to fight back tears when reporting that President Kennedy had been assassinated in Dallas? That clip remains one of the most powerful images of television history.

After Cronkite spent years covering the Vietnam War each evening, chronicling both the loss of life in Southeast Asia and the turmoil in the United States, he eventually stated publicly that it had been a blunder. President Lyndon B. Johnson reportedly told allies when he heard this, "If I've lost Walter Cronkite, I've lost the country."

Fair or not, I continue to look at news through a lens shaped by Walter Cronkite.

THAT'S ENTERTAINMENT!: BRINGING HOME THE BACON (BROTHERS) AND OTHERS FOR SIX DEGREES OF SEPARATION[7]

When I left the rehearsal for our recent movie *Everything You Always Wanted to Know About Separation of Church and State . . . But Were Afraid To Ask*, I was consumed by the thought that this was the most interesting collection of people in one place that I have been with in my entire life—and this was even before we factored in the musicians and Hollywood celebrities! The film was taped one evening, edited through the night, and then fed via satellite to movie theaters in thirty-seven cities the next day.

Perhaps even more importantly, the "champions" of religious freedom whose stories were being told had never met each other and had not recognized that the fight against an evangelistic teacher in New Jersey had much of the same feel as the battle against a Ten Commandments-wielding judge in Alabama or that proselytization efforts at the Air Force Academy in Colorado had the same sickening effect as did religious discrimination in Nevada. Listening to these courageous people talking to each other was mesmerizing.

And, then, of course, there were musicians, actors, and comedians who joined the First Freedom First affair. I had watched Jack Klugman long before *The Odd Couple*, in the great courtroom drama *Twelve Angry Men* (which was last year remastered on DVD for its fiftieth anniversary). I'm a big fan of

Kevin Bacon both as an actor and a musician, having seen him at Washington's best music room, the Birchmere, and at the Philadelphia Folk Festival.

Our program host, Peter Coyote, acts in terrific films and has the greatest voice for narration since Orson Welles (thus, his extensive work on Ken Burns's documentaries).

One more thing: Many of you have heard of the whimsical game "Six Degrees of Kevin Bacon," whereby players attempt to link another actor to Kevin through film roles. The idea is that Kevin is always only six films, or "degrees," away from every other living actor. After this event, I'm pleased to be just one degree from him—if those preview screenings really count as "films."

Following a True Compass: When Someone Had to Take the Lead, Ted Kennedy Was Always There[8]

The first time I met Sen. Ted Kennedy was back in the mid-1970s when I was working for the social justice arm of the United Church of Christ.

About twenty-five activists were meeting in a Senate conference room to hash out how to proceed on building support for full congressional representation for the District of Columbia. There were numerous squabbles about tactics and timing.

Then Kennedy swept into the room. Kennedy was known as a strong advocate for the District, and within minutes he assessed the situation and knew what to do. He did an astonishing off-the-cuff speech about the injustice of nearly one million people paying taxes and sending their children to war without having voting congressional representatives or senators to represent their interests. After those remarks, the groups started paying attention to the goal, not their institutional differences.

Over the years, in the numerous nonprofit groups I worked for, I had many opportunities to work with Kennedy's staff. They were extraordinary people themselves, who often stayed in their Senate positions for many years. They saw their work as a public service, not just a stepping stone to a slot as a highly paid K Street lobbyist.

Sometimes they would try to "protect" their boss from taking positions on controversial areas people like me would ask him to become involved with. Frequently, though, their views were ultimately rejected, as the senator would weigh in on why "someone" had to take the lead and that he was that "someone."

Ted Kennedy was a person with an instinctive sense of what the Constitution means. He came from a radically different background than the Rev. Dr. Martin Luther King Jr. Both, however, viewed the call for justice at its root not as just a religious matter but a demand to be faithful to the written promises of our founding document, the Constitution, and the wise expansions of rights through the amendment process.

"Equal protection" of the laws meant you treated all people fairly; "no laws" abridging freedom of speech and press meant even objectionable comments were not the subject of government regulation.

We saw this demonstrated in many ways. When Kennedy was not able to be in town the night of Americans United's fiftieth-anniversary dinner, he insisted on recording a very personal video for us.

"For fifty years, Americans United for Separation of Church and State has been a skillful, tireless, and indispensable ally in the ongoing struggle to protect religious liberty," Kennedy said. "All Americans are in your debt on this auspicious fiftieth-anniversary celebration."

At Americans United, we knew we could always count on Ted Kennedy to oppose various schemes giving tax aid to religious schools, school prayer amendments, and other threats to the church-state wall. He also helped lead the fight to keep Robert Bork off the Supreme Court.

But there was a very human side to him as well. In spite of the burdens of leadership on so many issues, the senator never lost touch with the individual people hurting in America.

No book could chronicle every instance of kindness by the senator. But I want to tell just one: I'm writing this just a few days before my son is getting married. Twenty years ago, he had been diagnosed with a rare form of muscle cancer.

Imagine what my wife and I went through. Imagine our feelings of despair. When Kennedy heard about the initial diagnosis, he offered to send my son a note about his own son's illness and urge him to be strong.

The offer was as unforgettable to me as any policy position he ever took. And when my son made a full recovery, Ted Kennedy couldn't have been more pleased to hear it.

That was the Ted Kennedy I knew. That was the Ted Kennedy I will miss. Americans have lost a man the likes of whom we will not see again for a very long time.

OF ALLIES AND ANNIVERSARIES: MEETING FRIENDS AT THE INTERSECTION OF RELIGION AND POLITICS[9]

I've always been a fan of the actor Richard Dreyfuss—even before he starred in *Jaws*.

Recently, I had the chance to meet him at an event in Washington, DC, sponsored by the Religious Action Center of Reform Judaism (RAC), a great ally in the fight to preserve religious liberty.

Dreyfuss was the master of ceremonies for a celebration marking the RAC's fiftieth anniversary. I was honored to have been invited to participate by the Center's longtime director, Rabbi David Saperstein. My role was to speak briefly about the importance of the Center's voice—and indeed all of the voices we can gather in defense of separation of church and state.

I was introduced by Jane Wishner, a long-time lawyer and activist who had been a legislative assistant for the Center back in the '70s. I first met her then and have encountered her in other events over the years. Jane explained a number of programs that got her and many other young people involved with the RAC's public policy work and then went on to say what a funny guy I was. When you get an introduction like that, it's a good thing if you just happen to have a few zingers for the crowd.

For example, I mentioned that I was stuck in an airport on the way to San Antonio a few days earlier and started playing around in my head with the idea of incorporating some reference to every one of Dreyfuss's films into my seven-minute address. I noted that this worked for a while with *The American President* and *Whose Life Is It Anyway?* but that I had to end the whole mental project when I realized he had also been in a film last year called *Piranha 3-D*. Not much to go with on that one.

Speaking of humor, at a reception before the program began, I ran into Sen. Al Franken (D-MN) whom, in a previous incarnation, I used to encounter at Christian Coalition meetings in Washington. (I assure you that he was getting comic material there, not trying to absorb the Coalition's bad history and constitutional analysis.) We chatted about how strange it was to see the same kind of people who were there in the '90s now roaming the halls of Congress with a Tea Party banner flying metaphorically over their heads.

Long-Form Television[10]

On a recent Saturday night, I was happy to see Phil Donahue being interviewed on CNN by Piers Morgan.[11]

Phil was great as always; his answers persistently brought a smile to my face. And the clips of his show (including one with Marlo Thomas as a guest before they ended up dating and marrying) reminded me of the numerous times I was on both his syndicated show and his unfortunately short-lived programs on MSNBC and the now-defunct NewsTalk Television network.

In those recollections, however, I was also saddened by the state of both daytime talk shows and evening cable news shows. It's not because it isn't fun to be on *Hardball with Chris Matthews* or *The Ed Show* or (occasionally) Fox News. It's because it is pretty difficult to say much beyond sound bites in the five minutes allotted these days for the average segment. (Some are even shorter at three minutes.)

What Phil did—and what William F. Buckley did in his two-hour, unedited specials—was to give a long forum to issues that mattered—and still do. A Buckley debate on evolution that I did more than ten years ago still elicits comments from people in audiences I speak to now.

Sing It Loud and Proud: AU Lifts Many Voices United for Separation of Church and State[12]

As many of you know, Americans United hosted a series of concerts around the country in late September to boost awareness about church-state separation, raise money for AU, and, well, have some fun.

My daughter Christina lives in Massachusetts. She sat down at the Voices United concert in Newton and began chatting with the man next to her, whom she did not know. He turned out to be Ellery Schempp, the plaintiff in the famous 1963 Supreme Court school prayer ruling *Abington Township School District v. Schempp*. I've known Ellery for years; I'm glad my daughter got to know him as well.

There are other great stories from what turned out to be a magical weekend. In Montgomery, Alabama, Morris Dees of the Southern Poverty Law Center arranged a show in a local theater he owns featuring blues great Guy Davis. Greg Lipper, AU's senior litigation counsel, went down for the show and told me he was blown away by Davis's artistry.

In Rehoboth Beach, Delaware, AU Director of Communications Joe Conn arranged to rent a local community center and hosted Anne Hills and David Roth. Roth drove across several states to play this gig.

Jackson, Mississippi, hosted Jenna Lindbo at the Julep Restaurant, a venue that often opens its doors to special events by the LGBT community. Jenna flew in for the show and came back raving about the energy she witnessed there.

In New Orleans, a very special show took place in Ward 8, featuring poet Chuck Perkins and accompanying musicians, as Perkins performed his unique brand of slam poetry with a strong focus on social justice.

I even got in on the act. At my home in Maryland, I hosted folk singer Tom Pacheco, an artist I can never hear enough from. More than a hundred friends crowded into my living room for this very special acoustic show.

The big finale was in Los Angeles. At the historic El Rey Theater, Americans United played host to Sarah Silverman and Russell Brand, two edgy and thought-provoking comedians and actors.

Both Sarah and Russell were incredibly gracious, down to Earth, and highly professional. It was a joy to work with them.

So why did we do this? As a long-time fan of folk music, I am aware of the power of that medium for social protest. Folk music—the people's music—provided the soundtrack to some of the great social justice struggles of our times. I wanted to tap into that spirit to increase awareness of Americans United's mission.

I'm aware that not everyone shares my fondness for folk, so I made sure that we included other genres. When I asked Boston-area singer/songwriter Catie Curtis to head up this project, she agreed: The more music the better. The more styles the better. The more performers the better.

Then we thought: Why limit Voices United to music? When Catie said she had a connection to Sarah Silverman, I knew we had to pursue that. The next thing I knew, Russell Brand was on board too, and we had a great finale for Voices United. Catie and folk singer Mary Gauthier shared the stage with Sarah and Russell, providing the perfect combination of fun and folk. It was an evening that will not soon be forgotten by all who attended.

In recent weeks I've had numerous emails, letters, and phone calls from people who wanted to thank Americans United for sponsoring this event. Some said they hadn't thought much about church-state issues before. Some said they weren't involved with Americans United. Now they wanted to be.

Some came for the music but left inspired to speak out. That's just what we wanted. People made connections; they made commitments to get involved; they vowed to learn more.

We couldn't have done this without Curtis. Catie's energy never failed to amaze me. I thought we'd be lucky to land one show in every state. Catie did that and more—she gave us seventy-four shows in fifty states (and DC). And oh, by the way, she played at three of them!

I also have to give a shout out to Todd Stiefel of the Stiefel Freethought Foundation, who provided a generous donation to get Voices United up and running. Some doubted this was possible; Todd's generosity proved them wrong.

GOING VIRAL: AU VIDEOS PROMOTE THE CAUSE— TO A BRAND NEW AUDIENCE[13]

Americans United decided to try its hand at making some viral videos. The first was created during an all-day taping in Los Angeles with Jane Lynch, the star of the popular television musical show *Glee*, and Jordan Peele, the brilliant comedian from Comedy Central.

Sarah Stevenson, who works in AU's Development Department, was there to watch the production, brief the participants, and give the many people involved a few Americans United goodies—not quite what the Academy Award "bling bags" contain but some nice items that show what we do here.

The three-and-a-half minute long video, "Jane Lynch and Jordan Peele: Epic Church-State Breakup," was based on a song written by Faith Soloway and was directed by her sister Jill Soloway, a Hollywood director/producer/ writer. The theme was the breakup of Lynch portraying "Church" (dressed in a flowing white gown and a wig that mirrored a certain hairstyle of a number of television preachers' spouses) and Peele's "State" (wearing a blue leisure suit and sporting a large flag belt buckle). It was a spoof of 1970s-era pop music, filmed in a nightclub whose owner supports our cause. The message: Even if church and state thought they belonged together, they actually need an epic breakup.

After some routine editing, the video debuted on May 30. The website *Funny or Die* premiered it for us. Soon it was everywhere—and people really seemed to like it. The last time I checked, the video had more than sixty-two thousand views on *Funny or Die*, and 85 percent rated it funny.

At about the same time, we announced a new series of concerts similar to our Voices United fundraisers last fall. On a lark, Stevenson sent an email to the website of the popular rapper Macklemore, who had recently released a song about marriage equality.

To our surprise, his staff wrote back and said he'd be happy to do a short video endorsing Voices United. With very little promotion from Americans United, that video took off as well, and, at this writing, is also racing toward three hundred thousand views on YouTube.

I'd be the last person to claim any dazzling competence or intense familiarity with the world of cyberspace, but I was blown away by the results of our viral video experiments. When you get a familiar message out in a new way, it can be surprising how many folks who ignored it earlier suddenly pay attention.

STRANGE PERSONS OF A "RELIGIOUS RIGHT" BENT

Of course, just as I've had the chance to meet some wonderful secularist advocates, I've also had the experience of commingling my life with some truly strange figures as well. There are the "big names" like Bill O'Reilly, the late Jerry Falwell, and well-known "public intellectual" Ann Coulter, and then the not-so-well-known Pastor Wiley Drake and General "Jerry" Boykin.

I was always told to "play nice" in the sandbox and on the jungle gym and that childhood lesson has been incorporated into my lifestyle, at least most of the time. I rage against their ideas but try to keep my public encounters low key because I believe I should reserve my "screaming rages" for telemarketers, people who text while driving next to me, and of course door-to-door magazine subscription salespeople.

Jerry Falwell died in the spring of 2007, and I wrote a reflection on my encounters with him. He, of course, appears in other places in this book and is also the subject of many anecdotes in my previous book, *Piety & Politics*. Here's what I thought was the most pathetic about Falwell:

OF MYTHS AND MEN: REFLECTIONS ON THE JERRY FALWELL ERA[14]

Jerry Falwell was declared dead at 12:40 p.m. on Tuesday, May 15. Bulletins about the gravity of his condition had abounded on news websites as soon as reports surfaced that he had been found unconscious in his office earlier in the morning.

Death is a singularly unpleasant matter for people, including journalists, to discuss. They expect that even the harshest critic of the deceased will listen to oft-repeated parental and social columnist advice: "If you have nothing good to say, say nothing."

On May 15, most of the people who actually had encounters with Falwell on radio and television followed that scenario. So did I—with some important qualifiers. I called him "passionate" and "never yielding" but noted that he "politicized religion and failed to understand the genius of our Constitution." I also pointed out that "I disagreed with just about everything Falwell stood for."

This relatively restrained criticism was anchored in the one hundred or so media clashes I had with the man over the last twenty years. It would have been foolish not to have acknowledged our deep divisions the day he died. Not everyone played nice. Pundit Christopher Hitchens appeared on CNN's *Anderson Cooper 360* and blasted Falwell with a ferocity I cannot ever remember seeing on television news.

To what end does anyone say anything about the dead? Let me try this: It is important to put a life in perspective immediately so that an uncorrectable mythology doesn't develop. With Falwell, most commentators said that he "apologized" for blaming civil libertarians, feminists, gays, and pagans for the horror of September 11 because this caused God to lift his mantle of protection.

But the "apology" wasn't really one. Falwell said he wished he hadn't named specific groups and acknowledged that God hadn't told him that his mantle had been lifted. Falwell's horrendous remark concluded that 9/11 gave "us probably what we deserve"[15] and for that I could find no apology to the victims or the public. Indeed, a fundraising letter under the signature of one of his sons after this so-called "apology" blamed the whole ruckus on evil liberals and insisted it had all been taken out of context.[16]

The first person to put me on the air live when Falwell's death was announced was Ed Schultz, one of the few successful progressive talk show hosts. He asked about my personal relationship with Falwell, and I had to concede that it wasn't warm. The very first sentence of my book *Piety & Politics* is, "The Reverend Jerry Falwell doesn't like me." He was always very belligerent with me on television. Over the years, he called me a liar, asserted I "was paid by Al Gore," and repeatedly insisted that I'm not really a minister.

Some of Falwell's conservative allies asked me why he seemed to dislike me so much. I'm not a psychologist, but I have thought that he hated the fact that I am not embarrassed to be both a Christian and an advocate for the right to believe or not believe anything or everything in matters of theology.

It is also important to point out that when a person dies who has had a conventionally "successful" life (and perhaps did have a major impact on electing many members of Congress and a few presidents), his or her "success" often comes at the expense of others. What Falwell would have described as "victories" were viewed very differently by others.

Women denied access to reproductive choice as Falwell worked to cut off federal funding and create an atmosphere of fear that led many doctors to stop performing abortions have reason to see themselves as his victims. So do members of the gay, lesbian, bisexual, and transgendered communities who saw zealots fueled by Falwell's narrow interpretation of the scriptures deny their rights. Speech matters; that is why it is important to protect it. When it comes from a powerful national pulpit, it can have tremendous power to heal or open wounds.

Falwell was not always in the business of mixing partisan politics and religion, or even policy discussion and salvation. In the 1960s, he told evangelicals to focus on winning souls for Christ and not work to elect your favorite politician to the White House. He changed.

First, he joined politically with other evangelicals to try to retain tax exemptions for racially discriminatory private religious schools. (To his credit, Falwell later renounced his support for segregation.) In 1979, he was given the chance to run the Moral Majority. He decided to focus on a very narrow range of hot-button social issues and employ increasingly ham-fisted demands that his moral views be written as legislative fiats—or politicians would suffer consequences at the polls.

One can only wonder what would have happened if he had worked from his powerful national pulpit on other issues, from peace to the environment, and had spoken out against policies he found unethical without partisanship or electoral threats attached.

I don't celebrate the death of people. I would have gladly celebrated the demise of Jerry Falwell's ideology, though. But it did not die with him. Unfortunately, the flammable mix of religion and politics will continue for the foreseeable future.

Falwell was so "out there" that he was a media favorite, but his ascendancy to the top level of the Religious Right lured some into thinking he (and his colleague the Reverend Pat Robertson) were strange national outliers and that fundamentalists they might encounter in their hometowns were more reasonable. This often turned out not to be the case and the following tale reminded me of this lesson:

OF DEATH AND TAXES: PASTOR DRAKE'S PARTISAN POLITICKING AND "IMPRECATORY PRAYERS" LEAVE ME COLD[17]

Wiley Drake, pastor of First Southern Baptist Church of Buena Park in California, and I go back a long way. He first took an interest in me when I criticized the highly partisan content and style of Christian Coalition voter guides back in 1998 at a National Press Club event in Washington.

Drake called such public criticism "an absolute ungodly approach, absolutely Satanic approach." He then urged his supporters to begin an "imprecatory prayer" campaign against me.

Even though seminary-trained, I was a tad uncertain about the meaning of this tactic. Imprecatory prayers, it turns out, are prayers that bad things— up to and including death—befall the "prayer" recipient. In other cultures, they would simply be called "curses" (and dolls might be involved).

Six months later, Pastor Drake and I were on CNN together one afternoon, and I happened to mention that he had been praying for my demise for some time. When I returned to my office, I discovered that he had faxed me a handwritten note informing me that he was "shocked" that I would bring up this "private matter" on national television. I was certain that I had not learned that rule at the seminary.

Pastor Drake is now back in the imprecatory prayer business, and two other AU staff members and I are the targets of his ire. Back in August, we sent a letter to the Internal Revenue Service asking it to investigate the possibly illegal intervention in a political campaign by Drake. He supported the election of presidential candidate Mike Huckabee on church stationery and on his church-based daily radio program.

Drake claimed these were "personal" endorsements, but it would be abundantly clear to any observer that the use of the church letterhead was intended to convey a "weightier" endorsement than that of a single cleric. The stationery also lists Drake as the "Second Vice President 2006/2007 Southern Baptist Convention" and, indeed, on one radio broadcast he told listeners that he was throwing his weight behind Huckabee in his role "as Second Vice President." So much for the "personal" nature of his endorsement.

We faxed our complaint to Drake as we sent it to the IRS, and the pastor sent out an angry press release two hours later calling for those imprecatory prayers against both Joe Conn and Jeremy Learing (whose real name is Leaming) and a presumptive continuance of the same against me.

His missive included sample prayers for the biblically semiliterate, which included, "Let his children be fatherless, and his wife a widow. Let his children be continually vagabonds, and beg; let them seek their bread also out of their desolate places."[18]

All this led me to two immediate questions. First, since he had spelled Jeremy's name incorrectly, was there a person named Jeremy Learing who should be notified? Second, did he really know my children? One is working at Google. The other is finishing law school at the University of Virginia.

We didn't learn much more until early February when an article appeared on a right-wing website informing readers that Drake's church was indeed under IRS investigation.

Drake's attorney, Erik Stanley of the Alliance Defense Fund, announced that all this was a "Big-Brotherish" response caused by Americans United. Drake announced the imprecatory prayer effort would be expanded.[19]

The pastor is not discussing the particulars of his case much under advice of counsel, but he did say that he "loves the media." Our latest tête-à-tête has gotten a reasonable amount of press coverage.

When distressed Christians write him and rebuke his tactics, he sometimes e-mails them back and notes that the tactic is God's, not his own. (As in, "don't blame me, take it up with God," washing his hands of the whole thing.)

On the other hand, we've had a number of people write us in similar disgust at Drake's tactics and including some sizeable contributions. (One even requesting that we send Drake one of our "a gift has been given to AU in your honor" letters).

Interjecting death prayers into the discourse over important legal and policy manners is pretty disgraceful. Pastor Drake has a competent legal team to defend his interests. If he prevails, he prevails, and what we thought was "wrong," the IRS did not.

In that event, I'm quite sure he will declare victory.

This preemptive strike of curses, however, is properly seen as alien to American political and spiritual life. As a people, we decry fatwahs against writers who do not toe a fundamentalist Islamic line. We denounce threats of violence announced by Hindu fundamentalists. To his credit, even Governor Huckabee didn't seem too pleased with the tactics telling the press that he preferred "the saving of souls rather than the damning of souls."

I'll be heading home now as I finish this column. An ice-storm is expected to start soon. As long as it doesn't rain frogs. . . .

I have not had the misfortune to have too many encounters with Ann Coulter. But she clearly is not a fan of mine, nor I of her. She is an insufferable and mean-spirited person. Here is an account of the bizarre column she did about me in 2009:

WHEN ANN COULTER ATTACKS: MY LATEST INTERACTION WITH AMERICA'S "PUBLIC INTELLECTUAL"[20]

I don't know what a "public intellectual" is, but Ann Coulter is frequently referred to as one. If this is true, I am hoping that I am not a "public intellectual."

Ann has occasionally taken potshots at me in the past. In writing an obituary for Dr. Jerry Falwell, she said that the only disagreement she ever had with him was that when he laid blame for the attacks of September 11 on various groups, including gays and feminists, he did not personally cite Sen. Edward Kennedy and Barry Lynn as the precipitating cause.

And after Hurricane Katrina (no, she did not blame me for the weather), Ann suggested that "Barry Lynn's church" probably didn't do much for the victims. (Actually, the United Church of Christ, in which I am ordained, gave

$4.4 million since 2005 in disaster relief, and the church even organized trips to New Orleans for volunteers to personally help the victims.)

A few weeks ago, Ann took her most recent jab at me. I noticed while checking my e-mail one morning that several people had forwarded me one of her columns. Why? Had she become a convert to church-state separation "gospel"?

Not quite.

Ann had written a column about people who hate their own kind—as in Southerners who concede the racism of the area, Vietnam veterans who talked about atrocities, and ministers (well, one to be precise) who are anti-religion. In the paragraph about me, she suggested not only that I wasn't a true minister, but also that I wasn't a Christian.

Ann wasn't suggesting I had violated some scriptural prohibition or that I didn't believe in some doctrine. She meant I was not Christian, but Jewish. She said, "The first person to post Barry Lynn's bar mitzvah photos or birth announcement (mazel tov!) wins a free copy of my latest book."[21]

How does one respond to this?

I suppose I could have held a "tea party" in protest or even started screaming during some congressperson's forum on healthcare. Or I could just use my vast interlocking media conglomerate of a radio talk program, a Beliefnet debate blog, and the Americans United's website for a spirited defense.

That's just what I did. In a blog, I confronted Ann with the truth. It included a photo of a birth certificate and the earliest-known photograph of my parents and me at a New Jersey beach.

The birth certificate was an ancient one from Cameroon that someone had found in the trash. I blurred the actual name of the holder and printed in bold letters "BARRY WILLIAM LYNN." The photograph was a phony, altered picture of two large-headed space aliens holding their "son," an alien with my face superimposed.

I noted in the blog that my purpose in all of this was to correct her misinformation. After all, I would not want her scholarly credentials sullied. (Of course, this is a joke, too, because her recent books on Joe McCarthy and evolution have been savaged by historians and scientists for their loopy conclusions and ridiculous "evidence.")

Arguably, the level of public discourse in this country has hit a new low. The late William F. Buckley Jr.'s Firing Line (which I did a number of times) was a wonderful opportunity to have two uninterrupted hours of actual debate. Charlie Rose's late night show on many PBS stations is an honest effort to give people a chance to hear what real thinkers have to say. We need more of this.

What we are getting, though, are more "short form" shout-fests. I am just waiting for a Fox show to feature Ann and a chimpanzee, in which Ann says, "If we really descended from apes, why are you still here?" And the monkey just smiles wistfully.

AWARDS

Let's face it—everybody likes a little recognition for what they do. When I walk out of my office and left twenty-five yards, I come to what we call the "Wall of Shame"—a section of space to which have been affixed a cache of hate mail. We aren't ashamed, by the way, to receive it; we're just ashamed of the rank idiocy of the people who write gems like:

Example #1:

"Dear Commie Pinkos at Americans United for Communism: Thanks for butting in our state of Maine with your wonderful values and getting involved with screwing with the kids at South Bristol Elementary School. Well done. P.S. Just so I'm clear—I do not support your group."

Example #2:

"This is your new group name: belugas of america
This is your commitment:
Democrats run on emotion, feelings, estrogen.
Flacid men
Feminists.
Open borders
Bilingual education
Protection of the smut industry

White men with dreadlocks
Legalize drugs
Anti family
Anti tradition
Anti christian
Pro muslim
Pro abortion rights
Anti flag
Pro gangsta rap
Pro hump and grind movies and tv shows etc.
Feelings feelings feelings
Broke back mountain ("Best western since lonesome dove")
Anti military . . .
Anti catholic . . .
Pro sexual predators . . . see vermont
Pro liberal whiny judges
Anti american
You are the real hate groups. You will bring this great
     country to it's (sic) knees
Barry and all like him can kiss my a**
Who in the hell do you think you are
Go back across the pond where you belong

And finally, example #3:

"Go climb a gum tree and get stuck at the top!"

On the more positive front, people who like what you do can make for some highlight of your career in the awards they deem you worthy of receiving—for being a "national irritant" to a "Medal of Freedom" designee to being labeled a "creative citizen."

What's better than being labeled a national "irritant" by your foes? Being recognized as one by your friends![22]
I had this honor recently when I was privileged to receive the Robert O. Cooper Peace and Justice Fellowship Award at Southern Methodist Uni-

versity. SMU Chaplain William Finnin told the news media that the award, named for a former chaplain at the Dallas school, is for people who put themselves in such a "position to the reigning power that makes them irritants to the status quo."

In light of that, here's an update on some of my irritating activity over the past few weeks. I'll start with a powerful group that's easy to irritate— Tony Perkins and the Family Research Council (FRC). During the course of the Harriet Miers nomination, it became known that White House strategist Karl Rove had called FRC board member James Dobson to assure the Colorado Springs Religious Right honcho that Miers is a conservative evangelical who goes to a prolife church.

I pointed out in the press that this use of religion to sell a Supreme Court nominee is the latest example of a religious litmus test articulated by President George W. Bush back in 2002 when he said he would only propose judicial nominees who "believe our rights come from God."

Perkins took umbrage and sent out an e-mail with a rather unflattering photo of me. He noted that Thomas Jefferson wrote in the Declaration of Independence that we are "endowed by [our] Creator with certain inalienable rights." Queried Perkins, "Better watch that one, Mr. Lynn. Can you impeach a dead President?"

That's cute. However, Jefferson's Creator was not viewed as a force meddling in American politics even in the late 1700s. Moreover, given his lifelong commitment to separation of church and state, Jefferson would never have supported the idea of a "religious test" for public office. Perkins is desperately trying to shift attention away from the utter hypocrisy of the Religious Right, which demanded that even speculation of how John G. Roberts's religion might affect his judging be off the table but now stands idly by while the administration sells Miers by highlighting where she goes to church.

I have also irritated Franklin Graham recently. Speaking at Jerry Falwell's Liberty University, Graham gave a combination meteorological/ theological assessment of Hurricane Katrina. He blamed New Orleans for engaging in "satanic worship" and "sexual perversion" and asserted, "God is going to use that storm to bring revival."[23]

Graham's Samaritan's Purse charity is in the area putting up roofs and giving children evangelistic tracts and stuffed lambs that play "Jesus Loves Me." Just days earlier, I had criticized the Federal Emergency Management Agency for having such unclear reimbursement guidelines for houses of worship that the government could end up funding evangelism. Basically, I was calling for accountability and the preservation of civil rights rather than just dumping tax dollars into collection plates.

Graham denounced my modest proposal as "ridiculous," and the product of a mind that "hates God." All this bluster and name calling could be a cover for Graham, who perhaps hopes that nobody notices that he has in the past received a cool $7 million in federal funds, yet claims all relief efforts should have as their "primary purpose" to "share the redeeming love of the Lord Jesus Christ."[24]

Finally, I have irritated Florida Gov. Jeb Bush—again. He chose C. S. Lewis's novel *The Lion, the Witch and the Wardrobe* for a statewide reading contest. Kids are supposed to read the book and submit essays, artwork, and videos about it in an effort to win prizes.

The problem is everyone acknowledges that this book is a thinly veiled allegory of Christianity's core concepts. Aslan the lion is a Christ-like figure, who is killed by evil forces and rises again. Lewis once noted that the series will "make it easier for children to accept Christianity when they meet it later in life."

I realize not everyone who reads the book sees the Christian connection, but I can't believe Jeb doesn't. Here is a man who simply doesn't appreciate the separation of church and state and who wants everything from faith-based prisons to faith-based child welfare programs and faith-based vouchers to subsidize religious schools. We asked the governor to use better judgment in the future and to add non-religious books to the contest this year so all Florida children can participate.

So far, the governor's office has refused to address the religion issue, commenting only that the Lewis book is a "classic story of good versus evil." (And one Christian talk show host told me Lewis's book couldn't be promoting the Gospels because it contains "animals that talk." Right.)

Sometimes one has to disturb even friends and colleagues. When AU got word recently that some senators who normally support church-state separation were backing a measure that would give religious school vouchers to displaced hurricane victims, I spoke out. Our protest, picked up by the media, helped stall the bill, which had been on a fast track.

"Irritant" can be a strong word. But the simple fact is that sometimes some powerful people need to be irritated. They might need to be prodded to action or reminded that their views don't square with the Constitution.

To Boise and Beyond: It's Far from Quiet on the Western Front[25]

A few of the events in a recent swing through the American West contained some out-of-the-ordinary footnotes. In Los Angeles, I was given the Leonard Rose Award by the Women's Reproductive Rights Assistance Project, a group that collects funds to help poor women, many the victims of assault or incest, pay for medical expenses linked to reproductive health.

Grants went to women in forty-eight states last year. That group was particularly interested in AU's efforts to preserve the independence of the federal courts, prevent politicking from the pulpit, and stop religiously based discrimination in President George W. Bush's "faith-based" initiative.

Boise also featured an unusual occurrence. My final appearance there was the annual banquet for the Idaho affiliate of the American Civil Liberties Union. I had noticed that the next ballroom over from our dinner was an event labeled "Angel Party." I assumed this was most likely a rehearsal dinner for a wedding in a family surnamed "Angel." Well, not exactly!

I was in the middle of my speech, commenting on some of the more bizarre recent ramblings of James Dobson and Pat Robertson. I mentioned that Robertson had just told people in Dover, Pennsylvania, that if a disaster struck the city God wouldn't help them. They had angered God, Robertson said, by tossing a pro-"intelligent design" slate out of office.

Suddenly, loud hymns began wafting through the walls from the event next door. Was this a divine comment signaling support for my criticism of Robertson? Again, not exactly. It turns out "Angel Party" is an annual right-wing fundraiser for a group called Birthright of Idaho, one of those dishonest "counseling" centers for pregnant unmarried women seeking advice who are never told about any options other than motherhood and adoption.

In 2012, I was very happy to receive a 2011 Roosevelt Medal of Freedom award for defending religious freedom. This is what I said when receiving the medal in Hyde Park, New York (former home of the Roosevelts):

I am deeply honored to receive this award. The freedom of religion accorded by the separation of church and state is always a fragile commodity, even more so at a time when at least four candidates from one major political party each believe God has chosen them to be the next president

The founder of Americans United was Glenn Archer, a law school dean from Kansas who gave up his promising political career there to spend the rest of his life in the cause of real religious freedom, concerned about religious influences in public schools, efforts to subsidize religious schools with tax dollars, and censorship based on theological critiques. He became friends with Eleanor Roosevelt, who had written in her newspaper column and in *Ladies Home Journal* that public schools should not teach religion and that when she sent her children to private schools she "never thought about asking the government to pay their tuition." Presciently, Mrs. Roosevelt once told Archer "the battle for church-state separation may have to be fought all over again." Indeed it has, in each generation.

Meanwhile, the president articulated as early as 1937 a proactive interpretation of tolerance—not viewing it as the gift of the powerful to the small, but as a core attribute of all men and women: "the lessons of religious tolerance—a toleration which recognizes complete liberty of human thought, liberty of conscience—some which by precept and example, must be inculcated in the hearts and minds of all Americans if the institutions of our democracy are to be nurtured and perpetrated."[26]

The Roosevelts would, I suspect, be gravely disappointed today. The political process itself is being poisoned by the corrosive effect some forms of religion are having on our greatest institutions of democracy. The schools, the judiciary, the social service net: all corroded by a kind of religion that claims to know all things and whose only complaint is that it does not run all things. We are entering a campaign season in which candidates routinely go to political gatherings in Iowa where preachers quiz them on personal piety as well as political philosophy, violating the core spirit of the Constitution's abhorrence of "religious tests for public office." Every issue from reproductive choice to the national debt has advocates drawing from scriptural tradition instead of critical thinking, sound analysis of data, and the commonly shared values of our Constitution. Judges are being removed from office for making unpopular decisions; the Tea Party has discovered a new bill of rights in their sock drawers that preserves corporate power and displaces the conscience of the very individuals who are America.

Our schools face a double assault of efforts to force religious indoctrination into textbooks of science and history and treat those institutions as "mission fields" for outside groups to subject a captive audience to proselytization and evangelical outreach. If they are not transformed in that way, advocates seek tuition tax credits, school vouchers, and other experimental mechanisms to end up forcing taxpayers to subsidize religious doctrine in schools, which do not even match their own academic claims.

In the social service arena, President Roosevelt, in June of 1941, signed the first executive order barring discrimination in employment by government contractors and grantees based on race, creed, color, or national origin. Regrettably, the Bush administration altered that to permit religious charities who are recipients of government funding for purportedly secular social services to discriminate in hiring, given preference to fellow believers and barring jobs to persons of other viewpoints. This scandalous practice continues in the current administration. Groups justify their hiring bias in the most peculiar ways: "We feel more comfortable working with people like us" or, in the case of the group World Vision—recipient of three hundred million tax dollars last year—proclaiming that if you tell people of your bias in advance, it's "not discrimination." Ms. Parks, we told you about where you could sit before you bought the ticket, so don't complain. We have all heard all of these excuses before.

I want to be free of the fear that some politician claiming to hear the voice of God will seek to impose her or his will on all, depriving the rest of Americans from exercising their own conscience. But for that freedom to be viable, all of us need to work to preserve it. I've had the honor of participating in this effort for most of my adult life. It is not a freedom built solely by judicial decisions or acts of Congress. It is ultimately kept alive when it, in the words of Justice Learned Hand: "does not die in the hearts of the people."

Puffins and Prizes: A Pat on the Back for "Creative Citizenship"[27]

I recently attended a great party in New York City. I got to listen to comedian Lewis Black (without having to pay $100 for a ticket); I got to chat with Mayor-Elect Bill de Blasio; I saw my friend Phil Donahue and discussed with him the trend of religious minorities and nontheists demanding, and getting, equal space for displays in publicly owned spaces that previously housed only nativity scenes in December.

This December 9, 2013, soirée was cosponsored by the Puffin Foundation and the Nation Institute. I was there for a reason: to accept an award that was extremely meaningful to me, one I was honored and humbled to receive.

The Puffin Foundation's main job is to award grants to artists and arts organizations. Anyone who has seen the doodles I make during staff meetings can attest that I'm no artist. But the foundation—which is named for the beautiful and hardy puffin, a species of bird found mainly in very cold regions of the world—also awards an annual prize for "creative citizenship" to an activist who challenges the status quo.

I was delighted to be named this year's recipient. A Puffin Foundation official, in introducing the person who would introduce me, focused primarily on my work at Americans United, making a specific reference to our innovative Voices United series of musical events, started in 2012.

I was quite amazed to get this award and could barely believe anyone considered me in the same category as civil-rights icon Robert Moses, playwright and AIDS-awareness activist Tony Kushner, writer and economic justice advocate Barbara Ehrenreich, and Planned Parenthood President Cecile Richards.

Cecile introduced me and told some stories about my life. She noted that in one of my books I had revealed that my mother, then in her late eighties, told me that she was once escorted to the outskirts of a Pennsylvania coal-mining town by the police and told never to return. Her "crime": distributing information about birth control. Cecile also reminded the five hundred people in attendance that I had once filled her in on how creationists explain the ability of Noah's Ark to hold so many animals: "They only took babies, including baby dinosaurs."

If you've ever heard me give a speech—as opposed to arguing with/ yelling at Sean Hannity or Pat Buchanan on television—then you know that I think humor is essential to public appearances. I picked that up from my father. My dad could not teach a Sunday School class or write the minutes for a civic club without embellishing the content with a joke or two.

Since Black had already decimated the phony "war on Christmas" during his time at the microphone, I had to do some last-minute edits to my prepared text. I noted that the owners of some for-profit corporations are arguing that their companies have a right of conscience to refuse to provide contraceptive coverage to their employees through company health insurance plans. They are actually claiming that corporations can practice religion.

The two cases the Supreme Court will hear on this topic in March involve a chain of craft stores owned by conservative Baptists and a Mennonite-owned firm that manufactures wood products for home construction.

My thought: "I will only give this credence when I see a do-it-yourself garden gnome sitting next to me in a pew at church or have the Adirondack lawn chair I sit in during the summer start singing hymns to me."

It was a very pleasant evening, as I think you can gather. I would have never expected a night like this when I was growing up. I didn't plan to become an activist, nor did I strive to get involved in controversial matters. It just happened that way.

ALTERNATIVE UNIVERSES: CINEMATIC ACHIEVEMENT AND A BIZARRE CAPITOL HILL HEARING

LOUIE, LOUIE!: MY "HELLISH" DAY TESTIFYING IN CONGRESS[28]

I always enjoy testifying before congressional committees about the Constitution. Until a few weeks ago, though, I have never had to testify about my personal religious views.

That changed on June 10, 2014, when US Rep. Louis B. "Louie" Gohmert (R-TX) got a chance to ask me questions at a hearing. The hearing, sponsored by the House Judiciary Committee's Subcommittee on the Constitution and Civil Justice, was supposed to be about "The State of Religious Liberty in the United States"—but for me it took on a bit of an inquisitorial tone.

I gave the standard five-minute summary of my testimony. During my remarks, I expressed skepticism about some of the statements by the three other witnesses (all chosen by the Republican majority), who asserted that there is a wide-ranging war on religion in America. I also issued a warning about how the radical redefinition of religious freedom crafted by people like them was the real danger to the First Amendment.

Then it was question-and-answer time.

There were a few inquiries about the state of school-prayer litigation and the faith-based initiative from Democratic representatives, but soon the rotation came around to Gohmert.

I knew that Gohmert has a reputation for taking ultraconservative positions on various policy matters, but I will admit to being a bit perplexed by the line of inquiry he pursued with me.

He began by quoting one of Thomas Jefferson's observations about

God. His point seemed to be that Jefferson hadn't really been a Deist after all. He then observed that Franklin D. Roosevelt had recommended that soldiers read the Bible and wanted to know, "Are you offended by that?"

I assumed that this line of questioning would lead to policy issues—perhaps a discussion of the role of religion in the military (which has been controversial lately). When I noted that I rather liked Roosevelt and had received a Freedom of Worship Award from the Roosevelt Institute a few years back, Gohmert noted that the award "wasn't awarded by Roosevelt himself." (No surprise there since FDR has been dead for nearly seventy years.)

It got even stranger. Soon Gohmert was talking about a *Seinfeld* episode where the character Elaine became upset to learn that her boyfriend was a Christian. This led to the real zinger: "Do you believe in sharing the good news that will keep people from going to hell, consistent with the Christian beliefs?"

Things were clearly unraveling fast. "I wouldn't agree with your construction of what hell is like or why one gets there," I replied. I was later able to add, "I personally do not believe people go to hell because they don't believe in a specific set of ideas in Christianity."

Gohmert then asserted, "So the Christian belief, as you see it, is whatever you choose to think about Christ—whether or not you believe those words he said that nobody, basically, goes to heaven except through me?"

I responded, "We could have a very interesting discussion some time, probably not in a congressional hearing" about theology. Getting the final word, Gohmert assured me that he did not mean to be "judgmental," adding, "I appreciate your indulgence."

I don't know the religious background of every member of the subcommittee, but I do know there are at least two Jewish and one Buddhist member. I hope Gohmert wasn't being "judgmental" about their after-death trajectory either.

The next day, there were dozens of blog posts about this exchange, generating hundreds of comments. Not surprisingly, the comments on sites like Glenn Beck's The Blaze generally lambasted me and praised the insights of Gohmert. Respondents on more progressive sites, like Rachel Maddow's blog, chastised, vilified, and otherwise rejected his "inquisitorial" techniques.

After an encounter like this, I always wonder what else I could have said or done. I got plenty of suggestions about this, too. Why didn't I demand that the Democrats leap to my defense and insist that Gohmert stop his line of questioning? Why didn't I echo the response of one witness at the infamous Joseph McCarthy hearings: "Have you no sense of decency, sir?"

I appreciated the advice, but I've concluded that I was probably on more solid ground with what I said. I had to assume that many of the subcommittee members have probably heard equally strange lines of inquiry from the gentleman from Texas before and were shaking their heads one more time.

The next day I appeared on MSNBC's *The Ed Show*, where I labeled Gohmert "kind of a walking talking example of why we need separation of church and state." Politicians, I noted, should not try to decide which theological beliefs are correct and which are not.

A protracted debate over theology seemed to be a less-than-productive way to spend the subcommittee's time and the taxpayers' money, so after the hearing, I told Gohmert I'd be happy to have lunch with him to discuss the nature of hell and biblical interpretation in a more appropriate venue.

Gohmert and I obviously don't agree on these questions. But we could still have an interesting discussion. I'll let you know if that conversation ever comes to pass. My lunch invitation has seemingly been lost in the mail.

At the Movies: My Latest On-Screen Appearance Is No Noah[29]

Many of you know that I am a film buff. Have me speak at an event and if there is a multiplex in the vicinity of the site of my hotel, I'll probably ask you to drop me off for a 10 p.m. showing of, well, pretty much anything.

In a recent column, I mentioned *Noah*, the new film starring Russell Crowe that generated enormous hostility from some Religious Right groups for taking license with the biblical version of the tale. These critics scored the movie for theological errors and a hefty dose of pro-environmental "propaganda."

One recent rainy Sunday afternoon, my wife and I saw it in a local IMAX theater. Although I don't agree with the Religious Right criticism, I did walk out underwhelmed.

But enough about watching a movie. How about being in one? I had that opportunity recently when I was contacted by EchoLight Studios, a company with a heavy investment by former US Sen. Rick Santorum that makes "Christian worldview" motion pictures.

EchoLight's first effort was a holiday offering called *The Christmas*

Candle. It was expensively advertised but a critical- and box-office bomb. In the wake of that fiasco, Santorum and his backers got a better idea: Make films and pitch them almost exclusively to megachurches that have their own audio and video set-ups. The studio's next offering will be available for church showings in September. And I'm in it.

No, this is not a work of fiction. *One Generation Away* is a documentary about "religious liberty"—more than likely claims of "religious persecution" of the Christian majority.

I had some hesitations, but when I learned that AU allies like Dan Barker of the Freedom From Religion Foundation and Mikey Weinstein had been interviewed I agreed as well. The director and crew came by AU's office with lights, two cameras, and a makeup artist in tow. I spent a few hours with them.

When you've been in the advocacy business as long as I have, you get pretty good at knowing what to say so that nothing—at least in theory—can be taken out of context or make you look like a total dolt. Of course, it's always possible to edit a film in a devious way in which parts of sentences are strung together with material in between left out; a kind of visual ellipsis. I don't expect trouble like that. Sarah Jones from AU's Communications Department sat during the interview; she thought it went well.

Let's be candid here: I would have preferred to have been offered a heftier role: an aging Batman, the inventor of a cure for cancer, a heroic (did I mention aging?) rescuer of a person tied to the train tracks. But you don't get to pick all your roles, so I am just playing "me."

In my youth, I had my mind changed dramatically about issues by hearing people I didn't expect to enjoy open my eyes and ears to some new ideas. Maybe somebody sitting in a pew at a church-turned-cinema will have the same experience. We all sing to the choir a lot and hope the members of that musical ensemble go out to sing to others. I will continue to speak to choirs and people belting out a different tune in the hopes that minds do sometimes change.

And if I get an Oscar nod for this project, I'm going to make sure that Santorum invites all of you to the after-party.

Concluding Thoughts
THE FUTURE LOOKS BRIGHTER

Who is winning the separation "war" and what does the future hold? Prior to the Reverend Jimmy Swaggart's two notorious (and well-publicized) encounters with "women of the night," I found it intriguing to watch his television show occasionally—mainly in hotel rooms where the only alternatives were the shopping channel and *Gilligan's Island* reruns. He was a decent piano player (although not quite up to his cousin, Jerry Lee Lewis) and a pretty fiery preacher. He was known to hold up a Bible during his sermons and say to his viewers—"You know what happens at the end of this book? We win!" He meant Christians.

Here at the end of this book, I'm here to tell you: "We secularists will win."

Here's my guardedly optimistic take on the future:

Things change—often quite slowly, but on balance I would submit that there will be more "separation of church and state" in 2035 than there is today.

However, what decisions are made in the next twenty years from courts will, of course, depend on who is elected and has the power to make and approve appointments for Senate ratification. Presidents who appoint judges, and the members of the Senate asked to confirm them, are often worried about getting labeled as "liberal" and thus losing the next election.

Secularism is a relatively simple construct. To me, it means that government needs to make purely secular, rational decisions on policies. It cannot rely on interpretation of anyone's holy book and use it as the basis for decision-making. When I appear at ACLU events, I often ask civil libertarians whether it would be constitutionally acceptable if the death penalty were abolished in their state solely because of comments by "religious" advocates for its abolition. For example, what if everyone who spoke in favor of terminating this practice cited the New Testament's admonition from Jesus that "let he who is without sin, cast the first stone," a warning that allegedly ended the lawful effort by government leaders to stone an adulteress to death? There is mixed reaction in most cases. When I posed that issue to Harvard Law professor Alan Dershowitz on a radio show once, he replied, "That's a good question for my next constitutional law exam."

During the 2014 midterm elections, a significant number of conservatives have replaced many "constitutional" liberals in the Senate and in statehouses.

But this has happened before. After nearly a quarter of a century here at Americans United, I see a silver lining in the data that has been collected, some even before this election occurred, and I want to share some of it with you.

When I started here, the biggest threat was that the House and Senate would both pass and send to the states for ratification a Constitutional amendment to return government-sponsored prayer to public schools. They failed in the House of Representatives, first in 1998, then in 1999, and finally in 2001, and in the Senate in 2006. There is little chance they will even try again in either chamber. The issue has no legs; it is a footnote to history and one we can feel confident that we have put it to rest. Of course, constant vigilance is still required to make certain that local school boards abide by the Supreme Court's decisions.

Since the victory we had in the Dover, Pennsylvania, "intelligent design" case, there have been very few successful efforts to teach it anywhere else. Even in Louisiana, where schools have theoretically been granted the opportunity to move to do so (by adding "supplemental"—that is, religious—material in biology classes), we and the Louisiana Civil Liberties Union have failed to find a single school district that has taken the bait. We jointly announced that together we will fight any school that does so. Although only half the public supports the "evidence" for evolution, the political will doesn't seem to exist to move this issue back into the courts. In 1999, 40 percent of Americans supported the evidence for evolution (with 19 percent eliminating God from the equation altogether); another Pew poll found in 2014 that 68 percent of young people supported the evolution construct for humans, 7 percent higher than the general public.[1]

Another positive note: I never believed that I would see in my lifetime anything like the support for marriage equality, now the law in thirty-seven states and the District of Columbia. Admittedly, many of those states are covered by decisions in federal appeals courts overturning policies or state constitutional provisions purporting to define "marriage" as the union of one man and one woman. The only argument left is religious—God doesn't want to define marriage any other way. I was happy to hear from an LGBTQ activist in California that the change in law largely began when his community started to use the argument that "separation of church and state" required that theological arguments about the "sacrament" of marriage could not be used to justify discrimination or other unequal treatment. The Supreme Court waded into this issue on April 28, 2015, choosing to hear the one federal appeals court case that upheld state bans on same-sex marriage. The other circuits and numerous district courts had relied on Supreme Court language in the decision declaring sections of the Defense of Marriage Act unconstitutional in 2013 to declare antimarriage equality provisions in flagrant violation of the constitution.

Many polling organizations find growing sentiment for marriage equality generally, with a staggering 64 percent support from evangelical millennials.[2]

Public opinion polls are also heavily on the progressive side on three other critical issues: the faith-based initiative, the Hobby Lobby case, and politicking from the pulpit. Two-thirds of Americans believe that if you get a grant or contract from the state or federal government you should not be allowed to give hiring preference to people of your own religious background and discriminate against people who have theological differences or no theology at all. Similarly, nearly two-thirds of Americans oppose allowing charities, including churches, from endorsing or otherwise supporting candidates for public office, and nearly half oppose churches even discussing initiatives and other public issues. Fifty-three percent of us think the Supreme Court was wrong in granting First Amendment "religious exercise" rights to for-profit companies like Hobby Lobby and its co-plaintiff, Pennsylvania wood products store, Conestoga Wood.[3] Fifty-eight percent of "millennials" believe that providers and corporations should be required to provide employees with healthcare plans that cover contraceptives.[4]

How do these translate legislatively? In the one vote we've had on preferential hiring, the House rejected the idea of permitting it in Head Start programs back in 2003. Regrettably, although President Obama as a candidate said he'd take care of this problem, he has since decided to continue the policy and has expanded the amount of funding that has gone to religious institutions. To his credit, he did sign an executive order recently that insists that government contractors not discriminate against LGBTQ employees, and it had no direct "religious exemption." Regrettably, he has not explained how claims of LGBTQ will be investigated, nor is it easy to distinguish impermeable bigotry from still permissible "religiously motivated" hiring discrimination. That discrimination is permitted by the continued use by the Obama administration of an Office of Legal Counsel memo from the Bush years that specifically allowed religiously motivated employment discrimination, relying on the federal Religion Freedom Restoration Act. Perhaps when President Obama thinks about this some more, he'll do another executive order unequivocally outlawing invidious religious discrimination as well. Nearly one hundred civil rights and civil liberties groups insisted that he do this.

Polling on the Faith-Based Initiative began in 2001, after President George W. Bush started the scheme. At that time, 48 percent of Americans supported it, while 44 percent disapproved. When Pew Research did an updated analysis in 2009, 74 percent of Americans opposed a central premise of the program—that is, the aforementioned preferential hiring.[5]

On the tax front, the Alliance Defending Freedom (ADF) has been urging local pastors to violate the non-politicking provision of the tax code and claims to have engaged more than 1,800 priests and preachers in their campaign in 2014, which, if accurate, is, far higher than in the past. If it is illegal to do this, why is the IRS not doing anything? We have insisted that they act to enforce the law; we continue to file complaints about illegal electioneering in religious institutions; we participated in a rule-making required after a technical decision was issued in one of our prior complaint cases; we have a letter from the IRS commissioner that he would start up these investigations again in June of 2014. Nothing—absolutely nothing—happened. We now have to make clear that this illegal activity may have helped elect pro-Religious Right candidates to the Senate during the mid-term elections. Do we really want this to happen again in 2016? This is another issue on which pollsters find a high degree of support for the separationist viewpoint. Nearly 66 percent of respondents in a recent poll said no to pulpit electioneering by nonprofits and close to half said these entities shouldn't even be able to take positions on issues (further than I think the First Amendment permits, by the way).

Senator Harry Reid, the Majority Leader, tried to have a vote on a bill sponsored by Senators Patty Murray of Washington and Mark Udall of Colorado to overturn the Hobby Lobby conclusion in July 2014 but failed to get the sixty votes necessary to achieve "cloture" and move to the merits. Interestingly, every Democrat voted to move forward—even such relatively constitutionally "imperfect" senators like Pennsylvania's Bob Casey and Arkansas's Mark Pryor—as did the Republican's Mark Kirk (IL), Lisa Murkowski (AK), and Susan Collins (ME). The bill was never voted on on its merits and, of course, in the House, Speaker John Boehner never held hearings on the proposal, much less allowed a vote.

With school vouchers, there actually was a defeat for a Hawaii 2014 initiative to divert scarce public school funds to support religious private prekindergarten. The measure lost 55 percent to 45 percent and became the twenty-eighth straight defeat for school vouchers since 1966. In two recent national polls, we've seen 55 percent opposition to vouchers rising to 66 percent if the question acknowledged that this would take money away from public education.[6]

There was also a 2014 defeat in Tennessee where an initiative was approved that would permit state legislators to impose more complicated conditions on the approval of the right to abortion (which we know from Hobby Lobby now includes prohibitions on some of the most common forms of birth control). However, millennials are significantly more "pro-choice" than any other group in the country according to the most recent Gallup poll. And by mid-2015, only 15 percent of millennial respondents took the view that abortion should be illegal under all circumstances.

When framed this way, it seems that we have achieved some remarkable things over the past few decades, and we have sensitized the public to understanding in commonsense ways what our arguments for separation really are. What we haven't done is find ways to get people to the polls, particularly the young people who overwhelmingly support our positions on issues.

In the long run, unless we lose momentum, we are going to prevail on preserving, and even strengthening, the separation of church and state. Americans United has spent over sixty years trying to get this done—trying to shift the courts and the court of public opinion in our direction.

ACKNOWLEDGMENTS

No book like this could be written without the support of the Americans United staff and Board of Trustees. They have allowed me to work here and have supported my decisions to implement new ideas and new visions. I thank all of them over all these years.

Of special note, however, is the special assistance of my executive assistant, Allendra Letsome. She is a tax lawyer and a former vice president of the National Organization of Women (NOW), who initially was just interested in working on a project for Americans United. This is that project. On many occasions, when I said, "I'll never get this finished," she would respond, "Yes, we can." Well, we did.

NOTES

CHAPTER 1: SCHOOLS ARE STILL A BATTLEFIELD, BUT WE ARE WINNING

1. Barry Lynn, "Religious Freedom and Church-State Separation: Keeping Our Balance," *Church & State*, December 1992.

2. Barry Lynn, "Welcome to Washington, President Clinton," *Church & State*, January 1993.

3. Lee v. Wiseman, 505 U.S. 577 (1992).

4. "Bush vs. Clinton: The Candidates Debate," *Reader's Digest*, October 1992.

5. Barry Lynn, "Praying for Common Sense in Congress," *Church & State*, December 1994.

6. Barry Lynn, "Storming the Hill: AU Goes to Congress," *Church & State*, July/August 1998.

7. Anne Marie Lofaso, *Religion in the Public Schools: A Road Map for Avoiding Lawsuits and Respecting Parents' Legal Rights* (Washington, DC: Americans United for Separation of Church and State, 2009), p. 33.

8. Lee v. Wiseman, 505 U.S. 577 (1992).

9. Santa Fe Independent School Dist. v. Doe, 530 U.S. 290 (2000).

10. Westfield High Sch. L.I.F.E. Club v. City of Westfield, 249 F. Supp.2d 98, 114 (D. Mass. 2003).

11. Doe v. Duncanville Independent School Dist., 994 F.2d 160 (5th Cir. 1993).

12. Cole v. Oroville Union High School District, 228 F.3d 1092 (9th Cir. 2000).

13. Adler v. Duval, 250 F.3d 1330 (11th Cir. 2001); Chandler v. Siegelman, 230 F.3d 1313, 1317 (11th Cir. 2000).

14. Westside School District v. Mergens, 496 U.S. 226 (1990).

15. Barry Lynn, "Memo to Government: If You Don't Want 'Weeds,' Don't Plant a Garden," *Church & State*, April 1996.

16. Christian Legal Society v. Martinez, 561 U.S. 661 (2010), 319 Fed. Appx. 645, affirmed and remanded.

17. Barry Lynn, "Battering the Wall of Separation: Child's Play?" *Church & State*, December 1999, https://www.au.org/church-state/December-1999-church-state/perspective/battering-the-wall-of-separation.

18. Barry Lynn, "In Times of Trouble, the Watchdogs Must Bark Even Louder," *Church & State*, November 2001, https://www.au.org/church-state/November-2001-church-state/perspective/in-times-of-trouble-the-watchdogs-must-bark-even.

19. Barry Lynn, "Memo to Congress: You're on Capitol Hill, Not Mt. Sinai," *Church & State*, July/August 1999, https://www.au.org/church-state/julyaugust-1999-church-state/perspective/memo-to-congress.

20. Stone v. Graham, 449 U.S. 39 (1980).

21. Barry Lynn, "Public Schools Teach Values Every Day," *Church & State*, June 1994.

22. Barry Lynn, speech, Save Our Schools: The People's Education Convention, Washington, DC, August 2012.

23. Barry Lynn, speech, Secular Student Association Convention, Columbus, OH, July 2013.

CHAPTER 2: THE EVOLVING DEBATE . . . ON EVOLUTION

1. Jim Holt, *Why Does the World Exist? An Existential Detective Story* (New York: Liveright, 2012).

2. Epperson v. Arkansas, 33 U.S. 97 (1968).

3. Barry Lynn, speech, National Association of Biology Teachers Convention, Portland, Oregon, 2003.

4. Epperson v. Arkansas, 33 U.S. 97 (1968).

5. Edwards v. Aguillard, 482 U.S. 578 (1987).

6. Webster v. New Lenox School District, 917 F.2d 1004 (7th Cir. 1990).

7. Peloza v. Capistrano School District, 37 F.3d 517 (9th Cir. 1994).

8. Moeller v. Schrenko, 554 S.E.2d 200 (Georgia Court of Appeals 2001).

9. Freiler v. Tangipahoa Parish Board of Education, 185 F.3d 337 (5th Cir. 1999).

10. Kitzmiller, et al. v. Dover Area School District, et al., 400 F. Supp. 2d 707, 115, 137 (2005).

11. Barry Lynn, "Of Arks, Unicorns, and K Street: Lobbying, Lecturing, and Litigating from a New Location," *Church & State*, March 2011, https://www.au.org/church-state/march-2011-church-state/perspective/of-arks-unicorns-and-k-stree.

12. Simon Brown, "Stormy Seas?: Discriminatory Hiring Practices at KY 'Ark Park' Put Its Tax Incentives in Doubt," *Wall of Separation* (blog), October 8, 2014, https://au.org/blogs/wall-of-separation/stormy-seas-discriminatory-hiring-practices-at-ky-ark-park-put-its-tax.

13. Frank Newport, "In U.S., 42% Believe in Creationist View of Human Origins," *Gallup*, June 2, 2014, http://www.gallup.com/poll/170822/believe-creationist-view-human-origins.aspx.

CHAPTER 3: IF WE CAN'T CHANGE
PUBLIC SCHOOL CURRICULA,
LET'S JUST DESTROY PUBLIC SCHOOLS

1. Jerry Falwell, *America Can Be Saved!* (Murfreesboro, TN: Sword of the Lord Publishers, 1979), p. 52–53.

2. 46th Annual PDK/Gallup Poll of the Public's Attitudes Toward the Public Schools, September 2014, pdkpoll.pdkintl.org.

3. Barry Lynn, "Voucher Vendetta: A Heated Debate at the High Court," *Church & State*, March 2002, https://www.au.org/church-state/march-2002-church-state/perspective/voucher-vendetta.

4. Barry Lynn, speech, Tampa Voucher Rally, 2003.

5. Brown v. Board of Education, 347 U.S. 483 (1954).

6. Gary Orfield and John T. Yun, *Resegregation in American Schools* (Civil Rights Project/ Harvard University, June 1, 1999).

7. John F. Witte, Joshua M. Cowen, David J. Fleming, Patrick J. Wolf, Meghan R. Condon, and Juanita Lucas-McLean, *MPCP Longitudinal Educational Growth Study*, Third Year Report (Fayetteville, AR: School Choice Demonstration Project at the University of Arkansas, April 2010).

8. Danielle Dreilinger, "Louisiana Voucher School Scores Remain Low in 2014," NOLA. com/ *Times-Picayune*, Nov. 3, 2014, http://www.nola.com/education/index.ssf/2014/11/louisiana _voucher_student_perf.html.

9. Molly Beck, "DPI: Wisconsin Voucher Schools Show Lower Test Scores Compared to Public Schools," *Wisconsin State Journal*, http://host.madison.com/news/local/education/blog/dpi -wisconsin-voucher-schools-show-lower-test-scores-compared-to/article_df494180-cd29-538a -80be-a923cded39aa.html#ixzz3WqiZDvMd.

10. Thomas Ott, "Cleveland Students Hold Their Own With Voucher Students on State Tests," *Plain Dealer* (Cleveland), Feb. 22, 2011, http://blog.cleveland.com/metro/2011/02/ Cleveland_students_hold_own_wi.html.

11. Patrick Wolf, Babette Gutmann, Michael Puma, Brian Kisida, Lou Rizzo, Matthew Carr, and Marsha Silverberg, *Evaluation of the DC Opportunity Scholarship Program: Final Report* (US Dept. of Education, June 2010).

Though the 2009 study showed a marginal gain for some students in reading (but notably, not for the program's targeted group, students from schools in need of improvement), the 2010 *Final Report* said, "There is no conclusive evidence that the [program] affected student achievement" and earlier findings of modest gains "could be due to chance" and were no longer statistically significant.

12. Senate hearing on community policing, December 9, 2014 (statement of Sen. Ted Cruz of Texas).

13. These statements are found both in the schoolbooks and curriculum produced by ResponsiveEd and Paradigm Accelerated Curriculum. See, Jonny Scaramanga, "Darwin Inspired Hitler: Lies They Teach in Texas," *Salon*, October 25, 2013, www.salon.com/2013/10/25/ Christian-textbooks-darwin-inspired-hitler/.

14. Barry Lynn, "Love Your Faith? Then Pay For It," *On Faith*, January 11, 2013, www.faith-street.com/onfaith/2013/01/11/love-your-faith-then-pay-for-it/12006.

15. Bill Duncan v. New Hampshire, Argued: April 16, 2014; Opinion Issued: August 28, 2014.

CHAPTER 4: THE RELIGIOUS RIGHT

1. Barry Lynn, "Ten Reasons to Be Suspicious of the Religious Right" (speech, Texas Civil Liberties Union, 2002).

2. Sexuality Information and Education Council of the United States (SEICUS), *A History of Funding for Abstinence-Only-Until-Marriage Programs* (2011).

3. Tom Dickinson, "Newt and Callista's Affair 'Was Common Knowledge' on the Hill," *Rolling Stone Magazine*, January 26, 2012.

4. Howard Kurtz, "Larry Flynt, Investigative Pornographer," *Washington Post*, December 19, 1998.

5. Howard Kurtz, "Report of Hyde Affair Stirs Anger," *Washington Post*, September 17, 1998.

6. Howard Kurtz, "Flynt Calls Rep. Barr a Hypocrite for Divorce Case Answers," *Washington Post*, January 12, 1999.

7. "Censorship Plan Sparks Opposition in Wichita Falls," *Church & State*, February 1999, https://www.au.org/church-state/february-1999-church-state/people-events/february-1999-people-events.

8. Americans United for Separation of Church and State, "TV Preacher Pat Robertson Expands on 'Gay Days' Comment," press release, June 23, 1998, https://www.au.org/media/press-releases/tv-preacher-pat-robertson-expands-on-gay-days-comments.

9. Pat Robertson, *The 700 Club*, CBN (Christian Broadcast Network), aired March 23, 1995.

10. Pat Robertson, *The 700 Club*, CBN, aired November 11, 1997.

11. Pat Robertson, *The 700 Club*, CBN, aired January 14, 1991.

12. Maralee Schwartz and Kenneth J. Cooper, "Equal Rights Initiative in Iowa Attacked," *Washington Post*, August 23, 1992.

13. Pat Robertson, *The 700 Club*, CBN, November 28, 1989.

14. Pat Robertson, *The 700 Club*, CBN, March 18, 1992.

15. Steven Benen, "Pat Gets Paid: TV Preacher Robertson Gets 'Faith-Based' Grant from Bush Administration, *Church & State*, November 2002, https://www.au.org/church-state/november-2002-church-state/featured/pat-gets-paid.

16. Barry Lynn, "Imagine the Right's Religion," *On Faith*, November 22, 2013, www.faithstreet.com/onfaith/2013/11/22/imagine-the-rights-religion/30020.

17. Sarah Jones, "Outrage Over Oath: Religious Right Objects to New Conscience Rules at Air Force Academy," *Wall of Separation* (blog), October 29, 2013, https://au.org/blogs/wall-of-separation/outrage-over-oath-religious-right-objects-to-new-conscience-rules-at-air.

18. Ibid.

19. Rep. Sam Johnson (R-TX) introduced the H.R. 1425, "Preserve and Protect God in Military Oaths Act of 2015," on March 18, 2015; Preserve and Protect God in Military Oaths Act of 2015, H.R. 1425, 114th Cong. (2015).

20. "Humanist Group Tells Ga. School to Stop Allowing Official Coach-Led Prayers," *Church & State*, October 2014, https://www.au.org/church-state/october-2014-church-state/people-events/humanist-group-tells-ga-school-to-stop-allowing.

21. "Tenn. Football Coaches Continue Praying with Players, Newspaper Says," *Church & State*, November 2013, https://www.au.org/church-state/november-2013-church-state/people-events/tenn-football-coaches-continue-praying-with.

22. Chris Oberholtz, "Mission Rejects Kansas City Atheist Group's Thanksgiving Help," KCTV 5 News, December 12, 2013, http://www.kctv5.com/story/23942826/mission-says-no-to-kansas-city-atheist-group.

23. Barry Lynn, "Uneasy Rider: Car Sick on the 'Road to Victory,'" *Church & State*, October 1995.

24. Barry Lynn, "'Road to Victory' 1996: Where's the Exit Ramp?" *Church & State*, October 1996.

25. Barry Lynn, "Not-so-Undercover at the Christian Coalition 'Road to Victory,'" *Church & State*, November 1998.

26. "Constitutional Amendment Restoring Religious Freedom," Hearing Before the House of Representatives, June 4, 1998 (statement of Rep. Bill Hefner of North Carolina).

27. Barry Lynn, "My Chat with Pat: Exchanging Views with Brother Robertson," *Church & State*, November 1999, https://www.au.org/church-state/November-1999-church-state/perspective/my-chat-with-pat.

28. Barry Lynn, "'The Enemy' Within: My Strange Trek to the Values Voter Summit," *Church & State*, November 2006, https://www.au.org/church-state/November-2006-church-state/perspective/'the-enemy'-within.

29. Barry Lynn, "Right-Wing Reunion: What I Saw at the 'Values Voter' Summit," *Church & State*, November 2007, https://www.au.org/church-state/November-2007-church-state/perspective/right-wing-reunion.

30. Barry Lynn, "Faith, Freedom and Front-Row Seats: I'm a 'Values Voter,' But Not the Kind I Met at these Events," *Church & State*, October 2010, https://www.au.org/church-state/October-2010-church-state/perspective/faith-freedom-and-front-row-seats.

31. Barry Lynn, "Always on Their Mind: 'Values Voter' Summiteers Fixate on Americans United," *Church & State*, October 2012, https://www.au.org/church-state/October-2012-church-state/perspective/always-on-their-mind-values-voter-summiteers.

CHAPTER 5: RELIGIOUS RIGHT TACTICS

1. Russell Shorto, "How Christian Were the Founders?" *New York Times Magazine*, February 11, 2010.

2. Barry Lynn, "Prophet Pat?: Buchanan Predicted the Current Wave of Odious Initiatives," *Church & State*, July/August 2012, https://www.au.org/church-state/julyaugust-2012-church-state/perspective/prophet-pat-buchanan-predicted-the-current-0.

3. Barry Lynn, "Historic Mistake: Old North Church and Our Tax Dollars," *Church & State*, July/August 2003, https://www.au.org/church-state/julyaugust-2003-church-state/perspective/historic mistake.

4. "Federal Grant for the Old North Church," press conference, Boston, MA, May 27, 2003.

5. Barbara Bradley, "Federal Grant for Historic Church Marks Shift in Policy," *Morning Edition*, NPR, May 28, 2003, http://www.npr.org/templates/story/story.php?storyId=1277076.

6. California Missions Preservation Act: Hearing on S. 1306, March 9, 2004, Before the Subcommittee on National Parks of the Comm. on Energy and Natural Resources, 108th Cong. (2004) (statement of Rev. Barry Lynn, Executive Director, Americans United for Separation of Church and State).

7. "Memorial and Remonstrance against Religious Assessments," June 20, 1785 *The Papers of James Madison*, vol. 8, *10 March 1784–28 March 1786*, ed. Robert A. Rutland and William M. E. Rachal (Chicago: University of Chicago Press, 1973), pp. 298–300.

8. "From James Madison to the House of Representatives, 28 February 1811," *The Papers of James Madison*, Presidential Series, vol. 3, *3 November 1810–4 November 1811*, ed. J. C. A. Stagg, Jeanne Kerr Cross, and Susan Holbrook Perdue (Charlottesville, VA: University of Virginia, 1996), p. 193.

9. Barry Lynn, "Don't Pass Me the Plate for Your Church's Upkeep," *Huffington Post*, February 16, 2011, www.huffingtonpost.com/barry-w-lynn/don't-pass-me-the-plate-fo_b_823558.html.

10. "From James Madison to the House of Representatives, 21 February 1811," *Papers of James Madison*, Presidential Series, pp. 176–77.

11. Barry Lynn, "Severe Storm Warning: Did Hurricane Sandy Demolish the First Amendment?" *Church & State*, April 2013, https://www.au.org/church-state/april-2013-church-state/perspective/severe-storm-warning-did-hurricane-sandy-demolish.

12. Dan Lamothe, "Exclusive: Lt. Gen. William Boykin, Past Delta Force Commander, Hit with Army Reprimand," *Washington Post*, May 23, 2014.

13. Ibid.

14. Barry Lynn, "Scaling the Summit: What I Learned at this Year's Far-Right Shindig," *Church & State*, November 2014, https://www.au.org/church-state/November-2014-church-state/perspective/scaling-the-summit-what-i-learned-at-this-years.

15. "Erwin Chemerinsky's *The Conservative Assault on the Constitution*," podcast interview by Adam Schlossman, SCOTUSblog, December 14, 2010, www.scotusblog.com/2010/12/podcast-interview---erwin-chemerinskys-the-conservative-assault-on-the-constitution/.

16. Jeremy W. Peters, "Eye on Legacy, Obama Shapes Appeals Courts," *New York Times*, September 14, 2014, p. A1.

17. Barry Lynn, "The High Court and Davey: Handing a Big Victory to the Optimists' Club," *Church & State*, April 2004, https://www.au.org/church-state/april-2004-church-state/perspective/the-high-court-and-davey.

18. Newdow v. Rio Linda Union School District, 597 F. 3rd 1007 (U.S. Court of Appeals, 9th Circuit) (2010), p. 3929.

19. Lee v. Weisman, 505 U.S. 577, 596 (1992).

20. Santa Fe Independent School Dist. v. Doe, 530 U.S. 290, 312 (2000).

21. Marsh v Chambers, 463 US 783, 794 (1983).

22. Lee v. Weisman, 505 US 577 (1992).

23. Transcript of Oral Argument at 45, Town of Greece, N.Y. v. Galloway, 134 S. Ct. 1811 (2014) (No. 12–696).

24. Douglas Laycock, "Equal Access and Moments of Silence: The Equal Status of Religious Speech by Private Speakers," *Northwestern University Law Review* 81, no. 1 (1986).

25. Town of Greece, N.Y. v. Galloway, 134 S. Ct. 1811, 1823–25 (2014).

26. Barry Lynn, "West of Fairness and Justice: New Documentary Showcases Dangers of Religious Hysteria," *Church & State*, March 2013, https://www.au.org/church-state/march-2013-church-state/perspective/west-of-fairness-and-justice-new-documentary.

CHAPTER 6: WHEN GOVERNMENT OFFICIALS PRAY, GET OUT THE TV CAMERAS

1. Barry Lynn, "Who Needs a National Day of Prayer?" *Huffington Post*, June 20, 2010, www.huffingtonpost.com/barry-w-lynn/who-needs-a-national-day_b_541107.html.

2. National Day of Prayer Task Force, "National Day of Prayer Under Attack; Judge Rules Statute Setting National Day of Prayer Unconstitutional; Americans Urge President Obama to Appeal," press release, April 15, 2010, *Capitol Hill Prayer Partners Daily Brief* (blog), chpponline.blogspot.com/2010/04/press-release-national-day-of-prayer.html.

3. Todd Richmond, "Federal Judge Rules Day of Prayer Unconstitutional," Associated Press, June 24, 2011.

4. Amanda Terkel, "Obama Publicly Condemns Uganda's Anti-Homosexuality Legislation: It Is an 'Odious' Bill," *ThinkProgress*, February 4, 2010, thinkprogress.org/politics/2010/02/04/80685/Uganda-prayer/.

5. Ibid.

6. Barry Lynn, "Why I'm Not Going to the National Prayer Breakfast," *On Faith*, February 2, 2012, www.faithstreet.com/onfaith/2012/02/02/why-im-not-going-to-the-national-prayer-breakfast/16831.

7. Jeff Sharlet, *The Family: The Secret Fundamentalism at the Heart of American Power* (New York: Harper, 2008); Jeff Sharlet, *C Street: The Fundamentalist Threat to American Democracy* (New York: Little, Brown and Company, 2010).

8. Ben Carson, *One Nation: What We Can All Do to Save America's Future* (New York: Sentinel, 2014).

9. Barry Lynn, "Congressional Chaplains: A Waste of Taxpayer Money," *Church & State*, January 1995.

10. Elizabeth Fleet, "Madison's Detached Memoranda," *William and Mary Quarterly* (1946).

11. Barry Lynn, "A New Commandment for Politicians: Thou Shalt Not Be a Hypocrite," *Church & State*, September 2001 https://www.au.org/church-state/September-2001-church-state/perspective/a-new-commandment-for-politicians.

12. "Congressman Aderholt Introduces Ten Commandments Defense Act," press release, March 7, 2002, http://aderholt.house.gov/s2002/congressman-aderholt-introduces-ten-commandments-defense-act1/.

13. Glassroth v. Moore (MD Ala. 2002).

14. Barry Lynn, "Judging Roy: Why the Court Ruled Against Moore's Monument," *Church & State*, December 2002, https://www.au.org/church-state/December-2002-church-state/perspective/judging-roy.

15. Barry Lynn, "The Commandments Cases: A Monumental Moment at the Supreme Court," *Church & State*, April 2005, https://www.au.org/church-state/april-2005-church-state/perspective/the-commandments-cases.

16. "Public Display of the Ten Commandments," *Washington Journal*, C-SPAN (March 2, 2005), http://www.c-span.org/video/?185676-2/public-display-ten-commandments&start=2199.

17. Rob Boston, "Nine Justices, Ten Commandments, Two Important Cases: Church-State Separation Hangs in the Balance as the Supreme Court Debates Decalogue Displays," *Church & State*,

April 2005, https://www.au.org/church-state/april-2005-church-state/featured/nine-justices -ten-commandments-two-important-cases.

18. Ibid.

19. Barry Lynn, "Commandments Clash: Parsing a Split Decision at the Supreme Court," *Church & State*, July/August 2005, https://www.au.org/church-state/julyaugust-2005-church-state/ perspective/commandments-clash.

20. "Headlines—Hot Docket," *The Daily Show with Jon Stewart*, Comedy Central, June 28, 2005.

21. Barry Lynn, "The Grinch Who Fobbed About Christmas: Falwell's Holiday Hokum," *Church & State*, January 2006, https://www.au.org/church-state/January-2006-church-state/perspective/ the-grinch-who-fobbed-about-christmas.

22. Gretchen Carlson, *Fox & Friends*, Fox News, November 28, 2012.

23. Barry Lynn, "My Profession of Faith: 'I Believe' Government Should Not Endorse Religion," *Church & State*, January 2009, https://www.au.org/church-state/January-2009-church-state/ perspective/my-profession-of-faith.

24. Salazar v. Buono, 559 U.S. 700 (2010).

25. Barry Lynn, "Of Crosses, Crescent Moons and Lou Dobbs: Religious Symbols Clang as the Supreme Court Hears a Church-State Argument," *Church & State*, November 2009, https:// www.au.org/church-state/November-2009-church-state/perspective/of-crosses-crescent -moons-and-lou-dobbs.

26. Salazar v. Buono, Transcript of Oral Argument, October 7, 2009, pp. 21–28.

CHAPTER 7: DOES THE RELIGIOUS RIGHT HATE EVERYBODY? ANSWER: YES

1. Dar Williams, *The Christians and the Pagans*, 1996.

2. *Ask the White House*, November 26, 2003, http://georgewbush-whitehouse.archives.gov/ ask/20031126.html.

3. Alan Cooperman, "Bush Aide Ignites Ire of Pagans," *Washington Post*, December 9, 2003, http:// articles.chicagotribune.com/2003-12-09/news/0312090069_1_pagans-towey-americans-united.

4. "Chesterfield County, VA, Refuses to Consider a Wiccan for Invocation," *Religious Tolerance. org*, October 4, 2002, http://www.religioustolerance.org/wicchest.htm.

5. Barry Lynn, "Wiccans and the VA: The Case for Decency and Common Sense," *Church & State*, September 2006, https://www.au.org/church-state/September-2006-church-state/ perspective/wiccans-and-the-va.

6. Pat Robertson, *The 700 Club*, CBN (Christian Broadcast Network), aired September 13, 2001.

7. Barry Lynn, speech, Social Studies Teacher Convention, Washington, DC, October 2001.

8. Barry Lynn, "A Year after Sept. 11, Some Folks Still Don't Get It," *Church & State*, September 2002, https://www.au.org/church-state/September-2002-church-state/perspective/ a-year-after-sept-11-some-folks-still-don't-get.

9. Welsh v. U.S., 398 U.S. 333 (1970).

10. Brian Montopoli, "Rick Santorum: Left Uses College for Indoctrination," *CBS News*, January 25, 2012, http://www.cbsnews.com/news/rick-santorum-left-uses-college-for-indoctrination.

11. Michael Lewis, *Flash Boys: A Wall Street Revolt* (New York: W. W. Norton, 2014).

12. R. Albert Mohler, Jr. "Can Christians Use Birth Control?" *AlbertMohler.com*, May 8, 2006, http://www.albertmohler.com/2006/05/08/can-christians-use-birth-control.

13. MO Rev. Stat. § 1.205.

14. Webster v. Reprod. Health Servs., 492 U.S. 490, 566, 571 (1989).

15. Barry Lynn, "The Assassination of Dr. Tiller: Do Religious Right Extremists Share Some of the Blame," *Church & State*, July/August 2009, https://www.au.org/church-state/julyaugust-2009-church-state/perspective/the-assassination-of-dr-tiller.

16. "George Tiller Was a Mass-Murderer, Says Randall Terry—We Grieve that He Did Not Have Time to Properly Prepare His Soul to Face God," ChristianNewsWire, May 31, 2009, www.christiannewswire.com/news/8967610531.

17. Associated Baptist Press, "Former SBC Officer Says Tiller Murder Answer to Prayer," Baptist News Global, June 2, 2009, baptistnews.com/archives/item/4119-former-sbc-officer-says-tiller-murder-answer-to-prayer.

18. Larry Keller, "Pastor Asks God to Smite President Obama," *Hatewatch* (blog), June 25, 2009, http://www.splcenter.org/blog/2009/06/25/pastor-asks-god-to-smite-president-obama/.

19. Barry Lynn, "Religious Liberty Award Acceptance Speech," 68th Annual Conference of the American Humanist Association, Phoenix, Arizona, June 2009.

20. "Lines Crossed: Separation of Church and State: Has the Obama Administration Trampled on Freedom of Religion and Freedom of Conscience?" Hearing Before the Committee on Oversight and Government Reform, February 16, 2012 (statement of C. Ben Mitchell, PhD), oversight.house.gov/wp-content/uploads/2012/02/2-16-12_Full_HC_Mandate_C_Ben_Mitchell.pdf.

21. "Lines Crossed: Separation of Church and State: Has the Obama Administration Trampled on Freedom of Religion and Freedom of Conscience?" Hearing Before the Committee on Oversight and Government Reform, February 16, 2012 (statement of Most Reverend William E. Lori, Bishop of Bridgeport), oversight.house.gov/wp-content/uploads/2012/02/2-16-12_Full_HC_Mandate_BishopLori.pdf.

22. Richard Wolf and Cathy Lynn Grossman, "Obama Mandate on Birth Control Coverage Stirs Controversy," *USA Today*, February 9, 2012, usatoday30.usatoday.com/news/Washington/story/2012-02-08/catholics-contraceptive-mandate/53014864/1.

23. Jerry Markon, "Health, Abortion Issues Split Obama Administration and Catholic Groups," *Washington Post*, October 31, 2011.

24. ACLU of Massachusetts v. Sebelius, US District Court of Massachusetts, March 23, 2012.

25. "Lines Crossed: Separation of Church and State: Has the Obama Administration Trampled on Freedom of Religion and Freedom of Conscience?" Hearing Before the Committee on Oversight and Government Reform, February 16, 2012 (opening statement of Rep. Darrell Issa), oversight.house.gov/hearing/lines-crossed-separation-of-church-and-state-has-the-obama-administration-trampled-on-freedom-of-religion-and-freedom-of-conscience/.

26. Kyle Mantyla, "Mat Staver Says Gay Marriage Is 'The Beginning of the End of

Western Civilization,'" *Right Wing Watch*, July 30, 2014, www.rightwingwatch.org/content/mat-staver-says-gay-marriage-beginning-end-western-civilization.

27. Ann Coulter, "Jerry Falwell—Say Hello to Ronald Reagan!" *Ann Coulter*, May 16, 2007, www.anncoulter.com/columns/2007-05-16.html.

28. 153 Cong. Rec. S12026 (statement of Senator Kennedy on the Matthew Shepard Act) (September 25, 2007).

29. Bob Knight, "Homosexuality" (panel), Reclaiming America for Christ Conference, February 28, 1999.

30. "Family Impact Summit: 'Jaunty Musclemen,' 'Gay Aliens,' and the 'Homosexual Agenda' in PowerPoint," *Right Wing Watch*, September 21, 2007, www.rightwingwatch.org/content/family-impact-summit-jaunty-musclemen-gay-aliens-and-homosexual-agenda-powerpoint.

31. Robert Gagnon, "How to make a valid secular case against cultural endorsement of homosexual behavior," 2004, http://www.robgagnon.net/SecularCase.htm.

32. "Traditional Values Coalition: Organizational Profile," *Right Wing Watch*, http://www.rightwingwatch.org/content/traditional-values-coalition.

33. "Family Research Council: Organizational Profile," *Right Wing Watch*, http://www.rightwingwatch.org/content/family-research-council.

34. "Focus on the Family: Organizational Profile," *Right Wing Watch*, http://www.rightwingwatch.org/content/focus-family.

35. "Bishop Wellington Boone," *Crooked Crosses: Taking Aim at Dominionism*, https://crooked-crosses.wordpress.com/crazies-for-god/bishop-wellington-boone.

36. "Religious Right Mourns Rep. DeLay's Decision to Leave Congress," *Church & State*, May 2006, https://www.au.org/church-state/may-2006-church-state/people-events/religious-right-mourns-rep-delayrsquos-decision-to.

37. R. Jeffrey Smith, "DeLay PAC Is Indicted for Illegal Donations," *Washington Post*, September 9, 2005, http://www.washingtonpost.com/wp-dyn/content/article/2005/09/08/AR2005090800973.html.

38. Juli Weiner, "Tom DeLay Conviction Overturned; *Dancing with the Stars* Elimination Stands," *Vanity Fair*, September 19, 2013, http://www.vanityfair.com/news/2013/09/tom-delay-conviction-overturned-dancing-with-the-stars-elimination-stands.

39. Abby Goodnough and William Yardley, "Federal Judge Condemns Intervention in Schiavo Case," *New York Times*, March 31, 2005, www.nytimes.com/2005/03/31/national/31schiavo.html.

40. Joel Roberts, "Schiavo Politics, Up Close," *CBS News*, March 25, 2005, http://www.cbsnews.com/news/schiavo-politics-up-close/.

41. Sarah Palin, "Statement on the Current Health Care Debate," Facebook, August 7, 2009, https://www.facebook.com/notes/sarah-palin/statementon-the-current-health-care-debate/113851103434.

42. Steven Ertelt, "*New York Times* Attacks *Washington Times* on 'Death Panels,'" August 14, 2009, www.lifenews.com/2009/08/14/bio-2921/.

43. "Common Good Death Camps," *The Revealer: A Review of Religion and Media*, May 29, 2010, http://therevealer.org/archives/4239.

44. Jim Towey, "The Death Book for Veterans," *Wall Street Journal*, August 18, 2009.

45. Ron Suskind, "Why Are These Men Laughing?" *Esquire*, January 1, 2003, ronsuskind.com/why-are-these-men-laughing/.

46. David Kuo, Tempting Faith: An Inside Story of Political Seduction (New York: Free Press, 2006).

47. Patient Protection and Affordable Care Act, Pub. L. No. 111–148 (2010).

48. "Views on End-of-Life Medical Treatments," *Pew Research Center*, November 21, 2013, http://www.pewforum.org/2013/11/21/views-on-end-of-life-medical-treatments/.

CHAPTER 8: THE BIG WALL-BANGERS

1. Barry Lynn, speech, "The Faith-Based Initiative Two Years Later: Examining its Potential, Progress and Problems," Pew Forum on Religion and Public Life and the Roundtable on Religion and Social Welfare Policy, March 5, 2003.

2. Bellmore v. United Methodist Children's Home of the North Georgia Conference, Inc., and Department of Human Resources, State of Georgia (2002).

3. Lambda Legal, "Why is a United Methodist Children's Home Practicing Bigotry?" *GayToday.com*, http://gaytoday.com/events/101602ev.asp.

4. "'Faith-Based' Fumble: Grant to Robertson Subsidizes Bigotry," *Church & State*, November 2002, https://www.au.org/church-state/November-2002-church-state/editorial/faith-based-fumble-grant-to-robertson-subsidizes.

5. *John McLaughlin's One on One*, PBS, February 2, 2001.

6. Lisa Richardson, "Religious Groups Get Federal Funds," *LA Times*, October 5, 2002, http://articles.latimes.com/2002/oct/05/local/me-religgrants5.

7. Chris McGreal, "Mission Congo: How Pat Robertson Raised Millions on the Back of a Non-Existent Aid Project," *Guardian*, September 5, 2013.

8. Bill Sizemore, "Religious Groups Benefit from Bush's Blessings," *Baylor Lariat*, January 19, 2006, http://www.baylor.edu/lariatarchives/news.php?action=story&story=38468.

9. Kai Wright, "On the Books," *The Nation Institute*, January 18, 2010, http://www.nationinstitute.org/featuredwork/fellows/1323/on_the_books/?page=entire.

10. Hamil Harris, "Black Churches Missing Out on Federal Aid," *Black Enterprise*, January 1, 2007.

11. "Faith Based Initiative Moves Forward at Agencies," Center for Effective Government, November 6, 2002, www.foreffectivegov.org/node/1082.

12. Dana Canedy, "The 2002 Elections: The Florida Vote; Bush Wins 2nd Term With Surge," *Miami Herald*, November 6, 2002.

13. ACLU of Louisiana v. Foster, US Dist. Ct. for the Eastern District of Louisiana (2002).

14. Joseph Farah, "Phony Faith-Based Initiative," *WorldNetDaily*, January 17, 2003, www.wnd.com/2003/01/16782.

15. What Would Jesus Drive Campaign Launch, Evangelical Environment Network and *Creation Care Magazine*, Detroit, November 20, 2002, http://www.whatwouldjesusdrive.info/intro.php.

16. US Department of Health and Human Services, "President Announces $100 Million in

Grants to Support Substance Abuse Treatment," press release, August 3, 2004, http://archive.hhs
.gov/news/press/2004pres/20040803c.html.

17. Ernest Herndon, "A Light in Louisiana," *Charisma*, September 30, 2003, http://www
.charismamag.com/site-archives/305-features/compassion-in-action/1023-a-light-in-louisiana.

18. Laurie Goodstein, "Judge in Wisconsin Voids a Religion-Based Initiative," *New York Times*,
January 10, 2002, http://www.nytimes.com/2002/01/10/us/judge-in-wisconsin-voids-a-religion
-based-initiative.html.

19. David Abel, "State Veterans Shelters Losing Faith Religious Groups to Get More Grants
From US," *Boston Globe*, January 13, 2003.

20. Barry Lynn, "Faith-Based Folly: Obama's Executive Order Leaves Much to Be Desired,"
Church & State, March 2009, https://www.au.org/church-state/march-2009-church-state/
perspective/faith-based-folly.

21. Barry Lynn, "Faith, Hope, and Charity: Why President Obama's 'Faith-Based' Agenda Must
Change," *Huffington Post*, April 4, 2010, www.huffingtonpost.com/barry-w-lynn/faith-hope-and
-charity-wh_b_450099.html.

22. Government Accountability Office, "Faith Based and Community Initiative: Improvements
in Monitoring Grantees and Measuring Performance Could Enhance Accountability" Report to Congressional Requesters, June 2006, http://www.gao.gov/new.items/d06616.pdf.

23. Krista Kapralos, "Non-Christians Need Not Apply," *Global Post*, June 17, 2010, http://
www.globalpost.com/dispatch/ngos/100110/world-vision-religion-foreign-aid.

24. Ibid.

25. Ibid.

26. Barry Lynn, "It's Time for Obama to Fix the Faith-Based Initiative," *Huffington Post*, March
29, 2010, www.huffingtonpost.com/barry-w-lynn/its-time-for-obama-to-fix_b_517249.html.

27. President's Advisory Council on Faith-Based and Neighborhood Partnerships, *A New Era of
Partnerships: A Report of Recommendations to the President*, March 2010, https://www.whitehouse.gov/
sites/default/files/partnerships-reform-office.pdf.

28. Ibid.

29. Government Accountability Office, "Faith Based and Community Initiative."

30. President's Advisory Council, "A New Era of Partnerships."

31. Sylvia M. Burwell, Memorandum for the Heads of the Executive Departments and Agencies regarding Implementation of Executive Order 13559, "Fundamental Principles and Policy-
Making Criteria for Partnerships with Faith-Based and Other Neighborhood Organizations," August
2, 2013, https://www.whitehouse.gov/sites/default/files/omb/memoranda/2013/m-13-19.pdf.

32. US Department of Justice, "Frequently Asked Questions: Nondiscrimination Grant Condition in the Violence Against Women Reauthorization Act of 2013," April 9, 2014, http://www
.justice.gov/sites/default/files/ovw/legacy/2014/06/20/faqs-ngc-vawa.pdf.

33. Barry Lynn, "Faith-Based Procrastination: Religious Job Bias in Taxpayer-Funded Programs," *On Faith*, December 27, 2012, www.faithstreet.com/onfaith/2012/12/27/faith-based
-procrastination-religious-job-bias-in-taxpayer-funded-program/11868.

34. E. J. Dionne and Melissa Rogers, moderators, "Four More Years for the White House
Office of Faith-Based and Neighborhood Partnerships," panel discussion, Brookings Institution,

December 17, 2012, http://www.brookings.edu/~/media/events/2012/12/17-faith-based
partnerships/20121217_faith_based_c.pdf.

35. President Kennedy Executive Order 10925, "Establishing the President's Committee on Equal Employment Opportunity," March 6, 1961.

36. US v. Lee, 455 US 252 (1982).

37. Barry Lynn, "Silent Witness: House Panel Can't Handle the Truth from Sandra Fluke—Or Me," *Church & State*, April 2012, https://www.au.org/church-state/april-2012-church-state/perspective/silent-witness.

38. Barry Lynn, "Religious Liberty and the Coming Corporate Theocracy," *Huffington Post*, March 13, 2014, www.huffingtonpost.com/barry-w-lynn/supreme-court-religious-freedom_b_4956018.html.

39. Jamie Fuller, "Here's What You Need to Know About the Hobby Lobby Case," *Washington Post*, March 24, 2014, http://www.washingtonpost.com/blogs/the-fix/wp/2014/03/24/heres-what-you-need-to-know-about-the-hobby-lobby-case/.

40. Ben Zimmer, "Where Did the Supreme Court Get Its 'Parade of Horribles,'" *Boston Globe*, July 1, 2012, http://www.bostonglobe.com/ideas/2012/06/30/where-did-supreme-court-get-its-parade-horribles/Y0jnIscamtgPEzO0PdtL9N/story.html.

41. US v. Ballard, 322 US 78 (1944).

42. Jerrold Nadler, "For the Second Time This Week, House Blocks 'Not My Boss's Business' Bill," *Congressman Jerrold Nadler: Proudly Serving the 10th District of New York*, July 17, 2014, nadler.house.gov/press-release/second-time-week-house-blocks-"not-my-boss'-business"-bill-procedural-vote.

43. Callie Beusman, "Clergy Pass Out Condoms at Hobby Lobby in Protest," *Jezebel*, July 3, 2014, http://jezebel.com/clergy-pass-out-condoms-at-hobby-lobby-in-protest-1599729956.

44. Tara Culp-Ressler, "The Most Creative Ways that People Are Protesting the Hobby Lobby Ruling," *ThinkProgress*, July 10, 2014, http://thinkprogress.org/health/2014/07/10/3458726/creative-hobby-lobby-protests/.

45. Kristine Guerra, "How Indiana's RFRA Differs from the Federal Version," *Indiana Star*, April 25, 2015, http://www.indystar.com/story/news/politics/2015/03/31/indianas-rfra-similar-federal-rfra/70729888/.

46. Molly Redden, "Catholic Church Argues It Doesn't Have to Show Up in Court Because Religious Freedom," *Mother Jones*, November 17, 2014, http://www.motherjones.com/politics/2014/11/catholic-school-fires-teacher-using-ivf-unusual-religious-freedom-defense.

47. United States Conference of Catholic Bishops, "Advance Notice of Proposed Rulemaking on Preventive Services File Code No. CMS-9968-ANPRM," May 15, 2012, http://www.usccb.org/about/general-counsel/rulemaking/upload/comments-on-advance-notice-of-proposed-rule-making-on-preventive-services-12-05-15.pdf.

48. Alexis de Tocqueville, *Democracy in America*, ed. J. P. Meyer, trans. George Lawrence (1835; New York: Harper & Row, 1969).

49. MacFarlane v. MacFarlane, 2009-Ohio-6647 (2009).

50. John Hurdle and Erik Eckholm, "Cardinal's Aide Is Found Guilty in Abuse Case," *New York Times*, June 22, 2012, http://www.nytimes.com/2012/06/23/us/philadelphias-msgr-william-j-lynn-is-convicted-of-allowing-abuse.html.

51. Ibid.

52. Bill Donohue, "Straight Talk about the Catholic Church," advertisement, *New York Times*, April 11, 2011, http://www.catholicleague.org/wp-content/uploads/2011/08/2011_04_11 _Donohue_StraightTalk.pdf.

CHAPTER 9: RELIGION IN POLITICS

1. Barry Lynn, "Memo to Candidates: Learn a Lesson from John F. Kennedy," *Church & State*, September 2000, https://www.au.org/church-state/September-2000-church-state/perspective/ memo-to-candidates.

2. Mark Jacoby, "GOP Senators Target Group Against Christian Coalition," *St. Petersburg Times*, July 20, 1999, http://www.sptimes.com/News/72099/news_pf/Worldandnation/GOP _senators_target_g.shtml.

3. Barry Lynn, "Subpoena Surprise: Fred Thompson Comes Knocking," *Church & State*, September 1997.

4. Barry Lynn, "Sen. Thompson and Co.: They Just Couldn't Handle the Truth," *Church & State*, April 1998.

5. Committee of Governmental Affairs (United States Senate), "Investigation of Illegal or Improper Activities in Connection with 1996 Federal Election Campaigns," Final Report, March 10, 1998, http://www.gpo.gov/fdsys/pkg/CRPT-105srpt167/pdf/CRPT-105srpt167-pt3.pdf.

6. Barry Lynn, "Investigating AU: Sen. Helms' Unfair Witch Hunt Project," *Church & State*, September 1999, https://www.au.org/church-state/September-1999-church-state/perspective/ investigating-au.

7. Barry Lynn, "The Helms Witch Hunt: A Happy Ending to an Unhappy Episode," *Church & State*, March 2000, https://www.au.org/church-state/march-2000-church-state/perspective/ the-helms-witch-hunt.

8. Hanna Rosin, "Christian Right's Fervor Has Fizzled," *Washington Post*, February 16, 2000, http://www.washingtonpost.com/wp-srv/WPcap/2000-02/16/019r-021600-idx.html.

9. Barry Lynn, "At the Falwell Follies: Jerry Finally 'Fesses Up on Fox News Channel," *Church & State*, September 2004, https://www.au.org/church-state/September-2004-church-state/ perspective/at-the-falwell-follies.

10. Barry Lynn, "TV Preachers, Elmer Gantry and U.S. Tax Law: My Day in Congress," *Church & State*, June 2002, https://www.au.org/church-state/june-2002-church-state/perspective/ tv-preachers-elmer-gantry-and-us-law.

11. Gerald Zeilzer, "The Quest for Power and Influence," *Liberty*, May/June 2003, http:// www.libertymagazine.org/article/the-quest-for-power-and-influence.

12. Barry Lynn, "It's Real Simple: Federal Tax Law Forbids Churches to Endorse Political Candidates," *Church & State*, November 2008, https://www.au.org/church-state/ November-2008-church-state/perspective/itrsquos-real-simple.

13. Barry Lynn, "'Pulpit Freedom Sunday': A Crusade to Turn Churches into Cogs in the Right

Wing's Political Machine," *Huffington Post*, September 30, 2008, www.huffingtonpost.com/barry-w
-lynn/pulpit-freedom-Sunday-a-c_b_129394.html.

14. Kyle Mantyla, "Religious Right's Odd Definition of 'Endorsement,'" *RightWingWatch*, September
23, 2008, http://www.rightwingwatch.org/content/religious-rights-odd-definition-endorsement.

15. Barry Lynn, "Church Electioneering and the IRS: Another Example of Tax Agency
Failure," *Huffington Post*, May 14, 2013, www.huffingtonpost/barry-w-lynn/church-electioneering
-and_b_3267250.html.

16. "Charles L. Worley, North Carolina Pastor: Put Gays and Lesbians in Electrified Pen to Kill
Them Off," *Huffington Post*, May 21, 2012, http://www.huffingtonpost.com/2012/05/21/north
-carolina-pastor-gay-rant-starvation_n_1533463.html.

17. "AU Urges IRS to Fix Policies Regarding Church Electioneering," *Church & State*,
December 2009, https://www.au.org/church-state/December-2009-church-state/people-events/
au-urges-irs-to-fix-policies-regarding-church.

18. Barry Lynn, "Falling From Grace: Partisan Prophets Plummeted at the Polls," *Church & State*,
December 2006, https://www.au.org/church-state/December-2006-church-state/perspective/
falling-from-grace.

19. James Dao, "Movement in the Pews Tries to Jolt Ohio," *New York Times*, March 27, 2005.

20. Barry Lynn, "God-Talk and Politicians: When Does Honesty Turn into Plain Old Pandering?"
Church & State, September 2007, https://www.au.org/church-state/September-2007-church-state/
perspective/god-talk-and-politicians.

21. David Kirkpatrick, "Consultant Helps Democrats Embrace Faith, and Some in the Party
Are Not Pleased," *New York Times*, December 26, 2006, http://www.nytimes.com/2006/12/26/us/
politics/26faith.html.

22. Transcript of Sojourners Presidential Forum, June 4, 2007, http://www.cnn.com/
TRANSCRIPTS/0706/04/sitroom.03.html.

23. Barry Lynn, "Romney, Religion, and John F. Kennedy: Two Speeches, Two Different Viewpoints," *Huffington Post*, December 6, 2007, www.huffingtonpost.com/barry-w-lynn/Romney
-religion-and-john-_b_75715.html.

24. John F. Kennedy, Address to the Greater Houston Ministerial Association at the Rice Hotel
in Houston, TX, September 12, 1960.

25. Barry Lynn, "My Response to 'The Response': What I Saw (and Felt) at Perry's Prayer Fest,"
Church & State, September 2011, https://www.au.org/church-state/September-2011-church-state/
perspective/my-response-to-'the-response'.

26. Subcommittee on the Constitution, Committee on the Judiciary, "State of Religious Liberty
in the United States," October 26, 2011 (opening statement of Hon. Trent Franks, rep. from Arizona),
http://www.gpo.gov/fdsys/pkg/CHRG-112hhrg70913/html/CHRG-112hhrg70913.htm.

27. Jonathan Mann, "Will Satan Stop Rick Santorum?" CNN, February 24, 2012, http://www
.cnn.com/2012/02/24/politics/mann-santorum-satan/.

28. Learned Hand, "Spirit of Liberty," speech, 1944, http://www.providenceforum.org/
spiritoflibertyspeech.

CHAPTER 10: WHY DOES ANYBODY SPEND THEIR ADULT LIFE DOING THIS?

1. Barry Lynn, "Connecting with History: A Visit with the Archers," *Church & State*, March 1993.

2. Glenn Archer, *Dream Lives On: The Story of Glenn Archer and Americans United* (Washington, DC: Robert B. Luce, Inc., 1982), p. 247.

3. Barry Lynn, "The Alabama Debate: From 'Shout Shows' to Comedy Central," *Church & State*, October 2003, https://www.au.org/church-state/October-2003-church-state/perspective/the-alabama-debate.

4. "Take Two Tablets," *The Daily Show with Jon Stewart*, Comedy Central, September 24, 2003.

5. Barry Lynn, "The March for Women's Lives: One Speech, Two Minutes, A Million Amens," *Church & State*, June 2004, https://www.au.org/church-state/june-2004-church-state/perspective/the-march-for-womans-lives.

6. Barry Lynn, "And That's the Way It Is: Walter Cronkite, An Anchor of Truth," *Church & State*, April 2007, https://www.au.org/church-state/april-2007-church-state/perspective/and-thats-the-way-it-is-walter-cronkite-an-anchor.

7. Barry Lynn, "That's Entertainment!: Bringing Home the Bacon (Brothers) and Others for Six Degrees of Separation," *Church & State*, May 2008, https://www.au.org/church-state/may-2008-church-state/perspective/that's-entertainment.

8. Barry Lynn, "Following a True Compass: When Someone Had to Take the Lead, Ted Kennedy Was Always There," *Church & State*, October 2009, https://www.au.org/church-state/October-2009-church-state/perspective/following-a-true-compass.

9. Barry Lynn, "Of Allies and Anniversaries: Meeting Friends at the Intersection of Religion and Politics," *Church & State*, June 2011, https://www.au.org/church-state/june-2011-church-state/perspective/of-allies-and-anniversaries.

10. Barry Lynn, "From C-SPAN to Salon Sanctuary: Finding New Ways to Spread Our Message," *Church & State*, February 2012, https://www.au.org/church-state/February-2012-church-state/perspective/from-c-span-to-salon-sanctuary.

11. Interview with Phil Donahue," transcript, *Piers Morgan Tonight*, CNN, January 7, 2012, www.cnn.com/TRANSCRIPTS/1201/07/pmt.01.html.

12. Barry Lynn, "Sing It Loud and Proud: AU Lifts Many Voices United for Separation of Church and State," *Church & State*, November 2012, https://www.au.org/church-state/November-2012-church-state/perspective/sing-it-loud-and-proud-au-lifts-many-voices.

13. Barry Lynn, "Going Viral: AU Videos Promote the Cause," *Church & State*, July/August 2013, https://www.au.org/church-state/julyaugust-2013-church-state/perspective/going-viral-au-videos-promote-the-cause.

14. Barry Lynn, "Of Myths and Men: Reflections on the Jerry Falwell Era," *Church & State*, June 2007, https://www.au.org/church-state/june-2007-church-state/perspective/of-myths-and-men.

15. Laurie Goodstein, "Falwell: Blame Abortionists, Feminist and Gays," *Guardian*, September 19, 2001, http://www.theguardian.com/world/2001/sep/19/september11.usa9.

16. Peter Carlson, "Bearing Witness to the Gospel According to Falwell," *Washington Post*, May 16, 2007, http://www.washingtonpost.com/wp-dyn/content/article/2007/05/15/AR2007 051502368.html.

17. Barry Lynn, "Of Death and Taxes: Pastor Drake's Partisan Politicking and 'Imprecatory Prayers' Leave Me Cold," *Church & State*, March 2008, https://www.au.org/church-state/ march-2008-church-state/perspective/of-death-and-taxes.

18. Wiley Drake, "Pastor Wiley Drake Calls for Imprecatory Prayer against So-Called Religious Liberty Watchdog Group," press release, Christian News Wire, http://www.christiannewswire .com/news/44143894.html.

19. Bob Unruh, "IRS Probes Minister for Backing Huckabee," *World News Daily*, February 12, 2008, http://mobile.wnd.com/2008/02/56260/.

20. Barry Lynn, "When Ann Coulter Attacks: My Latest Interaction with America's 'Public Intellectual,'" *Church & State*, September 2009, https://www. au.org/church-state/ September-2009-church-state/perspective/when-ann-coulter-attacks.

21. Ann Coulter, "Kathleen Parker: The Barry Lynn of the South," *Human Events*, August 12, 2009, http://humanevents.com/2009/08/12/kathleen-parker-the-barry-lynn-of-the-south/.

22. Barry Lynn, "Awesome Award: How I Became an 'Irritant to the Status Quo': A Personal Reflection," *Church & State*, November 2005, https://www.au.org/church-state/November -2005-church-state/perspective/how-i-became-an-'irritant-to-the-status-quo'.

23. "Graham: I Would Never Say This Is God's Judgment," CNN, October 4, 2005, http:// www.cnn.com/2005/US/10/04/cnna.graham/.

24. "About Us," *Samaritan's Purse*, http://www.samaritanspurse.org/our-ministry/about-us/.

25. Barry Lynn, "To Boise and Beyond: It's Far from Quiet on the Western Front," *Church & State*, December 2005, https://www.au.org/church-state/December-2005-church-state/perspective/ to-boise-and-beyond.

26. Franklin D. Roosevelt, "Letter to Michael Williams on *Religious Tolerance*," March 30, 1937, online by Gerhard Peters and John T. Woolley, *The American Presidency Project*, http://www.presidency .ucsb.edu/ws/?pid=15382.

27. Barry Lynn, "Puffins and Prizes: A Pat on the Back for 'Creative Citizenship,'" *Church & State*, January 2014, https://www.au.org/church-state/January-2014-church-state/perspective/ puffins-and-prizes-a-pat-on-the-back-for-creative.

28. Barry Lynn, "Louie, Louie!: My 'Hellish' Day Testifying in Congress," *Church & State*, July/ August 2014, https://www.au.org/church-state/julyaugust-2014-church-state/perspective/ louie-louie-my-hellish-day-testifying-in.

29. Barry Lynn, "At the Movies: My Latest On-Screen Appearance Is No 'Noah,'" *Church & State*, May 2014, https://www.au.org/church-state/may-2014-church-state/perspective/ at-the-movies-my-latest-on-screen-appearance-is-no.

CONCLUDING THOUGHTS

1. Pew Research Center, "Views on Religion, the Bible, Evolution, and Social Issues," *Beyond Red and Blue: Political Typology* (A Pew Research Study, 2014) http://www.people-press .org/2014/06/26/section-5-views-on-religion-the-bible-evolution-and-social-issues/.

2. *Time Magazine*, March 21, 2013.

3. http://msnbcmedia.msn.com/i/MSNBC/Sections/NEWS/A_U.S.%20news/US-news -PDFs/14133%20MARCH%20NBC-WSJ%20Poll%20(3-12%20Release).pdf.

4. Robert P. Jones and Daniel Cox, *How Race and Religion Shape Millennial Attitudes on Sexuality and Reproductive Health: Findings from the 2015 Millennials, Sexuality, and Reproductive Health Survey* (Washington, DC: Public Religion Research Institute, March 27, 2015), http://publicreligion.org/ site/wp-content/uploads/2015/03/PRRI-Millennials-Web-FINAL.pdf.

5. Americans United for Separation of Church and State, *The 'Faith-Based' Initiative: Churches, Social Services and Your Tax Dollars* (Washington, DC: Americans United, 2009).

6. William J. Bushaw and Shane J. Lopez, *Which Way Do We Go*, 45th Annual PDK/Gallop Poll of the Public's Attitudes toward the Public Schools (PDK/Gallup Poll, 2013).

INDEX

ABOUT THE AUTHOR

The Rev. Barry W. Lynn is the pastor the Religious Right loves to hate.

TV preacher Pat Robertson once called Lynn "lower than a child molester." Jerry Falwell once told Lynn he wouldn't let him preach anywhere near his church. One right-wing group was so worked up about Lynn that it launched a special project urging a conservative to adopt him.

That's well and good. Less charming are the two Religious Right activists who have publicly announced that they are praying for Lynn to die.

Why does Barry Lynn get so many people so worked up? Since 1992, Lynn has led Americans United for Separation of Church and State, a national watchdog group that defends freedom of conscience by supporting what Thomas Jefferson called "the wall of separation between church and state." That alone would be enough for some people.

But that's only part of Lynn's resume. Prior to his work at Americans United, Lynn worked in the legislative office of the American Civil Liberties Union, and before that he led efforts to get President Jimmy Carter to grant amnesty to Vietnam War resisters.

All of this may explain why the far right isn't exactly Lynn's biggest fan.

Add to this the fact that Lynn regularly bests Religious Right representatives on cable news shows—he's tangled with Bill O'Reilly, Megyn Kelly, and Laura Ingraham, to name just a few—and that just adds to the right wing's rage.

Lynn has led an interesting life. He may be the only American ever to win both a Freedom of Worship Award from the Roosevelt Institute and a Hugh M. Hefner First Amendment Award from the founder of *Playboy*. (No, he didn't get it at the Playboy Mansion.) A polished public speaker, he's likely to be found addressing a gathering of LGBT Christians one day and a confab of atheists the next.

And about that "reverend" business: It's real. Over the years, various leaders of the Religious Right have insisted that there's no way Lynn could actually be a minister. Well, this "fake" clergyman earned a master's in theology from Boston University School of Theology and is ordained by the United Church of Christ. Every year, he presides at weddings and funerals and preaches guest sermons in houses of worship of assorted denominations.

Lynn's also a lawyer, and he's no slouch in that department either. His degree is from Georgetown University Law Center, and he's admitted to the US Supreme Court bar. As Lynn like to remind critics, "I can forgive you this afternoon, but still go on to sue you in the morning."

A film buff and folk music fan, Lynn is a far cry from the radical the Religious Right makes him out to be. He and his wife have been married for forty-five years and have two children. It's hard to get more "traditional" than that.

For a quarter of a century, Lynn's life work has been to annoy the would-be theocrats and busybodies among us who would run our lives along the lines of their religion. He'd say that's not a bad way to make a living.